Treating Personality Disorde

This book considers personality disorders and how they are treated within the institutional context of prisons and hospitals and offers practical guidance on assessment, formulation and integrated treatment planning.

Treating Personality Disorder offers contributions from professionals in psychiatry, nursing and psychology as well as prison officers and service managers and areas of discussion include:

- delivering integrated treatment to people with personality disorders
- issues and challenges for the clinical professional
- the role of the psychiatrist in treating personality disorder

Treating Personality Disorder will provide a timely and valuable guide for all professionals involved in the treatment and management of serious personality disorders within an institutional framework.

Naomi Murphy is a consultant clinical and forensic psychologist with over fifteen years' experience of working with clients presenting with complex psychopathology. Naomi has been instrumental in developing services for people with personality disorder in the community, secure services and prisons. Naomi has a particular interest in the development of transdisciplinary teams.

Des McVey is a consultant nurse and psychotherapist with over twenty-five years' experience of working within and developing forensic services. He is a visiting lecturer at the University of York and regularly teaches on nursing and clinical psychology courses. Des has a particular interest in developing strategies that maintain treatment integrity.

Treating Personality Disorder

Creating robust services for people with
complex mental health needs

Edited by Naomi Murphy and
Des McVey

Routledge
Taylor & Francis Group

LONDON AND NEW YORK

First published 2010
by Routledge
27 Church Road, Hove, East Sussex BN3 2FA

Simultaneously published in the USA and Canada
by Routledge
711 Third Avenue, New York, NY 10017

First issued in paperback 2014

*Routledge is an imprint of the Taylor & Francis Group,
an informa business*

Copyright © 2010 Selection and editorial matter, Naomi Murphy and
Des McVey; individual chapters, the contributors

Typeset in Times by
RefineCatch Limited, Bungay, Suffolk
Cover design by Andrew Ward

British Library Cataloguing in Publication Data
A catalogue record for this book is available from the British Library

Library of Congress Cataloging-in-Publication Data
Treating personality disorder : creating robust services for people
with complex mental health needs / edited by Naomi Murphy & Des
McVey.
        p. ; cm.
    Includes bibliographical references and index.
1. Personality disorders—Treatment.   2. Community mental health
services.   I. Murphy, Naomi, 1970–   II. Mc Vey, Des, 1962–
    [DNLM: 1. Personality Disorders—therapy.   2. Community
Mental Health Services—organization & administration.
3. Mentally Ill Persons—psychology.   4. Patient Care Team.
5. Professional Role. WM 190 T7834 2010]
    RC554.T718 2010
    362.196′8581—dc22
                                                2009041542

ISBN: 978–1–138–87180–9 (pbk)
ISBN: 978–0–415–40480–8 (hbk)

This book is dedicated to:
Tom and Kathleen McVey, for demonstrating the concept of unconditional love
and
Jim and Kathleen Murphy, for nurturing independent thought and action

Contents

Contributors

Jacquie Evans is a consultant forensic psychologist, with twenty years' experience of working with violent offenders. She has served on a number of international study groups looking at the management of violent offenders. She is the author of several forensic publications. She worked on establishing a Masters in Applied Forensic Psychology at York University where she was an honorary lecturer.

Stephen Fox is a prisoner officer widely experienced in working with prisoners with complex difficulties. Posts include the former Separated Prisoners Unit, HMYOI Reading and HMP Whitemoor's Fens Unit (DSPD). Stephen has a particular interest in autistic spectrum disorders.

Val Hawes is a consultant forensic psychiatrist practising for Norfolk and Waveney Mental Health Trust. Val has held medical posts both nationally and internationally. She has a particular interest in ensuring that psychopharmacological interventions aid psychological treatment by reducing distress without stifling affect.

Leanne Jones is Head Occupational Therapist at the Fens Unit and has worked with people with personality disorder across community, hospital and prison settings for the past decade. She places a particular emphasis on occupationally focused practice influenced by psychological principles.

Des McVey is a consultant nurse and psychotherapist with over twenty-five years' experience of working within and developing forensic services. He is a visiting lecturer at the University of York and regularly teaches on nursing and clinical psychology courses. Des has a particular interest in developing strategies that maintain treatment integrity.

Naomi Murphy is a consultant clinical and forensic psychologist with over fifteen years' experience of working with clients presenting with complex psychopathology. Naomi has been instrumental in developing services for people with personality disorder in the community, secure services and prisons. Naomi has a particular interest in the development of transdisciplinary teams.

Jo Ramsden is a clinical psychologist currently working in a specialist service supporting people returning to the community from conditions of security. Jo provides regular teaching and training to non-psychologists on the use of psychological principles when working with people with personality disorder.

Jacqui Saradjian is a consultant clinical and forensic psychologist. Currently the Clinical Director of a unit for men with severe personality disorder, she has treated such clients for twenty years. Jacqui has a particular interest in trauma and the development of personality disorder.

Elizabeth Sneath is a consultant forensic psychologist with over nineteen years' experience working in forensic settings. She has developed particular expertise in working with multidisciplinary teams responsible for managing and treating disruptive and violent prisoners. Elizabeth has a particular interest in disseminating the benefits of clinical supervision to non-clinical staff.

Neil Watson is a psychologist working with older adults. He has previously worked with people with personality disorder within a prison setting.

'Before I came here, I'd cut off from all outside contact . . . things became blacker and blacker and then just prior to coming here I could not talk to anyone. I was only interested in any illicit drugs I could get. . . . Now? I've realized that it starts by building up relationships, getting to know the staff, not trusting anyone at first but then you realise that you do. . . . For the first time in my life I remember, I felt hurt. I did not recognise what to feel hurt was. When someone hurt me, I felt angry and missed the in-between part and what happened before is that I got angry and then I'd act but not feel the anger . . . I'm starting to learn the gentler side of myself . . . it's an exploration. I'm starting to look at myself more – you know at last I can tell someone how frightened I've always been, you know it's hard to say but it's a relief too.'

('Stuart', prisoner, Fens Unit, HMP Whitemoor)

Chapter 1

Introduction

Des McVey and Naomi Murphy

Personality disorder is a mental health condition that generates significant distress for the people who have the condition and also for those who are involved with them whether personally or professionally. It is also a condition that generates controversy. Classification and diagnosis of the condition remain areas of intense academic debate, as does whether or not this condition is treatable. Despite these disagreements, there is agreement that a significant percentage of the world's population present with maladaptive cognitions, behaviours and emotional states in attempts to manage their world and their interpersonal relationships, which result in them being diagnosed as personality disordered. Their use of maladaptive coping strategies means that people with this diagnosis are disproportionately involved with the criminal justice system and/or mental health services. People with such maladaptive coping strategies are also significantly represented in areas of life that require skill or creativity. This can be evidenced through the many talented musicians, actors and athletes featured in the media who present with self-destructive interpersonal relationships and lifestyles. It could be credibly argued that these artists express their distress through the creativity of their art or performance.

People with this disorder experience significant psychological distress which they manage by utilising dysfunctional coping strategies including: addictions (e.g. drugs, gambling, sex), violence, self-neglect, self-injury (in its many forms), suicide and homicide. Those who interact with them often become distressed by the impact of these behaviours and by the intensity of underlying emotions, such as sadness, fear, disgust, shame and anger, that the behaviours are designed to mask or avoid. This can be so aversive that those closest to them become overwhelmed and feel manipulated and/or hopeless and consequently denigrate the person with the condition, making pejorative statements that indicate they are not deserving of care or support. Indeed, within both the criminal justice and health services, these clients may be experienced as so problematic that they are repeatedly shuffled from one service to another.

In prisons, those with the most need of containment are often regularly moved from prison to prison as they are considered uncontainable. In the health services, people with this diagnosis are unique in that they are often admitted for treatment and then angrily discharged when they present with the very symptoms that are intrinsic to their condition. Services that do provide treatment will often be so selective in their admission criteria that those in the most distress, and thus presenting with the more severe symptoms, are excluded from the service. Until recently, this has been one of the few conditions that mental health professionals could opt out of treating by deeming the individual as untreatable. This must be a despair-inducing scenario for any human being when those with physical disorders with no known cure (e.g. terminal cancer) are none the less 'treated' and in receipt of care until their death. Professionals and clients alike have used the 'treatability' clause to engineer a discharge from services which has on occasion resulted in the individual committing violent offences against others or killing themselves.

Over the past decade, the British government has invested significantly in both the criminal justice and mental health services in order to develop interventions that will provide hope, treatment and recovery for people who have this condition even in its most severe form. New legislation requires that treatment must be available for those detained due to this condition and clinicians can no longer hide behind the issue of 'treatability'.

This book is written by clinicians who have many years of experience in providing effective services to these clients in the community, hospitals and prisons. It provides health professionals, health service managers and prison staff with in-depth information as to how to successfully establish and deliver such services and how to adapt current skills in order to deliver effective treatment that will relieve the clients' distress and reduce the risk that they pose to themselves and others. Pitfalls and areas of difficulty that will be encountered are considered and a theoretical understanding of the causes of these difficulties and practical strategies that can be implemented in order to avoid or minimise such experiences are offered. All contributors have focused not only on *what* needs to be done, but also *how* to do it. The book includes chapters dedicated to all the specific components essential to providing such a service and gives clear and cohesive advice about how to develop a seamless service whilst maintaining an overarching clinical philosophy. Importantly, teamwork is stressed throughout and chapters explicitly highlight the specific roles for professionals involved.

This book could be considered as controversial as many other aspects of personality disorder since it is argued that to develop an effective service means confronting commonly held beliefs about service delivery. It exposes the current illogical approaches taken by many service providers, clinicians and researchers in their attempts to develop a greater understanding of this condition and its treatability. The aim is not to be overly critical or attacking but to encourage readers to reorganise their thinking and incorporate strategies that will enable them to provide truly accessible, meaningful interventions and thus facilitate real recovery.

The purpose of this book is to show the potential and methods for treatment of people with personality disorder in different institutional contexts, where containment or management of personality disordered individuals has tended to be the response of mental health service providers. The key to successful treatment lies in the understanding of the special challenges presented by such individuals and in the provision of complex sophisticated treatment in the context of a cohesive integrated treatment model, as well as in the teamwork of the different professionals involved and in the organisation and resources of the service within which treatment is given.

This book challenges the prevailing belief that this client group can make little therapeutic gain by offering an approach to treatment that fosters optimism among staff and clients. The authors offer improved clarity and understanding of the complexities of providing treatment to this client group by focusing upon the process of treatment and principles that, when adhered to, may improve the outcome of this process. All chapters highlight opportunities to maximise the potential of both staff and clients within existing services. The book includes a treatment structure that enables treatment to be organised in a coherent, integrated framework and enables practitioners to assess, formulate and plan effectively for treatment of clients with multiple, complex needs. All of the chapters suggest methods to overcome the obstructions to treatment and challenges that these clients pose. The book incorporates consideration of risk and destructiveness to enable those staff working with forensic clients to address offending behaviour simultaneously with other problem behaviours. All authors advocate for a transdisciplinary team approach whereby each discipline has a clear role and its own unique contribution to make towards treatment. Within this approach, every interaction between every client and every staff member has therapeutic potential. Although the majority of the volume is aimed at improved clinical services, an overview of the management structures essential for the provision of clinical excellence is also provided.

Chapter 2 provides an overview of the difficulties faced by clinical staff and prison service personnel in working with clients on a daily basis. The chapter explores how these difficulties have contributed to service providers avoiding their responsibilities, and summarises action that can be taken to develop a service that is accessible and responsive to people with personality disorder whilst maintaining a staff group who feel safe enough to perform their roles confidently and competently.

Within Chapter 3, the process and content of robust assessment and formulation for clients with multiple, complex needs, including potential risk to self or others, are described within a suggested framework. The chapter covers not only formal methods of assessment that can be useful with this client group, such as psychometric tests, but also other ways of enhancing assessment, such as observations, collateral information and countertransference. Difficulties in assessing clients where motivation to participate in the assessment process is minimal or fluctuating are also addressed. The authors argue for the production of a written formulation that is accessible to the individual client and the staff team involved in his or her care, highlights potential obstacles to treatment that will need to be overcome, and predicts vulnerability to increased 'acting out' behaviour.

People with personality disorder are often excluded from treatments and programmes by virtue of their diagnosis. Many services paradoxically require that clients reform their behaviours prior to being considered as appropriate for intervention, for example the client must resist using aggression. The rationale behind this is that the client will be unable to conform to the requirements of many treatment approaches. Other service providers offer treatment only to those who meet one discrete disorder, for example the provision of dialectical behaviour therapy to people with borderline personality disorder. Within Chapters 4 and 5, the characteristics essential for a more accessible treatment programme are described. A significant issue pertaining to treatment services for people with personality disorder is that of maintaining treatment integrity when staff are operating from diverse theoretical influences. The authors of Chapter 4 identify eight theoretical principles that underpin the treatment needs of an eclectic client group with varying needs and motivation. They describe an overarching framework within which clinical interventions can be organised and structured to provide an integrated service that ensures adherence to these principles.

Within Chapter 5, the authors describe features that are essential if services wish to treat rather than merely manage personality disordered clients. They describe the importance of working towards an emotionally intimate relationship with these clients and suggest three key strategies if this is to be achieved: maintaining optimum affective arousal; working with the logical perspective of the client; and using explicit communication. Although controversial, the chapter offers the reader new techniques that will allow for meaningful and valid therapeutic relationships that encourage growth within the principles of most psychological models.

Most services for people with personality disorder are annexed onto traditional psychiatric and prison-based services and are required to adhere to the customary practice within the host institution. The authors of Chapter 6 discuss the challenges faced by organisations offering a service to personality disordered individuals within such a context and highlight how many customary practices are ineffective when applied to this client group. The authors also suggest a framework for effective service provision that adheres to the National Service Framework of good practice for mental health services established within the UK.

Working within a multidisciplinary team has increasingly become a key part of the role of most mental health professionals and the editors believe that one of the salient factors for delivery of an effective programme for the treatment of personality disorder is that of an effective team. Without a robust team *in situ*, the risks to the integrity of any approach are raised significantly. One cannot overestimate the importance of this infrastructure in the development of a service. The author of Chapter 7 discusses not only the advantages of working within a multidisciplinary team but also some of the challenges that can arise which are exacerbated in teams providing specialist services for personality disordered clients. She advocates for such services to adopt a higher level teamworking approach, transdisciplinary teamworking, and provides guidance on how to transform existing teams into high performing transdisciplinary teams.

Chapters 8, 9, 10, 11 and 12 discuss the unique contribution made by each profession within the transdisciplinary team. The authors of the first four of these chapters describe a clear and active role for their professional group within the treatment of personality disorder that does not entail having to train as a psychological therapist. The author of each chapter identifies how traditional practice is often focused upon the management of the client and the client's symptoms rather than change-oriented treatment addressing the cause of the individual's difficulties. Each author describes unique challenges encountered by members of their professional group and describes a course of action to enable the professional to improve the effectiveness of their contact with the client group. These chapters also provide a benchmark against which managers of services can appraise the effectiveness of their team. The author of Chapter 12 is not concerned with the role of the psychologist as assessor or therapist. Instead she focuses upon the opportunity for the psychologist to maximise the therapeutic potential of the team by using his or her knowledge of psychological theory and practice to enable others to improve the effectiveness of their interventions and to facilitate the harmonisation of care across the team.

The author of the final chapter describes some of the essential components of a service where staff are able to develop key skills and knowledge and have access to good systems for support and supervision. Within this chapter she also describes some of the barriers to effective support and supervision and suggests strategies for overcoming these.

All of the authors contributing to this book are experienced in working with clients with personality disorder across the full spectrum of services and are passionate about ensuring the highest standards of care. They are all practising clinicians who are successful in facilitating change in the most challenging of clients. We hope the reader will also feel confident and positive about rising to the challenge of treating these clients and be optimistic about the possibility of making their own contribution to treating people with personality disorder after reading this book.

Chapter 2

The difficulties that staff experience in treating individuals with personality disorder

Naomi Murphy and Des McVey

Introduction

Personality disordered patients evoke strong negative emotions and attitudes among many health care professionals. Such is their unpopularity that Fallon's inquiry into Ashworth Hospital (1999) observed that the legal concept of 'psychopathic disorder', created to cover patients with personality disorder when they fall within the remit of mental health law, is a term of 'abuse'. Cavadino emphasised the futility of re-labelling the concept of 'moral insanity', arguing that 'the more modern term is simply a prime example of moralism masquerading as medical science'. He continues,

> Perhaps we should strip away the mask completely, and for the term 'psychopath' substitute the word 'bastard'. For 'predominantly aggressive psychopath', read 'stroppy bastard'. For 'predominately inadequate psychopath': read 'useless bastard'. Would much be lost in the descriptive power of the terms? Would not much be gained in the honest expression of the essentially moral judgement and dehumanizing contempt with which we view 'the psychopath'?
>
> (Cavadino, 1998, p. 6)

This distaste of mental health service providers led to personality disordered people being denied access to services on grounds of lack of 'treatability' without any obligation for apparent lack of treatability to be evidenced or for alternative forms of treatment to be sought. In the UK, this led to several high profile cases in the 1990s where men diagnosed with personality disorder but considered untreatable caused public concern. This was followed by the Labour government investing considerable resources to ensure that mental health services are accessible and meaningful for those people with personality disorder as well as for those with mental illness. This chapter explores the difficulties that led to some service providers avoiding their responsibilities, and summarises action that can be taken to develop a service that is accessible to people with personality disorder, and which is well managed and staffed by confident, competent staff. Other chapters within this volume discuss potential solutions to the difficulties identified within this chapter in greater detail.

Challenges identified within the literature

The current authors have previously discussed the challenge of nursing personality disordered patients (Murphy and McVey, 2003). The abundance of literature focused on the difficulties posed to nursing staff relative to other disciplines may reflect the fact that often nurses carry most responsibility for managing these patients within inpatient settings and the community. Contact with psychiatrists may be restricted to reviewing the patient once a week or less. Other disciplines, for example psychologists, often have the luxury of choosing their caseload and may avoid patients by labelling them as 'lacking in psychological-mindedness' or 'treatment resistant' without having to consider the consequences in terms of mental health legislation or the clients' immediate needs. Across all levels of service, the reluctance of some professionals to take on personality disordered patients for therapy not infrequently leads to some of the most challenging clients being managed by staff with the least training.

Reviews of literature indicate that, in general, all mental health disciplines find working with personality disordered patients more challenging than working with other patients, and this appears consistent across all settings, English-speaking cultures and time (e.g. Alhadeff, 1994; Bland, 2003; Bowers, 2002; Brody and Farber, 1996; Cleary et al., 2002; Deans and Meocevic, 2006; Fraser and Gallop, 1993; Gallop et al., 1989; Gallop and Wynn, 1987; Greene and Ugarriza, 1995; James and Cowman 2007; Lewis and Appleby, 1988; Moran and Mason, 1996; O'Brien and Flöte, 1997, Pavolovich-Danis, 2004; Piccinino, 1990).

Much of the literature on difficulties in delivering treatment to these patients reflects clinicians' opinions rather than empirical evidence. Clinical opinion is substantiated by evidence to suggest many clinicians find them difficult to treat (e.g. 84 per cent of Australian nurses thought clients with borderline personality disorder were 'more difficult' to nurse than other client groups (Cleary et al., 2002); 80 per cent of Irish psychiatric nurses identified them as 'more difficult' to look after than other clients (James and Cowman, 2007)), but there is little research devoted to why this is the case.

It would be erroneous to conclude that caring for people with personality disorder is undesirable as an occupation merely because staff find this task more difficult. After all, some staff may respond to the challenge of a more difficult task. However, researchers attempting to explore the impact of attitudes on the care of people with personality disorder have found some disturbing results. For instance, Lewis and Appleby's (1988) survey found that 173 UK psychiatrists (of 240 sent their questionnaire) thought people diagnosed as personality disordered were less deserving of care than other psychiatric patients. People labelled as personality disordered within a vignette were more likely to be judged as manipulative, likely to pose a management problem, attention-seeking, less sympathetic, annoying and not deserving of NHS resources and were judged to be unlikely to complete or comply with treatment, when contrasted with the same vignette in which the individual was not labelled as personality disordered. Brody and Farber (1996) found comparative results using a similar approach in a survey of UK clinical psychologists.

Many of those writing about the experience of working with the personality disordered appear to be working within general adult mental health settings. One would hope that the attitudes among staff working within specialist settings would be less negative. Unfortunately, there is a paucity of research in this area. Bowers's (2002) thorough research into the variable attitudes of nursing staff employed in high secure hospitals does not appear to have been focused primarily upon staff working on wards dedicated to treating patients with personality disorder. However, it is known that up to 79 per cent of high security patients fulfil diagnostic criteria for at least one personality disorder (Mbatia and Tyrer, 1988; Taylor et al., 1998), and Bowers (2006) also found variable attitudes among operational staff within a prison-based personality disorder unit (between 2001 and 2003). This might indicate that, even within specialist services, staff find it challenging to maintain a positive attitude to people with personality disorder.

Challenges posed to staff

The presentation of people with personality disorder is such that those encountering them are faced with a number of key challenges which some staff and services find difficult to overcome.

I Professional training is inadequate for the task

The theme of inadequate professional training emerges frequently within the research literature, suggesting most nurses do not feel their training prepares them sufficiently for the role of managing and treating personality disordered patients (e.g. Krawitz, 2004; Miller and Davenport, 1996). Within Cleary et al.'s (2002) study, a sizeable minority (29 per cent) of Australian psychiatric nurses felt they lacked the training and experience to adequately care for this client group. Other studies (e.g. Deans and Meocevic, 2006) found that much higher percentages (56 per cent) of psychiatric nurses identified themselves as lacking this training, and James and Cowman's (2007) study of Irish nurses found that only 3 per cent of nurses had received any training on borderline personality disorder outside their undergraduate training. Bowers's (2002) study of UK nurses also found that psychiatric nurses in high secure hospitals (which included staff working on specialist wards) felt under-prepared for the role of treating people with personality disorder.

Research suggests that biology only partially accounts for personality disorder and that environmental factors play a significant role in mediating the aetiology and treatment of personality disorder. Although training courses are moving increasingly towards a bio-psychosocial perspective, the medical model has historically dominated. Thus, many qualified, experienced nurses lack a thorough understanding of relevant psychological theory. Nurses who lack awareness of psychological models have a tendency to apply the medical model even when faced with evidence of its ineffectiveness (Moran and Mason, 1996).

Many psychiatrists have a similar experience of medical training. Those pursuing training in a psychotherapeutic approach are perhaps more likely to share an understanding of personality disorder with psychologists (or psychological therapists) but those who have not undertaken such training are likely to find that, like nurses, they lack sufficient knowledge to contribute effectively to discussions about the management and treatment of these patients. In a staff group that lacked training on personality disorder, doctors and nurses had more negative attitudes towards personality disorder than professionals allied to medicine but their attitudes improved when provided with specific training (unlike allied professionals whose attitudes remained constant), suggesting there are some similarities across nursing and psychiatry (Commons-Treloar and Lewis, 2008)

Within the medical model of illness, once symptoms of a condition are identified, one can predict what treatment will cause the symptoms to be alleviated. Identifying the aetiology and treatment of personality disorder is more complex. The 'condition' does not have a uniform manifestation with discrete symptoms that can easily be identified, and identifying the appropriate course of treatment requires skills in understanding the multitude of contributory factors that led to its onset and will affect the course of treatment. Weaving together these factors to establish a testable formulation and individualised course of treatment is difficult in the absence of a broader understanding of the condition, and is a skill that is perhaps not encouraged by traditional biomedical training where the emphasis is upon the role of biology within a disorder.

Research demonstrates that clinicians are more likely to define clients as difficult if the patient challenges their sense of competence and control (e.g. Breeze and Repper, 1998; McAllister et al., 2002). A study by Gallop et al. (1993) identified that when psychiatrists and nurses were prevented from performing the role for which they perhaps felt best trained, they were left feeling incompetent as their training was of limited use. For nurses, those patients perceived as most difficult to treat were those with whom it was hardest to form a therapeutic relationship; for doctors it was those who did not respond to medication.

Although professions allied to medicine may have more positive attitudes than their nursing and medical colleagues and their professional training is broader than the biomedical approach, research has nevertheless highlighted that personality disorder is more likely to elicit negativity from such groups than other types of mental disorder (e.g. Brody and Farber, 1996), suggesting that lack of psychological knowledge is not the only contributory factor in determining why these patients are experienced as 'difficult'. Whilst psychologists' distaste for treating personality disorder may not be due to absence of psychological knowledge *per se*, experience suggests that a specific type of psychological knowledge is required that is not uniformly provided to psychologists, and this may play a role in psychologists finding this client group unappealing.

Theoretically, clinical psychologists and psychological and occupational therapists are equipped with a range of tools that enable them to assess, formulate and treat a broad range of patients. However, experience suggests that adaptations have to be made to most standard psychotherapeutic treatments in order to make therapy accessible to the client group. The emphasis within training programmes is usually upon screening out 'unsuitable', apparently unmotivated, 'treatment-resistant' clients in order to maximise the opportunity for trainees to gain confidence and competence within a restricted time frame.

Unsurprisingly, given the interpersonal nature of the disorder, many people with personality disorder find themselves excluded from therapy within this context by virtue of the symptoms of their disorder. This may be perpetuated within the broader NHS where general policies such as discharging patients who do not attend two consecutive sessions may work against these patients. Staff could ensure that services are more accessible by adopting strategies such as writing to patients advising them that they are deserving of treatment following missed appointments. Working with people with personality disorder therefore requires therapists to develop skills for working with clients who may previously have been labelled erroneously as 'treatment resistant' because they attempted to access what Diamond and Factor (1994) refer to as an 'unresponsive system'. Like nurses and psychiatrists, this entails many psychologists and therapists having to broaden their knowledge base beyond that which is provided by their basic training.

Because of the entrenched nature of the condition, therapeutic work addressing personality disorder is slow and labour-intensive. Our experience across a range of settings is that those within the community require three to six months (during which time they typically employ self-protective acting-out strategies) to begin to form a reasonable working alliance. Within medium secure settings and above, a period of twelve months may be necessary to develop a relationship in which the patient feels safe enough to consider meaningfully engaging. Most core professions do not offer placements that exceed twelve months in duration and, within many professionals' training schemes, the placements are significantly shorter. Therefore, not only do training schemes fail to provide staff with the knowledge that would enable them to access a more complex client group, but they also fail to provide them with the opportunity to develop the skills required to nurture and maintain a medium- to long-term therapeutic relationship.

2 Patients are low in reinforcement

Like all workers, mental health staff benefit from seeing a positive outcome in return for their investment of resources within the patient. The literature associates personality disorder with a lack of positive reinforcement which can make the work seem ungratifying to inexperienced staff for a variety of reasons.

Absence of progress

People with personality disorder have frequently been labelled 'untreatable' due to the limited utility of psychopharmacology (Commons-Treloar and Lewis, 2008; Diamond and Factor, 1994), or the failure to correctly formulate and adapt other unsuccessful therapeutic interventions. Labelling the patient as untreatable and thereby locating responsibility for lack of progress firmly with the patient may be more bearable than reconsidering our inaccurate formulations which would force us to confront our own inadequacies or the system's contribution to the patient's lack of progress. Policies regarding access to psychological therapy, the duration of therapy or the model of psychological therapy on offer to the client may not be fit for purpose when applied to these clients.

Imperceptible progress

Lack of experience in providing long-term treatment can lead to staff lacking the resilience to stick with clients when progress is slow and imperceptible, as staff are more accustomed to gauging progress with clients who are easily identified as psychologically minded, have discrete problems, or respond quickly to therapy or psychotropic medication. Slow progress has been identified as contributing to the perception that patients are difficult to treat (Colson et al., 1985; Pfohl et al., 1999) and imperceptible progress may be mistaken for an absence of progress by inexperienced staff.

Boyes (1994) argues that an inability to 'cure' the patient causes staff to feel frustrated. Watts and Morgan (1994) acknowledge this frustration in staff and suggest inexperienced or poorly supervised psychiatric staff are particularly prone to confusing their professional ability to heal with their own self-worth.

The narcissistic need to heal our patients may be compounded by the pressure of market forces within the current NHS climate to produce quick results. This has led to huge investment in brief cognitive behavioural interventions which people with severe personality psychopathology are unlikely to gain great benefit from. Key performance indicators are often focused upon an end point such as ensuring low non-attendance rates and completion of therapy within twelve sessions, rather than breaking the work down into discrete tasks such as (i) engaging the client, (ii) assessment, (iii) maintaining the client in therapy, and (iv) completion of therapy. When many primary care patients are quickly engaged in therapy, work with patients who require at least twelve sessions to build a foundation for therapy and ensure the patient attends regularly may not be as valued by managers.

Apparent progress

Whilst some patients appear to show no progress to the novice staff member, others appear initially to make rapid progress (which is clearly very reinforcing) before deteriorating back to their original condition and disappointing the staff involved in their treatment.

Borderline patients offered the same approach as mentally ill patients may become 'revolving door' patients with frequent admissions (Gunderson, 1984), which Gallop (1985) suggests may be a consequence of the brief honeymoon phase that frequently ensues when the patient is admitted to hospital. Our experience is that some patients may be relatively easily contained when they feel supported and their dependency needs are being met. However, when this dependency is threatened, for example at discharge, acting-out behaviour may return. This is particularly evident in patients who are reliant upon self-injury or antisocial activity to communicate their emotions. It has been suggested that such patients are 'made worse' by hospital admission (Fahy, 2004), but our perception is that when such patients deteriorate in this manner it is because treatment has been only *apparently* effective and the initial assessment and formulation failed to consider the underlying function of the acting-out behaviour or whether there would be any benefit to the client in only apparently progressing, for example a subjugating client who perceives he has to please others if he is to keep himself safe.

This tendency to lapse back into dysfunction may be especially difficult for staff working within secure services due to the associated potential for severe consequences which may include loss of life if risk assessments are inaccurate. A particular difficulty emerges for psychological therapists who may mistake gains in cognitive engagement and insight for adequate improvement without ensuring that ability to regulate emotions effectively is also developed. For instance, dialectical behaviour therapy is associated with short-term improvements when compared with treatment as usual, but these improvements may disappear by one year after discharge (Linehan *et al.*, 1991). Since the acting-out behaviours of forensic clients are largely responsible for their contact with services (affect drives the behaviour, cognitions merely trigger it), a failure to attend to the client's capacity to cope with overwhelming affect without recourse to destructive actions will undermine the efficacy of therapeutic interventions.

Rejection of staff

A number of personality disorder diagnoses (avoidant, schizoid and paranoid) are characterised by social withdrawal and shunning of relationships. This has also been linked to the labelling of patients as 'difficult to treat' (Colson *et al.*, 1985). Others are characterised by an interpersonal style fluctuating between approach and avoidance. Although personality disordered patients have the same need for closeness and intimacy as others, their childhood has often included experiences of extreme victimisation and neglect (not infrequently at the hands of multiple perpetrators) and so their expectation is that if others get too close they may be endangered. Others are unable to even acknowledge the desire for fear that it will not be met. The intense sense of worthlessness and shame that many of them experience, coupled with distorted beliefs about their own toxicity, often drives rejecting behaviour. Those who cope with feelings of defectiveness by utilising narcissistic overcompensation may leave therapists feeling their efforts are inadequate.

If these patients found it easy to maintain relationships with others, they would probably not require secondary care. To protect themselves from the vulnerability that emotional intimacy entails, some patients form superficially close, subjugative relationships but retreat when efforts are made to develop a more emotionally meaningful one, whilst others act to alienate others and then panic and attempt to lure them back. Inexperienced staff can lose sight of the rationale behind the patient's behaviour, and Piccinino (1990) observes that the approach-avoidant interpersonal style contributes to relationships characterised by crises and stormy episodes and involving intense feelings on behalf of both staff and patient. Staff may be asked for help and then find their efforts spurned through overtly hostile behaviour, missed appointments or non-compliance with treatment, leading to frustration and anger in staff (Glick *et al.*, 1984) and the perception that the patient is 'a bad patient' (Podrasky and Sexton, 1988; Sarosi, 1968; Schwartz, 1958). Kelly and May (1982) suggest it is this rejection of help that creates the perception that these patients are 'difficult' rather than the 'difficult behaviour' *per se*.

Lack of overt gratitude

Early childhood experiences of abuse, sexual exploitation, disrupted care and enforced self-sufficiency can leave personality disordered patients cynical and suspicious about displays of nurturance and focused upon their expectation of impending abuse and neglect. It is unusual for them to have had sincere displays of gratitude role-modelled within their relationships with caregivers.

Consequently, it is rare to receive an overt display of gratitude within the early stages of a relationship. This lack of gratitude is difficult to tolerate (Gallop *et al.*, 1989; Pfohl *et al.*, 1999; Sarosi, 1968), which is unfortunate, as genuine displays of gratitude and affection become a feature of more developed relationships where trust has been established and where the individual has grown to recognise their impact upon others.

3 Patients are high in demand

The lack of reinforcement and gratitude is exacerbated by egocentricity and entitlement which are defining symptoms of several personality disorders (narcissistic, antisocial and borderline). Such patients often either had no limits set in childhood (thus failing to develop the ability to recognise limits) or never had their needs met (thus learning 'if you don't look after yourself, no one else will do it'). Patients may overtly and explicitly demand that their needs are prioritised or may behave in ways that force staff to attend to their needs, for example engaging in deliberate self-harm or presenting with temper-tantrums. Within an institutional setting, this may create a dilemma for staff struggling to balance the needs of these patients alongside those of more withdrawn or avoidant patients (Bland and Rossen, 2005). Across all settings, staff may fear angry acting out could result in destructive behaviour.

Several authors attribute professional hostility to personality disorder to the perception of some patients as not only demanding but also 'manipulative' in ensuring their demands are met (Bowers, 2002; Deans and Meocevic, 2006; Diamond and Factor, 1994; May and Kelly, 1982; Nehls, 1999). McMorrow (1981) defines healthy manipulation, like most dictionaries, as 'purposeful behaviour directed at getting needs met'. Some authors consider that we are all manipulative but only those whose efforts to get their needs met are clumsy and transparent may find themselves labelled overtly as manipulative. This is reflected within Diamond and Factor's (1994, p. 97) discussion of how staff

> call patients manipulative if we feel that they want 'too much', that is, more than we feel we want to give. The problem is not just that they want too much but that they end up getting very little of what they want despite all their entreaties and demands. Patients who are labelled manipulative are unskilled in dealing with other people and often cause others to feel resentful or angry. People who are skilled in getting other people to do what they want are described as friendly, convincing, or influential and rarely as manipulative. If we view manipulative patients as having inexhaustible needs, there is little we can do except put up barriers to protect ourselves. However, if we view many of their demands as arising from deficits in interpersonal skills, our treatment then involves helping them develop better skills to get more of their needs met without producing so much anger in others.

These patients have often been raised within families or institutions that lacked clear, explicit boundaries that were equitably applied to all children. Instead, their experience is often that favouritism and scapegoating are rife and that the roles and boundaries of adults and children are inconsistently applied and may be interchangeable if the child has something to offer that is desired by the adult such as sex or nurturance. Is it therefore so surprising that some patients attempt to establish 'special' relationships with staff in which they offer secrets and flattery in exchange for privileges or the care-giver's opinions about colleagues? Or that they should attempt to obtain something from another staff member after their initial request has been denied? Those who are being courted by the patient may struggle to identify the patient as demanding, particularly if acknowledging they have been seduced threatens their professional identity. This can lead to conflict between staff if dynamics of favouritism and scapegoating are not explicitly discussed.

Bowers (2003) refutes the suggestion that manipulation is normal and attempts to overcome the lack of clarity within the literature by defining manipulation as behaviour constituted by 'purposeful, planned action', 'deception and/or coercion' *and* 'lack of concern for others', arguing that the disregard of the needs of others distinguishes the behaviour of the personality disordered. He describes six types of behaviour that were perceived as 'manipulative' by participants within high secure hospital settings: (i) bullying, e.g. use of threats, persistent challenges and requests, physical intimidation and actual violence; (ii) corrupting via bribery and persuasion; (iii) 'condition-ing' (grooming); (iv) capitalising on alternative hierarchies to undermine the position of those withholding access (e.g. use of advocacy and legal systems); (v) lying; and (vi) dividing (splitting). Within this article, Bowers reports that victims of manipulation report feelings of anger, fear, guilt, shame, humili-ation and disappointment and may be gossiped about or risk losing their job.

Whilst we would not dispute the occurrence of Bowers's taxonomy of 'manipulative behaviours' within personality disordered patients, especially those encountered within forensic systems, we would argue that these behaviours are not present within all patients and the use of the term manipu-lation is unhelpful since it is used in an imprecise and inconsistent way. Too often the use of this term acts as an obstruction to empathy and serves as a distraction from addressing offending behaviour since it confuses inept attempts to get one's needs met with aggressive, offending and offence-paralleling behaviour. It is more therapeutic for the client and more func-tional for staff to understand the underlying motivation behind each of these behaviours and address these explicitly.

4 Difficulties in perceiving the vulnerability of the patient

One could argue that the ability to see the vulnerability in personality dis-ordered patients contributes directly to a more positive attitude to this client group. Our perception is that it is this ability that is strengthened by strategies such as reading case notes and identifying with the patient which Bowers (2002) identifies as related to a more positive attitude in nurses and which perhaps contributes to the relatively more positive attitude of psychologists (Commons-Treloar and Lewis, 2008). The ability of staff to perceive the patient's vulnerability is hindered by the apparent competence of many patients, the aggressive actions of others and the failure of staff to consider that they may live in a different logical world from the patient.

Apparent competence

Young (1994) identifies ten schema modes that individuals may utilise within their interactions with others. He defines modes as 'the moment-to-moment emotional states and coping responses – adaptive and maladaptive - that we all experience. Often our schema modes are triggered by life situations to which we are oversensitive' (p. 37). Some modes are healthy for an individual, others are unhealthy. People without personality disorder rely mainly upon 'healthy adult' and utilise 'happy child' in situations requiring playfulness and spontaneity. These modes are typically adopted in situations where a person feels safe and unthreatened, and patients with personality disorder do have the ability to utilise these modes in such situations or when engaged in certain activities. For instance, a person with narcissist personality disorder may present as confident when performing an activity that draws upon a specific talent, but over compensate and present as a braggart or enraged when confronted by a situation in which they feel less competent.

Patients presenting in healthy adult mode may be initially identified as more 'normal' (DeLaune, 2004) than other psychiatric patients. Others, fearful of abuse or exploitation, may attempt to conceal their vulnerability and feign competence through use of overcompensatory and intellectualising coping strategies which mask their internal turmoil and may cause others to misinterpret their feigned competence as 'healthy adult'.

When healthy adult or even feigned healthy adult is contrasted with behaviours associated with maladaptive modes such as those described as needy, controlling or demanding, patients may be seen as deliberately not improving or as sabotaging their treatment (Fraser and Gallop, 1993; Greene and Ugarriza, 1995; Linehan, 1993; O'Brien, 1998), and staff may feel angry, duped or inadequate. They are more likely to label the patient as 'difficult' when they perceive the patient's symptoms to be within their own capacity to modify rather than those which are viewed as essentially outside their sphere of control (Markham and Trower, 2003; Podrasky and Sexton, 1988), and the capacity of the personality disordered patient to present at times in 'healthy adult' mode may ultimately undermine their credibility as a patient.

Offender identity

The inability of some patients to regulate their emotions effectively contributes to the manifestation of angry, offending behaviour for which they may or may not incur criminal convictions. Grinker and Werble (1977) note that intense anger constitutes the primary affective state for many with personality disorder and the behavioural consequences may make it difficult to hold in mind the vulnerability and neediness of the personality disordered patient. This may contribute to staff referring to patients by their offending behaviour in discussions among themselves, for example, 'What treatment will we offer to the rapists?'

Burrow (1991) describes the difficulties staff working within forensic settings experience in balancing the need for safety and security with the provision of care. It can take several years to acquire the skill of being able to hold in mind the vulnerability of the patient whilst simultaneously holding the capacity of the patient to be destructive. Staff may experience conflicting emotions as they fluctuate from one polarity to the other or find themselves in conflict with one another when different staff members prioritise competing poles.

When staff believe that the mentally ill are dangerous they are more likely to be socially rejecting, but this perception of dangerousness may extend to those who have no history of offending. Markham (2003) found that qualified mental health professionals perceived people with personality disorder to be more dangerous than those with mental illness, unlike unqualified staff who tended to perceive both groups as equally dangerous. Within the UK, the perception of personality disorder as an inherently dangerous disorder has probably been heightened by the government's high profile attempts to ensure the NHS and prison service provide for a formerly excluded client group. These have been accompanied by the creation of specialist services which were initially labelled 'Dangerous and Severe Personality Disorder Units'.

Inability to comprehend the patient's world

The context within which the personality disordered individual has been raised leads to such clients occupying a logical world that may differ significantly from our own. Children who grow up in families where they are consistently treated with love and respect and have their basic needs met grow up feeling valued as a person and believing that they are deserving of care and that others can be relied upon to provide help and support. When children grow up in abusive, neglectful or emotionally deprived families, they make sense of events by internalising a model of themselves as fundamentally unlovable and unworthy of having their needs met (Bowlby, 1988), and may develop an expectation that others will harm them if opportunities arise. When staff apply their own logical understanding of the world to their interactions with patients, they make the faulty assumption that patients will consider them to be safe because they are 'caregivers'. However, since the patient's experience is such that they may be operating in accordance with the logical rule that 'caregivers cannot be trusted', a conflict arises whereby the hostility of the patient is perceived to be primarily motivated as an attack on staff rather than an attempt at self-preservation when frightened. This dynamic is explored in greater detail within Chapter 5, but to be successfully worked with requires staff members to be able to tolerate the perception of themselves as potential abusers.

5 The work leaves staff feeling vulnerable

Personality disorder is characterised by difficulties in regulating emotion and individuals with this disorder often present as behaviourally impulsive or over-reliant upon anger as a means of coping with underlying affect that would otherwise leave them feeling vulnerable. Patients may vacillate from extreme dependency, characterised by an overwhelming neediness, to intense hatred of staff for not managing to fulfil such unachievable demands (Bland *et al.*, 2007). Working with these clients is often a test of the staff member's own ability to tolerate extremes of emotion. In particular, staff need to be able to manage not only the rapidly fluctuating mood but also the range of emotions that the patients struggle to tolerate – that is, those associated with vulnerability (in particular, fear, being hated and shame or humiliation) – without resorting to angry acting out as a means of coping.

Fear

A number of aspects of this work have the potential to induce fear in staff due to the risk to the physical or emotional integrity of the staff member.

FEAR OF VIOLENCE TO SELF

Many people with personality disorder manage their emotions via angry, impulsive, acting-out behaviour, particularly those whose behaviour leads to their detention within forensic services. Working with these patients therefore involves the risk of assault. Within forensic services, staff often cope with the threat of violence by rationalising aggressive incidents as the acts of a 'sick person'. Since personality disordered individuals can be difficult to construe as 'sick', their aggression may be more difficult to cope with, and Bowers (2002) found a perception that people with personality disorder may be more inclined to use a greater level of force than mentally ill patients. There is also a perception that people with personality disorder are more inclined to resort to instrumental aggression. However, when one explores incidents that appear initially to be motivated solely by gain, the violence often had its origins within apparently innocuous events that triggered overwhelming humiliation within the aggressor.

FEAR OF TRAUMATISATION

Some authors suggest that working with people with personality disorder is traumatising (Hartman, 1995; O'Brien and Flöte, 1997; Sexton, 1999). In addition to the risk of physical assault and the risk to one's professional integrity, many people with personality disorder have been victims of violence, sexual violence or extreme neglect (Soloff et al., 2002; Chapman et al., 2005; Zlotnick et al., 2003), and a significant number of service users have also been perpetrators. Working with victims of violence carries the risk of vicarious traumatisation (Hartman, 1995), and caring for victims of violence has been identified as frightening for staff (Nehls, 1998; O'Brien and Flöte, 1997). Gallop et al. (1995) found that approximately 40 per cent of a sample of nurses did not approve of routine enquiries about sexual abuse, citing fear of increasing a client's distress or acting intrusively as reasons for their beliefs. Some authors (Farquharson, 2004; Weaver et al., 1994) observe that the structure of institutional work entailing several hours of contact rather than a therapeutic hour, the severity of the psychopathology and the lack of distance between staff and patients make treatment in institutions especially difficult and may contribute to the reluctance of some staff to engage in such discussions. There is some evidence to suggest that even staff who have more restricted contact, such as psychiatrists, may be reluctant to engage in discussions with patients about their traumatic histories (Goater and Meehan, 1998); and, whilst working within a community forensic team, the first author was requested by the head of a psychology team not to refer any more individuals with traumatic histories for a while due to the manager's fear 'that all my staff will go off sick'. Similarly, within forensic settings, where patients and prisoners may have committed heinous offences, many health and operational staff function within their role by avoiding information that would keep them consciously alert to the dangerousness of those with whom they work.

FEAR OF LOSING PROFESSIONAL INTEGRITY

Nurses in O'Brien and Flöte's (1997) study reported feeling that the organisation held them personally responsible for the patient's safety, a view supported by Gutheil (1985) who states, 'the lay person's simplistic belief that suicide is suicide is shared at times by courts and attorneys'. Cooper (1995) and Sacks et al. (1987) refer to the scapegoating that can occur following a serious assault or suicide, and incidents of self-harm, which are not uncommon occurrences, can leave staff feeling frustrated, angry and incompetent (Cleary et al., 2002; Crowe, 1996). Staff may blame the victim of an assault for their injury, as it may be preferable to think that an assault could have been avoided if only the assaulted staff member had managed the situation better, rather than thinking that one could be unpredictably assaulted during the course of a normal working day.

Personality disordered individuals are a notoriously litigious client group and may misuse the media, complaints systems and organisations designed to facilitate supportive advocacy (Bowers, 2002) in efforts to punish or coerce staff into their desired course of action or to overcome feelings of powerlessness. This can leave inexperienced staff fearful of humiliation or expulsion from their professional body, and contributes to defensive (rather than defensible) decision making. Defensive decision making is likely to lead to a stressful and therefore poor decision-making process that inhibits the ability of a team to generate creative solutions to complex problems. Being on the receiving end of numerous complaints is not only stressful but also generates extra work that, if unformulated, may foster resentment in staff.

Piccinino (1990) observes how the patient's criticism and judgements of staff members as inept or inadequate can contribute to their colleagues questioning an individual's competence, particularly in teams where relationships are weak or fractured. Cooper (1995) notes how this can undermine a staff member's own confidence, and this is likely to be amplified within teams characterised by mistrust or when staff lack confidence in their own abilities or those of their colleagues.

Being hated

Some patients are unable to contain their hate for a needed person or an abuser (e.g. parent or other carer) and project this onto staff (Watts and Morgan, 1994). If hate is reciprocated, then responsibility for the hatred is shared and the patient can feel better about their own hatred. Patients may behave aggressively or passive aggressively in order to provoke hatred in the other and this again creates an intrapersonal conflict for staff.

Within forensic populations where the patient's capacity for hatred may actually have led to the physical annihilation of another, the experience of being hated may be exceptionally painful to tolerate. Groups of patients who have committed offences against others may use their hatred of another to bond and defend themselves from more vulnerable affect (e.g. hatred of female staff within a male population mainly convicted of rape and murder of female victims). However, even within non-offender populations, hatred of the staff member can contribute to a very unpleasant experience in which the staff member is subjected to frequent insulting, hostile comments and criticism (Neilson, 1991).

Shame and humiliation

Related to the fear of losing one's professional integrity is the shame that may be evoked when staff feel they have actually compromised their professional integrity with minor transgressions such as the fleeting loss of temper or by being confronted by their own limitations in performing their professional role.

The intense emotions that may be aroused in staff treating personality disordered patients, such as despair, anger, fear, guilt, shame and disappointment (Bowers, 2003; Johnstone, 1997), may in themselves elicit a strong sense of shame and inadequacy (Highley and Norris, 1957; Schwartz, 1958) and in some cases be experienced as profoundly humiliating. They also interfere with the use of sound clinical judgement (Gutheil, 1985), restrict the capacity of staff to be effective (Schwartz, 1958), and lead to the desire for revenge (Johnstone, 1997) or to staff distancing themselves from the patient (Fraser and Gallop, 1993; Gallop *et al.*, 1989; Johnstone, 1997; O'Brien and Flöte, 1997; Smith and Hart, 1994). Since these consequences are antithetical to the way staff are supposed to behave towards their patients, feelings of shame may thus be exacerbated and may be managed by staff becoming angry or avoiding the patient.

6 The work requires specific personal qualities and skills

Whilst it may be unusual for services to recruit staff with certain skills and attributes to work with people with personality disorder, the literature suggests that a specific range of skills and qualities are required. Implicit within the literature is an understanding that some staff are unsuited to working with this client group. Several authors suggest that nursing these patients requires such a high standard of professionalism that some staff may be unable to meet the requirements. For instance, Smoyak (1985) writes that 'Borderline patients separate the pros from the amateurs in psychiatric nursing', and there is reason to believe that this statement applies equally to other professional groups. The inter-related qualities, knowledge and skills identified below are attributes that we believe would contribute to a competent staff member across all mental health client groups, but such attributes become more necessary when working with people with personality disorder.

Desire to work with this client group

We have already established that this is an unpopular client group and, in some specialist services, staff may find themselves directed rather than choosing to work with this patient group (Moran and Mason, 1996). Others may find themselves encountering personality disordered patients within a more generic population. In such circumstances, it is likely that the patient will detect any negative attitudes in staff and this will have a detrimental effect on the therapeutic relationship. Research has established that people with borderline personality disorder are significantly better at identifying affect in faces than people without the disorder (Fertuck *et al.*, 2009) and additionally tend to see faces as less trustworthy.

Bowers (2002) identified a number of moral choices made by nurses that contributed to a positive attitude towards working with people with personality disorder. These included a commitment to equality (rather than a need for superiority over the patient), non-judgementalism (not engaging in moral evaluation of the patient), universal humanity (valuing people despite their diversity) and appreciation of the value of all individuals. Caine *et al.* (1981) also suggest that being liberal and socially oriented are positive qualities when working with personality disordered patients.

Good emotional regulation skills

Since the work is so emotionally challenging, there is a requirement for staff working with this patient group to have a good ability to recognise and tolerate their own emotions. It is not uncommon for staff, like patients, to either convert emotions that are associated with vulnerability, such as hatred, shame and fear, into anger (as this enables the staff member to feel more powerful), or resort to avoiding the patient (Smith and Hart, 1994). Paradoxically, staff members who resort to angry or avoidant responses to patients can end up reducing their self-esteem as they may feel guilty or perceive themselves as unprofessional. Making sure that support is available to staff within a service will not ensure that staff are able to make full use of this if they do not already have a reasonable ability to cope with strong affect and have a capacity to be emotionally honest.

Capacity for self-reflection

An essential component of effective emotional regulation is the capacity to reflect on oneself and observe what one is experiencing. Similarly, the ability to consider what one is also bringing to interactions with the patient is important (Piccinino, 1990; Gallop, 1985). This is emphasised within the work of Safran and Muran (2000) who indicate that discussing the emotional transaction between the client and staff member positively influences alliance and outcome. As with the ability to regulate emotions, providing staff with a forum for reflection, i.e. supervision, does not guarantee enhanced self-reflection although it is possible that training may have some benefits.

Related to the capacity for self-reflection is the ability to admit to errors. Admitting to errors enables staff to learn from their mistakes and develop the potential to diffuse anger-provoking situations with clients. It also prevents staff from expecting patients to keep secrets for them in order to conceal any errors they have made and thus reduces opportunities for misuse of patient power.

Robust self-esteem

Robust self-esteem is important in protecting staff from taking verbal attacks personally and enabling them to cope with feelings of being disliked or hated. This client group are prone to categorising staff into 'good' and 'bad' sub-groups and unfavoured staff are left in no doubt about their personal and professional weaknesses and failings and are subject to much hostility and criticism (Neilson, 1991). Staff may find clients misrepresenting them or providing accounts of interactions with them that are skewed by cognitive distortions or information that is presented out of context. When staff lack confidence in their relationship with their peers, they may fear these misrepresentations will be believed and become angry or defensive, thus exacerbating the situation.

Those who are emotionally fragile may not only perceive verbal attacks as more personal but also be vulnerable to attempts by patients to form 'special' relationships (Chitty and Maynard, 1986) in order to boost their self-esteem. This is particularly so when staff members are unable to acknowledge and confront their own vulnerability or fear of patients and instead find themselves drawn into collusive relationships that are designed to keep the staff member feeling safe or special. It is not unusual for boundary breaches to occur between staff and personality disordered patients. Whilst the apparent competence of many patients may be a contributory factor, within inpatient and prison settings, the risk of a sexual relationship being established is elevated when supervision does not directly and explicitly address questions of the staff member's self-esteem and emotional vulnerability and the sexual tensions between the client and staff member.

Robust professional identity

Self-esteem may be enhanced when one is in possession of a robust professional identity. Many teams are established with a range of professionals occupying generic mental health worker posts. Not only does this practice undermine the effectiveness of a team (see Chapter 7) but it may also contribute to the erosion of the staff member's professional identity and thus their self-esteem. Our experience is that possessing a robust professional identity enables staff to more easily identify appropriate interventions and thus acquire a sense of competence. A lack of self-efficacy is associated with impaired ability to manage the patient's anger (Smith and Hart, 1994), and staff who lack a strong professional identity may be drawn into role blurring which is associated with role strain and confusion (Moller and Harber, 1996).

Capacity to present as healthy parent

An essential ability required in providing treatment to these clients is having the capacity to relate with the patient as a healthy parent. Young (1994) refers to the concept of limited re-parenting as a vehicle for the effective delivery of treatment. However, superficial adoption of this role will be insufficient for these clients who have a tremendous propensity to interpret when a relationship is authentic and when it is contrived and are therefore capable of exposing the therapist who merely 'acts' the role. Thus, the clinician requires the capacity to foster the client and demonstrate the ability to acknowledge and encourage the lovable part of the patient. It is through this ability to provide a healthy interpersonal experience that the patient can begin to acknowledge themselves as lovable, thus shifting their internal identity to a more healthy one.

Ability to set limits

Maintaining firm boundaries is essential for a client group who have typically experienced a lack of boundaries or overly restrictive or inconsistent boundaries during childhood. Whilst a cohesive team may create a context where it is easier to set limits (Piccinino, 1990; Neilson, 1991), the interpersonal style that is adopted when setting limits is also important (Kaplan, 1986; Lancee *et al.* 1995). Some staff seem better equipped to set limits empathically without utilising a belittling, angry or punitive manner which can inflame an already tense situation. An analysis of seventy-three episodes of physical restraint within an inpatient setting concluded that the most frequent explanation for the patient's aggression was conflict over boundaries (Sheridan *et al.*, 1990).

   Bowers (2002) identifies two related characteristics that are important in staff being able to provide a good service to personality disordered patients: being able to be honest with patients even when this is difficult or costly; and having the bravery to confront patients and risk violence where necessary. Both of these qualities contribute to the ability to set limits empathically. Moran and Mason (1996) highlight how fear can prevent less brave staff from being honest in limit-setting 'for short-term comfort'. A failure to master one's fear has been linked to increased episodes of violence (Lancee *et al.*, 1995) and can increase the risk to staff who are able to set limits as they may be perceived by the patients as 'the bad guy' and a legitimate target of assault or abuse.

Willingness to embrace therapeutic challenges

Much of the knowledge and skills that are beneficial to staff in working with this client group can be provided via clinical supervision, mentoring and training. It is possible that these learning opportunities may also enable some staff to access more valuable personal qualities within themselves. However, these opportunities will only be of benefit if staff members are open to new experiences and ideas and have the courage to accept that their existing knowledge base and skill range may be inadequate. Bowers's (2006) study of prison officers found that those who had more liking for personality disordered prisoners and interest in them were more open to new experiences and ideas. It is likely that those who enjoy working with these clients find overcoming the challenge that this client group poses rewarding.

Possessing a psychological understanding of personality disorder

Krawitz (2004) found that providing training workshops which enabled clinicians to have a common foundation of knowledge, language and skills (even when they didn't identify themselves as having an interest in personality disorder) was positively received, and at the six months follow-up participants felt the workshop had considerably improved their clinical practice. A significant difference in attitudes, optimism, theoretical knowledge and clinical skills was observed at follow-up. Krawitz also found that increasing clinicians' knowledge of the medicolegal environment can decrease anxiety about possible medicolegal consequences and thereby increase clinicians' willingness to work in the area.

A thorough understanding of subjects related to personality disorder such as assessment and formulation, aetiology, awareness of the long-term nature of the condition, an understanding of the impact of poor emotional regulation and cognitive distortions on relationships with others, staff response patterns and treatment strategies can enable staff to feel more competent, less personally attacked and therefore increase their tolerance. These abilities are related to enhanced coping and continued involvement with the patient rather than avoidance and inadequate or abusive patient care (Fraser and Gallop, 1993; Gallop *et al.*, 1989; Smith and Hart, 1994). Knowledge of attachment theory is particularly useful since this enables staff to hold in mind the vulnerability of the patient and also guides their interventions when they are able to recognise the implications for their own role as a caregiver/ parental figure.

Ability to perceive vulnerability in the patient

Within forensic settings, reading about the patient's offences can cause clinicians to be fearful of or repulsed by the client. Even with non-forensic patients, the client's interpersonal style can be such that it is difficult to perceive the client's vulnerability. Experienced staff adopt strategies such as getting to know the patient before reading about the index offence, reminding themselves about the patient's own history of abuse, and formulating the function of the patient's rejecting behaviours.

Ability to identify true progress

Developing the skill to identify almost imperceptible progress and discriminate between apparent progress and true progress is an invaluable asset and enables staff to maintain therapeutic optimism and confidence in their risk assessment skills.

Some authors have expressed the desirability of employing experienced staff (Smoyak, 1985; Piccinino, 1990) which may improve the likelihood of the staff member having these skills already. However, it is important that their experience is of this client group as those who have become accustomed to working with other client groups may undergo an initial period of feeling immensely deskilled. Newly qualified staff are often keen to learn and may be more open to new experience. Research supports this and indicates that personality disordered patients do not necessarily need allocating to highly trained, experienced professionals (Commons-Treloar and Lewis, 2008; Krawitz, 2004).

Personal qualities may be harder to develop but our experience has been that this task is not necessarily impossible, particularly with qualities influenced by knowledge. Some staff initially appear unsuited to work with people with personality disorders but, within the right learning environment, more service user-focused attributes can be developed. What may be more essential is the presence of the aforementioned qualities in managers of services. Bravery and honesty may be developed in staff if managers and supervisors are brave enough to utilise honesty within their discussions of the individual staff member's clinical practice – for example, adopting a direct approach and pointing out when a staff member appears to have avoided appropriately challenging a client.

Consequences of challenges for patients and staff

A failure to overcome the difficulties arising when caring for these clients can have negative consequences for both staff and patients. Negative attitude to personality disorder is associated with diminished empathy and reduced standards of care (Alston and Robinson, 1992; Gallop *et al.*, 1989; Fraser and Gallop, 1993; Johnstone, 1997; Markham, 2003; Podrasky and Sexton, 1988) and may contribute to further undermining of the personality disordered client's ability to access respectful, nurturing treatment. Within Bowers's (2002) study, nurses who held negative attitudes were more likely to behave disrespectfully or punitively towards the patients, use the adjectives 'evil' and 'monstrous', and rely upon anger to cope. A positive attitude was associated with an enhanced standard of care in nurses (Bowers, 2002) and operational staff (Bowers, 2006). Reluctance to accept a patient for treatment, premature discharges and punitive restrictions on treatment may all represent attempts by staff to avoid their own negative affect (Kullgren, 1985;

Watts and Morgan, 1994). Within services where there is a general trend towards avoidance of such patients, the burden of care often falls most heavily upon those staff whose status affords them least autonomy, i.e. those with least training and experience. The efforts of psychologists to discharge themselves from the responsibility of those they identify as 'not psychologically-minded' within a community mental health team can mean that untrained support workers are left with the most difficult patients on their caseload.

Use of language (e.g. 'evil' and 'manipulative') can cause us to feel hopeless and give us permission to discount the individual's needs (Diamond and Factor, 1994). In 1988, Lewis and Appleby drew attention to the pejorative and derogatory ways in which people with personality disorder are referred to in print, and this continues to be reflected within contemporary discussions of this client group. At times, an author's dislike of the patient is reflected in a subtle tone to the text; for example, Bowers writes,

> Their behaviour is difficult, obnoxious, threatening and they are hard to manage in institutional settings . . . when at large in the community they cause problems for others through their antisocial and irresponsible conduct. Their incessant and contradictory demands upon health service resources . . . evoke negative reactions from all professions.
>
> (2002, p. 2)

Other authors are yet more explicit in their contempt for the patient. For instance, Tredgett (2001, p. 348) describes the symptoms of personality disorder as 'a lack of concern for the feelings of others, extreme egocentricity and lying, either to explain or excuse their own behaviour or to gain sympathy. There is often a tendency to blame others for problems they themselves have created.' Professionals reading such pejorative comments can be influenced to develop a negative mindset towards people diagnosed with these disorders. Importantly, such comments in academic journals enable staff to feel justified in utilising similar statements within clinical reports. The patient will sense the hostility towards them and may withdraw from the clinician. Other staff may also become affected by the negativity that is expressed towards the patient. Hinshelwood (2002) describes 'affect flow' in which emotions become contagious within a setting if staff do not overtly recognise and adequately process their emotional reactions to a patient.

In addition to the standard of client care suffering as a consequence of negative staff attitudes, nursing staff holding negative attitudes tend to experience more anger towards their patients (Bland *et al.*, 2007), feel deskilled (Breeze and Repper, 1998; O'Brien, 1998) and have more detrimental personal experiences when they encounter such patients (Bowers, 2002; Pfohl *et al.*, 1999). Prison officers who held negative views were more likely to suffer burnout, took more sick leave and were rated lower in terms of job performance than their more positive colleagues (Bowers, 2006). Bowers (2002) found that negative attitudes extended to the staff member's life outside work, and conversely found that staff who expressed positive attitudes towards their patients described becoming more assertive and compassionate within their personal lives as well as having lower levels of stress and greater well-being.

If the challenges are not managed effectively, there is likely to be not only an impact upon the level of patient care and the well-being of the staff but also an impact at an organisational level. Services that fail to keep staff and patients feeling safe and secure are unlikely to be able to recruit and retain good quality staff and are also likely to develop an 'image problem' which may lead to calls for closure (e.g. Fallon's inquiry into Ashworth hospital).

Managing the challenges effectively

Whilst individual clinicians, services or organisations may not be able to greatly impact upon professional training courses or cultural attitudes of professional groups, they do have the capacity to change the climate within their own sphere of influence, whether that is at team, service or organisational level. Creating an environment that ensures equitable effective services for personality disordered patients whilst maintaining a competent, motivated cohort of staff requires an assertive approach to resolving the difficulties. This has implications for staff selection, education and support; the structure, policies and procedures adopted by the service provider; and the choice of therapeutic interventions and the ways in which they are delivered.

There is no infallible method of staff selection but some strategies may reduce the risk of employing toxic staff. Staff selection needs to be at least partially based on the person's interpersonal skills and attitude to the client group with whom they will work. In the UK, guidance has been published (*Personality Disorder Capabilities Framework*; NIMHE, 2003) highlighting the skills that are required to work with these clients, and any employer offering services to personality disordered patients would benefit from reflecting upon their recruitment procedures and broadening these beyond an interview and presentation. Sneath (Chapter 13) offers suggestions about how staff selection can be improved and also ways in which staff' skills can be enhanced through formal training and mentoring and by ensuring supervision is effective, and includes attention to staff-generated treatment-interfering behaviours. She also identifies ways in which organisations can optimise the support opportunities available to staff.

In Chapter 6, McVey and Saradjian emphasise organisational strategies that can minimise the difficulties that are posed to staff working within services, such as planning services with an established coherent treatment model to guide preparations; having clear policies and procedures (particularly in relation to management of complaints) to guide practice and protect staff and service users; and ensuring service provision is sensitive to the difference between treatment and management of patients.

Murphy (Chapter 7) identifies why teamwork is often a more effective approach to treating these patients and outlines how to create a high performing team that can manage the challenges posed. She suggests that by preparing a team (planning team composition, staff selection, staff training, orientation of new staff), ensuring clarity within the team (of membership, accountability, role, operational policy and procedures, communication and decision making and relations with host organisation), reducing unnecessary differences between team members (ensuring a common catchment/client group, establishing shared goals, philosophy, knowledge) and providing participatory safety (via high frequency interactions, ensuring adaptive conflict resolution and protecting team integrity), teamwork can offer support in overcoming the challenges posed.

Providing effective care and treatment for people with personality disorder is one of the most challenging objectives in the field of mental health. However, when working within a bespoke service that identifies and addresses the labyrinth of therapy-interfering behaviours, working with this client group can provide staff with a tremendous sense of job satisfaction and countless opportunities for professional and personal growth.

References

Alhadeff, L. (1994) Managing difficult populations. *New Directions for Mental Health Services*, **63**, 71–79.

Alston, M. and Robinson, B. (1992) Nurses' attitudes towards suicide. *Omega*, **25**, 205–215.

Bland, A.R. (2003) Emotion processing in borderline personality disorders. Ph.D. thesis, University of South Carolina, Columbia, South Carolina.

Bland, A.R. and Rossen, E.K. (2005) Clinical supervision of nurses working with patients with borderline personality disorder. *Issues in Mental Health Nursing*, **26**, 507–517.

Bland, A.R., Tudor, G. and Whitehouse, D.M. (2007) Nursing care of inpatients with borderline personality disorder. *Perspectives in Psychiatric Care*, **43(4)**, 204–212.

Bowers, L. (2002) *Dangerous and Severe Personality Disorder*. London: Routledge.

Bowers, L. (2003) Manipulation: description, identification and ambiguity. *Journal of Psychiatric and Mental Health Nursing*, **10**, 323–328.

Bowers, L. (2006) Attitude to personality disorder among prison officers working in a dangerous and severe personality disorder unit. *International Journal of Law and Psychiatry*, **29**, 333–342.

Bowlby, J. (1988) *A Secure Base*. London: Routledge.

Boyes, A. (1994) Repetition of overdose: a retrospective five year study. *Journal of Advanced Nursing*, **20**, 462–468.

Breeze, J.A. and Repper, J. (1998) Struggling for control: the care experiences of 'difficult' patients in mental health services. *Journal of Advanced Nursing*, **28**, 1301–1311.

Brody, E.M. and Farber, B.A. (1996) The effects of therapist experience and patient diagnosis on countertransference. *Psychotherapy*, **33**, 372–380.

Burrow, S. (1991) The special hospital nurse and the dilemma of therapeutic custody. *Journal of Advances in Health and Nursing Care*, **3**, 21–38.

Caine, T.M., Wijesinghe, O.B.A. and Winter, D.A. (1981) *Personal Styles in Neurosis: Implications for Small Group Therapy and Behaviour Therapy*. London: Routledge & Kegan Paul.

Cavadino, M. (1998) Death to the psychopath. *Journal of Forensic Psychiatry*, **9(1)**, 5–8.

Chapman, A.L., Specht, M.W. and Cellucci, T. (2005) Factors associated with suicide in female inmates. The hegemony of hopelessness. *Suicide and Life-Threatening Behaviour*, **35**, 388–399.

Chitty, K. and Maynard, C. (1986) Managing manipulation. *Journal of Psychosocial Nursing*, **24(6)**, 9–13.

Cleary, M., Siegfried, N. and Walter, G. (2002) Experience, knowledge and attitudes of mental health staff regarding clients with a borderline personality disorder. *International Journal of Mental Health Nursing*, **11**, 186–191.

Colson, D.B., Allen, J.G., Coyne, L., Dearing, D., Jehl, N., Kearns, N.W. and Spohn, H.E. (1985) Patterns of staff perceptions of difficult patients in a long-term psychiatric hospital. *Hospital and Community Psychiatry*, **36**, 168–172.

Commons-Treloar, A.J. and Lewis, A.J. (2008) Professional attitudes towards deliberate self-harm in patients with borderline personality disorder. *Australian and New Zealand Journal of Psychiatry*, **42**, 578–584.

Cooper, C. (1995) Patient suicide and assault: their impact on psychiatric hospital staff. *Journal of Psychosocial Nursing*, **33(6)**, 26–29.

Crothers, D. (1995) Vicarious traumatization in work with survivors of childhood trauma. *Journal of Psychosocial Nursing*, **33(4)**, 9–13.

Crowe, M. (1996) Cutting up: signifying the unspeakable. *Australian and New Zealand Journal of Mental Health and Nursing*, **5**, 103–111.

Deans, C. and Meocevic, E. (2006) Attitudes of registered psychiatric nurses towards patients diagnosed with borderline personality disorder. *Contemporary Nurse*, **21(1)**, 43–49.

DeLaune, S.C. (2004) Personality disorders. In C.R. Kniesl, H.S. Wilson and E. Trigoboff (eds), *Contemporary Psychiatric Mental Health Nursing*. Upper Saddle River, NJ: Pearson Education, pp. 479–505.

Diamond, R. and Factor, R. (1994) Taking issue: treatment-resistant patients or a treatment resistant system? *Hospital and Community Psychiatry*, **45**, 97.

Fahy, T. (2004) Organisation of personality disorder services in general adult psychiatry services: Discussion paper. http://www.dh.gov.uk/dr_consum_dh/groups/dh_digitalassets/@dh/@en/documents/digitalassets/dh_4130849.pdf

Fallon, P., Bluglass, B., Edwards, B. and Daniels, G. (1999) *Report of the Committee of Inquiry into the Personality Disorder Unit, Ashworth Special Hospital*. London: Stationery Office.

Farquharson, G. (2004) How good staff become bad. In P. Campling, S. Davies and G. Farquharson (eds), *From Toxic Institutions to Therapeutic Environments*. London: Gaskell, ch. 2.

Fertuck, E.A., Jekal, A., Song, I., Wyman, B., Morris, M.C., Wilson, S.T., Brodsky, B.S. and Stanley, B. (2009) Enhanced 'Reading the Mind in the Eyes' in borderline personality disorder compared to healthy controls. *Psychological Medicine*, **39(12)**: 1979–1988.

Fraser, K. and Gallop, R. (1993) Nurses' confirming/disconfirming responses to patients diagnosed with borderline personality disorder. *Archives of Psychiatric Nursing*, **7(6)**, 336–341.

Gallop, R. (1985) The patient is splitting: everyone knows and nothing changes. *Journal of Psychosocial Nursing Mental Health Services*, **23(4)**, 6–10.

Gallop, R. and Wynn, F. (1987) The difficult in-patient: identification and response by staff. *Canadian Journal of Psychiatry*, **32**, 211–215.

Gallop, R., Lancee, W. and Garfinkel, P. (1989) How nursing staff respond to the label 'borderline personality disorder'. *Hospital and Community Psychiatry*, **40**, 815–819.

Gallop, R., Lancee, W. and Shugar, G. (1993) Residents' and nurses' perceptions of difficult to treat short stay patients. *Hospital and Community Psychiatry*, **44**, 352–357.

Gallop, R., McKeever, P., Toner, T., Lancee, W. and Lueck, M. (1995) Inquiring about childhood sexual abuse as part of nursing history: opinions of abused and non-abused nurses. *Archives of Psychiatric Nursing*, **9(3)**, 146–151.

Glick, J., Klar, H. and Braff, D. (1984) Guidelines for hospitalisation of chronic psychiatric patients. *Hospital and Community Psychiatry*, **35**, 934–936.

Goater, N. and Meehan, K. (1998) Detection and awareness of child sexual abuse in adult psychiatry. *Psychiatric Bulletin*, **22**, 211–213.

Greene, H. and Ugarriza, D.N. (1995) The 'stably unstable' borderline personality disorder: history, theory and nursing intervention. *Journal of Psychosocial Nursing*, **33(12)**, 26–30.

Grinker, R. and Werble, B. (1977) *The Borderline Patient*. New York: Jason Aronson.

Gunderson, J.G. (1984) *Borderline Personality Disorder*. Washington, DC: American Psychiatric Press.

Gutheil, T.G. (1985) Medicolegal pitfalls in the treatment of borderline patients. *American Journal of Psychiatry*, **142**, 9–14.

Hartman, C.R. (1995) The nurse–patient relationship and victims of violence. *Scholarly Inquiry for Nursing Practice: An International Journal*, **9**, 175–192.

Highley, B.L. and Norris, C.M. (1957) When a student dislikes a patient. *American Journal of Nursing*, **57(9)**, 1163–1166.

Hinshelwood, R. (2002) Abusive help – helping abuse: the psychodynamic impact of severe personality disorder on caring institutions. *Criminal Behaviour and Mental Health*, **12**, S20–S30.

James, P.D. and Cowman, S. (2007) Psychiatric nurses' knowledge, experience and attitudes towards clients with borderline personality disorder. *Journal of Psychiatric and Mental Health Nursing*, **14**, 670–678.

Johnstone, L. (1997) Self-injury and the psychiatric response. *Feminist Psychology*, **7**, 421–426.

Kaplan, C.A. (1986) The challenge of working with patients diagnosed as having a personality disorder. *Nursing Clinics of North America*, **21**, 429–438.

Kelly, M. and May, D. (1982) Good and bad patients: a review of the literature and theoretical critique. *Journal of Advanced Nursing*, **2**, 147–156.

Krawitz, R. (2004) Borderline personality disorder: attitudinal change following training. *Australian and New Zealand Journal of Psychiatry*, **38**, 554–559.

Kullgren, G. (1985) Borderline personality disorder and psychiatric suicides. An analysis of eleven consecutive cases. *Nord Psykiatrica Tidsskr*, **39**, 479–484.

Lancee, W.J., Gallop, R., McCay, E. and Toner, B. (1995) The relationship between nurses' limit-setting styles and anger in psychiatric inpatients. *Psychiatric Services*, **46**, 609–613.

Lewis, G. and Appleby, L. (1988) Personality disorder: the patients psychiatrists dislike. *British Journal of Psychiatry*, **153**, 44–59.

Linehan, M. (1993) *Cognitive Behavioural Treatment of Borderline Personality Disorder*. New York: Guilford Press.

Linehan, M., Armstrong, H., Suarez, A., Almon, D. and Heard, H. (1991) Cognitive behavioral treatment of chronically suicidal patients. *Archive of General Psychiatry*, **48**, 1060–1064.

Markham, D. (2003) Attitudes towards patients with a diagnosis of 'borderline personality disorder': social rejection and dangerousness. *Journal of Mental Health*, **12(6)**, 595–612.

Markham, D. and Trower, P. (2003) The effects of the psychiatric label 'borderline personality disorder' on nursing staff's perceptions and causal attributions for challenging behaviour. *British Journal of Clinical Psychology*, **42(3)**, 243–256.

May, D. and Kelly, M (1982) Chancers, pests and poor wee souls: problems of legitimisation in psychiatric nursing. *Sociology of Health and Illness*, **4(3)**, 279–301.

Mbatia, J. and Tyrer, P. (1988) Personality status of dangerous patients in a special hospital. In P. Tyrer (ed.), *Personality Disorders: Diagnosis, Management and Course*. London: Wright.

McAllister, M., Creedy, D., Moyle, W. and Farrugia, C. (2002) Nurses' attitudes towards clients who self-harm. *Journal of Advanced Nursing*, **40**, 578–586.

McMorrow, M. (1981) The manipulative patient. *American Journal of Nursing*, **81**, 1188–1190.

Miller, S.A. and Davenport, N.C. (1996) Increasing staff knowledge and improving attitudes towards patients with borderline personality disorders. *Psychiatric Services*, **47**, 533–535.

Moller, M.D. and Harber, J. (1996) Advanced practice in psychiatric nursing: the need for a blended role. *Online Journal of Issues in Nursing*. http://www.nursingworld.org/MainMenuCategories/ANAMarketplace/ANA Periodicals/OJIN/TableofContents/Vol21997/No1Jan97/ArticlePreviousTopic/ AdvancedPracticePsychiatricNursing.aspx

Moran, T. and Mason, T. (1996) Revisiting the nursing management of the psychopath. *Journal of Psychiatric and Mental Health Nursing*, **3**, 189–194.

Murphy, N. and McVey, D. (2003) The challenge of nursing personality disordered patients. *British Journal of Forensic Practice*, **5(1)**, 3–19.

National Institute for Mental Health in England (NIMHE) (2003) *Personality Disorder Capabilities Framework*. London: NIMHE.

Nehls, N. (1998) Borderline personality disorder: gender stereotypes, stigma and limited system of care. *Issues in Mental Health Nursing*, **19**, 97–112.

Nehls, N. (1999) Borderline personality disorder: the voice of patients. *Research in Nursing and Health*, **22**, 285–293.

Neilson, P. (1991) Manipulative and splitting behaviours. *Nursing Standard*, **16(8)**, 32–35.

O'Brien, L. (1998) Inpatient nursing care of patients with borderline personality disorder: a review of the literature. *Australian and New Zealand Journal of Mental Health Nursing*, **7(4)**, 172–183.

O'Brien, L. and Flöte, J. (1997) Providing nursing care for a patient with border-line personality disorder on an acute in-patient unit: a phenomenological study. *Australian and New Zealand Journal of Mental Health Nursing*, **6**, 137–147.

Pavolovich-Danis, S.J. (2004) On the border – borderline personality disorder. *Nursing Spectrum*, **5(3)**, 16–18.

Pfohl, B., Silk, K., Robbins, C. *et al.* (1999) *Attitudes towards Borderline Personality Disorder: A Survey of 752 Clinicians*. Geneva: International Society for the Study of Personality Disorders – 6th International Congress on the Disorders of Personality.

Piccinino, S. (1990) The nursing care challenge: borderline patients. *Journal of Psycho-social Nursing*, **8(4)**, 1666–1671.

Podrasky D.L. and Sexton, D.L. (1988) Nurses' reactions to difficult patients. *IMAGE: Journal of Nursing Scholarship*, **20(1)**, 16–21.

Sacks, M., Kibel, H., Cohen, A., Keats M. and Turnquist, K. (1987) Resident response to patient suicide. *Journal of Psychiatric Education*, **11**, 217–227.

Safran, J. and Muran, J. (2000) *Negotiating the Therapeutic Alliance*. New York: Guilford Press.

Sarosi, G.M. (1968) A critical theory: the nurse as a fully human person. *Nursing Forum*, **7(4)**, 349–363.

Schwartz, D. (1958) Uncooperative patients? *American Journal of Nursing*, **58(1)**, 75–77.

Sexton, L. (1999) Vicarious traumatisation of counsellors and effects on their work-places. *British Journal of Guidance and Counselling*, **27**, 393–403.

Sheridan, M., Henrion, R., Robinson, L. *et al.* (1990) Precipitants of violence in a psychiatric inpatient setting. *Hospital and Community Psychiatry*, **41**, 776–780.

Smith, M.E. and Hart, G. (1994) Nurses' responses to patient anger: from disconnect-ing to connecting. *Journal of Advanced Nursing*, **20**, 643–651.

Smoyak, S. (1985) Editorial: Borderline personality disorder. *Journal of Psychosocial Nursing and Mental Health Services*, **23(4)**, 5.

Soloff, P.H., Lynch, K.G. and Kelly, T.M. (2002) Childhood abuse as a risk factor for suicidal behaviour in borderline personality disorder. *Journal of Personality Disorder*, **16**, 201–214.

Taylor, P.J., Leese, M., Williams, D., Butwell, M., Daly, R. and Larkin, E. (1998) Mental disorder and violence. A Special (high security) hospital study. *British Journal of Psychiatry*, **172**, 218–226.

Tredgett, J. (2001) The aetiology, presentation and treatment of personality disorders. *Journal of Psychiatric and Mental Health Nursing*, **8**, 347–356.

Watts, D. and Morgan, G. (1994) Malignant alienation: dangers for patients who are hard to like. *British Journal of Psychiatry*, **164**, 11–15.

Weaver, P.L., Varvaro, F., Connors, R. and Regan-Kubinski, M. (1994) Adult sur-vivors of childhood sexual abuse: survivors, disclosure and nurse therapists' response. *Journal of Psychosocial Nursing*, **32(12)**, 19–25.

Young, J. (1994) *Cognitive Therapy for Personality Disorders: A Schema-focused Approach*. Sarasota, FL: Professional Resource Press.

Zlotnick, C., Johnson, D.M., Yen, S. *et al.* (2003) Clinical features and impairment in women with borderline personality disorder (BPD) and post-traumatic stress disorder (PTSD), BPD without PTSD and other personality disorders with PTSD. *Journal of Nervous and Mental Disease*, **191**, 706–713.

Chapter 3

Assessing personality disorder within a formulation framework

Jacquie Evans and Neil Watson

Introduction

Current prevalence statistics suggest it is inevitable that clinicians in community and secure services will encounter personality disordered people within their practice. It is estimated that 25 per cent of attendees at GP practices fulfil diagnostic criteria for personality disorder (Moran *et al.*, 2000), as do 30–50 per cent of outpatients (e.g. Koenigsberg *et al.*, 1985), 10–15 per cent of the general population, up to 50 per cent of imprisoned women and 78 per cent of sentenced male prisoners (Personality Disorder Services Framework; ESMHCG, 2005). Consequently, it is important that clinicians working in all settings have basic skills in assessing personality disorder as well as other mental health problems.

Clinicians working with this population experience challenging clients who may be denigrating, demanding, rejecting and aggressive or, alternatively, passive and detached in style. They are often referred to in highly negative and pejorative terms. Many service providers have previously relied on the exclusion from treatment clause of the Mental Health Act (1983) as a way of legitimising not offering services to this group of people. Conversely, other clinicians avoid diagnosing personality disorder as they feel ill equipped to do so (Duggan and Gibbon, 2008), or fear the label will be used by others to exclude the individual from treatment. With high prevalence rates, the amendments to the Mental Health Act (2007) and new treatment initiatives, it is important that service providers adopt an effective assessment model to identify the presence of the condition and design effective treatment.

We do not explore some of the fundamental theoretical questions about diagnosis and assessment within this chapter, for example stability of condition, the merits of categorical versus dimensional classification, evaluation of psychometric tools or conducting structured risk assessments and clinical interviews, since these are already effectively covered elsewhere (e.g. Beck *et al.*, 2004; Clark, 1999; Livesley, 2001; Millon and Davis, 2000; NICE, 2009a; Steiner *et al.*, 1995; van Velzen and Emmelkamp, 1996; Zanarini *et al.*, 2003). Instead, we outline a model of *how to* assess since this has largely been neglected within the literature. Utilising such a model enables clinicians to arrive at a formulation-driven understanding of personality disorder with a view to determining the client's treatment needs, aiding staff management and guiding treatment of the client irrespective of service context.

The importance of assessment and diagnosis

Assessment should enable clinicians to move beyond merely labelling people as personality disordered to identifying their difficulties and distresses within the context of their own unique world. Millon and Davis (2000) argue that 'assessment is the basis of therapy'. It is the role of the assessor to ensure that there is a holistic understanding of the patient which encompasses his risk, interpersonal and social functioning, symptoms and inner experiences.

Too frequently, assessment has merely led to a diagnosis. Diagnosis relied upon in isolation leads to therapeutic pessimism (NICE, 2009b) in both clinicians and clients, due to the association of this diagnosis with lack of 'treatability', and it should therefore be part of broader formulations of clients and their needs. Where formal diagnosis is not utilised, clients may be perceived as 'time wasters' or be referred to as 'having a P.D.' without receiving a thorough assessment and formulation of their personality. Such clients are defined by the perception of them as 'difficult' and are either provided with no treatment or given inappropriate treatment that may reinforce perceptions of failure.

The most commonly used diagnostic systems, DSM-IV (APA, 2000) and ICD-10 (WHO, 1990), both utilise categorical diagnosis, although there is scope for dimensional recording. The model presented draws upon categorical diagnosis since we utilise the DSM-IV definition of personality disorder as 'an enduring pattern of inner experience and behaviour that deviates markedly from the expectations of the individual's culture, is pervasive and inflexible, has an onset in adolescence or early adulthood, is stable over time and leads to distress or impairment' (p. 685), to structure our assessment. However, this model is equally applicable to dimensional material and can be used within both systems to develop a formulation to guide interventions. What *is* important is the ability to assess dysfunction of an individual in at least two of the following areas: cognition, affectivity, interpersonal functioning and impulse control. Equally, it is important to account for pervasiveness and severity of the disorder as episodic presentation may entice clinicians towards a diagnosis of mental illness. Furthermore, it is necessary to ensure patterns of functioning cause significant distress or affect the person's ability to function across a number of domains (e.g. occupation, intimate relationships and social functioning) since this indicates that the disorder has significant negative consequences for the person. Severity of personality disorder may be determined by a complex diagnosis across the main three clusters (as argued by Tyrer and Johnson, 1996) or by the level of dysfunction caused to the person.

Assessment also requires clinicians to attend to co-morbidity. Co-morbidity is common due to lack of specificity for personality disorder criteria and multiple personality disorder diagnoses are often encountered (Coid, 1992). Co-morbidity with Axis I disorders such as psychosis and violence (Nolan et al., 1999; Tengstrom, et al., 2000; Moran et al., 2003) and learning disability (Alexander and Cooray, 2003) is also widespread. Co-morbidity is more common in forensic settings, where the likelihood of dual diagnosis including personality disorder is increased (Coid et al., 1999; Singleton et al., 1998; Taylor et al., 1998). Thus, any effective assessment must include some exploration of this issue.

Assessment leading to formulation

As noted above, standardised systems for diagnosing individuals with specific disorders, such as DSM-IV (APA, 2000), enable clinicians from diverse backgrounds to identify the likely presentation of a client diagnosed with a specific personality disorder. However, diagnosis of personality disorder does not necessarily indicate how that client will present in specific situations or respond to specific interventions. Neither does it specify the exact course or nature of the intervention that is best suited to the client, or the therapy-interfering behaviours that are likely to occur during treatment. Consequently, a significant aspect of the assessment process is to develop a preliminary case formulation that can be tested out through additional assessment or responses to interventions. We propose the assessment model depicted in Figure 3.1 as a way of gathering material across four key domains to enable both diagnosis and the development of a clinical formulation.

Each method of assessment (collateral, patient/client interview, etc.) is analysed to determine how information for each domain (e.g. affective, cognitive, etc.) can be gathered, identified, evaluated and be available for interpretation across historical as well as current situations. For some services (e.g. community) it may not be possible to access objective observable data, but we advocate that services consider their resources and collect the optimum information available to them by drawing on at least two of the four sources.

Assessment context

Those who have previously been assessed by mental health services frequently report highly negative encounters with service providers (Nehls, 1999; NICE, 2009b). Primary and secondary care providers may lack the time, skills and resources to complete complex assessments and may see their role as supporting the client through their immediate distress whilst awaiting a referral to either secondary or tertiary care depending upon the perceived level of need. The frequent failure of services at these levels to identify the presenting

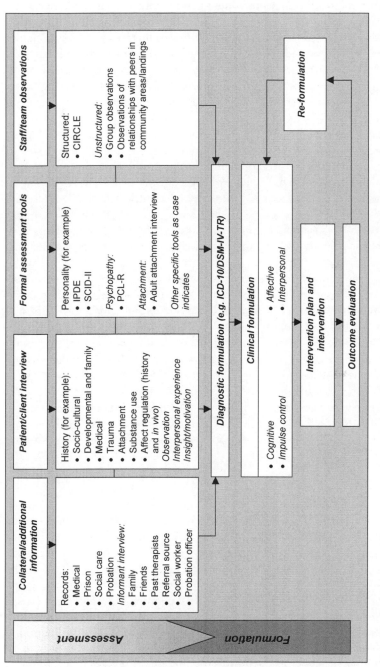

Figure 3.1 Diagram depicting different assessment strategies and links to the development of the diagnostic and clinical formulation, focusing upon the four domains of personality disorder. CIRCLE, Chart of Interpersonal Reactions in Closed Living Environments; IPDE, International Personality Disorder Examination; PCL-R, Psychopathy Checklist – Revised; SCID-II, Structured Clinical Interview for DSM-IV Axis II Personality Disorder.

difficulties of their clients as symptoms of personality disorder contributes to them being referred to inappropriate tertiary services that treat aspects of the disorder in an unsynchronised way, thus compounding their difficulties. For example, one service may insist that substance misuse is addressed before a second service will provide trauma-focused work and vice versa (Edgar and Rickford, 2009). Since both problems may require simultaneous treatment, the client may become pessimistic about the possibility of accessing treatment and deteriorate further, thus reducing their chances of accessing any care.

Once clients are labelled as 'difficult' (which may be unintentionally leaked or more directly expressed), future assessors may encounter a client resistant to diagnosis and have to overcome their own countertransference against engaging with clients that have been labelled as such. This allows clinicians and services to abdicate responsibility for therapeutic ruptures and locate responsibility within the client (Diamond and Factor, 1994; Lander and Nahon, 2005). Whilst clinicians may not specifically indicate that a client is untreatable, they may seek reasons not to offer services to personality disordered clients, for example, through utilising unrealistic service inclusion criteria or placing responsibility on the patient for non-engagement, resistance or a lack of responsivity. This is unnecessary if effective assessment is undertaken earlier in the referral process. NICE guidelines for antisocial personality disorder (2009a) suggest that primary services should be routinely exploring co-morbidity, current life stressors, relationships and life events and seeking information from other sources such as written records and carers, whilst secondary care services should, in addition, identify any contact with the criminal justice system or other specialist services for people with other personality disorders. Adopting the proposed model ensures NICE guidelines are fulfilled and increases the chance of clients with any form of personality disorder accessing the most appropriate treatment.

Collateral gathering

A key concern is that personality disordered clients are often inaccurate informants of their own problematic thoughts, feelings and behaviours (Livesley, 2001). Hence, collateral gathering/reviewing is critical at the onset of assessment. Independent sources of material may corroborate or contradict the patient's account and also offer historical evidence of the client's interpersonal style, behaviour and affect to enable a comparison over time (Hare, 2003; Zimmerman et al., 1986). Although clients with limited previous contact can present to services, this does not mean that collateral information on those clients will inevitably be unavailable, and it should be sought from alternative sources, for example 'informant' interview with relatives (NICE, 2009b).

Quality of collateral is more important than quantity. This can be gauged by determining the breadth of information covered in the report, as well as details of specific events or circumstances, such as the provision of concrete examples of the person's behaviour. A difficulty with collateral sources is establishing whether other authors have presented biased accounts of the client. Bias arises for a number of reasons including the client providing different information to different assessing clinicians (e.g. due to differing engagement with each assessor) and due to previous assessors basing reports on unsubstantiated opinion or subjective verbal reports. Having alternative sources of information enables assessors to establish the credibility of reports and informant disclosures, facilitates alternative perspectives from key informants to be processed, and provides opportunities to gather lifetime material from multiple sources other than the client. Where possible, it is useful to draw collateral from a number of sources including social services, psychiatrists, in- or outpatient carers, probation, etc.

'Collateral' is often used to describe informant responses to formal tests or interviews. This is a valuable source of information but may be time-consuming to achieve. Furthermore, the client may be resistant to providing informant sources and such sources (for example, the client's family) may have a vested interest in maintaining their own biases. Within some contexts, it is more difficult to access collateral. Patients presenting in both community and forensic settings may have had limited contacts with other agencies and these may be reluctant to provide material without the patient's consent. Where consent is not forthcoming, clinicians need to be mindful of their responsibility to ensure risk to self and others is adequately assessed and not be frightened of litigious patients who may refuse access. Mental health practitioners have a duty of care to protect the public as well as to uphold the rights of the patient.

Naïve or limited information can lead to difficulties in undertaking interviews. Inconsistencies or omissions may be unidentified and difficulties in completing a thorough assessment are exacerbated by cognitive distortions and interpersonal styles that may render the interviewer unable to challenge or seek explanations for inconsistencies or query minimisations and omissions. Prior information enables the clinician to plan for potential difficulties in the assessment and to consider areas where clients may be reluctant to provide full accounts of their difficulties. Equally, it is possible to be biased towards clients on the basis of other authors' descriptions of their history and presentation. Consequently, the background information that an assessing clinician utilises during assessment must be considered objectively against the presentation and history provided by the patient.

Collecting and evaluating collateral is time-consuming. The extent to which collateral gathering occurs prior to assessment must be considered within the service context, although NICE (2009a) recommend that all levels of service should utilise information from written records and carers in relation to those with suspected antisocial personality disorder. The need for multiple agencies to communicate is also noted as critical in the outcome of all public inquiries revolving around personality disordered individuals. Given the likelihood of these clients having multiple agency contacts, information can be confusing and complex to assimilate but critical if we are to prevent underestimations of the risk many clients pose to themselves and others.

Clinical developmental interviews

Clinical developmental interviews offer firsthand insight into the likely developmental paths of a person's cognitive distortions, affective instability, interpersonal functioning and impulse control, and so constitute a critical part of assessment within a formulation-driven model. We advocate collecting life-history data, paying particular attention to the quality of experiences rather than establishing a factual record of key milestones. In each developmental category, examples of experiences or episodes are sought exploring the four domains. For example, 'Can you describe a time when your mother [or main carer] displayed love and affection?' rather than: 'Was your mother affectionate?' The former approach allows for more exploration of memory systems, enabling the assessor to develop an understanding of what is said and how this relates to cognitions, whilst paying attention to the affective and interpersonal processes. Some assessment tools (see below) also involve collecting significant developmental information during use. This may augment the clinical interview and subsequently reduce the need to gather data on some areas suggested here. In forensic settings, this may be used to cross-reference and verify the consistency of the client's account. Where possible, it can be useful to have different aspects of the assessment completed by different staff. This enables assessors to consider the different experiences of the client and may offer insight into which therapist will best meet the needs of the client.

The developmental interview should be completed over more than one meeting to consider marked fluctuations in mental state (NICE, 2009b) and should include attention to the individual's care history; physical and mental health; life stressors; education; occupational activity; relationships in childhood and adulthood including parenting; psychosexual development; use of intoxicating substances; previous treatment initiatives; and, where relevant, forensic history (e.g. Murphy et al., 2009). Following a chronological sequence facilitates memory recall in clients, enables staff to attend to interpersonal behaviours and allows inconsistencies in reporting to be transparent. For some patients, deliberate lies are an integral part of their interpersonal style, which can add to the confusion of assessors who have no clearly identified interview method. More frequently, accounts may be reflective of cognitive distortions that colour how the individual experiences life.

These distortions may represent overcompensation for feelings associated with vulnerability, for example shame, and assessors who fail to recognise these will arrive at different conclusions and diagnoses than those who looked beyond initial impressions. For example, a patient assessed as having narcissistic personality disorder recounted an idealised and nurturing childhood, where he described all his needs being met. He verbalised having an idealised mother, but did so in angry and dismissive tones, hence the emphasis was upon understanding what interpersonal strategy had developed rather than interpreting content at face value.

High levels of arousal can be triggered during interviews and it is important that the interviewer acknowledges emotions that arise during assessment such as sadness, shame or fear. Interviewers often find it difficult to tolerate fear. Emotions evoked during assessment impact upon assessment by predisposing us to like or dislike certain clients, thereby influencing our judgement (Maier, 1990; Taylor, 1999). Thus, interviewer styles need to be both empathic and gently challenging whilst offering opportunities to validate and normalise the client's account. Colluding with the patient may reinforce denial or externalisation and must be avoided if a collaborative and trusting relationship is to be developed. In summary, effective diagnoses are made when clinicians actively listen to patients describing interpersonal interactions and observe their behaviour with the interviewer (Western, 1997).

Formal assessment tools

A wide range of self-report tools have been developed over the years and have been reviewed elsewhere (Livesley, 2001; Millon and Davies, 2000; NICE, 2009a). Such tools focus on either a particular personality disorder, such as the Diagnostic Interview for Borderline Patients – Revised (DIB-R; Zanarini et al., 1989), or are general diagnostic tools for the main personality disorders recognised within ICD-10 or DSM-IV, such as the International Personality Disorder Examination (IPDE; Loranger, 1999) and the Structured Clinical Interview for DSM-IV Axis II Personality Disorder (SCID-II; First et al., 1997).

Such measures represent efficient means of assessing due to speed and ease of completion. However, we argue that relying solely on formal assessment tools with this population can create diagnostic and treatment difficulties. First, individuals may exaggerate or minimise their symptomatology due to maladaptive schemata (see Young et al., 2003), either in the hope of eliciting care (e.g. those who feel emotionally deprived) or punishment, or in an attempt to avoid negative consequences such as shame or further detention. Secondly, these tools offer opportunities for normative interpretations (e.g. Psychopathy Checklist – Revised, PCL-R; Hare, 2003) but lack the individuality offered by idiopathic assessments. The tool may provide a specific personality disorder diagnosis but this can be inaccessible to the patient and thus experienced as a label (Nehls, 1999) that does not lend itself easily to formulating a treatment path designed to alleviate areas of risk and distress. Thirdly, these tools lack the ability to attend to the interpersonal functioning present within the assessment. For instance, the person may adopt a grandiose, superior style of interaction, and question the assessor's competence and the usefulness of the tool during assessment, and this may not be adequately represented within the specific tool employed. Hence, a vital opportunity for something interpersonally meaningful to be gained is missed. Assessment is about unpicking the behaviour and traits presented and making sense of them to inform a reliable diagnosis (Duggan and Gibbon, 2008). This requires both experience and confidence in assessors if they are to adopt triangulation of information and not rely solely on tool outcomes.

Diagnoses should also be clinically based, and not influenced by professional, personal, cultural or ethnic biases. Assessors must be sensitive to gender and cultural biases within assessment. For instance, male assessees are more likely to endorse antisocial and paranoid personality disorder items, whilst females are more likely to endorse schizoid personality disorder (Oltmanns et al., 2007); Caucasian men are 2.8 times more likely to be given a diagnosis of antisocial personality disorder than African Caribbean men (Mikton and Grounds, 2007). These studies suggest assessors must be mindful of biases in tools, their clients and themselves when undertaking assessment. Fairness within psychological tools is the extent to which a test is used in an impartial, just and equitable way, and therefore requires test users to be sensitive and consider the cultural or sub-cultural application of the tool. This does not mean that the tool ought to have been sampled on the group it is likely to be used with (a common argument about fairness); rather, one should reflect upon appropriateness whilst interpreting results.

Staff observations

Staff observations facilitate alternative assessment of clients within 'naturalistic' settings. This is particularly useful when facilitated over a long period rather than a short snapshot which may alert the client to the fact that he/she is being observed and enable attempts to modify presentation (such as faking 'well'). This method enables the assessor to access aspects of the personality the patient is unaware of (as the problem is not reported) or may have distorted in more formal assessments.

Interpersonal behaviours can be usefully observed and rated using formalised tools such as the Chart of Interpersonal Reactions in Closed Living Environments (CIRCLE; Blackburn, 1998). This approach assumes stability of interpersonal style and interpersonal manifestation. Such measures help observers understand presentation within the context of personality disorder and offer benefits in terms of managing risk and identifying treatment-interfering behaviours.

In order to undertake unbiased observations it is important that assessors guide staff into identifying both strengths and weaknesses exhibited by clients. Too often (certainly in forensic settings), staff are keen to report negative presentations rather than being open to the possibility that a client may have important protective features within his style of interacting, behaving or thinking. It is assumed that if a client is personality disordered, then all of his/her functioning is maladaptive. Thus, observations should not be evaluated in isolation from other sources that enable triangulation of all available information, thus allowing for rogue evaluations to be challenged and discredited.

Another factor potentially biasing staff observations is that of the staff member's own psychopathology. That is, staff may behave in sexist or racist ways that lead them to dismiss such behaviour in their patients as 'the norm'. It is essential that staff are both trained and offered guidance in what is necessary to observe and that any observational rating processes are not dependent upon one individual but at least two (independently rated). This also guards against the most influential staff member affecting the judgements of the team.

Within some services, observational assessments are costly and impractical – for example, when patients reside and work in the community. However, there may be opportunities to observe the patient in waiting areas and day centres, as well as utilising less formal contacts such as nurses and administrative staff.

Case formulation

All psychological models of therapy rely upon case formulation to guide treatment. There are case formulations available for specific personality disorders (e.g. Beck *et al.*, 2004; Sperry, 1999), which can potentially guide clinicians into formulating their client's presentation and problems; however, it is important for clinicians to individualise their case formulation rather than 'fitting' their client to the diagnosis and consequent treatment.

Individualised case formulations are pivotal in developing effective interventions to treat or manage individuals with personality disorder (Beck *et al.*, 2004; Castillo, 2003). The benefits of developing and utilising individualised case formulations have been demonstrated (e.g. Turkat and Msaito, 1985) and discussed in general terms elsewhere (e.g. Person, 1989), but little attention has been given to their specific role in the treatment of clients with personality disorder. The benefits of an effective case formulation to the client, the clinician and their team are outlined below.

Case formulation provides an overall picture of the client and their problems

Effective case formulation enables both client and clinician to develop insight into the client's problems. When a formulation is shared with a client, it conveys an overall, holistic understanding of the client's experiences and difficulties (Persons, 1989; Persons and Tompkins, 1997). This is an essential element in increasing the client's psychological well-being (Crits-Christoph, 1998), as it enables the client to develop both insight into their problems (thus enabling them to consider engaging in therapy to develop themselves) and, to an extent, some containment through more effectively understanding their difficulties (Ryle and Kerr, 2002). In clients with personality disorder, particularly those who engage in violent offending, the formulation also enables the client to safely re-connect with their vulnerability rather than projecting anger as a means of defending against the experience of feeling vulnerable.

The attributions of staff teams have been shown to influence the care that they provide towards clients (Marteau and Riordan, 1992). Sharing case formulations with a team enables staff to understand clients rather then perceiving them only through their presenting difficulties. This enables a team to engage and develop relationships with the clients that are less likely to reinforce the clients' schemata and consequent challenging behaviour.

Case formulation identifies relationships between problems and the planning/selection of a treatment modality/intervention

Clients with personality disorder can feel overwhelmed by the complexity of their difficulties and the influence these have on multiple aspects of their life. Formulations enable clients and therapists to link and chain events into patterns, which can be experienced as containing for the client. High quality case formulations, including a conceptualisation of the underlying mechanisms of the problem, reduce the likelihood of ineffective intervention strategies being applied (Needleman, 1999) and enable selection of the appropriate form of intervention, the intervention strategy and intervention point (Persons, 1989). This is important as clients with personality disorder often require complex interventions and the timing of the different intervention strategies is vital in terms of achieving a positive outcome. For example, it is important to develop a trusting therapeutic relationship and treat a client's trauma experiences prior to engaging in treatment that focuses upon any offending, otherwise factors underpinning the offending are likely to remain untreated.

There is a tendency towards specialisation of clinical services which can result in services becoming compartmentalised. As noted previously, clients with personality disorder may present with co-morbid difficulties. For example, a client with borderline personality disorder and co-morbid eating disorder and substance misuse may present at one of three specialist services. Each team may have a potential treatment responsibility for the client; however, each service may be reluctant to accept the client until he/she has undertaken treatment with one of the other services. Such presentations can cause difficulties between services and may reinforce the perception of services and client that the client's difficulties are not treatable. A case formulation communicated between services would potentially enable them to understand patterns and core themes relevant to the problems (e.g. that both substance misuse and eating disorder were overt behaviours designed to manage the client's high levels of internalised shame associated with distorted cognitions arising from sexual abuse), and enable more effective treatment planning and selection through shared care.

Case formulation strengthens the therapeutic alliance

Therapists often struggle to establish good therapeutic relationships with personality disordered clients and case formulations assist in strengthening the therapeutic alliance (Wills and Sanders, 1997; Needleman, 1999) prior to engaging in therapy. Ryle and Kerr (2002) suggest the experience of being attended to by the therapist can be a powerful and unique experience, particularly with clients who have histories of abuse or deprivation. Sharing a formulation can enable a client to feel understood (Ryle and Kerr, 2002; McCluskey, 2005) and connected to the therapist. Case formulations enable therapists to feel more empathic toward their clients by developing a thorough understanding of their history and trauma and the historically adaptive function of the client's interpersonal style (Needleman, 1999), rather than focusing upon the potentially aversive interpersonal experiences.

Sharing case formulations within a team enables the broader staff team to engage with clients who have often been experienced as interpersonally difficult. For example, a man with a history of volatile and threatening behaviour towards staff, in addition to a long history of self-harm and parasuicidal behaviour, was diagnosed with histrionic, borderline and paranoid personality disorders. The diagnosis, when shared with the team, did not enable the team to understand the client's difficulties, nor did it enable them to engage with the client and intervene with him. Sharing his formulation with the team enabled staff to understand that the client's history of neglect and abuse led him to develop schemata that disposed him to crave dependency whilst anticipating that others would reject, abuse or abandon him. He consequently behaved in a manner that reinforced these schemata, through drawing staff into caring for him (increasing his sense of dependence), then becoming rejecting and angry towards staff (and self-harming) in order to distance himself from them. This enabled him to feel safe since his perception that he would be rejected or abandoned by others was confirmed and his world seemed predictable. These behaviours developed as a means of avoiding experiencing pain associated with the loss of being cared for and the egocentric belief that others cannot care for him because he is fundamentally defective. The formulation enabled staff to understand the client and empathise with his difficulties whilst interacting with the client at a level that acknowledged and validated these core meanings.

Case formulation enables prediction of behaviour and responses including non-compliance with treatment

Clients without personality disorder can find it difficult to complete homework tasks and engage in treatment. This is exacerbated in clients with personality disorder. Their personality style has developed as a survival mechanism to cope with traumatic life experiences and has proven itself to be adaptive previously (if maladaptive in the present situation as an adult). As a consequence of this, engaging in treatment designed to ameliorate the impact of personality is likely to cause clients to feel highly anxious and may lead to avoidance or superficial engagement in treatment. Case formulation enables clients and therapists to predict areas where non-compliance with treatment or difficulties with engagement in the therapy may arise (Persons, 1989). Complex formulations can indicate explicitly where there are likely to be therapy-interfering behaviours (Linehan, 1993) and when overcoming a problem is likely to present more problematic behaviours before improvement is observed. This aspect of the formulation can be especially useful for the team as it enables staff to feel in control and thus motivated when handling difficulties that have been considered and hypothesised in relation to applying a specific intervention.

Case formulation enables understanding and treatment of relationship difficulties

Case formulation enables the therapist to understand and work directly upon relationship difficulties (Persons, 1989). This is particularly useful with clients with personality disorder where interpersonal difficulties are a core problem. Difficulties in the therapeutic relationship are expected and predicted through effective case formulation. For example, with a highly anxious, paranoid, narcissistic client, one would predict that attempts to engage the client by offering support with their anxiety may be perceived as attempts to manipulate them (paranoid perception), or as belittling their ability to look after themselves (narcissistic perception), and result in the client being highly hostile and critical of the therapist. Given this prediction, the therapist will need to alter their style in order to meet the need of the client at that time. As treatment progresses, other therapist styles and interventions may be adopted (depending upon the formulation) to intervene with other aspects of the client's presentation.

Case formulation also enables therapists and clients to understand how the client's previous experiences are being re-enacted in the present relationship in order to maintain a set of beliefs. For example, if a person has been rejected throughout their childhood they may behave in ways that are designed to elicit rejection, or be rejecting toward others. This aspect of the formulation also enables the team to understand how and why a client may behave differently at different points in therapy or at different points in their relationship with the client, and consequently assists them in engaging and intervening with the client.

Case formulation allows for redirection of unsuccessful treatment following re-formulation

The process of formulation does not end with assessment. Additional information is gathered during the course of assessment and evaluated as to whether it supports or contradicts the current formulation (Persons, 1989). Where treatment is unsuccessful, the formulation (or re-formulation) enables evaluation of whether the current intervention is, or is likely to be, successful and, as a result, may indicate that alternative interventions should be considered. Where individuals with personality disorder have been exposed to ineffective treatment, this may provide additional support for their beliefs about their defectiveness and the inability of others to meet their needs. Re-formulation encourages the consideration of factors that may undermine the current intervention and reflection upon whether the therapist's current style or the current intervention is ineffective, rather than reinforcing the belief that the client is 'untreatable'. This is particularly valuable when previous assessments have not followed an in-depth formulation-driven assessment and have failed to attend to the possibility of a personality disorder at the expense of a more superficial diagnosis of mental health (such as depression). This process also enables the instillation of hope in the client, the therapist and the team as it assists recognition that alternative interventions are likely to be available and may be more effective due to the increased information gleaned from the re-formulation.

It is likely that case formulation complexity will vary according to setting, due to issues to do with the increased prevalence of co-morbidity in forensic versus community settings (Coid et al., 1999; Singleton et al., 1998), the availability of multiple sources of information and the accompanying issue of assessing and predicting the risk of violence in such settings, and accounting for this within formulations. Similarly, time available to assess and formulate a client and their difficulties is likely to vary across settings. Unfortunately, in some settings this may result in brief formulations being developed that fail to capture the complexity of the client, their difficulties, their therapy-interfering behaviours and their interactions with services. This has implications for both client and service.

There are several general guides to formulation (e.g. Persons, 1989; Beck, 1995; Safran and Segal, 1990; Needleman, 1999), which will not be discussed in detail as it is assumed that readers have basic formulation skills. It is advocated that clinicians utilise flexibility during assessment and formulation, which relies upon the clinician judging the level of complexity required for the formulation, depending upon: service setting; time constraints; availability of multiple sources of information; and complexity of presentation and problems.

Guidance on personality disorder assessment case formulation

Ideally, we advocate for developing complex individualised case formulations, as these enable a fuller consideration of targets for intervention and likely obstacles to intervention (i.e. therapy-interfering behaviours). Within the formulation, it is particularly important to focus upon the four core domains of personality disorder, and the assessment process we have suggested here should enable experienced clinicians to draw information from multiple assessment sources to fit a model that explains the development of specific patterns within these domains in great detail. Our general formulation model is depicted in Figure 3.2. This identifies how information drawn from different aspects of assessment can be linked into the different core domains of personality disorder. The process of formulating the client involves moving beyond personality disorder diagnosis to considering how specific aspects of the client's difficulties have developed, are maintained and interact with each other to make up their presentation.

In addition to drawing together the assessment information under each of the four domains, the formulation should also include the following.

Developmental history and functionality of the problem areas

When formulating a client's personality difficulties it is useful to hypothesise the key factors that have determined the development of the currently dysfunctional facet of the person's difficulties. Box 3.1 illustrates the issues of considering the developmental history and functionality of the problem, and the inter-relationships between core areas. Through considering the functionality and developmental trajectory of the personality problem areas within the formulation, the client and the therapist are enabled to understand how

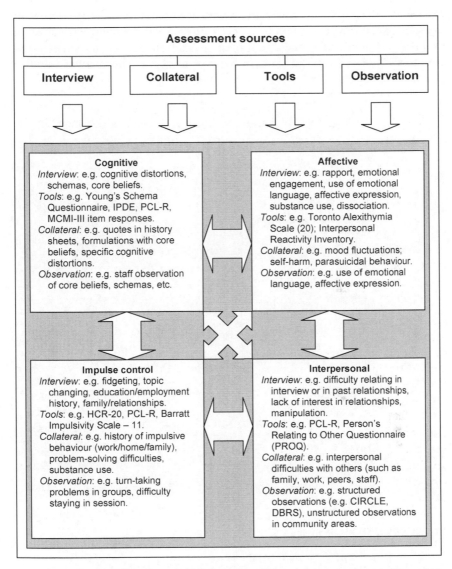

Figure 3.2 Graphical depiction of how assessment information is drawn together within the formulation to elaborate upon the four core domains of personality disorder. CIRCLE, Chart of Interpersonal Reactions in Closed Living Environments; DBRS, Dangerous Behaviour Rating Scale; HRC-20, Historical, Clinical, Risk Management-20; IPDE, International Personality Disorder Examination; MCMI-III, Million Clinical Multiaxial Inventory – III; PCL-R, Psychopathy Checklist.

the client has arrived at her present circumstances and to understand how her current difficulties have previously been adaptive and functional. This can increase potential engagement, enhance co-operation between the client and the team and reduce the perception of the client's behaviour as solely problematic.

Box 3.1   Brief example of formulation illustrating need for developmental trajectories and functionality of personality disorder problem domains

June, a 37-year-old client with borderline personality disorder, experiences extreme dissociative experiences that diminish her ability to connect meaningfully with others and manage her everyday life. She was abused and abandoned as a child and began to dissociate as this protected her from painful emotion. As an adult, there are different expectations from others regarding her interactions with them and her continued dissociative experiences cause her to re-experience rejection due to others struggling to remain connected to her. This serves to maintain the mistrust/abuse and abandonment schemata she developed as a child. These schemata subsequently cause her to find difficulties engaging with services and carers, as she believes that they will eventually abandon or abuse her. Consequently, when she begins to establish trusting relationships with staff, her anxiety will increase as she is increasingly expectant of the likelihood of abuse or abandonment and more intensely aware of the loss of care/support she would experience from this. She may subsequently attempt to avoid this experience through increased dissociation within sessions (to manage the affect), or early on in sessions attempt to ridicule or criticise the therapist in order to bring about the loss of the relationship before she becomes more emotionally committed to it.

Strengths and weaknesses

Different clients may present with a variety of strengths and weaknesses whilst having the same clinical diagnosis. When developing the formulation and focusing upon each domain of personality disorder, it can be useful to consider which areas of the client's presentation show least impairment and can be considered to be areas of relative strength. This enables clients and staff to experience hope and increase awareness and facilitate development of stronger domains. The client may then be better equipped to tolerate the increased stress that is experienced when making changes.

Inter-relationships between the core personality domains

A key task of formulation is developing and considering patterns of relationships between the core domains. Significant consideration must also be given to the context of assessment and treatment (in order to consider how this may potentially maintain or intervene upon the client's problems). Box 3.1 show how links may be drawn between an individual's core beliefs, affect regulation ability, impulsivity and interpersonal functioning. Elaboration of these patterns enables clinicians to understand at which points the most effective intervention can be applied. With clients who have multiple and complex difficulties it can also be useful to consider how these patterns may develop during the course of a session, such that the emotional and interpersonal aspects of the client's presentation may shift rapidly during the course of the session as the client fluctuates between their different ways of relating to others. This can enable the therapist to predict moment by moment responses to interventions and allow the therapist to alter their style and intervention during the sessions.

Interpersonal context

The interpersonal component of formulation is frequently ignored within general formulations of problems. When working with clients with personality disorder, it is vital to consider the interpersonal dimension – in particular to consider how each of the other domains maintains and is maintained by the client's behaviour and others' responses to that behaviour. For example, a client's belief about the likelihood of others sexually abusing him may cause him to be extremely unhygienic and hostile (thus allowing him to feel safe since no one will approach him), but result in increased suspiciousness and fear of others arising from isolation. Elaboration upon this enables the client to understand the function of their behaviours and the responses elicited, and can also enhance the therapist and team's ability to predict behaviours and develop interventions that recognise and address these difficulties with the client.

Therapy-interfering behaviours

The formulation should also consider how the client's difficulties *within* and *across* domains may increase the likelihood and type of therapy-interfering behaviours at different points in the therapy. Predicting these behaviours enables the client, therapist and team to feel more in control and more able to respond effectively to the client's needs. Thus, therapy is likely to be more effective for the client. An important contributory factor in the development of therapy-interfering behaviours is the patient's capacity to tolerate self-hatred. This can be a particular issue with forensic clients who struggle to tolerate the shame and hatred they experience toward themselves (particularly in relation to their offending). This can result in projections into the therapy and others that result in the client perceiving others and therapy as dangerous.

Summary

Overall, this chapter has demonstrated that an assessment of personality disorder across cognition, affectivity, interpersonal functioning and impulse control can be achieved more effectively if undertaken with a view to providing a case formulation. We have offered a multimodal model of assessment operating through multiple systems as outlined in Figure 3.1. We believe this strengthens the accuracy and reliability of diagnosis although we acknowledge this is a complicated process requiring clinicians to attend to data from multiple sources, analysing these sequentially across four domains (see Figure 3.2) looking for corroboration and discounting idiosyncratic information. Drawing this data into a complex formulation not only makes sense of the diagnosis but also has the advantage of enabling clients to work more collaboratively by enhancing their understanding and overcoming some of the barriers that lead to treatment failure, enhanced risk and multiple service contacts. We have raised clinicians' awareness of a number of biases and barriers that may affect our understanding of the client, such as gender and culture, but have assumed individuals will explore these for themselves. The overall aim of our model is to enhance possibilities for services and clients to have compassion for the patient/self, promote opportunities for engagement and change, and prevent labelling and rejection.

References

Alexander, R. and Cooray, S. (2003) Diagnosis of personality disorders in learning disability. *British Journal of Psychiatry*, **182(44)**, s28–s31.

American Psychiatric Association (2000) *Diagnostic and Statistical Manual of Mental Disorders (4th edn Text Revision) – DSM-IV-TR*. Washington, DC: American Psychiatric Association.

Beck, A.T., Freeman, A. and Davis, D.D. (2004) *Cognitive Therapy of Personality Disorders*, 2nd edn. London: Guilford Press.

Beck, J.S. (1995) *Cognitive Therapy: Basics and Beyond*. New York: Guilford Press.

Blackburn, R. (1998) Criminality and the interpersonal circle in mentally disordered offenders. *Criminal Justice and Behaviour*, **25(2)**, 155–176.

Castillo, H. (2003) *Personality Disorder: Temperament or Trauma*. London: Jessica Kingsley.

Clark, L.A. (1999) Dimensional approaches to personality disorder assessment and diagnosis. In C.R. Cloninger (ed.), *Personality and Psychopathy*. Washington, DC: American Psychiatric Press, pp. 219–244.

Coid, J. (1992) DSM-III diagnosis in criminal psychopaths: a way forward. *Criminal Behaviour and Mental Health*, **2**, 78–79.

Coid, J., Kahtan, N., Gault, S. and Jarman, B. (1999) Patients with personality disorders admitted to secure forensic psychiatry services. *British Journal of Psychiatry*, **175**, 528–536.

Crits-Christoph, P. (1998) The interpersonal interior of psychotherapy. *Psychotherapy Research*, **8**, 1–16.

Crittenden, P.M. (1998) Adult attachment interview: coding manual for the dynamic-maturational method. Unpublished manuscript, available from the author.

Diamond, R. and Factor, R. (1994) Taking issue: treatment-resistant patients or a treatment resistant system? *Hospital and Community Psychiatry*, **45**, 97.

Duggan, C. and Gibbon, S. (2008) Practical assessment of personality disorder. *Psychiatry*, **7(3)**, 99–101.

Eastern Specialised Mental Health Commissioning Group (ESMHCG) (2005) *Personality Disorder Services Framework*. www.esmhcg.nhs.uk/PD_Capacity_Plan_June_05.pdf

Edgar, K. and Rickford, D. (2009) *Too Little, Too Late: An Independent Review of Unmet Mental Health Need in Prison*. London: Prison Reform Trust.

First, M.B., Williams, J.B. and Spitzer, R.L. (1997) *Structured Clinical Interview for DSM-IV Axis II Personality Disorders (SCID-II)*. Washington, DC: American Psychiatric Press.

Hare, R. (2003) *Hare Psychopathy Checklist – Revised (PCL-R)*, 2nd edn. Toronto: Multi-Health Systems.

Koenigsbeurg, H.W., Kaplan, R.D, Gilmore, M.M. *et al.* (1985) The relationship between syndrome and personality disorder in DSM-III: experience with 2,462 patients. *American Journal of Psychiatry*, **142**, 207–212.

Lander, D. and Nahon, N. (2005) *The Integrity Model of Existential Psychotherapy in Working with the 'Difficult Patient'*. London: Routledge.

Linehan, M.M. (1993) *Cognitive Behavioural Treatment of Borderline Personality Disorders*. New York: Guilford Press.

Livesley, J. (2001) *Handbook of Personality Disorders. Theory, Research, and Treatment*. London: Guilford Press.

Loranger, A.W. (1999) *International Personality Disorder Examination Manual: DSM-IV Module*. Washington, DC: American Psychiatric Press.

Maier, J.J. (1990) Psychopathic disorders: beyond counter-transference. *Current Opinion in Psychiatry*, **3**, 766–769.

Marteau, T.M. and Riordan, D.C. (1992) Staff attitudes towards patients: the influence of causal attributions for illness. *British Journal of Clinical Psychology*, **31**, 107–110.

McCluskey, U. (2005) *To Be Met as a Person*, London: Karnac Books.

Mikton, C. and Grounds, A. (2007) Cross-cultural clinical judgement bias in personality disorder diagnosis by forensic psychiatrists in the UK: a case-vignette study. *Journal of Personality Disorders*, **21(6)**, 697–700.

Millon, T. and Davis, R. (2000) *Personality Disorders in Modern Life*. London: Wiley.

Moran, P. (1999) *Antisocial Personality Disorder: An Epidemiological Perspective*. London: Gaskell.

Moran, P., Jenkins, R. and Tylee, A. *et al.* (2000) The prevalence of personality disorder among UK primary care attenders. *Acta Psychiatrica Scandinavica*, **102**, 52–57.

Moran, P., Leese, M., Tennyson, L., Walters, P. and Thornicroft, G. (2003) Standardised assessment of personality – abbreviated scale (SAPAS): preliminary validation of a brief screen for personality disorder. *British Journal of Psychiatry*, **183**, 228–232.

Moran, P., Leese, M., Lee, T., Walters, P. *et al.* (2004) Standardised Assessment of Personality Abbreviated Scale (SAPAS): preliminary validation of a brief screen for personality disorder. *British Journal of Psychiatry*, **1**, 184–186.

Murphy, N., Ramsden, J. and McVey, D. (2009) Formulation Interview Guide. Available to download from www.pdmh-consultancy.com

National Institute for Health and Clinical Excellence (2009a) *Antisocial Personality Disorder: NICE Clinical Guideline 77*. London: NICE.

National Institute for Health and Clinical Excellence (2009b) *Borderline Personality Disorder: NICE Clinical Guideline 78*. London: NICE.

Needleman, L.D. (1999) *Cognitive Case Conceptualisation*. Mahwah, NJ: Lawrence Erlbaum.

Nehls, N. (1999) Borderline personality disorder: the voice of patients. *Research in Nursing and Health*, **22**, 285–293.

Nolan, K.A., Volavka, J., Mohr, P. *et al.* (1999) Psychopathy and violent behaviour among patients with schizophrenia or schizoaffective disorder. *Psychiatric Services*, **50**, 787–792.

Oltmanns, T.F., South, S.C. and Turkheimer, E. (2007) Gender bias in diagnostic criteria for personality disorders: an item response theory analysis. *Journal of Abnormal Psychology*, **116(1)**, 166–175.

Persons, J.B. (1989) *Cognitive Therapy in Practice: A Case Formulation Approach*. New York: Norton & Company.

Persons, J.B. and Tompkins, M.A. (1997) Cognitive-behavioural case formulation. In T.D. Eells (ed.) *Handbook of Psychotherapy Case Formulation*. New York: Guilford Press.

Ryle, A.T. and Kerr, I.B. (2002) *Introducing Cognitive Analytic Therapy: Principles and Practice*. Chichester: Wiley.

Safran, J.D. and Segal, Z.V. (1990) *Interpersonal Process in Cognitive Psychotherapy*. New York: Basic Books.

Singleton, N., Meltzer, H., Gatward, R. *et al.* (1998) *Psychiatric Morbidity among Prisoners*. London: Office of National Statistics.

Sperry, L. (1999) *Cognitive Behaviour Therapy of DSM-IV Personality Disorders*. Philadelphia, PA: Brunner/Mazel.

Steiner, J.L., Tebes, J.K., Sledge, W.H. *et al.* (1995) A comparison of structured clinical interview for DSM-III-R and clinical diagnosis. *Journal of Nervous and Mental Disease*, **183(6)**, 365–369.

Taylor, P.J. (1999) Personality disorder: struggles with definition and determining its prevalence. *Criminal Justice Matters*, **37**, 10–15.

Taylor, P.J., Leese, M., Williams, D., Butwell, M., Daly, R. and Larkin, E. (1998) Mental disorder and violence. A special (high security) hospital study. *British Journal of Psychiatry*, **172**, 218–226.

Tengstrom, A., Grann, M., Langstrom, N. *et al.* (2000) Psychopathy (PCL-R) as a predictor of violent recidivism among criminal offenders with schizophrenia. *Law and Human Behaviour*, **24**, 45–58.

Turkat, I.D. and Maisto, S.A. (1985) Personality disorders: application of the experimental method to the formulation and modification of personality disorders.

In D.H. Barlow (ed.), *Clinical Handbook of Psychological Disorders: A Step-by-Step Treatment Manual*. New York: Guilford Press, pp. 503–570.

Tyrer, P. and Johnson, T. (1996) Establishing the severity of personality disorder. *American Journal of Psychiatry*, **153(12)**, 1593–1597.

van Velzen, C.J.M. and Emmelkamp, P.M.G. (1996) The assessment of personality disorders: implications for cognitive and behaviour therapy. *Behaviour Research and Therapy*, **34(8)**, 655–668.

Western, D. (1997) Divergences between clinical and research methods for assessing personality disorders: implications for research and the evolution of Axis II. *American Journal of Psychiatry*, **154**, 895–903.

Wills, F. and Sanders, D. (1997) *Cognitive Therapy*. London: Sage.

World Health Organization (1990) *International Statistical Classification of Diseases and Related Health Problems (10th Revision)*. Geneva: WHO.

Young, J.E., Klosko, J.S. and Weishaar, M.E. (2003) *Schema Therapy: A Practitioner's Guide*. London: Guilford Press.

Zanarini, M., Gunderson, J.G., Frankenberg, F.R. *et al.* (1989) The revised diagnostic interview for borderlines: discriminating borderline personality disorder from other Axis II disorders. *Journal of Personality Disorders*, **3**, 10–18.

Zanarini, M.C., Vujanovic, A.A., Parachini, E.A., Boulanger, J.L., Frankenburg, F.R. and Hennan, J. (2003) Zanarini Rating Scale for Borderline Personality Disorder (ZAN-BPD): a continuous measure of DSM-IV borderline psychopathology. *Journal of Perosnality Disorder*, **17(3)**, 233–242.

Zimmerman, M., Pfohl, B., Stangle, D. *et al.* (1986) Assessment of DSM-III personality disorders: the importance of interviewing an informant. *Journal of Clinical Psychiatry*, **47**, 261–263.

Chapter 4

Delivering integrated treatment to people with personality disorder

Jacqui Saradjian, Naomi Murphy and Des McVey

Introduction

Many texts devoted to the treatment of personality disorder offer guidance specific to each personality disorder defined within the two international classification systems. However, many people with personality disorder exhibit difficulties that do not conform to one discrete diagnosis but are representative of multiple diagnoses. This causes difficulties for clinicians in deciding which treatment pathway to follow. Attempts to treat may be further thwarted when clinicians become absorbed in managing presenting behavioural difficulties by psychological or pharmacological interventions, but fail to address psychopathology underpinning the disorder. In such cases, 'treatment' is often unsuccessful; the individual is deemed to have 'failed', and is subsequently labelled 'untreatable'. Treatment failure often occurs because the 'treatment' does not truly address the aetiological factors that have contributed to the development of that condition within that specific individual.

The purpose of this chapter is not to provide a manualised intervention to be uniformly applied. Instead a psychological framework is suggested which could be adopted within any service context, to enable individualised treatment in the context of a psychological formulation of the presenting personality psychopathology.

Principles underpinning treatment needs

There is currently no established treatment model proven to be superior in treating people with personality disorder (Livesley, 2003; NICE, 2009a, 2009b) or in reducing the risk presented by those who have severe personality disorders (Burke and Hart, 2000; NICE, 2009a, 2009b). In addition, classification, and hence diagnosis anomalies, impact greatly on the evidence base in relation to this client group. The population researched are unlikely to be homogeneous which contributes to the inconsistent results and non-replicated findings, common to this client group. Thus, research findings should be considered indicative rather than definitive.

The lack of identifiable treatment means that service providers need to be innovative whilst theoretically rigorous in providing interventions. It is proposed that an appropriate strategy is to consider those factors common to people with personality disorder; the aetiological factors and consequent cognitive, emotional, interpersonal and behavioural strategies that they have adopted to manage their world; and, using the best evidence available, provide concomitant interventions. Treatment aimed specifically at changing an individual's personality disorder often fails to give sufficient attention to achieving a reduction in risk to self or others, whilst treatments targeted at risky behaviour often overemphasise behaviour management and fail to address core aspects of personality. Effective treatment must accommodate all the needs of the client group. These needs form the principles that should underpin any treatment.

Principle 1: Treatment must be capable of addressing the needs of a population meeting a diverse range of diagnoses and with a diverse range of presenting problems

People with a diagnosis of personality disorder present with heterogeneous problems in cognition, regulation of affect, interpersonal relationships and behaviour. The diverse behaviours that form the criteria for personality disorder diagnosis can range from irrational suspicions and mistrust of others (paranoid), to pervasive psychological dependence on others (dependent); a lack of interest in (schizoid) or fearful avoidance (schizotypal) of social relationships, to a desperate need for others' attention (histrionic); a pervasive pattern of grandiosity and need for admiration (narcissistic), to social inhibition, feelings of inadequacy and extreme sensitivity to negative evaluation (avoidant); extreme 'black and white' thinking, instability in relationships, self-image, identity and chaotic behaviour (borderline) or a total disregard for rules and the rights of others (antisocial), to a rigid conformity to personally defined morals and rules and excessive orderliness (obsessive).

People's presenting behaviours rarely fit exclusively into one of the diagnostic categories available to clinicians attempting to identify personality disorder via the two primary models of classification (ICD-10, WHO, 1990; DSM-IV, APA, 2000). Magnavita (2004) suggests that despite the construct of personality disorder being one which most clinicians in the field inherently understand, the actual diagnosis remains 'more of a clinical art than a science' (p. 4). The categorical model of diagnosis in these manuals is problematic. It is atheoretical, providing no coherent rationale for the criteria for each category. Categories are not mutually exclusive and lack well-defined boundaries between them. Consequently, there are significant levels of co-morbidity of diagnosis. Categorisation relies on the presence or absence of criteria, thus there is no formal way of determining severity. Importantly, since not all criteria in any category are essential, two people may have the same diagnosis but distinctly different constellations of problems. Equally, similar problems may have different aetiologies and functions for different individuals. In both these situations, individuals would require different interventions for the same 'diagnosed disorder', therefore the clinical utility of diagnoses using this categorical system is limited. Livesley (2003) suggests these problems arise from attempting to categorise behaviours that primarily stem from dimensional characteristics. Proponents of the dimensional approach suggest that classification should be based on the underlying dynamic dimensional systems that generate the behaviours leading to the diagnosis. Dimensional models have been based on the biological basis of temperament or on factor analyses of comprehensive sets of personality traits. Such dimensional models are explanatory of the full range of personality traits, normal and abnormal, supporting the view that personality disorders are extreme variants of normal personality functions that become maladaptive within the societal and cultural context of the individual. Dimensional models are consistent with current findings in the areas of genetics and neurobiology. However, there is still no consensus as to which specific dimensions are paramount to the understanding of personality or provide the most utility for clinical practice. Debate on this issue continues as the development of DSM-V progresses (e.g. Livesley, 2007; Skodol, 2009; Widiger and Lowe, 2008).

Psychopathy is not included as a personality disorder in either of the diagnostic manuals. Nevertheless, the construct of psychopathy as defined by Cleckley (1976) is widely accepted to be a form of personality pathology (also described in both categorical and dimensional terms) (Lynam and Derefinko, 2006). The characteristics that typify psychopathy (glibness, superficial charm, grandiose sense of self-worth, pathological lying, conning/manipulation, lack of remorse or guilt, shallow affect, callousness/lack of empathy, failure to accept responsibility for one's actions) represent dysfunctional patterns of affect, cognition, interpersonal relationships and behaviour – the general defining criteria for personality disorder. Similar arguments can be made in relation to the heterogeneity of people with this diagnosis and also in relation to the categorical and dimensional debate (e.g. Edens *et al.*, 2006) to those discussed more generally in relation to personality disorder. Thus, as the characteristics associated with psychopathy are personality characteristics, the treatment programme described here also incorporates the treatment of people meeting criteria for psychopathy.

If treatment is to meet the needs of this diverse population, it therefore needs to be formulation-based and to address the aetiological basis of the psychopathology rather than the phenotypic presentation. A model for assessment within a formulation framework (that can also incorporate psychopathy) is described in Chapter 3.

Principle 2: Treatment must be capable of addressing a disorder caused by a range of aetiological factors

Interventions for people with personality disorder should be based on individualised clinical formulations derived from assessment of the individual, including thorough attention to the developmental trajectories that have contributed to the individual's current psychopathology. Recent research suggests that the aetiology of personality is undoubtedly multi-factorial (Hart, 2008). Personality (i.e. cognitive style, emotional management, interpersonal style and behaviour) is formed by a complex interaction between genetic predisposition, neurobiological differences, intra-psychic experience and interpersonal experience, with influences from each domain impacting upon one another (e.g. Sameroff, 2009). Thus, individual neurobiological differences impact on behaviour and experience. However, behaviour and experience also bring about change in neurobiological systems (Schore, 2003; Seigal, 2003) which may occur across the lifespan (Cozolino, 2006; Etkin *et al.*, 2005). There is no reason to believe that disorders of personality are developed by any alternative process. While the process remains the same, one or more of the constituents of that process are the pathogens that interact to form the emotional, cognitive, interpersonal and behavioural reactions that society deems personality disordered. The key factors identified as significant in the development of personality disorder are genetic predisposition, attachment experience, traumatic events, family constellation and dysfunction and socio-cultural and political forces (Magnavita, 2004). These factors are considered to be 'interactive (and) interrelated' (Magnavita, 2004, p. 16). Whilst nothing can alter genetic vulnerability, treatment of other aetiological factors can effect real change.

Biological basis of personality

GENETICS

Genes are templates carrying the 'instructions' for manufacturing proteins within any living organism. The information they hold creates the myriad of characteristics of an individual. Some genes are determined (e.g. eye colour); some genes are expressed only via interaction with other genes and/or with environmental experience. These experiences determine which genes are activated. If genes are not activated, they can remain dormant (Hart, 2008).

Whilst there is some evidence for genetic influences on the development of personality disorder clusters (e.g. Jacob *et al.*, 2005), the research base is inconsistent. Due to the problems with categorisation, it has been proposed that personality traits underlying personality disorders should be identified, and then potential genetic influences investigated (Reif and Lesch, 2003). Research has led to evidence of genetic contribution (ranging from 40 per cent to 60 per cent) to various personality traits (e.g. callousness, stimulus seeking, anxiousness) (Plomin *et al.*, 1994; McGuffin and Thapar, 1992; Livesley, *et al.*, 1993; Bouchard and Loehlin, 2001). Indeed, Plomin and Kosslyn (2001) argue that one of personality psychology's most important findings in the last three decades has been that virtually every aspect of personality is heritable. Once more, however, there have been problems with the consistency of these findings, leading to the suggestion that multiple genes are involved, each gene conferring only a small increase in risk (Noblett and Coccaro, 2005). Equally, there is the possibility that a single gene influences multiple traits associated with personality disorder and the likelihood of gene–gene interactions. Research has also demonstrated that the manifestation of genetic influences on personality characteristics requires environmental risk (Reif and Lesch, 2003; Viding and Frith, 2006). For example, a twin study demonstrated that the impact of physical maltreatment on risk for conduct problems in children was strongest among those at high genetic risk (Jaffee *et al.*, 2005). Also, an adoption study reported that adverse adoptive home environment led to antisocial traits in only those adoptees who had a genetic vulnerability for antisocial personality disorder (Cadoret *et al.*, 1995). Conversely, genetic liability to antisocial behaviour becomes evident only in the presence of an environmental trigger, such as maltreatment (Kim-Cohen *et al.*, 2006). In summary, genes are responsible for the potential to develop neuropsychological processes but the exact neurobiological development of the individual will depend on the environment to which those genes are exposed (Plomin and Asbury, 2005).

Studies considering genetic influence on antisocial behavioural characteristics of psychopathy have found a positive correlation. Genetic studies of the affective-interpersonal characteristics that constitute the primary differentiating aspects of this disorder are rare. Those that have been undertaken (e.g. Blonigen *et al.*, 2005), like studies involving antisocial behaviours, have found a similar gene–environment interaction (Waldman and Rhee, 2006).

TEMPERAMENT

Temperament refers to individual differences in behavioural and emotional tendencies that are biological in origin, but there is no agreement as to the factors that constitute temperament. Buss and Plomin's (1984) model proposes three temperament traits: emotionality, sociability and activity. People with high sociability prefer the company of others to solitary life; high emotionality is reflected as a tendency to experience negative emotions, particularly fear and anger; and high activity is expressed as energetic and vigorous behaviour in daily routines. Other theorists have added: rhythmicity, the presence or absence of a regular pattern for basic physical functions; approach and withdrawal, initial response to a new stimulus; adaptability, the degree of ease or difficulty of adjustment to change; intensity, the energy level of a response, be it positive or negative; mood, the degree of pleasantness or unfriendliness in behaviours; attention span, the ability to stay with a task, with or without distraction; distractibility, the ease of distraction from a task by environmental stimuli; sensory threshold, the amount of stimulation required for a response. None of the models of temperament has reached universal acceptance. Although temperament is not personality, these biological systems are the basis of personality characteristics and propensity for social interaction which lead to the development of personality. Despite being biologically based, and present at birth, these characteristics are not immutable and are open to environmental influences. Temperament theorists recognise that social experiences can and will change a child's temperament and that temperament can even be affected by intra-uterine experience (e.g. Werner *et al.*, 2007). Treatment must therefore be sensitive to individual differences in temperament and aimed to optimise the most functional aspects of people's individual styles.

NEUROBIOLOGY OF PERSONALITY SYSTEMS DISORDER

Depue and Lenzenweger (2001) state that 'personality disorder represents emergent phenotypes of multiple neurobehavioral systems' (p. 167). Neuro-imaging techniques have led to those neurobehavioural systems being studied in people with personality disorder. Differences have been found in areas of the brain responsible for the regulation of affect, cognitive processing and behaviour: the frontal lobes and the limbic system. However, these findings are correlational and the aetiology of these differences is difficult to determine.

Social experience, stress and trauma have significant impact on both the structure and functioning of the brain. Secure early attachments are deemed essential for the development of neural networks in the right orbitofrontal region within the prefrontal cortex, an area associated with social and moral behaviour (Anderson *et al.*, 1999). The orbitofrontal region links to the major regions of the brain, including the associational cortex, limbic circuits and brain stem areas, and enables 'more complex "higher order" abstract processing of the neocortex to be integrated with the "lower order" somatic and emotional functions of the deeper structures' (Seigal, 2001, p. 88). With poor early attachments, it is unlikely these brain structures will function effectively in most people with personality disorder.

Additionally, most people who develop personality disorder experience childhood abuse and neglect. Teicher *et al.* (2006) report that such experiences induce a cascade of physiological effects, including changes in hormones and neurotransmitters, that mediate development in vulnerable brain regions; the greater the severity of the abuse, the greater the impact on brain function. Even childhood exposure to repeated verbal abuse has been found to impact on brain structure (Choi *et al.*, 2009). Teicher *et al.*'s (2006) early research implicated damage to the temporal lobes and the limbic system in wide-ranging difficulties including emotional processing (and the appraisal of meaning and value of stimuli) and information processing for social cognition (including affiliation and theory of mind). Abuse and neglect have also been associated with impaired development of the corpus callosum, the major information pathway between the two brain hemispheres (e.g. Teicher *et al.*, 2004). It is suggested that this impairs the integration of the two halves of the brain, resulting in dramatic shifts in mood and personality. Furthermore, it is believed that repeated abuse causes over-activation of the amygdale, thus producing a fast response to danger and causing the amygdala to signal danger even when there is no apparent threat (Perry *et al.*, 1995).

Bremner and colleagues found that individuals with a history of childhood abuse had reduced volume of hippocampus, the brain area involved in learning and memory. The hippocampus also has important links to the prefrontal cortex which mediates emotion and the stress response (Bremner *et al.*, 1995, 1999). Additionally, abuse has been found capable of damaging the cerebellar vermis, an area of the brain involved in emotion, attention and the regulation of the limbic system (Anderson *et al.*, 2002).

It has been suggested that overwhelming stress early in life also alters production of both the stress-regulating hormone, cortisol, and key neurotransmitters such as epinephrine, dopamine and serotonin, the neurochemicals associated with mood and behaviour (Stien and Kendall, 2003). Disturbances in these systems have been implicated in all-or-nothing responses (Perry *et al.*, 1995), typical of those with personality disorder. These biochemical imbalances can have other profound implications; for example, lower serotonin levels can lead to impulsive aggression towards self and others. Teicher *et al.* found that abuse survivors were twice as likely as non-abused individuals to have abnormal electroencephalogram readings, typically associated with aggression and self-destructive behaviour.

Thus, childhood adversity has significant impact on the developing brain in systems that are associated with the cognitive, emotional and behavioural characteristics of personality disorder. As the brain remains plastic throughout the lifespan, these changes are not necessarily irreversible; interventions such as psychotherapy can change neurobiology (Cozolino, 2006). Treatment must therefore include processes now known to impact positively on neurobiological systems.

Attachment: social interaction and the development of personality

Siegal (2001) presents an integrated view of how human development occurs within a social world, in transaction with the functions of the brain that give rise to the mind. This framework suggests the essential experiential ingredients that facilitate the development of the mind, emotional well-being and psychological resilience during early childhood and throughout the lifespan.

Key to this development are interpersonal relationships and the development of secure attachments (Bowlby, 1969). Kernberg (1996) argues that disturbed attachment relationships are fundamental to personality disorder, a view supported by most major theorists. As attachment is crucial for the development of self, disturbed attachments lead to disturbed self-systems (Bateman and Fonagy, 2004).

An attachment relationship is a one-to-one relationship with a carer. An infant is innately motivated to form such attachment with carers for survival and security in times of anxiety. Bowlby (1988) describes attachment as forming a 'secure base'; Winnicott (1965) describes the child's need for 'a holding environment'. To develop a secure attachment, the carer needs to be sensitive and responsive to the infant's needs (Bowlby, 1969) and able to establish attunement at the level of affect (Schore, 1997). Parental responses lead to the development of patterns of attachment which in turn lead to internal working models which guide the individual's feelings, thoughts and expectations in later relationships. These internal models, akin to templates, lead to expectations of self and others (Bowlby, 1969) which are dynamic and can change via alternative experiences throughout the lifespan. However, the primary models act as a filter through which experiences are subsequently and additionally interpreted. Experiences congruent with internalised models, in particular models of the self, are most likely to be accepted as valid. Incongruous experiences are likely to be judged as spurious and thus rejected, denied or else reframed in a manner that maintains congruity. Hence, without powerful mediating factors which stimulate challenge, early models are resistant to change. There is also strong evidence for the intergenerational transmission of attachment patterns (Van Ijzendoorn, 1995).

Secure attachments enable the self to develop in a manner that can manage complexity, reflection, flexibility and adaptation. Individuals without secure attachments have more rigid patterns of responding (Seigal, 2003), impaired ability for meta-cognition (Main, 1991) and other forms of cognitive processing (e.g. Grossman et al., 2005), impaired affect regulation (Schore, 2003); impaired relationships (Ainsworth, 1989; Bretherton, 1987); impaired ability to reflect on the relationship between external and internal reality; and impaired verbal elaboration of affect, leading to behavioural difficulties (Fonagy, 2001). These effects continue to influence behaviour, thought and feeling in adulthood (Fraley et al., 2000) and characteristics of those with personality disorder.

Despite the heterogeneous nature of people with personality disorder, there is commonality in some of their characteristics. These include lack of ability to develop empathy, and moral and social awareness, and, in some, a lack of 'conscience'. There is evidence that these functions of mind require the development of the neural networks in the prefrontal region of the brain (Anderson et al., 1999; Dolan, 1999). Secure attachment is necessary for the development of the complex circuitry, including that of the prefrontal regions, that enables these social and moral behaviours. People with personality disorder have rarely experienced secure interpersonal attachments either in childhood or indeed throughout the lifespan and therefore capacity for social and moral behaviour is compromised. Treatment therefore must be capable of enabling these clients to form attachment bonds and the emotional containment to enable more appropriate development and fundamental change.

Dysfunctional family

Extending beyond individual relationships with parental figures, the culture of the familial environment in which the child develops also has significant impact. Despite scarcity of research, clinicians typically describe their clients with personality disorder as coming from dysfunctional families. Recent data relating to a cohort of men with severe personality disorder verify this clinical impression (Maden *et al.*, 2009; Burns *et al.*, 2009). Dysfunctional families are characterised by conflict, violence, domineering control, erratic or no boundaries, neglect, overt abuse, parental absence and parental psycho-pathology including alcoholism, substance abuse, criminality and untreated mental health problems. Dysfunctional environments produce anxiety which can lead to the child developing psychological defences, many of which correlate with personality pathology.

The family constructs the child's world; for that child, that world is the norm. Children's knowledge of that world is assimilated into their internal world, creating a memory system of complex units that is built up of behaviours, images, tastes, smells, attitudes that are associated with particular emotion/s, 'unconscious sets' (Matte Blanco, 1975) or schemata (Piaget, 1969) which form a person's conscious and unconscious models of the world. Schemata organise current knowledge and provide frameworks for future experiences. These models develop and change as new experiences are assimilated but existing schemata limit the perceptual possibilities via cognitive defences. Interpersonal schemata, related to internal working models, are developed through interpersonal relationships and are self-perpetuating and drive behaviour. The interpersonal schemata of children in dysfunctional families are adaptive within those environments but become maladaptive in the wider community. Specific maladaptive interpersonal schemata are associated with particular personality disorders (e.g. Petrocelli *et al.*, 2001).

Treatment should therefore include strategies to address the interpersonal schemata developed within dysfunctional family systems.

Trauma

Trauma is a key factor in the aetiology of personality disorder (e.g. Battle *et al.*, 2004; Bierer *et al.*, 2003). It has been suggested that personality disorder would be better understood as a complex post-traumatic stress reaction

(Herman, 1992). Herman describes children abused within their families as experiencing a 'familial climate of pervasive terror'. Terror can also be experienced by children abused outside the family who have no physical or emotional refuge. Such terror inhibits children's normal development as they make adaptations to their ways of thinking, identity, managing emotions, interpersonal relationships and behaviour whilst maintaining the optimum proximity to their caregivers to ensure survival. These 'adaptations', described by Herman (1992) as Complex Posttraumatic Stress Disorder, map onto the characteristics that define personality disorder (Shea *et al.*, 1999). Chronic trauma impacts on neurobiological development, inhibiting the integration of sensory, emotional and cognitive information (Vasterling and Brewin, 2005). Whilst these adaptations are functional within abusive environments, they become dysfunctional and maladaptive when utilised within other environments.

Nevertheless, not all people who experience trauma develop personality disorder; pre-existing vulnerabilities or protective factors can mediate. Vulnerability could be genetic, or due to poor attachment relationships, other dysfunctional family constellations and/or social and cultural environments. Conversely, protective factors develop as a result of more secure attachment relationships and/or positive family and social relationships (e.g. Peters *et al.*, 2005), good intellectual and problem-solving ability, humour, strong identity and positive perception of self, good emotional regulation skills, positive interpersonal relationships and social support (King *et al.*, 2004). Those who have a 'good enough' family, or other relationships that support and care for the person through and after the trauma, are unlikely to develop complex personality changes (Silverman and LaGreca, 2002). An 'easy' temperament is deemed to be a protective factor and a 'difficult' temperament a vulnerability factor for adaptation to misfortune. Interestingly, a difficult temperament is associated with greater likelihood of abuse in an abusive family and more accidents (Losel and Bender, 2003).

Some research indicates that not everyone with personality disorder has experienced trauma (e.g. Paris, 1998). Nevertheless, clinicians working with those with severe psychopathology report extensive traumatic histories (e.g. Maden *et al.*, 2009; Burns *et al.*, 2009). Several hypotheses may account for this discrepancy. For example, some people who experience trauma do not categorise it as such, or the trauma was so extreme or so early that it is not consciously memorable to that individual. One client described his childhood as 'happy' and 'trauma free', speaking of his mother as 'loving and caring'. Social services records state that at age 3, he was found alone in a flat where he had been left unattended for a week. Several other entries recording prior incidents of rejection and extreme neglect were in his files. He had numerous foster carers and returned home, aged 8, when his mother was in a stable relationship. He was returned to care, aged 12, due to delinquent behaviour for which he blamed himself.

Extreme neglect

Extreme neglect is a trauma often overlooked. Such neglect means that the infant/child experiences terror of annihilation, a defining characteristic of traumatic experiences. This terror needs to be repressed in order to survive without an adult on whom to depend. Interestingly, in the experience of the authors, the majority of those in a prison unit providing therapeutic intervention with men with severe personality pathology (including many who score highly on a measure of psychopathy) have experienced extreme early neglect and show minimal overt fear reactions.

Neglect may be the most destructive form of child abuse (e.g. Perry, 2002). Whilst research connecting early and continuing emotional neglect with the development of psychopathic traits is in its infancy, the connection has strong face validity. Emotionally neglected children cannot develop attachment relationships and therefore do not develop those brain structures necessary to develop empathy, moral and social awareness and conscience (Anderson *et al.*, 1999; Dolan, 1999), and have dysregulated affect (Schore, 2003), rigid cognitive processes (Main, 1991) and poor sense of self (Seigal, 1999). These children have to survive with little support from adults. Therefore, as they develop, they learn to meet their needs by lying, conning, charming others and becoming manipulative, often 'outwitting' adults. If these strategies fail, they resort to illegal behaviours and aggression to survive, with no sense of guilt or remorse. Profoundly neglected children initially show low levels of activity but eventually seek stimulation (Crittenden, 1988). Antisocial activities can provide some of the excitement needed. With no one to offer comfort, children who have to survive in this way learn to suppress fear and other distressing emotions. To mask fear, these children develop an omnipotent and grandiose 'false-self'. Relationships become functional rather than emotional and tend to be shallow and self-serving. Thus, it can be seen that the characteristics associated with psychopathy can be developed as a consequence of early and continuing neglect.

Treatment must therefore include strategies to directly address traumatic experiences within safe containing relationships.

Socio-cultural and political forces

The impact of socio-cultural and political environments on the development of personality disorder is evidenced by differential prevalence of personality disorder typologies in different societal groups (Paris, 2001). Whilst socio-cultural and political environments alone will not lead to the development of personality disorder, environment creates the conditions that impact on the expression of genetic and developmental vulnerabilities. Political, economic and social circumstances impact on parenting, social supports and societal norms and, in turn, influence attachment, identity and cognitive, affective, behavioural and interpersonal strategies. For example, whilst infants' attachment behaviour is innate, they learn to express their needs in ways that have been shaped by parental behaviour influenced by societal norms (e.g. working mothers are unable to feed on demand). In addition, parental ability to be sensitive to children's needs is dependent on their stress which will, in part, be influenced by social and economic pressures. Paris (2001) describes the impact of 'rapid social change' on adolescents who have had dysfunctional and traumatic childhoods and who no longer have strong community guidance and support. Such adolescents will be highly likely to attach to sub-cultures which reinforce rather than challenge potential developing personality pathology.

The development of self and identity will depend not only on intra-familial relationships, but also relationships with extended social networks and sub-cultures (Bronfenbrenner, 1979), 'the generalised other' (Mead, 1934). The generalised other is the collective roles, beliefs and attitudes of those in the person's environment, immediate and extended. Through interaction with the wider environment, people internalise the common expectations held within each particular socio-cultural context. There will be specific socio-cultural expectations of, and attitudes towards, the individual's gender, social status, ethnicity, nationality and any social groups to which he or she is affiliated. In interpersonal interactions, the individual acts to minimise anxiety and threats to self-esteem; consequently, these attitudes and expectations will influence behaviour and become incorporated into the individual's personality characteristics. For example, societal values, norms and expectations help shape the individual's response to emotional adversity. In societies where the male stereotype is powerful and dominant, rage engendered in those who experience powerlessness may be expressed by aggressive or exploitative behaviours towards others. Where the female stereotype inhibits expressions of aggression, women who have similar rage due to similar experiences may respond by self-harming. Thus, the socio-cultural and political environment in which development occurs has an influential impact on the person's internal working model of self and others and thus on his or her self-schemata. In differing environments, different aspects of the person's behaviour can be reinforced; thus 'different selves' or aspects of self are predominant in different environments. People who have experienced such extreme adversity as to develop severe personality pathology may present very differently in different environments.

Treatment must therefore provide opportunities for understanding the impact of environment on development but also of alternative emotional experiences of relationships with a wider community.

Principle 3: Treatment should prioritise aetiological factors rather than solely managing symptomatic acts of destructiveness towards self or others

In De Zulueta's (2006) review of the literature on violence, she states, 'what these findings show is that human destructiveness, like psychological trauma, cannot be understood without recognising the intrinsic importance of human relationships in our development and in our sense of well-being' (p. viii). She concludes that violence originates in trauma. To reduce violence, one must reduce the personal distress that the perpetrator of violence experiences. Van der Kolk (1996) also draws this conclusion. Both De Zulueta and van der Kolk refer to evidence supporting the link between trauma and increased aggression: a deficit in empathy, increased addictive and self-destructive behaviours, a tendency to re-enact abuse (either as victim or perpetrator), impaired trust, reduced sense of responsibility and a lack of identity. This is true of numerous other presenting problems such as poor personal hygiene (sexual abuse), dependency (emotional neglect), obsessional behaviour (physical and emotional abuse), paranoia (abuse and bullying), and sexual domination or subjugation (sexual abuse). This catalogue of deficits or increased vulnerabilities is consistent with the difficulties experienced by those diagnosed as having personality disorder; the more severely disordered, the more severe the trauma appears to have been. Managing the symptoms will not change underlying distress and the individual will be vulnerable to employing those or other strategies at times of distress. People are not only traumatised by their victimisation but also by acts that they have perpetrated against themselves and others (Evans, 2006). This trauma also needs addressing. Van der Kolk states:

> The key element of the psychotherapy of people with post traumatic stress disorder is the integration of the alien, the unacceptable, the terrifying and the incomprehensible into their self-concepts. Life events initially experienced as alien, imposed from outside upon passive victims, must come to be 'personalized' as integrated aspects of the individuals' history and life experiences.
>
> (1996, pp. xv–xvi)

Unless integration occurs, the individual will continue to pose a potential risk of harm.

Thus, changing behavioural symptoms without addressing traumatic histories provides short-term management at the expense of lasting change.

Principle 4: Treatment must be capable of addressing the needs of a population with varying levels of motivation and engagement, including periods of crisis

Despite the distress that people with personality disorder experience, motivation to engage in treatment fluctuates even in those initially most motivated to change. Clients may not feel they are deserving of therapy or perceive they will be rejected as soon as the team get to know them for 'who they really are'. Work to enhance motivation prior to commencing treatment is important but motivation is unlikely to be consistently maintained in the absence of consistent attention through various strategies and, in particular, through the development of appropriate therapeutic attachment relationships.

Interventions directed at changing fundamental aspects of a person's personality are extremely anxiety-provoking. Clients will undoubtedly be fearful at times during intervention, and motivation will wane; indeed their motivation at times will be to stop treatment. Many people with personality disorder are impulsive and when treatment becomes stressful they will ask for 'time-out' or engage in less pro-social ways of avoiding therapy, such as refusing to engage in sessions or formally withdrawing from treatment. At times, solicitors may be employed to try to achieve termination of treatment. Self-harming, sexually or physically aggressive behaviours or knowingly contravening significant boundaries may all be utilised to orchestrate removal from treatment. Many services discharge clients at this point. However, it is at these times of crisis, when they are in greatest need of treatment.

Any treatment offered must be able to accommodate fluctuating motivation and periods of crisis when people are at their most emotionally vulnerable. If people are rejected from treatment when their motivation wanes (as some therapies advocate), or during crisis, then psychological damage to the client could occur and result in increased risk to self or others. Clients can of course choose to leave therapy but treatment offered must provide a means of ensuring that they are given every opportunity to work through periods of crisis.

Thus, treatment must be capable of containing clients during periods of crisis and provide strategies to re-engage those clients when motivation wanes.

Principle 5: Treatment must enable individuals to meet their survival needs

Gilbert (1989) takes an ethnological approach, describing all behaviour as related to the two primary fundamental needs: to survive as an individual and to survive as a species. Research and clinical evidence support the notion that to meet these primary needs humans have had to develop strong social networks. Consequently, four biosocial goals have evolved related to social interaction and have become equally fundamental to survival. These bio-social goals are: (i) caregiving; (ii) care receiving; (iii) power over others (leading to status and thus access to resources) and over the environment (leading to a sense of competence); and (iv) co-operation, i.e. connection to a group. Because these needs are so fundamental to survival, experiences that meet these needs lead to positive emotions and a sense of well-being (reward) and thus we have a propensity to repeat those experiences. Experiences antithetical to these needs are dangerous to survival so generate negative emotion (and are thus experienced as punishment). The nature of the negative emotion (disgust, fear, shame, sadness, anger) directs action but also engenders a desire to avoid those experiences. All behaviours can, when thoroughly analysed, be traced back to meeting these fundamental needs or to modulating the negative emotional state generated from such needs not being met. Block (2002) suggests that the behaviours associated with personality have the function of affect regulation in order to maintain affect at a tolerable level. At times there can be a conflict in achievement of different biosocial goals; at these times cognition, whether consciously processed or not, and emotion, will influence the choice of behaviour. The choice is often highly complex and will be determined by the need which at that moment is most important for survival. For example, a child may submit to humiliating sexually abusive experiences at the hands of an adult, and thus forgo power and control needs, in order not to alienate the abuser. This is particularly so if the abuser is a parent or person on whom the child is totally dependent for shelter, food or protection (i.e. basic survival).

Research demonstrates that social learning is achieved by direct experience, vicarious experience and instruction. From birth, a person is constantly learning, through interaction with caregivers, others and the environment, how to get their needs met to ensure survival. They also learn how to protect themselves from adverse experiences. In adversity, human beings adapt to survive. There is significant evidence that people with personality disorder are exposed to chronic adversity in childhood. The adaptations that the individual makes in order to minimise risk of harm and maximise survival are the very characteristics that are subsequently labelled personality disordered.

The implications of Gilbert's and Block's work and also of Young et al.'s (2003) schema-focused approach, which draws heavily upon attachment theory, are that personality has the function of maintaining optimal proximity to others. Indeed, De Zulueta (2006) proposes that the dysfunctional behaviours adopted by people with personality disorder are attempts to maintain relationships with others that have evolved in unusually adverse childhood relationships. These suggested functions of personality and the facilitation of survival have significant implications for treatment.

Treatment must enable clients to identify and adopt more appropriate strategies for meeting these needs (e.g. Eldridge and Saradjian, 2000).

Importantly, treatment must enable individuals to develop an improved self-construct, to form healthier attachments to others and to develop effective affect regulation.

Principle 6: Treatment must be equipped to disconfirm the perceptions, expectations and constructions of each individual if the individual is to achieve lasting change

People generally maintain their current styles of relating, even when these are highly dysfunctional (Benjamin, 2006). This is because new patterns of interacting are extremely anxiety-provoking even if they ultimately lead to healthier relationships (Young *et al.*, 2003). Carson observes that 'maladaptive behaviour persists over lengthy periods, because it is based upon perceptions, expectations or constructions of the characteristics of other people that tend to be confirmed by the interpersonal consequences of the behaviour emitted' (Carson, 1982, cited in Safran, 1998, p. 9). Thus, treatment must find ways to disconfirm the perceptions, expectations or constructions of others that the personality disordered individual holds.

Young observes that interpersonal schemata

> are comfortable and familiar, and when they are challenged, the individual will distort information to maintain the validity of these schemata. The threat of schematic change is too disruptive to the core cognitive organization. Therefore the individual automatically engages in a variety of cognitive manoeuvres to maintain the schema intact.
>
> (1994, p. 9)

He describes a number of interpersonal strategies (clustered around themes of schema-avoidance, schema-maintenance and schema-compensation) that are adopted by individuals in order to maintain their beliefs about themselves, the world and how they will be treated by others. In interpersonal interactions, individuals utilise an interpersonal style that elicits a response from others that is consistent with their schemata.

Services often unwittingly reinforce rather than challenge these schemata in that staff are readily drawn into clients' psychopathology. For example, humour and/or flirtation is used to keep staff feeling safe rather than addressing the emotion that the client is trying to avoid (Chapter 5), and services discharge clients when they become actively symptomatic (Chapter 6).

Treatment should enable the person's beliefs about self, others and the world to be regularly challenged, thus providing as many disconfirming responses as possible.

Principle 7: Treatment attempting to change personality must contain opportunities for new emotional experiences

Reviewing the literature on stability of personality disorder, Oldham and colleagues concluded that personality disorder traits are stable over time and developmental periods but can create 'intra and inter-personal conflicts that generate personality disorder-symptomatic behaviours (that are less stable over time)' (2005, p. 112). This can be seen in clients who have the same underlying pathology but act in different ways depending on the contingencies within each environment in which they find themselves.

McCrae and Costa's (2003) longitudinal study of personality found that personality does not change in the absence of a profound, emotional experience. They describe a number of emotionally-charged situations that may lead to personality change: 'Catastrophic events – illnesses, wars, great losses – may alter personality as may effective therapeutic intervention' (McCrae and Costa, 2003, p. 106) Recent findings from neuroscience suggest that the brain remains plastic, or open to influences from the environment, throughout life (Roffman *et al.*, 2005). This plasticity may involve not only the creation of new synaptic connections among neurons, but also the growth of new neurons across the lifespan. Thus, development is an ongoing process, particularly within close, emotionally involving relationships. Therapy is one such relationship that can bring about functional neurobiological change (Cozolino, 2006; Roffman *et al.*, 2005).

Safran and Greenberg's (1991) discussion of cognitive therapy highlights the importance of affect in achieving therapeutic change. They write that,

> No change seems possible without emotions . . . while thinking usually changes thoughts, only feeling can change emotions; that is, only the emergence of new emotional experiences, by adding new tonalities of feelings to the unitary configuration of core emotional themes, can affect their self-regulation facilitating a re-ordering in personal meaning processes.
>
> (pp. 60–61)

Safran and Greenberg's theory has significant implications for the treatment of people with severe personality disorder. The therapeutic relationship can provide an alternative attachment relationship within which those new emotional experiences can be reflected, empathised with and understood. People with severe personality disorder have, in most cases, little access to their affective state. They lack awareness of emotions other than anger and tend to behave in ways to avoid experiencing any negative affect. Even those whose presentation might indicate a struggle with overwhelming affect, such as those with a diagnosis of borderline personality disorder, lack the capacity to experience the full breadth of emotions experienced by others. Their emotions either fluctuate rapidly or become fixated upon one single emotion that they have strategies to manage.

Whilst cognitive therapy is useful for individuals capable of experiencing a normal range of affects, pure cognitive therapy is limited in its efficacy with individuals who lack the ability to identify and experience emotions (Young, 1994). Many people with personality disorder complete cognitive, behavioural and psychodynamic therapies at an intellectual level, making efforts to change their thoughts, but have not achieved emotional change. Based on the assumption that emotion facilitates change, any programme for these clients needs to incorporate a significant emotional component and allow for new emotional experiences. This requires that the individual is prevented from presenting in his or her preferred interpersonal style in order that he can access the underlying emotions that are being avoided at either a conscious or unconscious level (Block, 2002).

Treatment must therefore enable individuals to experience appropriate and contingent emotions within safe containing relationships.

Principle 8: Treatment must be consistently applied across a team

Gabbard (1989) describes how clients can present one aspect of the self to some team members and a completely different aspect of the self to others. This intra-personal split becomes enacted within teams, and members may begin to work at cross-purposes, often to the point of becoming dysfunctional and counter-therapeutic. This is a common and often unconscious strategy employed by people with personality disorder to maximise their control over situations and minimise their anxiety and shame. However, these strategies are dysfunctional and thus decrease treatment efficacy.

It is essential that in cases where treatment is delivered by a team rather than a lone practitioner, the team have an integrated framework that enables them to provide treatment consistently, thus minimising opportunities for splits (see Chapter 7; NICE, 2009a, 2009b).

Theoretical framework of intervention: cognitive interpersonal therapy

Allen Frances, quoted in Benjamin, states:

> The essence of being a mammal is the need for and the ability to participate in interpersonal relationships. The interpersonal dance begins at least as early as birth and ends only with death. Virtually all the most important events in life are interpersonal in nature and most of what we call personality is interpersonal in expression.
>
> (1993, p. vii)

People with personality disorder have chronic interpersonal dysfunction which is the driving force behind pathological cognitions, affect regulation and behaviours that characterise the disorder. Since personality is formed and maintained as a consequence of interpersonal processes which adapt the plastic neurobiological system, the brain, the only processes by which personality can be changed or modified are the same interpersonal processes by which it was formed and maintained. Thus, the treatment of people with personality disorder needs to be rooted within appropriate, emotionally intimate, attuned relationships.

People with severe personality disorder require intensive psychological treatment and most theorists in this area advocate multiple therapeutic contacts offering a range of interventions (Benjamin, 1993; Millon and Davis, 2000). Indeed, Livesley (2001) suggests one overarching theory should be adopted to organise therapy, thus ensuring 'an integrated approach using a combination of interventions drawn from different approaches, and selected whenever possible on the basis of efficacy, may be the optimal treatment strategy. The challenge is to deliver diverse interventions in an integrated way whilst managing individual patients' (p. 570) Thus, providing a manualised treatment approach capable of meeting such multiple needs would be difficult if not impossible.

Cognitive interpersonal theory offers a useful framework to drive the delivery of treatment because it meets the needs of treatment based upon the above assumptions. Cognitive interpersonal theory allows for interventions to be targeted at not only cognitions but also affect and interpersonal behaviour. Interventions from cognitive, psychodynamic and behavioural approaches can therefore be accommodated within this framework relatively easily since all major psychological models share some common features with cognitive interpersonal models. This framework allows for specific interventions that address relationships, trauma, cognitions, affect, regulation, and dangerous behaviours to self and others, and does not preclude the use of medication.

Importantly, the cognitive interpersonal approach:

- allows for explicit acknowledgement that current dysfunctional behaviours were at one time adaptive and represented a child's best attempt to cope with adversity.
- is based on the premise that people are at best ambivalent about change and that some level of resistance, albeit subconscious, is the norm; consequently a high level of motivation is not required to participate in therapy since this can be developed via a cognitive interpersonal approach.
- prioritises the therapeutic alliance, and difficulties within the relationship between client and therapist are expected, anticipated and explicitly addressed.
- is sufficiently flexible to guide treatment for a diverse range of individuals

with a diffuse range of problems with varying degrees of insight and motivation and is thus accessible to all.

- enables those individuals who find it difficult to establish a collaborative relationship, or are reluctant to attend formal therapeutic sessions, to be included, as treatment can be applied informally on an *ad hoc* basis by all staff whilst a deeper level of collaboration is established.
- is relatively easily understood by even those with minimum psychological knowledge and is accessible to both staff and clients.
- facilitates strategies that assist staff in resisting the responses that clients attempt to elicit from them, equipping staff to provide clients with the opportunity for new emotional experiences that challenge their perceptions of self and others.

Putting treatment into practice

Seigal (2003) states the importance of the twelve 'C's of effective psychotherapy – connection, compassion, contingency, cohesion, continuity, coherence, clarity, co-construction, complexity, consciousness, creativity, and community – and describes their neurobiological correlates in producing healing. The framework described encompasses these factors.

The importance of individual case formulation

The central role of formulation in driving the treatment of people with personality disorder is prominent within psychological literature. Castillo (2003) highlights how successful services for this population are those that make decisions based on case formulation. Case formulation involves using evidence-based theoretical frameworks to organise all information collected in relation to the client (interviews, psychometrics, observations and documentation) in order to formulate explanatory hypotheses for factors that underlie and maintain the client's psychopathology, in order to guide interventions. Individualised case formulations need to be developed and owned by the team. Case formulations are dynamic not static and will be developed over the course of treatment. Clients can play an active role in the development and elaboration of their own formulation. The case formulation should drive all interventions and therefore needs to be shared with all staff involved in client care to maximise the potential of every interaction.

Treating attachment disorder

Individual therapy – process

The key role of the individual therapist is to develop a secure attachment relationship with the client. Intimate attachments are the key to individual development (Bowlby, 1969, 1988). Whilst the most influential attachment figures are those developed in infancy, if significant secure attachments can be made at any time during life, fundamental changes can be brought about, not only psychological but also physiological. Neborsky (2003) suggests that secure attachments are mediated by serotonin, norepinephrine and dopamine in the limbic system, deficits of these neurotransmitters being associated with anxiety, depression, impulsivity and aggression. Seigal (2003) hypothesises that 'the therapeutic interpersonal experience enables integrative fibres to actually grow and thus enable new abilities to be attained' (p. 3)

The attachment relationship formed between therapist and client is the emotional 'holding environment' and 'secure base' from which the client can work through life experiences including trauma and consequent adaptations that an individual has made in order to survive. Thus, the process of individual therapy should be based on those strategies known to be effective in developing secure attachments. Secure relationships: (i) are based on collaborative, contingent communication; (ii) involve verbal sharing of the internal experience of each member of the dyad – reflective dialogue; (iii) offer repair when communication is disrupted, as it inevitably will be; (iv) allow for the development of a coherent narrative: connecting past, present and future is one of the central processes of the mind in the creation of the auto-biographical form of self-awareness; (v) share both the negative and positive experiences of living and the ability to remain connected during moments of uncomfortable emotion. Thus, negative emotional states can be shared and distress soothed (based on Seigal, 2001).

It is crucial that the client is enabled to experience attunement at the level of affect, which was lacking during early development – a prerequisite if he or she is to develop empathy for self and thus others. These clients may engage cognitively but will initially be extremely resistant to engaging emotionally. However, failure to engage at that level will impede therapeutic change. Therapists need to consistently and persistently utilise appropriate therapeutic strategies to ensure that affective engagement is achieved (see Chapter 5).

Individual therapy – content

Cognitive interpersonal therapy focuses on the connection between the person's current interpersonal behaviours and the development of those behaviours in earlier experience. Originally growing out of psychodynamic theory, difficulties are regarded as arising from deep, unresolved issues. Therapy involves taking a detailed history; exploring resistance to treatment; clients' patterns in relationships; clients' current interpersonal experiences, particularly the relationship with the therapist; the cognitive and affective components that are attached to behaviours, i.e. the client's interpersonal schemata; analysing the transactions between therapist and client and selecting a response that would not be predicted upon the basis of the client's interpersonal style (Carson, 1969); exploration of the client's fantasies; and most importantly, developing an emotionally intimate therapeutic relationship (Safran and Segal, 1990). This also involves working therapeutically with the trauma that the client has experienced, experiencing in the present the emotions repressed in the past within the containment of the secure attachment to the therapist (see below).

The aim of therapy is to fundamentally change the client's internal working models of self and others, and consequently their relationships, with the therapeutic relationship as the instrument of change. In residential units, it is crucial that relationships with *all* staff in contact with those individuals follow these same processes in their interactions.

Treating consequences of dysfunctional family systems

Relationships with staff

The evidence base for the importance of relationships in bringing about therapeutic change is strong (Haugh, 2008). Whilst the individual therapy relationship will become the secure attachment base, all other relationships that the clients have with staff should mirror secure attachments within an extended family. Treating the effects of chaotic dysfunctional family relationships requires the staff team to provide the clients with a consistent, ordered and eventually predictable environment in which they are able to develop healthier relationships with staff. All interpersonal interactions are viewed as opportunities for therapeutic change. The processes for developing such relationships are the same as those that form any other secure attachment relationship (see above). Given that the interpersonal style of most people with personality disorder is extremely challenging, getting them into any truly therapeutic relationship will be beset with difficulties. Due to their experiences within their own families and wider communities, these clients will be highly mistrustful of staff and fearful of such relationships. They will anticipate and try to draw rejection. Attempts to lever them into therapeutic relationships, via strategies such as contracts, are unlikely to be helpful as they become an obvious point of challenge. Nevertheless, with persistence and following the strategies described, even the most psychopathic individuals have been able to form such relationships. Strategies must be adapted to appeal to the client's curiosity by presenting him or her with an unfamiliar situation – for example, an environment where staff do not get drawn into the client's psychopathology and act in a therapeutic manner contrary to that which would be predicted by the client, thus disconfirming rather than confirming the client's schemata developed within their family. This requires psychologically minded staff, educated in the treatment model and flexible enough to adapt their normal professional training to encompass cognitive interpersonal strategies.

To enable staff to deliver this intervention it is essential to have an open confidentiality policy so that all staff working with the clients fully share all information. Without such an explicit policy, treatment will be compromised as it is highly likely that clients will draw staff into responding in ways that will confirm rather than contradict their dysfunctional schemata. The absence of such a policy will also greatly increase the likelihood of team split dynamics. Whilst this may be a controversial strategy for some professionals, clients tend to feel safer in units adopting this policy. This may be in part because secrets have been so destructive in their lives, in part because they have less potential for splitting. It may also be because knowing so many people are aware of their experience and accept them and respond positively towards them helps ameliorate shame.

Group work

Group work is an important vehicle for ameliorating damage resulting from dysfunctional families. Groups formed should, as far as possible, be maintained throughout the person's treatment. The group replicates a sibling group and the group facilitators take the role of parental figures who offer nurturance, sensitivity, emotional intimacy, explicit communication, empathy, challenge, boundary containing, and unconditional acceptance of the person (if not the behaviours) that are characteristic of healthy families. Like all families, there will be discord and ruptures within these groups but it is the healthy resolution of discord and ruptures that is healing for these clients. In addition to the therapeutic content, offering treatment in a group where there is a focus on relationships and group dynamics is reparative of dysfunctional family environments.

Treating trauma

Trauma involves an experience which generates intense fear. If there are no available attachment figures, extreme emotion cannot be processed and thus, for survival, it is repressed and/or dissociated from and the person appears emotionally detached. Over time, intrapersonal, interpersonal and behavioural adaptations occur which protect the individual from fear and also grief, anger and shame associated with the trauma (Neborsky, 2003). Neborsky (2003) proposes that to treat trauma, the client has to access those unconscious emotions. Brewin (2005) suggests attention also needs to be focused on managing intrusive flashbacks and nightmares and enabling conscious reappraisal of the experience. He proposes therapeutic interventions based on the neuropsychology of trauma. He advocates for exposure treatment to enable the sensory cues associated with the past trauma to be brought into the present within a safe emotional space and consequently re-encoded in a way that makes them verbally accessible. He proposes that doing so constructs 'detailed verbal memories which can then be used to exert inhibitory control over involuntary sensory and perceptual memories associated with amygdala activation' (Brewin, 2005, p. 283). This process must be gradual in order to ensure sufficient emotional arousal to access the traumatic memories but not over-arousal which will lead to further dissociation and failure to reprocess the images as verbal memories. With highly traumatised clients, this process needs to be regularly repeated, stopping when the person is no longer able to reflect consciously on the experience. As trauma reduces the capacity to hold and process information (working memory), the gradual approach to trauma processing is most effective. Brewin suggests that clients often have specific 'hot spots' associated with particularly intense emotions and these can provide a useful initial focus of attention. He cautions that cognitive reprocessing in relation to the trauma needs to occur when the client is emotionally reliving the traumatic event; if not, the person will not feel differently about the experience.

With people with severe personality disorder, these processes will not be possible unless the client has a secure attachment relationship within which the therapist can provide the emotional holding necessary for these processes. Conducting treatment with severely traumatised individuals without such a relationship risks ineffective treatment or even re-traumatisation. In conjunction with individual therapy, relevant aspects of the trauma and the sequelae can usefully be worked with in groups. This enables the clients to work on reducing shame and feeling less isolated.

Treating consequences of socio-cultural environments

Whilst little can be done directly to change the wider socio-cultural and political environment, understanding the role this has played in the client's development is an important part of every aspect of the therapy. Residential services should develop a strong ethos of community and a sense of belonging for both staff and clients. A culture of pro-social behaviour and pride in the unit is also important.

Clients need exposure to wider environments in which to consolidate and generalise newly developed interpersonal strategies and behaviours. Therefore education, employment opportunities, workshops, and social activities and opportunities can be made available to clients, initially on and then both on and off the unit. Clients should be encouraged to self-monitor within these fora and practise new skills in interacting.

One area where the socio-cultural and political environment can be influenced is in promoting evidence that people with personality disorder, including those who present with aggressive behaviours, can be treated effectively. National guidelines (NICE, 2009b) cite Crawford and Rutter's (2007) review of services in the NHS in which they describe the reluctance to work therapeutically with those who have antisocial personality disorder or a history of violence or aggressive behaviour. Such attitudes further stigmatise this client group and reinforce shame, sadness and hopelessness. Such feelings increase a sense of isolation, resentment and anger and perpetuate antisocial behaviour. Working within the framework described, people with all forms of personality disorder can be effectively treated.

Working with dangerous behaviours towards self and others

People with severe personality disorder are almost always a risk to self and/or others. Traditional programmes that directly address these behaviours in people with less severe psychopathology are less useful for this client group. They tend to drop out of treatment at this stage or, whilst initially appearing to contain the behaviour, at times of grave emotional 'need' regress to previous dangerous behaviour (Harris *et al.*, 1991, 1992; Looman *et al.*, 2005).

Those with severe personality disorder have learnt through experience, consciously or unconsciously, that the harmful behaviour has modulated negative emotional arousal. This learning began in early years and has been fundamental to their development. Studies have found that young people with poor attachments, who have lived in dysfunctional families and experienced trauma, are at great risk of expressing hostility with their peers and have the potential for interpersonal violence as they mature (Lyons-Ruth and Jacobovitz, 1999). Unresolved trauma also provides key motivational factors for self-harm (Klonsky, 2007). Seigal (2001) proposes that unresolved trauma remains at a lower mode of processing. Unresolved conditions may make it likely that entry into these states will occur with minimal provocation. Seigal states that 'entry into such lower-mode states may produce excessive emotional reactions, inner turmoil, dread, or terror, as well as an ensuing sense of shame and humiliation. In such conditions, individuals may be prone to "infantile rage" and aggressive, intrusive, or outright violent behaviour' (p. 89), which they direct towards themselves or others. He proposes that 'the process of resolution (of the trauma) may involve the achievement of a more integrated form of functioning that makes these lower-mode states less likely to occur' (p. 89).

Treatment of trauma has particular implications for the development of empathy for both self and others. As victimisation of others is related to a person's own victimisation, if that person has not assimilated the trauma, he or she will lack empathy for self and thus be unable to develop empathy for others. Without such work, a person may acquire some intellectual understanding of what it means to be victimised but is unlikely to relate to the emotional ramifications of victimisation. Thus, if the risk of dangerous behaviours is to be reduced, the key focus of therapy must be to resolve trauma whilst also addressing resultant interpersonal difficulties and maladaptive cognitive and emotional strategies. Changing this early learning requires multimodal complex interventions.

In addition to individual and group interventions focusing on unresolved trauma, behaviours can be targeted on a daily basis. When people are prevented by their environment from engaging in more extreme forms of dangerous behaviours, they can modify the behaviours but engage in a similar process. These parallel behaviours are symbolically representative of dangerous behaviours. The behaviours witnessed can appear relatively innocuous but they follow the same emotional regulation function and are driven by the same underlying cognitive and interpersonal belief systems as the more dangerous behaviours. For example, the woman convicted of arson who floods her room, or in a group 'sets it alight' by making a contentious statement, knowing it will cause 'uproar' among her peers. A man who stabbed his wife to death after a perceived insult may 'blank' a female member of staff who he perceives insulted him. A man may stop self-harming but get into 'fights' he knows will result in him being injured. The emotional and cognitive factors that lead to those behaviours are identified and become targets for intervention. Staff are made aware of the risk-paralleling behaviours for each client. They are then in a position to recognise those parallel behaviours and work to help clients understand the interpersonal interpretations and judgements that lead to negative emotions driving the behaviour. Recognition of these behaviours and working with the emotional states underlying these behaviours are vital to bring about genuine change. In addition, clients can be helped to develop alternative strategies to manage their cognitions and affect until more fundamental change can be facilitated. However, development of such strategies without resolution of the trauma will almost certainly result in eventual relapse.

Working with crisis

Crisis management is a crucial component of treatment (Livesley, 2003). Due to the challenge posed to clients' core response patterns, they often experience acute emotional crises. In crisis, any individual tends to resort to their preferred learned behaviour which the individual has experienced and knows (consciously, preconsciously or unconsciously) will modulate high levels of affect. These clients revert to individually functional but socially dysfunctional behaviours – for example, bullying, increased sexual activity, violence, self-injury, isolation, psychotic episodes and substance misuse. It is during these times of crisis that the core pattern of maladaptive behaviours is fully exposed and explored. Clients require close supportive work and alternative experiences to enable real change to occur. This is akin to the process of trauma re-exposure previously described. Clients experience numerous periods of crises varying in intensity. Their changing responses to crises, and the strategies employed to cope during these periods, are crucial indicators of change. In the absence of crisis episodes, the person may be being contained and managed but it is unlikely that they will be being treated effectively. It is only when a person can regularly respond in a socially functional manner to crisis situations and those responses become as well learned as the socially dysfunctional responses that a person's risk can be observably reduced.

Summary

Endeavours to identify appropriate treatment for people with personality disorder are unlikely to be successful unless treatment is formulation-driven and reflects the individual needs of each client, the context within which the psychopathology was developed, and factors that maintain the personality psychopathology. Successful treatment will not focus merely on symptoms but will address underlying causes of these symptoms over a lengthy period if therapeutic change is to be effected.

References

Ainsworth, M.D.S. (1989) Attachments beyond infancy. *American Psychologist*, **44**, 709–716.

American Psychiatric Association (APA) (2000) *Diagnostic and Statistical Manual of Mental Disorders (4th edn Text Revision) – DSM-IV-TR*. Washington, DC: American Psychiatric Association.

Andersen, S.L., Lyss, P.J., Dumont, N.L. and Teicher, M.H. (1999) Enduring neuro-chemical effects of early maternal separation on limbic structures. *Annals of New York Academy of Sciences*, **877**, 756–759.

Anderson, M., Teicher, M.H., Polcari, A. and Renshaw, P.F. (2002) Abnormal T2 relaxation time in the cerebellar vermis of adults sexually abused in childhood: potential role of the vermis in stress-enhanced risk for drug abuse. *Psychoneuro-endocrinology*, **27(1–2)**, 23–44.

Anderson, S.W., Bechara, A., Damasio, H. and Tranel, A.R. (1999) Impairment of social and moral behavior related to early damage in human prefrontal cortex. *Nature Neuroscience*, **2**, 1032–1037.

Bateman, A.W. and Fonagy, P. (2004) *Psychotherapy for Borderline Personality Disorder: Mentalization Based Treatment*. Oxford: Oxford University Press.

Battle, C.L., Shea, M.T., Johnson, D.M. *et al.* (2004) Childhood maltreatment associated with adult personality disorders. *Journal of Personality Disorders*, **18(2)**, 193–211.

Benjamin, L.S. (1993) *Interpersonal Diagnosis and Treatment of Personality Disorders*. New York: Guilford Press.

Benjamin, L.S. (2006) *Interpersonal Reconstructive Therapy: An Integrative, Personality-Based Treatment for Complex Cases*. New York: Guilford Press.

Bierer, L.M., Yehuda, R., Schmeidler, J. *et al.* (2003) Abuse and neglect in child-hood: relationship to personality disorder diagnoses. *CNS Spectrums*, **8(10)**, 737–754.

Block, J. (2002) *Personality as an Affect-processing System: Toward an Integrative Theory*. Hillsdale, NJ: LEA.

Blonigen, D.M., Hicks, B.M., Krueger, R.F. *et al.* (2005) Psychopathic personality traits: heritability and genetic overlap with internalizing and externalizing psychopathology. *Psychological Medicine*, **35(5)**, 637–648.

Bouchard, T.J. and Loehlin, J.C. (2001) Genes, evolution and personality. *Behavior Genetics*, **31**, 243–273.

Bowlby, J. (1969). *Attachment and Loss: Attachment*. New York: Basic Books.

Bowlby, J. (1988) *A Secure Base: Parent-Child Attachment and Healthy Human Development*. New York: Basic Books.

Bremner, J.D. and Narayan, M. (1998) The effects of stress on memory and the hippocampus throughout the life cycle: implications for childhood development and aging. *Development and Psychopathology*, **10**, 871–886.

Bremner, J.D., Krystal, J.H., Southwick S.M. and Charney, D.S. (1995) Functional neuroanatomical correlates of the effects of stress on memory. *Journal of Traumatic Stress*, **8**, 527–554.

Bremner, J.D., Southwick, S.M. and Charney, D.S. (1999) The neurobiology of post-traumatic stress disorder: an integration of animal and human research. In P. Saigh and J.D. Bremner (eds), *Posttraumatic Stress Disorder: A Comprehensive Text*. New York: Allyn and Bacon, pp. 103–143.

Bretherton, I. (1987) New perspectives on attachment relations. In J. Osofsky (ed.), *Handbook of Infant Development*. New York: Wiley, pp. 1061–1100.

Brewin, C. (2005) Implications for psychological interventions. In J. Vasterling and C. Brewin (eds), *Neuropsychology of PTSD*. New York: Guilford Press, pp. 271–291.

Bronfenbrenner, U. (1979) *The Ecology of Human Development*. Cambridge, MA: Harvard University Press.

Burke, H. and Hart, S.D. (2000) Personality disordered offenders: conceptualization, assessment and diagnosis of personality disorder. In S. Hodgins and R. Müller-Isberner (eds), *Violence, Crime and Mentally Disordered Offenders*. Chichester: Wiley, pp. 63–85.

Burns *et al.* (2009) Men who reach criteria for DSPD; preliminary research findings from the DSPD High Secure Project Seminar. Westminster, London, 7 September 2009.

Buss, A.H. and Plomin, R. (1984) *Temperament: Early Developing Personality Traits*. Hillsdale, NJ: LEA.

Cadoret, R.J., Yates, W.R. *et al.* (1995) Genetic-environmental interaction in the genesis of aggressivity and conduct disorders. *Archives of General Psychiatry*, **52**, 916–924.

Carson, R.C. (1969) *Interaction Concepts of Personality*. Chicago: Aldine.

Carson, R.C. (1982) Self-fulfilling prophecy, maladaptive behavior and psychotherapy. In J.C. Anchin and D.J. Kiesler (eds), *Handbook of Interpersonal Psychotherapy*. New York: Pergamon, pp. 64–77.

Castillo, H. (2003) *Personality Disorder: Temperament of Trauma*. London: Jessica Kingsley.

Choi, J., Bumseok, J., Rohan, M. *et al.* (2009) Preliminary evidence for white matter tract abnormalities in young adults exposed to parental verbal abuse. *Biological Psychiatry*, **65(3)**, 227–234.

Cleckley, H. (1976) *The Mask of Sanity*. St Louis: Mosby.

Cozolino, L. (2006) *The Neuroscience of Human Relationships*. New York: Norton.

Crawford, M. and Rutter, D. (2007) Lessons learned from an evaluation of dedicated community-based services for people with personality disorder. *Mental Health Review Journal*, **12**, 55–61.

Crittenden, P.M. (1988) Family and dyadic patterns of functioning in maltreating families. In K. Browne, C. Davies and P. Stratton (eds), *Early Prediction and Prevention of Child Abuse*. Chichester: Wiley, pp 161–198.

Depue, R. and Lenzenweger, M. (2001) Neurobiology of personality disorders. In J. Livesley (ed.), *Handbook of Personality Disorders*. New York: Guilford Press, pp 136–176.

De Zulueta, F. (2006) *From Pain to Violence: The Traumatic Roots of Destructiveness*. Chichester: Wiley-Blackwell.

Dolan, J. (1999) On the neurology of morals. *Nature Neuroscience*, **2**, 927–929.

Edens, J.F., Marcus, D.K. *et al.* (2006) Psychopathic, not psychopath: taxometric evidence for the dimensional structure of psychopathy. *Journal of Abnormal Psychology*, **115(1)**, 131–144.

Eldridge, H. and Saradjian, J. (2000) Working with women who sexually abuse children. Part 7 in D.R. Laws, S.M. Hudson and T. Ward (eds), *Remaking Relapse Prevention with Sex Offenders*. Thousand Oaks, CA: Sage.

Etkin, A., Pittenger, C., Polan, J. and Kandel, E.R. (2005) Toward a neurobiology of psychotherapy. *Clinical Neuroscience*, **17**, 145–158.

Evans, C. (2006) What violent offenders remember of their crime: empirical explorations. *Australian and New Zealand Journal of Psychiatry*, **40(6)**, 508–518.

Fonagy, P. (2001) *Attachment Theory and Psychoanalysis*. New York: Other Press.

Fraley, R., Shaver, P. and Phillip, R. (2000) Adult romantic attachment. *Review of General Psychology*, **4(2)**, 132–154.

Gabbard, G.O. (1989) Splitting in hospital treatment. *American Journal of Psychiatry*, **146**, 444–451.

Gilbert, P. (1989) *Human Nature and Suffering*. Hove: LEA.

Grossman, K., Grossman, K.E. and Kindler, H. (2005) Early care and the roots of attachment and partnership representations. In K.E. Grossman, K. Grossman and E. Waters (eds), *Attachment from Infancy to Adulthood*. New York: Guilford Press, pp. 98–136.

Harris, G.T., Rice, M.E. and Cormier, C.A. (1991) Psychopathy and violent recidivism. *Law and Human Behavior*, **15**, 625–637.

Harris, G.T., Rice, M.E. and Cormier, C.A. (1992) An evaluation of maximum security therapeutic community for psychopaths and other mentally disordered offenders. *Law and Human Behavior*, **16**, 399–412.

Hart, S. (2008) *Brain, Attachment, Personality*. London: Karnac.

Haugh, P.S. (2008) The relationship not the therapy? What the research tells us. In P.S. Haugh (ed.), *The Therapeutic Relationship: Perspectives and Themes*. Ross-on-Wye: PCCS Books, pp. 9–23.

Herman, J.L. (1992) *Trauma and Recovery*. New York: Basic Books.

Jacob, C., Muller, J., Schmidt, M. *et al.* (2005) Cluster B personality disorders are associated with allelic variation of monoamine oxidase A activity. *Neuropsychopharmacology*, **30**, 1711–1718.

Jaffee, S.R., Caspi, A., Moffitt, T.E. *et al.* (2005). Nature x nurture: genetic vulnerabilities interact with child maltreatment to promote conduct problems. *Development and Psychopathology*, **17**, 67–84.

Kernberg, O. (1996) A psychoanalytic theory of personality disorders. In M. Lenzenweger and J.F. Clarkin (eds), *Major Theories of Personality Disorder*. New York: Guilford Press, pp. 106–140.

Kim-Cohen, J., Caspi, A., Taylor, A. *et al.* (2006) MAOA, maltreatment, and gene–environment interaction predicting children's mental health: new evidence and a meta-analysis. *Molecular Psychiatry*, **11**, 903–913.

King, D.W., Vogt, D.S. and King, L.A. (2004) Risk and resilience factors in the etiology of chronic PTSD. In B.T. Litz (ed.), *Early Interventions for Trauma and Traumatic Loss in Children and Adults*. New York: Guilford Press, pp. 34–64.

Klonsky, E.D. (2007) The functions of deliberate self-injury. *Clinical Psychology Review*, **27**, 226–239.

Livesley, J.W. (2001) A framework for an integrated approach to treatment. In J.W. Livesley (ed.), *Handbook of Personality Disorders: Theory, Research, and Treatment*. New York: Guilford Press, pp. 570–600.

Livesley, J.W. (2003) *Practical Management of Personality Disorder*. New York: Guilford Press.

Livesley, J.W. (2007) A framework for integrating dimensional and categorical classifications of personality disorder. *Journal of Personality Disorder*, **21(2)**, 199–224.

Livesley, J.W., Jang, K.L., Jackson, D.N. and Vernon, P.A. (1993) Genetic and environmental contributions to dimensions of personality disorder. *American Journal of Psychiatry*, **150**, 1826–1831.

Looman, J., Dickie, I. and Abracen, J. (2005) Responsivity issues in the treatment of sexual offenders. *Trauma, Violence, and Abuse*, **6(4)**, 330–353.

Losel, F. and Bender, D. (2003) Resiliance and protective factors. In D.P. Farrington and J. Coid (eds), *Preventing Adult Antisocial Behaviour*. Cambridge: Cambridge University Press, pp. 130–204.

Lynam, D.R. and Derefinko, K.J. (2006) Psychopathy and personality. In C.J. Patrick (ed.), *Handbook of Psychopathy*. New York: Guildford Press, pp. 133–155.

Lyons-Ruth, K. and Jacobovitz, D. (1999) Attachment disorganization. In J. Cassidy and P. Shaver (eds), *Handbook of Attachment Theory and Research*. New York: Guilford Press, pp. 520–554.

Maden *et al.* (2009) Common data set findings of men who reach criteria for DSPD; preliminary research findings from the DSPD High Secure Project Seminar. Westminster, London, 7 September 2009.

Magnavita, J.J. (2004) *Handbook of Personality Disorders*. New York: Wiley.

Main, M. (1991) Metacognitive knowledge, metacognitive monitoring, and singular (coherent) versus multiple (incoherent) models of attachment. In C.M. Parkes, J. Stevenson-Hinde and P. Marris (eds), *Attachment across the Life Cycle*. London: Routledge, pp. 127–159.

Main, M. and Hesse, E. (1990) Parents' unresolved traumatic experiences are related to infant disorganized attachment status. In M.T. Greenberg, D. Cicchetti and E.M. Cummings (eds), *Attachment in the Preschool Years*. Chicago: Chicago University Press, pp. 161–182.

Matte Blanco, I. (1975) *The Unconscious as Infinite Sets*. London: Karnac.

McCrae, R.R. and Costa, P.T. (2003) *Personality in Adulthood*. New York: Guilford Press.

McGuffin, P. and Thapar, A. (1992) The genetics of personality disorder. *British Journal of Psychiatry*, **160**, 12–23.

Mead, G.H. (1934) Play, the game, and the generalized other. In C.W. Morris (ed.), *Mind, Self and Society from the Standpoint of a Social Behaviorist*. Chicago: Chicago University Press, pp. 152–164.

Millon, T. and Davis, R.D. (2000) *Personality Disorders in Modern Life*. New York: Wiley.

National Institute for Health and Clinical Excellence (2009a) *Borderline Personality Disorder: Treatment and Management. NICE Clinical Guideline 78*. London: NICE.

National Institute for Health and Clinical Excellence (2009b) *Antisocial Personality Disorder: Treatment, Management and Prevention. NICE Clinical Guideline 77*. London: NICE.

Neborsky, R.J. (2003) A clinical model for the comprehensive treatment of trauma using an affect experiencing-attachment theory approach. In M. Solomon and D. Siegel (eds), *Healing Trauma*. New York: Norton, pp. 282–321.

Noblett, K.L. and Coccaro, E.F. (2005) The psychobiology of personality disorders. In M. Rosenbluth, S.H. Kennedy and R.M. Bagby (eds), *Depression and Personality*. Washington, DC: APA, pp. 19–42.

Oldham, J.M., Skodol, A. and Bender, D.S. (2005) *The American Psychiatric Publishing Textbook of Personality Disorders*. Washington, DC: APA.

Paris, J. (1998) Does childhood trauma cause personality disorders in adults? *Canadian Journal of Psychiatry*, **43**, 148–153.

Paris, J. (2001) Psychosocial adversity. In W.J. Livesley (ed.), *Handbook of Personality Disorders*. New York: Guilford Press, pp. 231–241.

Perry, B.D. (2002) Childhood experience and the expression of genetic potential. *Brain and Mind*, **3**, 79–100.

Perry, B.D., Pollard, R. *et al.* (1995) Childhood trauma, the neurobiology of adaptation and 'use-dependent' development of the brain: how 'states' become 'traits'. *Infant Mental Health Journal*, **16(4)**, 271–291.

Peters, R., Ross, B.J., Leadbeater, R. and McMahon, J. (2005) *Resilience in Children, Families, and Communities*. New York: Springer.

Petrocelli, J.V., Glaser, D.A. *et al.* (2001) Early maladaptive schemas of personality disorder subtypes. *Journal of Personality Disorders*, **15**, 6546–6559.

Piaget, J. (1969) *The Psychology of the Child*. New York: Basic Books.

Plomin, R. and Asbury, K. (2005) Nature and nurture. *Annals of the American Academy of Political and Social Science*, **600(1)**, 86–98.

Plomin, R. and Kosslyn, S. (2001) Genes, brain and cognition. *Nature Neuroscience*, **4(12)**, 1153–1155.

Plomin, R., Owen, M.J. and McGuffin, P. (1994) The genetic basis of complex human behaviours. *Science*, **264(5166)**, 1733–1739.

Plutchik, R. (1980) A general psychoevolutionary theory of emotion. In R. Plutchik and H. Kellerman (eds), *Emotion: Theory, Research and Experience*. New York: Academic Press, pp. 3–33.

Reif, A. and Lesch, K.P. (2003) Toward a molecular architecture of personality. *Behavioral Brain Research*, **139**, 1–20.

Roffman, J.L., Marci, C.D. *et al.* (2005) Neuroimaging and the functional neuroanatomy of psychotherapy. *Psychological Medicine*, **35**, 1385–1398.

Safran, J. (1998) *Widening the Scope of Cognitive Therapy*. New Jersey: Jason Aronson Inc.

Safran, J.D. and Greenberg, L.S. (1991) Affective change processes. In J.D. Safran and L.S. Greenberg (eds), *Emotion, Psychotherapy and Change*. New York: Guilford Press, p. 339–362.

Safran, J.D. and Segal, Z.V. (1990) *Cognitive Therapy: An Interpersonal Process Perspective*. New York: Basic Books.

Sameroff, A.J. (2009) *The Transactional Model of Development*. Washington, DC: APA.

Schore, A.N. (1997) Early organization of the nonlinear right brain and development of a predisposition to psychiatric disorders. *Development and Psychopathology*, **9**, 595–631.

Schore, A.N. (2003) *Affect Regulation and the Repair of Self*. New York: Norton.

Shea, M.T., Zlotnick, C. and Weisberg, R.B. (1999) Commonality and specificity of personality disorder profiles in subjects with trauma histories. *Journal of Personality Disorders*, **13(3)**, 199–210.

Siegel, D.J. (1999) *The Developing Mind: Towards a Neurobiology of Interpersonal Experience*. New York: Guilford.

Siegel, D.J. (2001) Toward an interpersonal neurobiology of the developing mind. *Infant Mental Health Journal*, **22(1–2)**, 67–94.

Siegel, D.J. (2003) An interpersonal neurobiology of psychotherapy. In M.F. Solomon and D.J. Siegel (eds), *Healing Trauma*. New York: Norton, pp. 1–56.

Silverman, W.K. and LaGreca, A.M. (2002) *Helping Children Cope with Disasters and Terrorism*. Washington, DC: APA.

Skodol, A. (2009) *Personality Disorders in DSM-V: Emerging Perspectives*. 11th International Congress of International Society for the Study of Personality Disorders, New York City, 21–23 August.

Stewart, S.H. and Conrod, P.J. (2002) Experimental studies exploring the functional relationship between Post Traumatic Stress Disorder and substance use disorder. In P.C. Ouimette and P.J. Brown (eds), *Trauma and Substance Abuse*. Washington, DC: APA, pp. 29–55.

Stewart, S.H. and Conrod, P.J. (eds), (2005) Special Issue: State-of-the-art and future directions in substance abuse treatment. *Journal of Cognitive Psychotherapy*, **19(3)**, 195–198.

Stien, P.T. and Kendall, J.C. (2003) *Psychological Trauma and the Developing Brain*. London: Taylor and Francis.

Teicher, M.H., Dumont, N., Yutaka, I. *et al.* (2004) Childhood neglect is associated with reduced corpus callosum area. *Biological Psychiatry*, **56(2)**, 80–85.

Teicher, M.H., Samson, J.A., Polcari, A. and McGreenery, C.E. (2006) Sticks, stones, and hurtful words: relative effects of various forms of childhood maltreatment. *American Journal of Psychiatry*, **163(6)**, 993–1000.

van der Kolk, B. (1996) Preface. In B. van der Kolk, A. McFarlane and L. Weisaeth (eds), *Traumatic Stress: The Effects of Overwhelming Experience on Mind, Body and Society*. New York: Guilford Press.

Van Ijzendoorn, M.H. (1995) Adult attachment representations. *Psychological Bulletin*, **117**, 387–403.

Vasterling, J.J. and Brewin, C.R. (2005) *Neuropsychology of PTSD*. New York: Guilford Press.

Viding, E. and Frith, U. (2006) Genes for susceptibility to violence lurk in the brain. *Proceedings of the National Academy of Sciences*, **103**, 6085–6086.

Waldman, I.D. and Rhee, S.H. (2006) Genetic and environmental influences on psychopathy and antisocial behavior. In C.J. Patrick (ed.), *Handbook of Psychopathy*. New York: Guilford Press, pp. 205–228.

Werner, E.A., Myers, M.M., Fifer, W.P. *et al.* (2007) Prenatal predictors of infant temperament. *Developmental Psychobiology*, **49(5)**, 474–484.

Widiger, T.A. and Lowe, J.R. (2008) A dimensional model of personality disorder: proposal for DSM-V. *Psychiatric Clinics of North America*, **31(3)**, 363–378.

Winnicott, D.W. (1965) *The Maturational Process and the Facilitating Environment*. London: Hogarth Press.

World Health Organization (WHO) (1990) *International Statistical Classification of Diseases and Related Health Problems (10th Revision)*. Geneva: WHO.

Young, J.E. (1994) *Cognitive Therapy for Personality Disorders: A Schema-focused Approach*. Sarasota, FL: Professional Resource Press.

Young, J.E., Klosko, J.S. and Weishaar, M. (2003) *Schema Therapy*. New York: Guilford Press.

Chapter 5

Fundamental treatment strategies for optimising interventions with people with personality disorder

Naomi Murphy and Des McVey

Introduction

Personality disorder is characterised by profound difficulties within the interpersonal sphere. These difficulties in relating to others pose a challenge to services and practitioners attempting to offer treatment. Clinicians advocating several models of therapy – e.g. dialectical behaviour therapy (Linehan, 1993), integrity model of existential psychotherapy (Lander and Nahon, 2005), mentalisation based treatment (Bateman and Fonagy, 2004) and transference focused psychotherapy (Clarkin *et al.*, 2006) – describe detailed strategies for individual or group therapists to improve the quality of the therapeutic relationship with personality disordered patients. However, there is an absence of guidance that can be utilised beyond the boundaries of formal psychological interventions which contributes to staff who are not trained to deliver psychological therapies struggling to identify how to ensure their contacts with clients are therapeutic.

Our experience of working with this client group leads us to propose that focusing upon establishing emotional intimacy, and attempting to overcome the obstacles to intimacy encountered in relationships with clients, is crucial in allowing all staff required to interact with personality disordered clients to provide a meaningful contribution to their treatment. Three primary interactive strategies are essential in developing emotional intimacy: optimising affect, working with the logical perspective of clients, and using explicit communication. These strategies also optimise the potency of formal psychological interventions, both individual and group therapies, thus enabling therapists to enhance their interventions and reach even those clients who are viewed as inaccessible to treatment.

The need for emotional intimacy in therapeutic relationships

All human beings require emotional intimacy and closeness to live a healthy life. Dahms (1972) notes that emotional intimacy is not merely a 'sentimental preoccupation' but, rather, is an 'overlooked requirement for survival'. Healthy, close interpersonal relationships are characterised by intimacy and such relationships allow the participants to experience warmth, tenderness and a heightened awareness of themselves (Meares, 2003). Lerner defines emotionally intimate relationships as ones in which

> we can be who we are within the relationship and allow the other person to do the same. 'Being who we are' requires that we can talk openly about things that are important to us, that we take a clear position on where we stand on important emotional issues, and that we clarify the limits of what is acceptable and intolerable to us in a relationship. 'Allowing the other person to do the same' means that we can stay emotionally connected to that other party who thinks, feels and believes differently, without needing to change, convince or fix the other. An intimate relationship is one in which neither party silences, sacrifices or betrays the self and each party expresses strength and vulnerability, weakness and competence in a balanced way.
>
> (1989, p. 3)

Fosha (2000) observes that having close, emotionally intimate relationships enables us to cope with adversity and even tragedy that we may encounter during our lives.

The difficulties that personality disordered individuals experience typically cut across affective, cognitive and behavioural domains to impact profoundly upon their interpersonal relationships. Whilst each domain of difficulty represents a range of associated problems that can be debilitating to live with, it is the fusion of the three problem areas within interactions with others that is arguably most incapacitating since this restricts the individual's ability to achieve emotional intimacy and thus gain real benefits from contact with others, including those professionals with whom they come into contact.

Despite emotional intimacy being an important feature of interpersonal relationships, psychotherapeutic literature has instead focused upon another component of the therapeutic relationship, that is, the therapeutic alliance. The alliance incorporates the patient's ability to work in therapy; the bond between the patient and therapist; the therapist's ability to empathically understand; and goals and tasks which are agreed between the two (Gaston, 1990). Robust research has demonstrated that the alliance is one of the most significant factors in relation to treatment process and outcome (e.g. Stiles et al., 1998; Horvath and Bedi, 2002). However, the therapeutic relationship has been observed to include more than an alliance (Smith et al., 2006).

Those who perceive the therapeutic requirement to consist of more than an alliance discuss the need to establish an emotionally intimate relationship with the patient (Bateman and Fonagy, 2004; Clarkin et al., 2006; Fosha, 2000; Greenberg, 2002; Meares, 2003; Safran and Segal, 1996; Wachtel,

2008). Magnavita (2000) argues that intimacy is the *currency* of corrective therapeutic experiences. Despite this, definitions of emotional intimacy within the therapeutic literature are scarce. Lander and Nahon (2005) define emotionally intimate therapy as that in which efforts are focused upon closing the gap between the therapist and the client, and advocate for incorporating honesty and responsibility into practice to create such a relationship.

Whilst establishing an authentic, emotionally intimate therapeutic relationship does not require clinicians to share personal details of their lives, it does require the clinician to be willing to share his or her emotional self in relation to the client and the client's shared experiences and emotional responses. Emotionally intimate relationships feature understanding or knowing, whereby the two parties 'get' each other; within the therapeutic relationship, connectedness between the client and therapist requires the therapist to endeavour to find a way to meet the client in the logical world he or she inhabits, and to find a way to make their own logical world apparent to the client. Emotionally intimate relationships are also characterised by the two parties tolerating the strong emotions that inevitably arise as the relationship deepens. For the client, this includes overcoming the fear of being hurt, shamed or rejected by the clinician; the clinician must in turn have a willingness to know and accept the many aspects of the client and remain connected even when those aspects make him or her feel deeply uncomfortable. Finally, emotionally intimate relationships involve an ability to communicate clearly despite the idiosyncrasies of the relating parties; within the therapeutic relationship this involves the clinician finding a way to create a channel of dialogue that is clear and transparent and where opportunities for misinterpretation are thus minimised.

Absence of emotional intimacy within the lives of people with personality disorder

Whilst emotional intimacy is necessary for a healthy life, developing an emotionally intimate relationship in any context requires that *both* participants have the capability and the desire to be close and connected whilst managing to retain a healthy separation of the self (Magnavita, 2000). Typically, people with personality disorder lack both a consistent desire to be in an emotionally intimate relationship and the ability to develop and maintain such a connection. A significant factor in developing an interpersonal style that prevents others from getting close has been the nature of their relationships in childhood which have generally been devoid of appropriate emotional intimacy. Attachment theory plays a key role in the development of personality (Bowlby, 1980, 1988). In summary, Bowlby theorised that the experiences of relationships that a person has during their childhood, and especially those with primary caregivers (either in the family or in residential settings), influence their patterns of interaction beyond the family and into later life, by causing the development of 'internal working models' or 'schema' (Young, 1994) which allow children to learn about who they are and to predict how others will respond to them in future interactions.

Within the concept of an internal working model or schema, the perception of self and the perception of others are both intrinsically interactional. Where children are exposed to good enough caregiving and experience a reasonably consistent degree of love and respect, they acquire a schema for themselves and their interpersonal interactions constructed around a belief that they are valued as a person and deserving of care. They also learn that displays of emotion can elicit help, comfort and support; thus care-seeking at times of distress is reinforced and children learn to experience emotions, articulate their emotional needs and develop skills for coping with emotions within proximity to a primary caregiver whom they associate with feeling safe.

When caregivers are inconsistently responsive, excessive emotionality is reinforced and the primary emotion experienced by the child is combined with anxiety about whether the caregiver will respond. This results in an insecure attachment style, or 'feeling but not dealing', as Fosha (2000) labels it. When children grow up in abusive or neglectful families, they make sense of events by internalising a model of themselves as fundamentally unlovable and unworthy of having their needs met. They also learn to deny that they have emotional needs as a means of coping with overwhelming emotions in a situation in which their emotional needs will remain unmet. Within such an environment, displays of emotion may lead to the caregiver becoming uncomfortable and withdrawing or punishing the child, and so expression of affect can become dangerous as it directly threatens the relationship with the caregiver and the physical integrity of the child. Fosha (2000) observes that this can cause children to become terrified of affect. Because intense emotions are overwhelming and threaten relationships with caregivers, she notes that people choose to preserve the integrity of their attachment ties at the expense of their affective self experiences which are sacrificed.

Attachment theory suggests that proximity to others plays an important role in our ability to survive. However, the optimal proximity to others that the personality disordered individual was forced to adopt as a child was more distant than that adopted by children who received good enough parenting. Children raised within abusive contexts are left with a profound fear of intimacy and a mistrust of others which conflicts with their desire for comfort and understanding (Bateman and Fonagy, 2004). They learn that the optimal proximity to others is one that is close enough to allow one to have one's physical needs met but distant enough to restrict the capacity of the other to threaten one's physical integrity or cause one emotional distress. They thus acquire a range of strategies that maintain the other at optimum distance. It is often the strategies that individuals use to keep others at an optimum distance that lead to others labelling the individual as having a difficult interpersonal style or diagnosing them as personality disordered, and Block (2002) proposes that personality would in fact be better understood as a means of regulating affect that arises in relation to others.

The interpersonal schemata developed during childhood as a consequence of those attachment relationships form the basis of strategies that affect the individual's ability to form relationships. The adult's pattern of relating is consequently characterised by beliefs and feelings that originated within the dysfunctional family of origin. Experiences that are consistent with a schema are most likely to be accepted as valid since they enable the schema to be maintained without question, thus providing an illusion of safety arising from the perception that the world is predictable. Experiences that are incongruent with a schema are more likely to be questioned or misinterpreted in order to maintain the schema.

The ability to attain and sustain an intimate relationship therefore evolves during our early childhood attachments. Meares (2003) writes that early traumatic experiences within relationships with caregivers cause the individual's sense of self to be stunted and dependent upon intrusive thoughts that tell the person how useless or worthless he or she is. Meares observes that these thoughts are distracting and restrict the ability of the individual to develop the capacity for intimate dialogue.

The combination of lack of motivation for closeness, coupled with poor interpersonal skills, and low self-worth developed as a consequence of childhood relationships restricts the ability of people with personality disorders to develop emotionally intimate relationships with those with whom they interact. Consequently, for many, entering the therapeutic environment represents a rare opportunity to access interactions that could be characterised by emotional intimacy.

The therapeutic situation can be particularly intense and may activate a fear of intimacy and closeness in people who are relatively well-functioning. For those with a personality disorder, this anxiety can be terrifying and can cause some clients to determinedly resist attempts by clinicians to draw closer (Bateman and Fonagy, 2004). Becoming involved in an emotionally intimate therapeutic relationship may also be difficult for clinicians working with people with personality disorder.

Establishing closeness is first challenged by the lack of capacity that many clients have to share intimate dialogue (Meares, 2003), which can leave staff not knowing how to proceed in order to foster intimacy. It is also hard to maintain a desire for closeness when one is faced with threatened or actual aggression from clients towards themselves or others. When clients fall within the remit of secure services, staff may be constantly reminded of their capacity for destructiveness through acting-out behaviours or discussions of offending and this evokes strong feelings in staff such as anger, fear and revulsion. Clinicians are also faced with the challenge of balancing the client's needs for intimacy against the demands of some clients to be special and have a relationship that resembles a personal friendship (Bateman and Fonagy, 2004). In both these conditions, clinicians may withdraw from intimacy and become distant, cold and uncaring in order to protect themselves from emotional distress, actual harm or breaching professional boundaries. In such circumstances, it is not uncommon to hear staff members say, 'I don't have to like them to do my job'. Alternatively, staff may manage their fear and anxiety by becoming over-involved with the client. This may take the form of disclosing excessive personal information (which is justified as an attempt to collaborate with the client) or becoming angry and hateful towards the client. Staff who are routinely reliant upon anger and hatred to cope with proximity to the client typically scoff at the notion of becoming emotionally involved with the client without recognising the huge emotional involvement they have, albeit a negative one.

The task for clinicians is to find a way to maintain their own motivation to engage in an emotionally intimate relationship with clients and demonstrate that such relationships can be safe. This entails managing the strong emotions experienced by both clinician and client and finding ways to overcome the dysfunctional interpersonal strategies that the client utilises to feel safe, in order to close the space between ourselves and our clients. The strategies described below are suggested as a means of achieving this task and guiding clinicians towards developing and sustaining emotional intimacy between them and their clients. The strategies are inter-related and each should be utilised throughout the duration of the relationship.

Strategy 1: Maintain optimum affect

Arguably the most therapeutically beneficial aspect of an intimate relationship between a client and clinician is the opportunity for relational emotion to be generated. Emotion literature concludes that the adaptive experience of emotion is necessary to attain psychological functioning and wellbeing (Barrett and Campos, 1987; Ekman, 1984; Lazarus, 1991; Safran and Greenberg, 1991; Schore, 2003a, 2003b; Tangney and Fischer, 1995; Tomkins, 1962, 1963). It organises, motivates and guides our behaviour since each emotion is associated with an action tendency or 'readiness to act' (Goleman, 1995) that can be more powerful than logic in influencing our decision making and courses of action (Foa and Kozak, 1991; Greenberg and Safran, 1987; Safran and Segal, 1996). It plays a primary role in self-regulation as well as regulating the experience of others by impacting on caregivers and our ability to communicate (Safran and Segal, 1996; Schore, 2003a, 2003b); and it makes us feel real and alive by enhancing our internal liveliness and spontaneity (Ferenczi, 1931; Fosha, 2000; Winnicott, 1960). Those who experience difficulties in processing their emotions therefore present as psychologically impaired.

Since all psychological difficulties include an emotional component, it is difficult not to conclude that for therapy to be effective, emotion must play a significant role. This view is endorsed by Guidano who states that

> No change seems possible without emotions . . . while thinking usually changes thoughts, only feeling can change emotions; that is, only the emergence of new emotional experiences, by adding new tonalities of feelings to the unitary configuration of core emotional themes, can effect their self-regulation facilitating a re-ordering in personal meaning processes.
>
> (1991, pp. 60–61)

Those authors who argue for an intimate relationship with the client are implicitly advancing a case for the role of emotion in therapeutic relationships since they emphasise that cognitive understanding alone is inadequate to effect profound change, particularly when the difficulties are manifest within the interpersonal sphere. Safran and Greenberg assert that 'emotionality is involved in every aspect of mental processing' (1991, p. 59). Much of the knowledge we require to be able to relate to others is likely to be procedural and must therefore be experienced since 'knowing how to be with someone' (Stern et al., 1998) is dependent upon 'implicit relational knowing' that includes emotional, interactive and cognitive information (Lyons-Ruth, 1998). Wachtel (2008) argues therefore that therapy aimed solely at increasing insight is unlikely to be effective for all the same reasons that books containing explicit instructions are unlikely to have great success in assisting people to overcome psychological complaints such as social anxiety. Instead, he argues, like others, that the needs of clients are such that a real, authentic relationship with the client, in which emotion plays a prominent role, is essential if therapy is to be effective (Alexander, 1961; Fosha, 2000; Lander and Nahon, 2005; Lyons-Ruth, 1999; Safran and Greenberg, 1991; Stern et al., 1998; Yalom, 2001).

In addition to emotionally involved relationships allowing the client to develop procedural knowledge about intimate relating, learning to tolerate the emotions that arise in relation to others enables the client to understand their feelings rather than be overwhelmed by them (Kennedy-Moore and Watson, 1999) and to acquire the tacit rules that guide the processing of emotional information (Safran and Segal, 1996). Emotion allows us to understand the motives and intentions of others (Costello, 2000), brings renewed energy, and when tolerated leads to a sense of mastery and empowerment (Fosha, 2000). Witnessing the therapist's management of emotions in relation to the patient can convey that emotions do not have to be destructive, overwhelming or incapacitating. In addition, exposure to emotions that have previously been intolerable allows one access to improved patterns of relating and new action tendencies (Kennedy-Moore and Watson, 1999). For instance, being able to tolerate sadness allows one's need for comfort to become visible, whilst being able to tolerate anger enables one to behave assertively.

Greenberg is particularly eloquent when summarising the need for emotion in therapy. He writes,

> to change in therapy, clients cannot just talk intellectually about themselves and their feelings; they need to viscerally experience what they talk about and use their feelings to identify and solve problems. The difference between talking about something and experiencing it in therapy is similar to the difference between talking about what it is like being knocked over by a wave on the beach and actually experiencing being knocked over by one. In therapy, people who change often need to experience being knocked over by emotional waves before they find their feet.
>
> (2002, p. 8)

One could argue that this is particularly true when considering the therapeutic needs of people with personality disorder since they experience profound difficulties in both the ability to process emotions and also the ability to achieve connectedness with others and this has far-reaching consequences that impact across their lives. Their difficulties range from over-controlled, restricted affect; through dependence upon one dominant affect such as anger or sadness; to impulsive, overwhelming, rapidly fluctuating affect. Consequently, many have advanced the case for a real, authentic relationship characterised by emotional involvement within formal psychological therapies. Insight-based therapy and cognitive therapy work well with people who are capable of experiencing a normal range of affective states but are likely to be limited in their efficacy with people with personality disorder who lack the ability to identify and experience emotions. Inexperienced staff may resort to crude reductionism when learning new skills and techniques and this can lead to emotion being neglected and bad habits being formed. So additional measures are needed to ensure adequate emotion is present within therapy sessions. We argue that the need to focus upon maintaining emotion extends to interactions beyond therapeutic sessions and is an essential task for all staff engaging with the personality disordered individual.

A real authentic relationship elicits emotion as a consequence of relating. The interpersonal style adopted by the individual with personality disorder represents their best effort to maintain their anxiety about relating to a level that they are sure they are able to cope with. The task of the clinician is to enable the client to tolerate increased closeness and anxiety thereby facilitating the client's access to a new emotional experience that will permit him or her to realise that intimacy does not have to be frightening and can in fact be fulfilling.

Maintaining affect at an optimum level does not come naturally to many who care for people with personality disorder since it not only involves working against the client's resistance to forming a more emotionally intimate relationship but also requires the staff member to address their own reluctance to connect with people who may elicit strong negative emotions. In order to ensure that emotion is not avoided, and that optimum affect is maintained wherever possible, staff members must identify interpersonal strategies used by both the client and themselves that restrict opportunities for emotion and intimacy.

Identify behavioural obstacles to affect

A number of common behavioural strategies are used to restrict opportunities for affect to arise between staff and clinicians. The obstacles posed are greatest within individual therapy sessions where interpersonal closeness is most threatening due to the expectation that proximity will last for an hour and uncomfortable subjects may be discussed. However, variations of these strategies occur across all interactions with staff.

Strategies that disrupt the consistency of contact

Both the client and staff may disrupt the consistency and predictability of interactions to weaken the relationship between them. Within therapy, the client variant of this strategy includes turning up late, double-booking appointments, not turning up at all, leaving early, or pushing for more time and being granted it. Therapists have their own version; in addition to forgetting appointments or turning up late or finishing early, they may move appointments at will or poorly schedule other commitments, such as taking a week off for study leave two weeks after returning from annual leave.

Beyond the therapeutic sessions, clients may avoid contact by sleeping, being overly busy or only being prepared to engage with staff when accompanied by others. Staff may procrastinate about meeting, or be busy or engaged in administrative tasks out of sight of clients.

Strategies that neutralise the content of conversation

Within therapy, both the client and the therapist may neutralise session content by allowing the session content to become overly predictable. The client may do this by rehearsing what they will discuss in advance or perhaps bringing a diary to control the topics that are discussed. Therapists may over-plan for sessions, making sessions totally predictable. Both individuals may focus on cognitive content at the expense of emotion, giving the impression that therapy is teaching, problem-solving or an intellectual debate. In addition, displacement activities may be introduced: coffee may be allowed to 'relax' the client, or wipe-boards and paperwork may be utilised to present a context broader than the interaction between client and therapist.

Both within and beyond therapeutic sessions, uncomfortable topics such as sexuality, abuse, intimidation and the interpersonal relationship may be avoided by both staff and client, as might be the use of emotive language. Conversational distractions such as tangential or theoretical discussions, persistent complaining, telling 'tall' stories, 'filling the silence', flirting and being humorous may also be allowed to prevent discussions from becoming more emotionally meaningful.

Strategies that stifle non-verbal communication

Both staff and client may remove opportunities for connecting over affect by inhibiting their non-verbal communication. Over-controlled speech or posture and a lack of eye contact may prevent both staff and client from ascertaining the emotional response of the other. A mismatch of non-verbal and verbal communication may be ignored; thus the client who laughs when relaying something tragic may be met by a smile rather than a more appropriate reference to the mismatch.

Identify strategies that restrict the range of emotion

The concept of 'security operations' was used by Sullivan (1953) to describe not only the behavioural strategies that individuals utilise to reduce their anxiety in interactions with others but also other interpersonal strategies. People with personality disorder often have restricted strategies for interacting with others and are over-reliant upon defence mechanisms and the use of interpersonal styles that fall at the extreme end of a continuum and which prevent others from getting close to them. For instance, an individual may be tied to dominance or submissiveness rather than being able to draw upon a mixture of each pole as necessary. The inability of individuals to modify and adjust their behaviour within a moderate range is characteristic of people with personality disorder, whereas a healthy individual may be relatively submissive within a meeting with her line manager but be able to draw upon assertiveness when complaining about a poorly cooked meal in a restaurant. People rely on restricted interactional strategies because during childhood these enabled them to achieve respite from terror, shame, humiliation and sadness. However, as Fosha (2000) observes, 'the price tag is exorbitant'. Chronic reliance upon these strategies enables painful affect to be avoided but the adaptive function and action tendencies of these emotions become lost to the individual, thus impairing their capacity to relate spontaneously and closely to others. A key requirement for clinicians attempting to develop emotional intimacy with clients is to notice what interpersonal strategies are being used by the client to 'pull' the clinician into responding in a certain way, thus maintaining a particular affect that the client is accustomed to and ultimately preserving interpersonal distance from the clinician (Kiesler, 1988; Safran and Segal, 1996).

A number of authors (e.g. Safran and Segal, 1996; Wachtel, 2008) observe that interpersonal problems are manifest in such a way that it is inevitable that those with whom the client interacts have an emotional response that activates 'complementary' behavioural responses (Kiesler, 1988). The principle of complementarity was defined by Kiesler as behaviour that pulls a restricted set of behavioural responses or action tendencies (Safran and Segal, 1996) from those with whom the individual interacts. The restricted range of responses will represent those interpersonal behaviours that the client finds least threatening. Thus, a woman with a childhood history of abandonment by her father and her mother's subsequent boyfriends may be hostile and sullen in her interactions with male staff in order to prevent them getting close enough to hurt her when they tire of working with her – something she believes is inevitable. The male staff may manage the hostility by avoiding this client. Thus, the woman's experience that men cannot be trusted to stick around is reinforced. Although the woman may desire a stable relationship with a man, her anxiety about being rejected is such that she chooses not to acknowledge this aspiration.

Not only is it inevitable that staff working with such clients get drawn into engaging in a complementary manner, but it is desirable to get 'caught in the emotional force field sufficiently that, for a period of time, [he or she] becomes a participant in the problematic pattern, an accomplice' (Wachtel, 2008, p. 228). Participating in such an interaction with the client enables the staff member to truly understand the client's interpersonal problems and be able to identify how the maladaptive interpersonal style is maintained. In order to do this, staff must be capable of observing their own emotional states and action tendencies whilst engaging with the client, and also of finding a means of disrupting this interactional sequence and instigating dialogue about it. The client who responds to a therapeutic rupture by voicing angry thoughts such as 'this service is so fucking useless and cannot manage to help the muppets it is supposed to be caring for' can generate extreme anger in staff. However, if staff can empathise with the vulnerable part of the client who believes he is beyond help, they may find a healthy response.

Being able to work authentically with these clients requires huge emotional resources within staff members. Staff may be exposed to strong negative emotions such as fear, shame and hatred, particularly when their clients engage in highly destructive behaviours. Poor clinical care arises when staff lack awareness of their emotional states, their motivations and their own security operations, or, as identified by Henry *et al.* (1990), when they have a hostile self-image. Such staff are likely to respond without recognising the complementary nature of their response and thus fail to use the interaction to gain further insight into the client's difficulties. Being aware of one's feelings in relation to the client requires that the staff member is willing to engage authentically with the client and to accept and tolerate a range of emotions that may at times be deeply unpleasant or even frightening and which may threaten their own self-concept. For instance, staff who perceive it is 'bad' to be sexually attracted to clients may have difficulty recognising sexual feelings towards the client. Consequently, such staff will be unable to disrupt the interpersonal transaction and address the security operations being utilised by the client. Failure to do so leaves staff at risk of engaging in sexualised interactions with the client. At best this may be manifest in a flirtatious relationship that lacks therapeutic value. At worst a full blown sexual relationship may ensue. Services that fear sexuality often contribute to such circumstances by failing to permit discussion of sexual feelings and this can exacerbate the risk of clients becoming embroiled in serial sexual relationships with professional carers.

Similarly those who have difficulty tolerating feelings like fear, shame or hatred may not be able to acknowledge these in themselves and will find it hard to disrupt the interpersonal transaction or engage the client in a meaningful dialogue about his or her problem. For instance, staff who find it difficult to tolerate feelings of shame may resort to defensive anger to protect themselves when encountering clients with a narcissistic aspect to their presentation who utilise highly personal belittling statements or criticism of past behaviours: for example, 'I can see how you may be perceived by your colleagues as incompetent' or 'You must be such a disappointment to people. You can't control your own weight and if you can't manage your own obesity, how can you help me with my eating habits?' When staff are unable to disrupt such interpersonal transactions, they are likely to respond punitively, thus confirming the narcissist's underlying perception that he is worthless. In addition, relying upon a strategy that utilises defensive, secondary affect prevents the staff member from processing and resolving the true primary emotions the client has elicited in him or her (e.g. shame or hurt) and so he or she remains stuck with negative feelings towards the client. Since this is antithetical to how staff are supposed to feel towards their clients, negativity towards the client may be exacerbated as well as negativity towards the self.

Those who find it difficult to tolerate or recognise fear may keep the relationship 'cosy' in order to avoid eliciting the client's anger. When working with those who commit serious offences, it is inevitable that staff will upon occasion feel frightened of their clients if they have truly engaged with all aspects of the client. For example, a man who has raped a number of women is unlikely to have effectively addressed his offending behaviour if he has not been able to access the destructive part of him within relationships with female staff or been experienced as frightening by them. Instead, it is likely that the client and staff have subconsciously entered a bargain that involves both parties relying upon the use of security operations to ensure adequate distance is maintained to prevent the client from feeling threatened by the staff member and the staff member from feeling frightened of the client.

Fosha (2000) observes how intense positive affects can àlso contribute to distance in therapeutic relationships as people may feel embarrassed, self-conscious and vulnerable. Reparation of ruptures is an essential task of therapy and both staff and clients need to have, or develop, the capacity to experience positive emotions in relation to one another. Difficulties in tolerating warmth and non-sexualised affection inhibit the therapeutic potential of relationships between staff and patients, and staff comfort with closeness has been established as important in developing a therapeutic alliance (Dunkle and Friedlander, 1996)

Identify secondary and instrumental affect

Some clients may appear to be emotional in interactions but the affect present is secondary (defensive affect) or instrumental (pseudo-affect) rather than primary affect. Primary affect is distinguished by its prompt arrival and short-lived duration. It includes visceral experience and imagery, provides a sense of energy that suggests action and is accompanied by textured specific cognitions rather than global, stereotyped ones (Fosha, 2000; Greenberg, 2002). Regardless of how painful primary emotions may be, expressing them leads to relief.

Personality disordered clients often use secondary emotions to protect themselves from feeling vulnerable. It is not uncommon for clients falling within the remit of forensic services to be over-reliant upon anger (secondary affect) as a means of protecting themselves from affective states such as fear and shame which they associate with feeling vulnerable. Similarly, staff may cope with vulnerable affects such as shame following the belittling interactions of a narcissistic patient or fear during the verbally abusive outburst of an antisocial patient by utilising anger with the patient as a defence.

Other clients may present with inauthentic emotions that they perceive as more socially desirable or that are designed to have an impact upon others (instrumental affect). For example, some clients get stuck with overt secondary shame (rather than primary shame) about sexual abuse, rather than experiencing anger, as they perceive anger as likely to incur the disapproval or rejection of others. Interactions with such others may revolve around the client presenting in such a way that the staff member becomes aware of perceiving that the client is comfortable portraying herself as a victim.

Failure to notice that one is being presented with instrumental or secondary affect may occur if there is a benefit to the staff member, such as avoidance of a primary affective state that the clinician finds difficult to bear, or when confronting the use of instrumental affect would challenge the clinician's own narcissism. Clients who rely on instrumental affect often leave staff experiencing positive feelings about 'how well therapy is going' when the patient's previous repertoire of challenging behaviours might lead one to anticipate greater difficulties.

It is common to meet clients who have a narrative to describe their abuse or offending that is not matched by congruent affect. These clients often appear to have great intellectual understanding of how their experiences have affected their current presentation and are commonly experienced as high in psychological-mindedness. Previous therapeutic encounters, where searching for primary affect was neglected, may have reinforced the use of instrumental affect. Reports of such encounters will often document the client's good insight and compliance with therapy, when one might anticipate more ruptures and crises if primary affect was being presented and there was an authentic relationship between the clinician and the client.

When secondary or instrumental affect is being utilised, rather than relief being achieved via expression of affect, the client presents as frustrated, 'stuck' with chronic, possibly even deteriorating bad feeling, and no clear action is suggested (Fosha, 2000; Greenberg, 2002). Fosha describes how pseudo-affect can be recognised by the experienced staff member: 'when emotionality is not authentic, the attuned therapist cringes. Just as out-of-tune singing is grating to a musical ear, so inauthentic affect makes the attuned therapist viscerally ill at ease; yet genuine affect draws one in' (Fosha, 2000, p. 159).

The task in working with clients is to help them become aware of their defensive use of anger or shame or whatever other emotional state they are stuck with and enable them to recognise the underlying, primary affect through discussions that normalise a broader range of emotional responses and interactional styles. Being able to discern true primary affect from secondary or instrumental affect requires that staff members have a good awareness of their own emotional responses and reactions, and have a heightened capacity to tolerate the full range of emotions including fear, shame and hatred. In addition, it is necessary that staff have the confidence to explore with the client their perception of the client as inauthentic or stuck, where necessary, as discussed in Strategy 3.

Remove obstacles to liking the client

For staff to be able to offer something therapeutic to the client, they need to be capable of liking the client and allowing the client to matter to them (Yalom, 2001). Without this capacity, an emotionally intimate encounter is unlikely to occur as the staff member is unlikely to be receptive to accessing a true experience of the client and prepared to work with the consequences of the interaction (Mearns and Cooper, 2005). Frequently difficulties are experienced in liking clients due to strong negative emotional responses being evoked in interactions.

Staff strategies that rely upon intellectualisation can be helpful in making negative feelings towards clients more bearable and can facilitate suppression of the action tendency to pull away from the client. Intellectualising strategies include reminding oneself that negative affect directed towards the self is a consequence of empathic failure in previous caregivers, and Clarkin *et al.*'s (2006) suggestion of assuming there is a normal self-representation 'imprisoned within the patient's nightmarish world [since] this assumption permits the [staff member] to systematically confront the patient's imprisonment in this world' (p. 84). Finding ways to remain mindful of the client's vulnerability can also be useful, such as reading case material where the client's own traumatic history is discussed. Therapists have a key role in communicating the client's vulnerability to the broader team who may more frequently experience the client's aggression and consequently find it more difficult to perceive vulnerability in a person they may be frightened of.

Another way for individuals to maintain awareness of the client's vulnerability is to try to identify 'the inner child' of the client. Childhood trauma and abuse often leave an individual with the sense of being 'stuck' at a much younger age. The repertoire of challenging behaviours the individual presents with often symbolise the age that the person is stuck at. Thus, it is not uncommon to be presented with temper tantrums, sibling rivalry (in residential settings), lies in the presence of evidence to the contrary, and other egocentric behaviours. Typically, when individuals with personality disorder are asked how old they *feel*, they will indicate an age that will enable staff to make sense of the disruptive behaviour within the context of that individual.

Naïve staff rely solely on intellectual coping strategies to remain connected to clients as such coping strategies are unlikely to adequately prepare staff for maintaining long-term relationships with people who elicit profound emotions such as fear, envy, hate, shame and love within them. A failure to truly engage with the client's affect renders the relationship inauthentic and deprives clients of opportunities for therapeutic growth. Neglecting the affect is particularly detrimental in forensic settings where the client's strong affect may actually have led to the physical annihilation of a previous individual and where working with the affect offers important information for risk assessment. Instead, affect that poses a challenge to liking the client must form a central focus of interactions. This is discussed in more detail under Strategy 3.

Engage with primary affect in discussions

Whilst there is a place for providing clients with formal education about emotions, for example dialectical behaviour therapy (Linehan, 1993), such interventions rely upon bolstering up the use of intellectualising defences which are already over-relied upon by some clients and may be ineffectual in assisting the client in resolving strong primary affect. Instead, clinicians are required to focus upon primary affect and maximise opportunities for this to be experienced to as much intensity as the client can tolerate (Fosha, 2000).

People with personality disorder typically experience impairments in four categories of emotional regulation skills. Cognitive impairments include a lack of intellectual knowledge about emotions, lack of emotional language, lack of value of emotions and lack of ability to recognise and acknowledge emotions in others. Expressive impairments include difficulties in verbal communication about emotions and over-reliance upon behavioural and somatic communication. Physiological impairments include the inability to regulate arousal and hyper-sensitivity and hypo-sensitivity to emotions. Finally, experiential impairments include difficulties in recognising and acknowledging affect in self, difficulties discriminating between affective states, difficulty tolerating affect associated with vulnerability, limited capacity for self-soothing, and difficulty discerning between primary, secondary and instrumental affect.

Actively developing emotional regulation skills involves staff identifying, labelling and normalising emotions, and communicating the value of emotions via their own use of affect. Staff are required to be proactive in encouraging clients to engage with their primary affect and should comment on affect that is incongruent with their conversation or lacks adequate intensity. For instance, when working with the client who smiles and cracks a joke when discussing sad events, staff should not collude with the use of humour but normalise the primary affect by commenting upon what a sad experience that must have been. Clarkin *et al.* (2006) observe that when clients are able to experience affect, the clinician must match the client's emotional intensity as the client's absorption in affect may cause calm, quiet staff to be experienced as dismissive. In some cases, clients lack the ability to muster up any affect and will be experienced as boring and monotonous. This dynamic should be discussed but also the clinician may have to inject emotion by exploiting opportunities where affect ought to have arisen. The ability to focus upon primary affect will inevitably be easier if clinicians have taken steps to prevent distractions from primary affect via other strategies.

Strategy 2: Synthesise the logical worlds of the client and clinician

Collins's English dictionary defines logic as: 'The branch of philosophy concerned with analysing the patterns of reasoning by which a conclusion is properly drawn from a set of premises, without reference to meaning or context' (1992, p. 887). This suggests that basic logical processes require an individual to arrive at conclusions regarding events or situations by relying upon some given assumptions. These assumptions are derived from reasoning using the concept of probability. For example, if a child is exposed to nurturance from smiling faces the child will logically conclude that smiling faces indicate safety. However, if the only smiling face a child was exposed to was that of a sexual abuser, that child may logically conclude that smiling faces indicate threat and disgust. Some idiosyncratic logical understanding therefore evolves out of personal experience, suggesting that on occasions, some individuals (or groups of individuals) may be utilising different logical understandings of events and behaviour (schema) and hence predict different outcomes due to different life experiences. The clinician with a good enough upbringing may hold the logical belief, 'If I greet my new client with a smile, tell her I will provide her with care, advise her that anything we discuss will be confidential, she will feel safe.' However, the client subjected to child sexual abuse may recall the smiling man who abused her, who protested his sexual advances were a sign of caring and impressed upon her that it must be kept secret, and thus may logically conclude that she may be at risk of sexual abuse from this clinician.

Countless errors arise from the disparity between the logical worlds inhabited by the client and the staff group when assessing and treating people with personality disorder. Failure to identify these errors can create communication difficulties, cause irreparable ruptures or the development of pseudo-intimate relationships, contribute to poor decision making and risk assessments, and lead to the application of inappropriate interventions that are at best ineffective and may be iatrogenic. These errors contribute to the difficulties that people with personality disorder have experienced in accessing treatment. Some of the most significant of these errors are described below.

Logical error 1: Assumption that people with personality disorder have both the desire and ability to suppress symptoms of their disorder in order to receive 'care'

People with personality disorder are generally referred to mental health services at times of significant distress when their behaviour has become at best erratic and at worst dangerous. Behaviours with which they commonly present include alcohol and substance misuse, aggression and violence (including self-harm), non-compliance with imposed rules, over-dependence upon prescribed medication, and disengagement from treatment – behaviours highly indicative of a personality disorder diagnosis. Some agencies, however, refuse admission to people who display these behaviours, and others insist clients do not present such symptoms whilst in their care, and if they do so, they are discharged. A comparable scenario would be to set up a service for people with schizophrenia that excludes or discharges those who experience auditory hallucinations.

Logical error 2: Assumption that detention is a deterrent and liberty is motivational

For many with personality disorder, prison is viewed as a refuge and a place to belong. Many establish significant attachments to prison officers. Consequently, the notion of release can generate fear of loneliness and lack of support. Some even find sanctuary by orchestrating moves to segregation units, the prison's internal punishment system, in order to feel safer, as they fear fellow prisoners or being out of control. Thus, they defy society's logic, that imprisonment is a deterrent. Similar processes occur within mental health services; some people with personality disorder who have low self-worth are unable to accept care other than when it is imposed upon them by detention. Whilst many staff work to enable clients to achieve their freedom, some patients actively sabotage their efforts. Typically, patients with border-line personality disorder apply to be discharged from section in order to test whether their care team will fight for their detention, thus demonstrating that they care. Members of statutory bodies such as Mental Health Review Tribunals, the Healthcare Commission and the Mental Health Act Commission prioritise patients' freedom and choice but can fail to recognise that the logic which informs their decisions may be different from the logic guiding the requests that are being considered (see Chapter 6).

Logical error 3: Assumption that our speech and language reflect the same logic

Bateman and Fonagy (2004) advise therapists not to make simple assumptions regarding clients' statements. People with a diagnosis of personality disorder frequently apply a different understanding of common language from the clinicians charged with assessing them and making decisions about their treatment and care. For example, one man who killed his father described his father as 'somewhat strict' but said he had an otherwise 'normal upbringing'. When the client was asked for an example of 'strict', he showed the therapist his extremely scarred hands, burnt by his father holding them under a grill when, as a young child, he found him playing with matches. When asked for another example, he described being hospitalised due to his father throwing him downstairs in a fit of rage. He exonerated his father from responsibility by attributing this punishment to his own 'naughty' behaviour. Another client described her mother as 'very loving' and said she had told her constantly that she loved her. Further exploration led to uncovering that her mother had sexually abused her virtually every day since infancy until she was hospitalised aged 24. Every time that she sexually abused her daughter, she told her she loved her. Failure to explore the client's 'communication' will reduce the likelihood of that individual accessing the most appropriate treatment.

Logical error 4: Assumption that performing activities of daily living improves well-being

Whilst performing daily activities such as keeping one's self and one's living space clean and engaging in meaningful employment is associated with good mental health, services can become over-focused on these targets at the expense of facilitating real improvement in clients' well-being. This is due to failure to consider the logic behind these perceived self-care 'failures'. For example, it is logical to some people with a sexual abuse history to maintain either their body or living space in a poor state of hygiene in order to repel sexual predators. Equally, for some people who were sexually abused at night, it is logical to stay awake, keeping alert to intruders, and to sleep in the day in a common area where more people are present, thus creating a greater sense of safety.

Staff preoccupied with ensuring clients comply with rules about hygiene and activity can become increasingly angry towards those clients who do not conform. Clients may feel defective for their inability to meet staff's needs. Interventions reflecting an understanding of the client's logical world could validate clients' strategies for managing their fear, reassure them they can be kept safe and encourage them to experiment with alternative behaviours.

An inability to understand the client's 'logic' can also contribute to poor risk assessments. For example, in secure hospitals, the logic applied is that clients need to be able to keep safe within their bedrooms before being granted ground or community leave. However, a client routinely self-harms in her bedroom as it triggers reminders of being locked alone in her bedroom as a child with no access to a toilet, food, water or activities for days at a time. That client may never achieve access to the grounds or community despite having no history of self-harming in these areas or absconding. Without understanding this 'logic', the client's liberty could be unnecessarily restricted.

Logical error 5: Assumption that the kinds of relationships and ways of relating that make us feel safe and comfortable have this effect on our clients

The inability of those considered 'psychopathic' to feel and recognise fear (e.g. Ogloff and Wong, 1990) is routinely cited as a way to differentiate between 'them' and 'us' and has the ultimate effect of dehumanising these clients. This conclusion derives from research which demonstrated that people with psychopathy have deficits in fearful face recognition (e.g. Blair et al., 2001; Van Honk and Schutter, 2006). The assumption that researchers and clinicians rely upon when concluding this is that what is frightening to the non-personality disordered is frightening to the personality disordered and vice versa. Many people with personality disorder are accustomed to being faced with hostility, deceptiveness, rejection and aggression and have a script or range of strategies to employ to help them cope with such situations. When they are not met with such treatment, they become bewildered and anxious as they have no schema to make sense of these interactions and often assume the situation is unsafe. Our experience is that images associated with warmth and intimacy are often more frightening to those with personality disorder. Consequently, a smiling face may trigger fear responses in individuals who are unaccustomed to this.

People can only accept acts of kindness that are commensurate with their sense of self and value, and they become suspicious of acts of kindness that seem disproportionate to their personal beliefs. For some clients, the act of smiling can generate thoughts such as 'Why is he smiling at me? What does he want?' A failure to attend to the mismatch of logic can result in clinicians inadvertently using language and gestures that, when interpreted within the client's logical framework, are provocative and distressing. For example, a female client with paranoid personality disorder and a history of sexual abuse by her father and brother developed a reasonably positive relationship with her male named nurse who attended to her needs and supported her during episodes of crisis. However, his supervisor observed that, despite the nurse's efforts, the relationship remained fairly superficial, and suggested the client was fearful of being sexually abused by the nurse. In supervision, the male nurse denied this possibility and insisted that his patient felt safe with him. He stated, 'I am like a brother to her!' and then realised the implications of his statement. The nurse discussed this dynamic with his client who expressed relief as she believed he was indeed grooming her for sexual favours. The client believed she was worthless and, as such, any positive attention must be driven by an ulterior motive.

Another assumption often made by staff is that women are 'safe'. The societal stereotype of women as nurturers, protectors and carers, there to meet the needs of others, often at personal expense, is rarely the direct experience of these clients. Female staff often make the assumption that they are perceived in line with the stereotype and avoid the fact that many of these clients have been emotionally, physically and sexually abused by women – women who have primarily been in roles of carer, within and outside of the family. Sexual abuse by women, and hence the perception that female staff may be perceived as sexual predators, is the most difficult for staff to accept, despite repeated evidence that this is a significant issue in the lives of these clients (e.g. Saradjian, 1996).

Similarly, the involvement of families in the care of patients is often prioritised because of our own assumptions that parents are loving and supportive and our assumption that the polite, well-mannered, socially skilled individuals who come to visit our clients could never be abusive, particularly not mothers. The degree of family involvement should be dictated by the formulation and staff should acknowledge not only that abusers are not always instantly apparent but also that some individuals have experienced trauma within relationships with parental figures that may be perpetuated if the adult child is not supported in maintaining their own well-being within the context of this relationship.

Logical error 6: Assumption that absolute confidentiality is desirable

Client confidentiality is an important aspect of professional health care and individuals have the right to experience care without being fearful that their disclosures may be discussed beyond those involved in their care or that their confidence may be treated disrespectfully. However, the care of clients receiving team-based services is hampered when clinicians believe in absolute confidentiality (i.e. the clinician does not share information with other team members). Usually the exception to this occurs when the clinician is told something that suggests the client or another is at direct risk of harm. However, issues of risk are rarely so clear-cut. A novice therapist advised by her supervisor to adhere to absolute confidentiality failed to share with a team in a medium secure unit that her male client had been sexually abused by his mother, as his mother had little contact with him. Unfortunately, whilst the therapist was on holiday, his mother visited and an unknowing nurse asked him to give his mother a hug. The client then severely assaulted the nurse.

For many clients with personality disorder, sexual abuse has played a significant role in the aetiology of their condition. This abuse is often carried out within the family unit or by a perpetrator familiar to the victim. In order to evade exposure, the perpetrator constructs the abuse within the confines of a secretive relationship and the child thus learns that secrets are shameful (Fisher, 1990). As such, many clients become fearful when they enter into a strictly confidential relationship with a clinician, as their logical understanding of confidentiality is that it entails painful, shameful secrets. When staff maintain absolute confidentiality they also collude with the client's distorted belief that being a victim of sexual abuse is something to be ashamed of.

Logical error 7: Assumption that therapy should be comfortable

NICE guidelines (2009b) for borderline personality disorder suggest the client should be comfortable with their therapist and have a choice of therapy. Indeed, in the UK, it is not uncommon for female clients with histories of abuse by males to be offered a female therapist to allow them to feel safe and be comfortable with their therapist. However, this approach offers limited opportunity for growth as the female therapist may not facilitate an experience for the client in which she can challenge her distorted beliefs regarding men. The female patient is unlikely to be exposed to the high levels of fear, anxiety and associated cognitions relating to males whilst in session with a female therapist. This approach is similar to keeping an agoraphobic client away from any open spaces for the duration of his treatment, thus colluding with the distorted belief that open spaces are dangerous. The treatment goal for such clients should in fact be to experience an intimate therapeutic relationship with a man, within which distorted beliefs can be disconfirmed, problematic affect can be tolerated and resolved, and the use of safety behaviours can be challenged. Providing a therapeutic relationship that is designed to ensure the client feels comfortable with their therapist may thus be colluding with maladaptive safety behaviours. Similarly, some settings provide abused women with services staffed only by women. Whilst these may be helpful in the short term by allowing women to feel safe and comfortable, such services will do little to address core treatment needs, as implicitly they communicate that men are dangerous. A comparable situation arises within the field of forensic health care where it is essential that clients work with therapists who in some manner represent their abusers and victims.

Logical error 8: Assumption that the exhibition of therapy-interfering behaviour means the client does not want treatment

One of the difficulties teams experience when working with people with personality disorder is overcoming behaviours exhibited that restrict the efficacy of treatment attempts. Indeed, it is such behaviours that often led to teams utilising the 'not-treatable' clause in the 1983 Mental Health Act. Typically, therapy-interfering behaviours are interpreted from the clinical team's logical perspective and assumptions are made regarding prognosis. Examples of misinterpretations include the following.

The client is too hostile to work in individual therapy

It is often the case that the client will present with hostile behaviours that can generate anger and fear in the therapist. However, this hostility is frequently a defence against fear of clinicians rather than a conscious attempt to generate conflict. In the client's logical world, this hostility allows them to feel safe in the presence of perceived danger. If the client had the capacity to express his fear through excessive crying and panic, would the team suggest that the client was too tearful to work in individual therapy? Rather than being too hostile for clinicians to work with safely, the client is too frightened. Interventions that are primarily focused on reducing the client's fear will paradoxically provide more safety to staff than those primarily focused upon keeping staff safe.

*The client does not turn up for sessions because they are not
committed to therapy*

Many clients have such high levels of self-disgust and shame that they believe
if they enter into an intimate therapeutic relationship they will contaminate
the therapist. Often they cannot tolerate feeling shame and feeling worthless
and believe they are wasting staff time. They may also not turn up for sessions
as they believe that the therapist's positive approach is merely a grooming
behaviour. Those who have experienced very neglectful and abusive childhoods may experience an attentive therapist as 'dangerous', thus not being
able to attend sessions as opposed to not wanting to attend sessions. Rather
than discharge the client, successful services find ways to communicate that
the client is safe and of value; for example, within inpatient settings, by
remaining in the therapy room for the duration of the session regardless of
whether the client is present in the room or not.

Therapy is not working if the client's behaviour gets worse

Many staff working with people with personality disorder have been trained
within the context of the disease model and, as such, recognise the maladaptive behaviours presented by people with personality disorder as their
symptoms. These staff often believe that, like an illness, a reduction in symptoms indicates improvement in the underlying condition, and an increase in
symptoms may indicate the condition is worsening. Treatment for personality
disorder can be viewed as akin to treatment for conditions that require surgery. Recovering from surgery is painful and may leave the patient feeling
worse than prior to surgery but surgery is a necessary stage if the patient is
to make a recovery. Likewise, when addressing the fundamental issues of the
client at a cognitive and emotional level, one would anticipate that a period
of crisis may precede a period of positive change.

Logical error 9: Assumption that ruptures are always counter-therapeutic

One should not underestimate the importance of therapeutic ruptures within
the treatment process particularly when working with forensic clients. Indeed,
staff teams should monitor for the absence of ruptures as an indicator that
therapy may be ineffective. The absence of ruptures in therapy may suggest
that both clinician and client are employing safety behaviours to avoid dealing with the difficult dynamics associated with the treatment of personality
disorder. It is important for clinical teams to acknowledge that when providing change-oriented treatment to people with personality disorder, anxiety
levels will at some point increase (particularly when the clinical team resist
colluding with psychopathology associated with behaviours designed to

confirm maladaptive schemata). It is important to recognise that clients admitted with personality disorder who do not present with management difficulties throughout their treatment are likely not to be engaged at a meaningful level despite presenting with pro-social behaviours. What is more likely, is that they have an adaptive interpersonal style to assist them in coping in institutions or supportive relationships which is absent when faced with the anxiety of independence. For example, the prisoner with a history of committing violent offences in the community may present as compliant and hardworking when imprisoned and may obtain a trusted employment position such as cleaner. This man may experience prison as emotionally containing and obsessive cleaning may be employed as a safety behaviour that distracts him from emotions that might otherwise be diverted into anger. Unless exposed to the affect that is associated with vulnerability by reducing his opportunity to be continually working and 'people-pleasing', this man may complete his sentence without addressing the fundamental dynamics of his offending. Preventing him from being preoccupied with hard work will be more challenging for staff as it may well cause ruptures. It will be in these ruptures that effective treatment and risk reduction work will be undertaken. Staff should not consider ruptures as merely a failing of therapy but as a process of therapy when working with complex psychopathology. Like therapy-interfering behaviours, ruptures should be anticipated and predicted via a complex case formulation. Ruptures are distinct from therapy-interfering behaviours in that they occur later in therapy when the client has engaged with staff and has established a reasonable working relationship.

Synthesising the conflicting logical worlds

Working towards synthesising logics can cause immense anxiety in staff as they are required to challenge their own representation of the world (Safran and Segal, 1996). Some staff find this task more difficult than others. Particular difficulties are posed when staff are fearful of exposing or tolerating their own vulnerability, fearful of ridicule, fearful of creating ruptures, unable to identify the vulnerability of the client, and unable to consider that they or their colleagues may be perceived as, or indeed are, potential abusers. Whilst staff reactions may be to instantly dismiss the notion that they or their colleagues could be abusers, the authors would draw the reader's attention to the number of staff who engage in sexual relationships with personality disordered clients. A failure on the part of clinicians to tolerate this idea allows for environments to be created where minor boundary breaches and unhealthy staff motivations pass unnoticed or unaddressed, thus leading to a culture where more serious boundary transgressions are able to flourish.

Safran and Segal (1996) suggest that to be empathic with clients, staff require the capacity to become immersed within the client's world. A number of steps can be taken to improve one's capacity to understand the logical world of one's clients.

Be prepared to accept and acknowledge that your logical world represents only your reality

Safran and Segal (1996) suggest that,

> the only way for therapists to truly accept patients as the final arbiters of their own reality is to be genuinely open to the possibility that the patient knows something about reality that the therapist does not. If therapists believe this, then there is as much possibility that their own models of the world will be changed as a result of a patient's therapy as there is that a patient's will be. Instead of socializing the patient's view of reality, this stance allows therapists to become available to patients in such a way that helps each patient discover his or her own reality creatively and constructively.
>
> (p. 9)

Many clients have experienced childhoods where alcohol, violence and sex were role-modelled as strategies for managing affect and where they have been required to adopt interpersonal and behavioural strategies that have allowed them to survive extremely traumatic experiences. Within the client's worldview, these behaviours are adaptive as they have managed to prevent their untimely death or prevented them from feeling the emotional pain of abuse. Thus, in order to develop a meaningful relationship with the client it will be important to initially validate the function of the behaviour within the client's world (albeit without condoning it) before exploring with the client how ineffective it is when applied in a less dysfunctional relationship. Examples include: using violence to problem-solve makes sense as a short-term strategy if you have learned that beating your wife makes her too scared to leave you; not bathing for weeks at a time makes sense if you want to stop people from getting so close to you that they abuse you; 'cutting up' makes sense when you hate yourself and you feel better when you believe you are punishing yourself.

Examine security operations for clues to the client's logical world

Generally the behaviour displayed within adult relationships reflects themes that were present earlier in the client's life, as such behaviour enables the person to maintain their sense of who they are. Safran and Segal (1996) suggest that current interpersonal behaviour can be used as 'windows' into the client's logical world. For example, aggressive behaviour may indicate that the client was frequently frightened during childhood; flirtatious behaviour may indicate a background where one was valued for sex; clingy, dependent behaviour or avoidant, dismissive behaviour may reflect a childhood characterised by frequent changes in carer; and entitled behaviour may suggest the client was emotionally and physically deprived during childhood or exposed to inconsistent limit setting. Hypothesising about the origins and function of current problematic behaviour may allow staff to begin a communication with the client about their history and the meaning of their behaviour for them. This process also enables staff to identify suitable interventions to employ which can be discarded if proved unfounded. For example, the client who states, 'Treatment is a waste of fucking time. You idiots will not be able to help me', may be more successfully engaged by staff who acknowledge the client's fear and hopelessness (for example, by responding, 'I do not think you are a waste of time nor do I think you are beyond help, you sound very frightened'), than by those who become defensive or punitive.

Seek clarification of your understanding of their relationships with significant others

Errors often occur because staff fail to ask clients to clarify or qualify their accounts of relationships with significant others. Clarkin *et al.* (2006) discuss the need to see if the client acts in a manner that is at odds with our expectations of what they have described. Employing a method such as that advocated by Crittenden (1998), whereby individuals are asked to provide episodes to substantiate the adjectives they assign to their carers, can be useful in exposing cognitive distortions that are utilised to minimise the danger within the relationship, as in the earlier application of the word 'strict'. In our experience, individuals frequently minimise the behaviour of carers or exonerate them by attributing the cause of adult behaviour to their childhood self. Similarly, utilising a similar strategy to explore romantic relationships with adults falling within the remit of forensic services may expose a greater level of antisocial behaviour within these.

Incorporate logic into practice

Effective staff find ways to incorporate the client's logic into practice. Thus, the therapist who ensures pre-prepared letters are sent out to her client during holidays reminding her of their next appointment allays her client's fears that her therapist has abandoned her, and the named nurse who arranges the next time he will meet with his patient at the end of each discussion communicates that he wants to spend time with him. NICE (2009b) emphasise the need to complete tasks that you commit yourself to. A failure to honour commitments for whatever reason (even when the client does not *appear* so bothered) shows a lack of ability to fully understand the world of perpetual disappointment that the client operates within.

Finding ways to integrate the logical understanding of the client and the clinician is an essential tool in working with the personality disordered patient. Fonagy *et al.* (1995) observe that 'the biological need to feel understood ... takes precedence over almost all other goals' (pp. 268–269). Achieving this task is easier when one makes use of explicit communication as a means of ensuring synchronicity between client and clinician.

Strategy 3: Utilise explicit communication

To maintain optimum affect and synthesise the logical worlds of the clinician and the client, the use of explicit communication is essential. Explicit communication is a key strategy for ensuring that what is implicitly known to one party is made transparent and known to the other, and also that inhibitors of emotion can be identified and addressed.

Training programmes for mental health clinicians generally emphasise the development of listening skills in order to understand the client's experience, but remarkably little attention is focused upon how to communicate this understanding (Wachtel, 1993) or how to improve the potency of therapeutic interactions. This is unfortunate as Meares (2003) notes: 'language provides the possibility of intimacy' (p. 121). The emphasis upon the client's communication is also reflected within texts for talking therapies which, as Wachtel observes, focus generally upon the client's communication and mainly only attend to the therapist's communication in terms of timing and tact. Staff communications beyond formal psychological therapies are less frequently discussed. Where the content of communication is touched upon, it is generally restricted to self-disclosure, a concept that is closely related to explicit communication.

Self-disclosure has been a contentious concept within the field of psychotherapy (see Beutler *et al.*, 2003; Greenberg, 1995; Jackson, 1990). Within the USA, the Psychopathology Committee of the Group for the Advancement of Psychiatry concluded that although

> self-disclosure has traditionally been viewed as forbidden ... in many clinical situations, considerable benefit may stem from therapist self-disclosure. ... Although the dangers of boundary violation are genuine, we are concerned that self-disclosure is underutilised or misused because it lacks a framework. ... The literature acknowledges that complete non-self-disclosure is a myth; even the most conservative analysis reveals much about the therapist.
>
> (2001, pp. 1489–1490)

Shadley (2000) identifies several types of self-disclosure: (i) intimate interaction; (ii) reactive response; (iii) controlled response; and (iv) reflective feedback. Rowan and Jacobs (2002) suggest that most training courses advocate for *reflective feedback*, i.e. the clinician offers his or her impressions of client issues or asks questions that reveal a point of view but don't provide information or reveal emotional reactions to the client. However, *reactive response*, whereby verbal and non-verbal responses reveal emotional connectedness within the relationship (without revealing the personal experiences of the therapist's own life), may be a more useful clinical style (Hill, 1989). We argue that reactive response is a necessary requirement of work with people with personality disorder and that this kind of communication belongs in a broader category of essential communications with clients that can be labelled as 'explicit communication'.

Explicit communication has two components. First, it requires clinicians to utilise dialogue that is as straightforward and unambiguous as possible (Greenson, 1967), in order to increase understanding and reduce misunderstanding or a conflict of logic. Second, naming and making explicit the transactions and emotions that occur within the interaction between clinician and client (Greenberg, 2002; Safran and Segal, 1996) is required to increase the degree of affect present in the encounter and to prevent affect from being avoided or neutralised. This latter task inevitably involves some degree of self-disclosure since any interpersonal transaction has at least two participants.

The necessity of explicit communication in treating personality disorder

There are a number of reasons why explicit communication is necessary to ensure interactions between staff and clients have optimum therapeutic potency.

Understanding between client and clinician is enhanced

We have established that the consequence of the client and the clinician operating within different schemata or logical worlds can be poor assessments and inappropriate interventions. It is recognised that within many innocuous interactions there is often a divergence between what is said and what is meant (Carston, 2002), and also that overt, focal messages that individuals intend to convey include a meta-message that reveals an attitude about the focal message (Safran and Segal, 1996). Safran and Segal observe that it is often the meta-message that offers most scope for therapeutic growth.

Utilising explicit communication enables both parties to be clear about both the focal message and the meta-message and the logical world that each inhabits, thus allowing governing rules to be exposed and the logical worlds to be synthesised. As each party becomes more familiar with the other, the ability to hypothesise meaning and intent behind behaviour in future situations becomes increasingly possible. So the clinician learns that the client becomes aggressive when she is feeling frightened, and the client learns that when other people smile, they may be trying to put her at ease rather than grooming her for sex.

It assists clients in understanding their impact on others

People with personality disorder frequently lack an awareness of their impact upon others. In particular, those who feel powerless or frightened are often unaware that the defensive strategies they employ are producing the same feeling of powerlessness or fear in others. Explicit discussion about staff emotions in relation to the client with the client frequently acts as a trans-formational opportunity as such disclosures allow the client rare insight into how others experience him or her.

It reduces client's ability to rely upon security operations

By making explicit the nature of the interactions between the client and the clinician, the clinician minimises the client's capacity to utilise security operations which restrict the therapeutic relationship. For instance, explicit conversations with a man with dependent personality disorder about his passivity in interactions with others and the impact on the clinician of the client's submissive, childlike posture enabled the man to consider how his current interpersonal style may be preventing him from forming a desired relationship with a woman. Naming the specific behaviours he drew upon in direct interactions motivated the man to modify his interpersonal style sig-nificantly. Too frequently, clinicians rely upon attempting to communicate these messages in a subtle form (the reasons for this are explored below), thus contributing to clients' reliance upon 'game-playing' and failing to challenge the dysfunctional behaviour. Those who utilise explicit communication are frequently experienced as more transparent in their interactions since under-lying motivations are clearer and hence there is less need for clients to rely upon 'game-playing' strategies in their attempts to expose clinicians' 'perniciousness'.

It allows for greater authenticity between client and clinician

Disclosing felt-responses to the client allows the opportunity for a relation-ally deep encounter to be developed (Mearns and Cooper, 2005) in which the humanity of both client and clinician can be made transparent to the other. The clinician's willingness to engage in real discussions with the client and reveal something of himself in relation to the client communicates a desire to truly invest in the client, which can be a profound experience for clients with low self-regard. Lander and Nahon (2005) observe that, 'One has to give the other something or someone to relate to; otherwise it is like the sound of one hand clapping' (p. 32). Fisher suggests that by *consciously choosing* to share, 'we offer the gift of intimacy to our patients' (1990, p. 12). Wachtel suggests that within a therapeutic relationship, 'It is perfectly possible to reveal certain aspects of oneself where that is deemed clinically appropriate without opening every back room of one's psyche for the patient's inspection' (1993, p. 220). This willingness to speak appropriately of ourselves may be more powerful than the content of what we say (Clarkin *et al.*, 2006; Stricker, 2003) and offers more profound therapeutic opportunities than information that is unintentionally revealed (for instance, our accent, clothing, demeanour and use of silence all convey information about us).

It encourages sharing of emotions

People are often reluctant to engage in direct, face-to-face discussions of the relationship between themselves and others and this is mirrored within therapeutic relationships where clients and clinicians may be fearful that an exploration of their feelings in relation to each other may cause alienation (Safran and Segal, 1996). Discussing emotions that arise within the context of the relationship is beneficial to both clinician and client since the sharing of emotions facilitates closeness and also allows for unpleasant emotions to be processed. We are not advocating for permission for clinicians to say whatever they like under this guise, and emphasise the need for interventions to be guided by integrity and to be directly concerned with improving the relationship with the client (e.g. Lander and Nahon, 2005). Despite this, whilst the emphasis should rightly be placed upon the client's needs, discussion of one's feelings in relation to the client can be useful in maintaining positive regard for one's client.

People with personality disorder experience profound difficulties in recognising, discerning and tolerating emotions associated with vulnerability. Children who have been maltreated produce fewer utterances about negative affect than those who have not (Beeghley and Cichetti, 1994). Cichetti and Toth (1995) suggest that maltreated children manage anxiety caused by parental disapproval of negative affect by modifying their language and possibly their thinking in order to inhibit expressions of affect. This lack of ability to discuss emotions continues into adulthood. The clinician's willingness to disclose that he or she is experiencing vulnerable affect in relation to the client, for example sadness or fear, requires of the clinician a huge capacity to trust others. Investing such trust within the relationship not only allows clients to see that these emotions can be tolerated but also encourages them to have the courage to trust in the therapist (Yalom, 2001). It also role-models a way of discussing feelings for those clients whose abilities to do so are impoverished. Wachtel (2008) believes this is a particularly powerful experience for clients when they perceive that the clinician '*could have gotten away with*' not acknowledging an emotion but instead chooses to do so.

It improves accuracy of assessment

In addition to encouraging client disclosure of emotions, when used to elicit information explicit communication can facilitate access to historical information which is necessary for formulation and effective intervention. Explicit questions about areas that may be vulnerable to different representations and different logics – for example, the quality of relationships and abusive experiences – may be particularly useful in attempting to understand the schema within which the individual is operating. Frequently, staff fail to make routine enquiries about abuse (for example, Goater and Meehan (1998) found that only 17 per cent of clients were recorded as having been asked about a history of sexual abuse), contributing to limited formulations of their clients (see Chapter 3).

It encourages reflection

Lander and Nahon (2005) discuss the role that honesty plays in maintaining health and well-being and draw attention to one of the primary tasks of therapy which is to enable the client to be more honest with one's self since lying to one's self creates identity problems.

Many clients with personality disorder have experienced abuses in childhood which were characterised by secrecy. Maintaining such secrets prevents the individual from developing the capacity for intimacy, as the individual is not truly able to allow himself to be known to others (Frawley, 1990). Fisher (1990) also observes how children learn to keep feelings, ideas and behaviour secret in order to avoid being punished or rejected. He comments that this accumulation of secrets leads to impairments in the capacity for reflection and to the authenticity of the child becoming constricted; 'the greater the degree of "secrets", the greater the degree of alienation from the self. The greater the alienation of the self, the greater the alienation from others (therefore) the greater the loss of real intimacy in relationships' (Fisher, 1990, p. 4). Being open and honest about what one is experiencing in relation to the client allows clients to see that it is possible to be open without fearing reprisals and also provides them with role-modelling to assist them in achieving this whilst encouraging them to engage in a process of reflection.

Failure to use explicit communication reinforces psychopathology

A failure to discuss negative affect arising within contact between client and clinician can perpetuate the client's belief that his emotions are too dangerous to be tolerated (Clarkin *et al.*, 2006). For obvious questions to remain un-asked and obvious affects to pass without overt comment, the client and clinician must both engage in a pseudo-intimate relationship reliant upon game-playing, cryptic communication and a lack of authenticity

– behaviours that people with personality disorder are frequently criticised for adopting.

Why do clinicians avoid explicit communication?

Whilst advocating for the use of explicit communication, we recognise that such an approach can initially seem counter-intuitive and anxiety-provoking for a number of reasons.

Fear of saying too much

The anxiety of novice clinicians contributes to them seeking firm rules and guidance about their new role. The use of self-disclosure has historically been a contentious issue and perhaps it is therefore unsurprising that most therapeutic training courses advocate for not sharing personal information about one's feelings with the client (Rowan and Jacobs, 2002). Many of us have encountered staff who reveal far too much information about their own personal issues during their own crises, which can cause problems for clients, and this can frighten inexperienced or naïve clinicians into greatly restricting the information that is revealed.

Some staff become drawn into punitively disclosing feelings of boredom and anger in order to hurt the client or exact revenge and one may be fearful of behaving in such a way. Wachtel (2008) cautions on the need to ensure the disclosure is not 'acting out' or a self-indulgence that is justified as being in the interest of the client. That is not to say that feelings of boredom and anger cannot be discussed, but one should be clear about one's motivation for disclosing such feelings and be certain that disclosure is aimed at understanding and resolving relational difficulties rather than punishing the client.

Inability to tolerate our own vulnerability

Chapter 2 highlighted the difficult emotions that are elicited in staff working with personality disordered clients, in particular fear, hatred and shame. This may be amplified in working with clients who pose a risk to self or others. Our reluctance to tolerate these emotions may contribute to us not asking questions that we do not feel ready to hear the answers to, such as information about abuse or offending. Mearns and Cooper (2005) suggest that 'it is often the ability to work with such feelings that distinguishes more experienced therapists from less experienced ones' (p. 129).

The ability to tolerate one's own fear is particularly important (Campling, 2004) and is essential when working with those who offend. If one is unable to access the offender in the client, then it is unlikely that one has enabled the individual to address his or her dangerous behaviour and it is likely that both client and clinician are utilising security operations to ensure the client does not become angry. Even work with people who don't offend requires staff to be capable of openly acknowledging the strength and powers held by the client. Failure to do so may arise from staff's inability to tolerate feeling helpless and thus experience their own impotence, a dynamic all individuals deplore feeling (Bloom, 1997). This can result in discussions of the power dynamic being avoided.

Research by King-Casas *et al.* (2008) demonstrated through use of games analysis[1] that individuals with borderline personality disorder playing the role of trustee break co-operation with an investor more quickly and this makes the investor less likely to want to invest. Typically, if the investor continued to risk his investment, the person with borderline personality disorder could be coaxed into returning a greater proportion of the investment. We would argue that a similar transaction occurs within the therapeutic relationship. The therapist has to be willing to tolerate their own vulnerability that is exposed when they make efforts to win over a client who may be resistant to forming a relationship with them. Initial risk taking, in an attempt to communicate a desire to relate on behalf of the therapist, can pay dividends in terms of coaxing the client into a more meaningful interchange, where ultimately the client is able to take the risk of trusting the therapist.

Reluctance to be known by the client

Some staff seem reluctant to engage authentically with the client. Perhaps this is due to anxiety about the client exploiting this relationship or reluctance to experience strong emotions. However, Dunkle and Friedlander (1996) found that staff who were comfortable with closeness formed more positive alliances than those who were not, whereas defensiveness in staff was associated with poor alliances (Eaton *et al.*, 1993).

Fear of humiliation/getting it wrong

Mearns and Cooper (2005, p. 132) suggest that 'people tend to have developed a lack of trust in the "reasonableness" of their feeling reactions to others'. Lack of confidence in one's ability to read the client or the situation can contribute to staff offering weak interventions that allude to, or hint at, possibilities that may pass unnoticed by the client if inaccurate. This approach suggests a lack of ability to trust in the patient (despite expecting people who have frequently been abused to trust in us) since the fear arises either from an expectation of mockery (either voiced or thought) or from a fear of influencing suggestible clients.

Our experience is that explicit communication is effective even with the most psychopathic of clients. Those clients who seek to humiliate others find opportunities regardless of whether explicit communication is used or not. Indeed, explicit communication is often experienced as bold and confident due to the directness of this approach which perhaps suggests to more psychopathic individuals that the user is less of an easy target. Because this style of communication is more transparent, clients appear to perceive there is less of a need to rely on game-playing strategies to uncover the clinician's underlying motivations and beliefs.

Those clients who are more compliant and suggestible are often more capable of disagreeing when they truly feel safe. Explicit discussion of clients' compliance may also enable them to find ways to express themselves more independently.

Incorporating explicit communication into practice

A number of steps must be taken to ensure explicit communication is incorporated robustly within clinical practice.

Be explicit about boundaries

The need for clear boundaries is frequently discussed in relation to people with personality disorder (Crawford *et al.*, 2007). There is recognition that boundaries are an essential component of treatment and management of personality disorder, and a failure to communicate these expectations to the client can have disastrous consequences, such as the dangerous situation created at Ashworth High Secure Hospital discussed within the Fallon inquiry (Fallon *et al.*, 1999). The rules and boundaries of any service, and the subsequent expectations of clients, must be made explicit and transparent, and boundary violations must have clear consequences. Most services are relatively clear about the boundaries imposed on their clients. For instance, many services advise clients that behaving aggressively or turning up inebriated will lead to termination of service. It is essential that when boundaries are discussed with clients, attention is given to conceptualising boundaries within each client's logical perspective. This requires advising each client about how he or she may challenge boundaries: for example, 'I know that you have a history of being rejected by services after only a short time and are probably expecting us to reject you too, so it's going to be a challenge for you to turn up for your appointment each week. Maybe when that situation arises, and you don't feel like turning up one week, you could call me so that we can discuss this?'

Equally important is the need for the staff team to be explicit regarding *their own boundaries*. 'While patients are told what is expected of them, they are not told what they can expect from the staff members' (Podrasky and Sexton, 1988, p. 16). When one considers the aversive experiences of relationships that people with personality disorder have previously encountered, it is easy to see how our assumption that we are perceived as safe figures is fundamentally flawed. Mearns and Cooper emphasise that a meeting at relational depth is something we must earn the right to: 'we should not fall into the myth of self-transparency and assume that others can see our trust-worthiness too' (2005, p. 114). Any discussion of our boundaries with the client therefore needs to be contextualised within the context of a tentative formulation about the client. Some common boundary discussions include advising clients that you will:

- offer them care and support but will not have a sexual relationship with them;
- not be disgusted with them should they discuss their trauma;
- not bully, intimidate or humiliate them;
- not physically harm them;
- not be dishonest;
- inform them should you become frightened of them;
- not laugh at their distress with your colleagues.

Engaging in such discussions in the early stages of the relationship (i.e. as soon as possible) allows the client a new experience and equips them with an understanding that this clinician has some insight into their logical world. Discussing our own boundaries and, in particular, the fact that we will not engage in a sexual relationship with the client often causes great anxiety to staff for fear of embarrassment. When pressurised by supervisors to make such a statement to a client who has a history of sexual abuse by someone of the same gender as the clinician, inexperienced staff often water down this statement by telling the client, 'I will not abuse you'. Such a statement reveals a failure of the clinician to truly immerse himself within the client's world as many clients who have been sexually abused attribute responsibility to them-selves for being vulnerable to accepting abuse. The authors have used this strategy numerous times over many years with a range of clients across set-tings. Neither has ever experienced the client as responding with humiliating behaviour. Typically, clients are relieved or at least appreciative that their history and perspective are being acknowledged. Even if the client doesn't believe the clinician's statement, discussing this gives the client permission to raise anxieties in relation to staff behaviour.

The strategy identified earlier of focusing upon the vulnerable child within the client can be particularly helpful in thinking about boundaries and en-abling clinicians to access healthy dialogue that can be comforting and sup-portive. We wouldn't think twice about offering reassurance to a 7-year-old child to tell him we are not going to have sex with him, but can find it hard to identify vulnerability within an adult who may be over six foot with nineteen-inch biceps. Understanding the biceps in the context of a comfort blanket as opposed to a representation of power can often allow the therapist to enter the client's logical world and access the dialogue that they need to utilise to keep the client safe.

Ensure communication is characterised by integrity

Explicit communication and the use of greater disclosure by the clinician only becomes dangerous if the communication lacks what Lander and Nahon (2005) define as integrity. They describe interventions as having integrity when they are characterised by honesty and responsibility and are motivated by a desire to be closer to the patient. They argue that 'honesty alone is not good enough. It must be used responsibly and with the intent to close the space with others. Used alone it can be a dangerous weapon' (2005, p. 34). Like Clarkin *et al.* (2006), they argue that interventions should be arrived at by thinking about one's own contribution to interactions and reflecting upon one's response to the client, as well as the content, tone, spirit and timing of interventions, and whether to comment at all.

Greenberg (2002) advises that in deciding whether to comment, clinicians should not only consider whether the explicit communication is in the interest of the client, rather than primarily motivated by the staff member's self-interest, but also ensure their own affect is primary, rather than secondary, defensive affect. The clinician must also ensure that their communication is comprehensive and that their motivation is transparent. Greenberg points out that saying one is bored or irritated does not in itself constitute comprehensiveness and that staff also need to communicate concern about the statement hurting the client and clarify that the communication has been shared out of a desire to improve the communication rather than a wish to destroy it.

For staff to be able to engage in explicit communication with integrity, the individual needs to have an awareness of their own internal experience, which requires a certain level of personal development, intellectual ability and moral values (Greenberg, 2002). Integrity is enhanced by robust effective supervision where supervisors are also utilising explicit communication and are effective at drawing their supervisee's attention to their security operations that are in operation with their clients (see Chapter 13).

Focus explicit communication on the thoughts, feelings and security operations being elicited within the relationship

When used with integrity, making explicit statements about the experiential relationship between clinician and client enhances feelings of closeness and intimacy and reinforces a direct style of relating as intimacy comes to be associated with safety and pleasure (Fosha, 2000). Fosha advises that it is more satisfying to say something to somebody than merely to think it or feel it because the full cycle of processing core affect is completed, as the action tendency embedded within the affect has also been enacted. Wachtel (2008) believes this experience can be liberating for staff working with clients. Most staff do not find it too challenging to reveal their sadness in response to clients' discussions of difficult experiences they have had, and perhaps those of us who opt to become mental health professionals have an enhanced capacity to tolerate feelings of sadness. Staff appear to experience greater difficulties in being open when their responses are more complex, when they fear that revealing the emotion or thought would hurt the client or when revealing the response would entail feeling more vulnerable.

Clarkin *et al.* (2006) comment that revealing one's confusion and uncertainty about how to respond is an acceptable disclosure. However, the communication that most frequently offers scope for transformation and growth is explicit discussion about aspects of the client that make them difficult to be close to, for instance, times when the client is experienced as boring, frightening, self-pitying or humiliating. All of these experiences can be spoken about and should not be 'off-limits' provided one's disclosure is motivated by a desire for closeness rather than a desire to hurt. This motivation should be shared with the client. For example, 'You came into therapy because you wanted to be able to improve your relationships with others and I want to be able to help you with this. One of the things that seems to happen in our relationship is that you switch off your emotions and tell me long detailed stories. This can leave me feeling like I want to switch you off as the lack of emotion makes this interaction boring. I wonder if this is your way of protecting yourself from me? I notice that you spend a lot of time with Joanne and am guessing she must have a very different experience of you?'

Preston-Shoot (1999) proposes that an open discussion of the power issues is essential in developing a shared sense of purpose in therapeutic relationships. If the client believes they have little acknowledged power within the relationship it is likely that they will act in a manner that ensures acknowledgement, for example, not attending, or being hostile, violent or threatening. Therefore, explicit discussions of the power dynamic are essential. Such discussions may be generated by exploring one's own action tendencies within the relationship in supervision before discussing these with the client. For instance, by questioning oneself about the impact of a client's self-harming behaviour – for example, 'This client uses acts of self-harm to manage his distress. Is my fear of him self-harming restricting me from being honest with him? What security operations am I employing to prevent him from self-harming?' – the clinician should be able to identify a means of initiating conversation about the power dynamic: for instance, 'I am aware that at present you have little value for yourself and often manage your emotions through acts of self-injury and suicide attempts. This behaviour is very powerful. I am scared of your self-destructive behaviours as I worry that if I say anything you find uncomfortable you may self-harm.'

*Be honest with yourself about whether you are keeping the
relationship cosy*

It is not unusual for people with personality disorder to be experienced as
physically frightening and intimidating, and Campling (2004) notes that
communications about fear are particularly useful. However, despite high
levels of anxiety and fear in response to these clients' behaviour, our experience is that almost all staff initially struggle to discuss or explicitly acknowledge their feelings of fear and anxiety. Indeed, the ability to acknowledge
these emotions is generally inversely related to the degree of threat. So, while
anxiety about the client engaging in non-life-threatening self-harming may be
openly discussed, fear caused by threat to our physical integrity is rarely
acknowledged. This is mirrored in daily life. A woman in a car accident on a
busy dual carriageway resulting in a badly damaged car, albeit no physical
injuries to her, manages to carry on with her working day as if nothing had
happened. The rush of epinephrine, as a consequence of fear elicited during
the accident, prevents the individual from recognising she is frightened until
safe at home in the evening when suddenly she becomes tearful.

Most of us are lucky enough not to have encountered physically threatening events on many occasions. Consequently, we are not accustomed to
tolerating our fear or recognising cues that may tell us we are frightened. To
be able to work effectively with forensic clients, it is essential that clinicians
hone their ability to do so. Developing this ability in ourselves requires us to
look objectively for signs that security operations may be in use. For instance,
reminding yourself of what your spouse's/friend's/parents' response may be
to aspects of your work may be of assistance in attempting to identify an
alternative perspective. It can be helpful to ask yourself questions such as:

> If I happen to upset my client he might attack me. Is this restricting the
> content of my dialogue? What security operations am I employing to
> prevent being assaulted?

or,

> This man has raped several women at knife-point. Why don't I feel
> frightened sitting in a room with him on my own? What strategies is he
> using to ensure he doesn't behave aggressively towards me? What strat-
> egies am I using to stop myself feeling frightened?

Using supervision to find answers to these questions and establish what is
being experienced in relation to the client enables clinicians to move from
'cosy' relationships with little capacity for real growth to authentic relationships where common interpersonal problems can be resolved through
initiating dialogue with the client. For example:

I think it is possible that if I upset you in the session you may become violent and attack me. It's important that we discuss this as, if I don't feel safe enough to share openly what I am thinking and feeling, I am not going to be able to help you.

or,

In the past when you've lost your temper, you have ended up committing sexual offences. It's difficult for me to identify the part of you that gets out of control and offends when he's upset and I wonder what strategies you might be using to keep us both safe? I know you don't like that part of yourself and may be frightened that if you get upset you could become dangerous but we need to find a way to explore that part of you if we are to find a way for you to keep yourself and others safe in the future.

These discussions are difficult to have with clients as staff often believe their own vulnerability will be exposed. However, within the context of treating personality disorder, the inability to have such discussions is more likely to expose one's vulnerability and also model to the client that one must hide vulnerability rather than discuss it. Paradoxically, being courageous about one's vulnerability communicates to the client that the clinician is strong.

Ensure explicit communication is reflected in written documentation

It is insufficient for explicit communication to be restricted to oral communication and a robust service will include documentation that reflects this need. Chapters 6 and 7 discuss the need for clear, transparent policies to assist in the smooth running of the organisation and the team. Documentation relating to the client, for example, the Care Programme Approach (CPA) review and multidisciplinary review paperwork, also needs to reflect explicit communication. NICE (2009b) identify the need for CPA reviews to include manageable short-term steps to be taken. Too frequently, teams establish broad areas of improvement – for example, 'improve ability to regulate emotions' – rather than focusing upon discrete steps: for example, '(i) explore in therapy how you coped with your emotions as a child; (ii) begin to notice *when* you are experiencing emotions; (iii) begin to notice differences between these emotions; practice tolerating those emotions that make you feel vulnerable', and so on.

Summary

To be effective as a clinician working with people with personality disorder it is essential that one is able to create and tolerate emotionally intimate relationships with these clients. When clinicians find ways to increase the level of emotion in the relationship between them and their clients, ensure they have an understanding of the client's logical world and utilise explicitness to improve communication, clients are offered an invaluable opportunity to engage in a meeting of relational depth and thus access a situation of real therapeutic potential.

Note

1 Within the Bayesian model of gaming behaviour described, the Investor chooses to invest money, for example $20, in a Trustee. The money is tripled in the transaction as it passes to the Trustee. The Trustee must then return a proportion of the money to the Investor. Typically ten rounds are played. Successful co-operation requires the capacity to sense, value and respond to social gestures but co-operation is easily ruptured. Subjects without a personality disorder typically choose to pay back one-third of the original investment.

References

Alexander, F. (1961) *The Scope of Psychoanalysis*. New York: Basic Books.

Barrett, K.C. and Campos, J.J. (1987) Perspectives on emotional development: II A functionalist approach to emotions. In J. Osofsky (ed.), *Handbook of Infant Development*. New York: Wiley, pp. 555–578.

Bateman, A. and Fonagy, P. (2004) *Psychotherapy for Borderline Personality Disorder*. Oxford: Oxford University Press.

Beeghley, M. and Cichetti, D. (1994) Child maltreatment, attachment and the self system: emergence of an internal state lexicon in toddlers at high social risk. *Development and Psychopathology*, **6**, 5–30.

Beutler, L.E., Malik, M., Alimohamed, S. *et al.* (2003) Therapist variables. In M.J. Lambert (ed.), *Handbook of Psychotherapy and Behaviour Change*. New York: Wiley, pp. 227–306.

Birbaumer, N., Viet, R., Lotze, M. *et al.* (2005) Deficient fear conditioning in psychopathy: a functional magnetic resonance imaging study. *Archives of General Psychiatry*, **62(7)**, 799–805.

Blair, R.J., Colledge, E., Murray, L. *et al.* (2001) A selective impairment in the processing of sad and fearful facial expressions in children with psychopathic tendencies. *Journal of Abnormal Child Psychology*, **29**, 491–498.

Block, J. (2002) *Personality as an Affect Processing System*. Mahwah, NJ: Lawrence Erlbaum.

Bloom, S. (1997) *Creating Sanctuary: Toward the Evolution of Sane Societies*. New York: Routledge.

Bowlby, J. (1980) *Attachment and Loss. Vol. 3. Loss: Sadness and Depression*. London: Hogarth Press.

Bowlby, J. (1988) *A Secure Base*. London: Routledge.

Bretherton, I. (1985) Attachment theory: retrospect and prospect. *Monographs of the Society for Research in Child Development*, **209(50)**. Chicago: University of Chicago Press.

Butler, S.F. and Strupp, H.H. (1991) The role of affect in time limited dynamic psychotherapy. In J. Safran and L. Greenberg (eds), *Emotion, Psychotherapy and Change*. New York: Guilford Press, ch. 4.

Campling, P. (2004) A psychoanalytical understanding of what goes wrong: the importance of projection. In P. Campling, S. Davies and G. Farquharson (eds), *From Toxic Institutions to Therapeutic Environments*. London: Gaskell, ch. 4.

Carston, R. (2002) *Thoughts and Utterances*. Oxford: Blackwell.

Cichetti, D. and Toth, S. (1995) A developmental psychopathology perspective on childhood abuse and neglect. *Journal of the American Academy of Adolescent Psychiatry*, **34(5)**, 541–565.

Clarkin, J., Yeomans, F. and Kernberg, O. (2006) *Psychotherapy for Borderline Personality*. Washington, DC: American Psychiatric Publishing.

Collins Softback English Dictionary (1992) Glasgow: HarperCollins.

Costello, P.C. (2000) Attachment, communication and affect: implications for psychotherapy. Dissertation submitted to the Graduate Faculty in Psychology, City University, New York.

Cramer, P. (2006) *Protecting the Self*. New York: Guilford Press.

Crawford, T.N., Rutter, D., Price, K. *et al.* (2007) *Learning the Lessons: A Multi-method Evaluation of Dedicated Community-based Services for People with Personality Disorder*. London: National Coordinating Centre for NHS Service Delivery and Organisation.

Crittenden, P.M. (1998) Adult attachment interview: coding manual for the dynamic-maturational method. Unpublished manuscript.

Dahms, A.M. (1972) *Emotional Intimacy*. Boulder, CO: Pruett Publishing Company.

Dunkle, J.H. and Friedlander, M.L. (1996) Contribution of therapist experience and personal characteristics to the working alliance. *Journal of Counselling Psychology*, **43**, 456–460.

Eaton, T.T., Abeles, N. and Gutfreund, M.J. (1993) Negative indicators, therapeutic alliance and therapy outcome. *Psychotherapy Research*, **3**, 115–123.

Ekman, P. (1984) Expression and the nature of emotion. In K. Scherer and P. Ekman (eds), *Approaches to Emotion*. Hillsdale, NJ: Erlbaum, pp. 319–344.

Fallon, P., Bluglass, B., Edwards, B. and Daniels, G. (1999) *Report of the Committee of Inquiry into the Personality Disorder Unit, Ashworth Special Hospital*. London: Stationery Office.

Ferenczi, S. (1931) Letter from Sándor Ferenczi to Sigmund Freud, 15 September, 1931. In E. Falzeder and E. Brabant (eds), *The Correspondence of Sigmund Freud and Sandor Ferenczi*, Vol. 3: *1920–1933*. London: Belknap Press of Harvard University Press, p. 417.

Fischer, K.W. and Tangney, J.P. (1995) Self-conscious emotions and the affect revolution. In J.P. Tangney and K.W. Fischer (eds), *Self-conscious Emotions*. New York: Guilford Press, ch. 1.

Fisher, M. (1990) The shared experience and self-disclosure. In G. Stricker and M. Fisher (eds), *Self-disclosure in the Therapeutic Relationship*. New York: Plenum, ch. 1.

Foa, E.B. and Kozak, M.J. (1991) Emotional processing: theory, research and clinical implications for anxiety disorders. In J. Safran and L. Greenberg (eds), *Emotion, Psychotherapy and Change*. New York: Guilford Press, ch. 2.

Fonagy, P. *et al.* (1995) Attachment, borderline states and the representation of the emotions and cognitions in self and other. In D. Cicchetti and S.L. Toth (eds),

Emotion, Cognition and Representation. Rochester, NY: University of Rochester Press, pp. 371–414.

Fosha, D. (2000) *The Transforming Power of Affect: A Model for Accelerated Change*. New York: Basic Books.

Frawley, M. (1990) From secrecy to self-disclosure: healing the scars of incest. In G. Stricker and M. Fisher (eds), *Self-disclosure in the Therapeutic Relationship*. New York: Plenum, ch. 16.

Gaston, L. (1990) The concept of the alliance and its role in psychotherapy: theoretical and empirical considerations. *Psychotherapy*, **27**, 143–153.

Gerhardt, S. (2004) *Why Love Matters: How Affection Shapes a Baby's Brain*. Hove: Brunner-Routledge.

Goater, N. and Meehan, K. (1998) Detection and awareness of child sexual abuse in adult psychiatry. *Psychiatric Bulletin*, **22**, 211–213.

Goleman, D. (1995) *Emotional Intelligence: Why it Can Matter More than IQ*. New York: Bantam Books.

Greenberg, J. (1995) Self-disclosure: is it psychoanalytic? *Contemporary Psychoanalysis*, **31**, 193–205.

Greenberg, L. (2002) *Emotion-Focused Therapy*. Washington, DC: American Psychological Press.

Greenberg, L. and Safran, J. (1987) *Emotion in Psychotherapy*. New York: Guilford Press.

Greenson, R. (1967) The working alliance and transference neurosis. *Psychoanalytic Quarterly*, **34**, 155–181.

Guidano, V.F. (1991) Affective change events in cognitive therapy. In J. Safran and L. Greenberg (eds), *Emotion, Psychotherapy and Change*. New York: Guilford Press, ch. 3.

Henry, W., Schacht, T. and Strupp, H. (1990) Patient and therapist introject, interpersonal process and differential psychotherapy outcome. *Journal of Consulting and Clinical Psychology*, **58**, 768–774.

Hill, C.E. (1989) *Therapist Techniques and Client Outcomes*. Newbury Park, CA: Sage.

Horvath, A.O. and Bedi, R.P. (2002) The alliance. In J.C. Norcross (ed.), *Psychotherapy Relationships that Work*. New York: Oxford University Press, ch. 3.

Jackson, J.M. (1990) The role of implicit communication in therapist self-disclosure. In G. Stricker and M. Fisher (eds), *Self-disclosure in the Therapeutic Relationship*. New York: Plenum, ch. 7.

Kennedy-Moore, E. and Watson, J.C. (1999) *Expressing Emotion. Myths, Realities, and Therapeutic Strategies*. New York: Guilford Press.

Kiesler, D.J. (1988) *Therapeutic Metacommunication: Therapist Impact Disclosure as Feedback in Therapy*. Palo Alto, CA: Consulting Psychologists Press.

King-Casas, B., Sharp, C., Lomax, L. *et al.* (2008) The rupture and repair of co-operation in borderline personality disorder. *Science*, **321**, 806–810.

Kohut, H. (1977) *The Restoration of the Self*. New York: International Universities Press.

Lander, N.R. and Nahon, D. (2005) *The Integrity Model of Existential Psychotherapy in Working with the 'Difficult Patient'*. London: Routledge.

Lazarus, R.S. (1991) *Emotion and Adaptation*. New York: Oxford University Press.

Lerner, H.G. (1989) *The Dance of Intimacy*. London: Pandora Press.

Linehan, M. (1993) *Cognitive Behavioural Treatment of Personality Disorder*. New York: Guilford Press.

Lyons-Ruth, K. (1998) Implicit relational knowing: its role in development and psychoanalytic treatment. *Infant Mental Health Journal*, **19**, 282–289.

Lyons-Ruth, K. (1999) The two-person unconscious. *Psychoanalytic Inquiry*, **19**, 576–617.

Magnavita, J. (2000) *Relational Therapy for Personality Disorders*. New York: Wiley.

Meares, R. (2003) *Intimacy and Alienation*. London: Routledge.

Mearns, D. and Cooper, M. (2005) *Working at Relational Depth in Counselling and Psychotherapy*. London: Sage.

Nathanson, D.L. (1996) About emotion. In D.L. Nathanson (ed.), *Knowing Feeling: Affect, Script and Psychotherapy*. New York: W.W. Norton, pp. 1–21.

Ogloff, J. and Wong, S. (1990) Electrodermal and cardiovascular evidence of a coping response in psychopaths. *Criminal Justice Behaviour*, **17**, 231–245.

Patrick, C., Cuthbert, B. and Lang, P. (1994) Emotion in the criminal psychopath: fear image processing. *Journal of Abnormal Psychology*, **103(3)**, 523–534.

Podrasky, D.L. and Sexton, D.L. (1988) Nurses' reactions to difficult patients. *Image: Journal of Nursing Scholarship*, **20(1)**, 16–21.

Preston-Shoot, M. (1999) Recreating Mayhem? In D. Webb and R. Harris (eds), *Mentally Disordered Offenders: Managing People Nobody Owns*. London Routledge, ch. 5.

Psychopathology Committee of the Group for the Advancement of Psychiatry (2001) Re-examination of therapist self-disclosure. *Psychiatric Services*, **52**, 1489–1493.

Rowan, J. and Jacobs, M. (2002) *The Therapist's Use of Self*. Maidenhead: Open University Press.

Safran, J. and Greenberg, L. (1991) *Emotion and the Process of Therapeutic Change*. New York: Academic Press.

Safran, J. and Segal, J. (1996) *Interpersonal Process in Cognitive Therapy*. Northvale, NJ: Aronson.

Saradjian, J. (1996) *Women Who Sexually Abuse Children: From Research to Clinical Practice*. London: Wiley.

Schore, A. (2003a) *Affect Regulation and the Repair of the Self*. New York: Norton.

Schore, A. (2003b) *Affect Dysregulation and Disorders of the Self*. New York: Norton.

Shadley, M.L. (2000) Are all therapists alike? Revisiting research about the use of self in therapy. In M. Baldwin (ed.), *The Use of Self in Therapy*. New York: Haworth Press.

Smith, T.L., Barrett, M.S., Benjamin, L.S. and Barber, J.P. (2006) Relationship factors in treating personality disorders. In L. Castonguay and L.E. Beutler (eds), *Principles of Therapeutic Change that Work*. New York: Oxford University Press, ch. 10.

Stern, D.N., Sander, L.W., Nahum, J.P., Harrison, A.M., Lyons-Ruth, K. *et al.* (1998) Non-interpretive mechanisms in psycho-analytic therapy: the 'something more' than interpretation. *International Journal of Psychoanalysis*, **79**, 903–921.

Stiles, W.B., Agnew-Davies, R., Hardy, G.E., Barkham, M. and Shapiro, D.A. (1998) Relations of the alliance with psychotherapy outcome: findings in the second Sheffield Psychotherapy Project. *Journal of Consulting and Clinical Psychology*, **66**, 791–802.

Stricker, G. (2003) The many faces of self-disclosure. *Journal of Clinical Psychology/In session*, **59(5)**, 623–630.

Sullivan, H.S. (1953). *The Interpersonal Theory of Psychiatry*. New York: Norton.

Tangney, J. and Fischer, K.W. (1995) *Self-conscious Emotions*. New York: Guilford Press.

Tomkins, S.S. (1962) *Affect, Imagery and Consciousness: Vol. 1. The Positive Affects*. New York: Springer.

Tomkins, S.S. (1963) *Affect, Imagery and Consciousness: Vol. 2. The Negative Affects*. New York: Springer.

Vaillant, G.E. (1992) *Ego Mechanisms of Defence*. Washington, DC: American Psychiatric Press.

Van Honk, J. and Schutter, D.J. (2006) Unmasking feigned sanity: a neurobiological model of emotion processing in primary psychopathy. *Cognitive Neuropsychiatry*, **11(3)**, 285–306.

Wachtel, P.L. (1993) *Therapeutic Communication*. New York: Guilford Press.

Wachtel, P.L. (2008) *Relational Theory and the Practice of Psychotherapy*. New York: Guilford Press.

Winnicott, D. (1960) The theory of the parent child relationship. *International Journal of Psycho-analysis*, **41**, 585–595.

Yalom, I. (2001) *The Gift of Therapy*. London: Piatkus.

Young, J. (1994) *Cognitive Therapy for Personality Disorders*. Sarasota, FL: Professional Resource Press.

Chapter 6

Organisational challenges to providing services for personality disordered people

Des McVey and Jacqui Saradjian

Introduction

People with a diagnosis of personality disorder have different needs com-pared to people with a diagnosis of mental illness but nevertheless have been catered for by traditional psychiatric services, where they have often been inadequately managed rather than effectively treated. It is principally because they did not respond to these services, that these clients have been deemed 'untreatable' – an inevitable consequence of receiving services not designed to meet their needs. People with personality disorder are not a homogeneous group; therefore one service model will not be appropriate for all. Those with the most severe psychopathology require a residential facility (hospital or prison unit) to ensure safe containment to implement effective treatment; those with less severe psychopathology are more appropriately treated in outpatient and/or day services. The organisational challenges discussed are primarily relevant to the provision of residential services but are also relevant to other contexts.

A framework for effective service provision

Safe and effective clinical services require strong, supportive managers with good clinical knowledge including awareness of the inevitable organisational difficulties intrinsic to providing services for these clients within a wider system. These difficulties are typically systemic reflections of the clients' dynamics and, when recognised as such, are managed more effectively.

The National Service Framework (NSF) for Mental Health (1999) pro-vided ten principles of good practice to guide all clinical services and will form the framework within which the organisational challenges of providing services for people with personality disorder will be discussed.

Planning services with involvement of service users and their carers

Planning the service – developing a secure base

The clients' needs should be paramount in any service planning. Once the client group has been identified and a budget boundary established, the most suitable service – outpatient, inpatient, etc. – can be determined. The next stage is frequently the search for a physical base; however, the primary client need is treatment and, until a treatment model is known, the requirements of a physical base cannot be established. The treatment model will determine the number of treatment rooms needed, staff composition and staff space requirements.

Therefore, it is suggested that the clinical lead and service manager should be appointed as soon as possible in order to establish an evidence-based treatment model which will guide other decisions about the service. Equally importantly, all staff then recruited will be aware of the treatment model to be delivered. If a service is set up without the framework of a known treatment model, it will be more difficult to inculcate previously employed staff into the required model; consequently frictions can develop which may be exploited by the clients. By establishing the treatment model at the earliest opportunity, a secure base can be formed within which a cohesive service can be delivered.

Service user involvement

There is a tendency to avoid the recommendation to involve service users when developing services within secure establishments. Nevertheless, service user views can be canvassed by interview or in writing or by using representatives who have been through treatment and no longer present with such severe psychopathology that they require detention.

Numerous publications present the views of service users, albeit few attend to the views of those at the most severe end of the spectrum (Maltman *et al.*, 2008; Barlow *et al.*, 2007; NIMHE, 2003; Castillo, 2003). The articles have common themes: wanting appropriate treatment whilst feeling physically and psychologically safe; fearing stigmatisation; fear of negative staff attitudes; feeling hopeless but needing optimism that treatment can be effective; and wanting a realistic expectation of time scale for change. These service user requirements can readily be incorporated into service planning.

Service user organisations (Borderline UK, WISH) can also provide useful contributions although some individuals may be constrained by their experiences and unresolved conflicts and make counter-therapeutic recommendations, for example that services for women with personality disorder should employ only female staff. This implicitly conveys that all men are dangerous and prevents the women from experiencing healthier relationships with men. Equally, it implies that women are not dangerous, thus ignoring the histories of women who have been abused and bullied by women. Managers must ensure that advice from whatever source is robustly evaluated.

Carer involvement

Involvement of carers in service planning for this client group is extremely difficult as there are rarely suitable personal carers to involve. Most clients with more extreme forms of psychopathology were abused by early carers, and have wittingly or unwittingly abused those with whom they had relationships as adults, or have spent much of their lives in institutions, so typically 'carers' have been staff. Thus, it seems appropriate to involve members of staff with considerable experience of caring for this client group in service planning.

The service should deliver high quality treatment and care which is known to be effective and acceptable

Treatment programmes should be based on the best information available as to the aetiology of the disorder, in conjunction with outcome studies that indicate effectiveness of the proposed intervention for that client group. The treatment model should be a fully articulated, accessible, auditable document. People with personality disorder are a disparate group, therefore treatment must be adaptable to the needs of each individual (see Chapter 4).

The organisational challenge is to provide an infrastructure that ensures adherence to the treatment model. This requires creating and implementing both policies and governance structures for monitoring them. Policies must address all aspects of the unit's work: the operational policy; the roles and responsibilities of each group and team member; the referral and assessment process; the implementation of each treatment component; documentation relating to clients' progression; the functions of each meeting; staff recruitment, training, supervision; and service user involvement and complaints.

Particular challenges for adherence to treatment model

Team ruptures

Ensuring team adherence to a treatment model within a service for people with personality disorder is particularly problematic due to the clients' propensity to expose 'split-dynamics' in the team which reflect 'splits' within the clients. Splits occur when clients, mostly unconsciously, present differently to different people. By placing themselves outside teams, managers are better placed to manage splits by objectively considering potential causes of ruptures and facilitating solutions to ensure effective treatment is maintained. Typical team ruptures arise when:

(i)   Staff collude with, and act-out, the patients' resistance to treatment by constantly questioning treatment.
(ii) There is failure to address staff non-adherence to the treatment model, e.g. senior staff with limited knowledge of personality disorder defend against feeling de-skilled by initiating interventions within their areas of expertise.
(iii) Senior or experienced staff are drawn into a split-dynamic and use their position to enforce their views.
(iv) Staff are unable to recognise the power of ever-present raw affect, focusing instead upon cognitive and behavioural processes.
(v)   Staff do not recognise that personal issues are being affected by a client and attack or collude with the client (particularly problematic when the staff member carries authority with other staff through position or popularity).
(vi) Some staff have personal issues that make them unsafe to work in these services. These staff can appear dedicated to clients but may cause conflict with colleagues, breach boundaries, objectify the clients or be incessantly punitive.

The power of the split dynamic cannot be overstated. Managers should protect teams by regularly monitoring team process, auditing minutes of team meetings and clinical decisions to assess adherence to the treatment model.

When in conflict, these clients often turn to managers for support. Managers need to absorb and contain the client's and their own affect rather than feel driven to intervene. Intervention will draw the manager into the split-dynamic thus exacerbating the team rupture. Managers should be explicit with staff, directly addressing those issues underlying the rupture and ensuring teams openly discuss and resolve the ruptures. If there is an impasse, the team may need supervision facilitated by someone external to the team but internal to the service.

Complaints as a treatment-interfering strategy

People with personality disorder tend to be hyper-vigilant to perceived threat and are prone to noticing even slight errors and inconsistencies by staff. Whilst many patients would ignore or merely comment on such issues, these clients, depending on their emotional state, may formally complain. These complaints can temporarily inhibit therapy. In situations where clients have made formal complaints, therapists can find themselves in the invidious position of being unable to make appropriate interventions due to the complaint investigation. Therefore, speedy resolution of complaints is essential. Frequently, complaints are driven by the following motivations:

(i) *To feel power over the staff team.* Some individuals develop a reputation for making aggressive complaints, progressing them to the highest level. These clients usually have a rigid cognitive understanding of their needs and the responsibilities of services. They study policies and legalities specific to their detention, often holding greater knowledge than staff. This can generate immense anxiety in staff; some fear engaging meaningfully with these clients for fear of litigation; some acquiesce to contra-therapeutic requests; and some collude with the client's complaints to feel safe. These clients often employ solicitors to pursue their complaints, further increasing staff anxiety. This leaves the client feeling powerful and in control but restricts their treatment as it is this need to maintain control that underlies their psychopathology.

(ii) *To create a level of chaos.* Some clients use complaints to generate chaos, making numerous simultaneous complaints, often about minute, overlapping issues to different managers who may be unaware of the other complaints. They then compare complaint responses and use inconsistencies to generate further complaints which can lead to chaos. Focusing upon the increasing number and complexity of complaints allows avoidance of treatment that they find emotionally difficult.

(iii) *To attack effective therapists.* Some clients make complaints when their therapists begin to penetrate their defences and develop an appropriately emotional therapeutic relationship. These complaints are driven by unresolved anger towards past carers and/or fear of emotional intimacy. Clients create a therapeutic rupture by making a formal complaint against the therapist and/or demanding a change of therapist. If not understood in context, these complaints can undermine treatment by resulting in a change of therapist and/or the client not addressing the relationship, thus inhibiting therapeutic growth.

(iv) *Using complaints to parallel offend.* When in an emotional state that may in the community lead to offending behaviour, an individual may recreate the process of offending using alternative behaviours whilst in an institution. Some clients use the complaints process to parallel offend, by targeting a member of staff who holds emotional salience for him or her. For example, a man who is angry with women may target a female staff member and make a complaint. If that complaint is not upheld, then the same staff member may be subjected to increasingly persecutory complaints. Whilst it is important that each complaint is investigated in case there is substance to the complaint, the staff member also needs protection. If there is no substance, the client should be dealt with managerially as a 'persistent complainer'; meanwhile the behaviour should become the focus of therapeutic intervention.

(v) *Avoiding responsibility for behaviour.* Complaints are often made when clients are at a stage in therapy where taking emotional responsibility for harmful behaviour to self or others is expected. Their inability to tolerate shame associated with the behaviour motivates them to engage in battles of integrity with their caregivers. They use the complaints system as a distraction and to maintain victim status. This style of complaint can generate fear in staff to the extent that they avoid addressing the behaviour.

Robust complaints policies and procedures, including a strategy for addressing persistent complainants, are required. Without these, there will be ambiguity, which increases the clients' opportunities to use complaining as a therapy-interfering strategy. Complaints need to be considered within the context of the client's psychopathology whilst ensuring that legitimate complaints are effectively addressed. Responses should be consistent with the treatment model to prevent clients using complaints to avoid effective treatment. Those responsible for answering complaints must have an in-depth understanding of the client group and the treatment model; equally, each complaint must be considered objectively and with regard to the unit's policies/procedures and the professional codes of conduct of staff members involved. Complaints should be regularly audited and lessons learnt fed into service development.

Whilst in most health care services a low number of complaints may indicate a high quality service, this may not be true for a personality disorder service. An increase in complaints is often juxtaposed with a decrease in dysfunctional behaviours such as self-harm or physical and sexual aggression. Despite complaints being stressful for staff, such an increase is often indicative that treatment is being effective in that it is pushing clients' defences but these clients are exercising more appropriate routes to manage their affect and resolve conflict.

People with personality disorder often appear powerful and intimidating, but this presentation almost always masks an inherent sense of powerlessness. Consequently, they frequently instruct lawyers to pursue their complaints, believing this increases their power. Clients can also use lawyers as surrogate parents, referring to them on occasions where they would benefit therapeutically from resolving the conflict independently. Managers frequently have to deal with legal letters which, reflecting the client's affect, can be demanding and accusatory in their style. Understandably, lawyers have limited knowledge of treatment relating to personality disorder and make requests for their clients that can restrict treatment or, if acquiesced to, would be iatrogenic. Therefore detailed responses are needed, requiring in-depth knowledge of the client and treatment.

The split-dynamic can be evident between clinicians and legal representatives when the client presents differently to each party and, in the absence of clinical training, lawyers rarely recognise the process or the potential for their interventions to be detrimental to their client. For example, clients with low self-worth and fear of abandonment often 'test' whether clinicians genuinely care by applying to tribunals to discharge them from section. Lawyers, blind to this motivation, fight for release. If discharged from section, the client is devastated, perceiving it as proof that neither staff nor the lawyer care enough to ensure treatment is maintained.

Whilst the authors support clients' access to legal representation, lawyers need assistance from managers to understand their client's psychopathology so that they are fully informed of the real consequences of their advice for their clients.

Ensuring clients receive treatment rather than management

Some services providing interventions for people with personality disorder aim to manage symptoms rather than treat the disorder. This prevents some organisational management problems but does little to reduce the client's risk or personal suffering. When discharged, clients frequently deteriorate as the underlying pathology has been untreated. It is therefore essential that managers ensure that the interventions offered constitute treatment rather than management.

Management-focused services aimed at symptom reduction are likely to be viewed as smooth-running services which efficiently contain clients. Within this model, interventions focus on reducing behaviours such as self-harm, sexual and physical aggression, complaining and conflict, but do not address underlying psychopathology. Behaviour is the manifestation of distress; if that distress is left untreated, any behavioural change is unlikely to be sustained. By managing symptoms, staff are protected from the inherent difficulties associated with treating these clients, whereas not addressing the underlying psychopathology leaves the protection of the public, and indeed the individual, limited to the duration of the detention.

Services that provide treatment tend to be more complex. Underlying dysfunctional cognitive, affective and interpersonal processes are attended to in order to enable clients to experience painful primary affect such as fear, shame and sadness, since inability to tolerate this affect led to their dysfunctional behaviour. Such an approach generates a certain level of chaos and anxiety which managers need to accept. Oppressive management aimed at minimising incidents prevents effective treatment. Treatment is initially more risky than management for staff and clients, but, if carried out within the individual formulation of each client, it provides an opportunity to address core problems, ensuring change is not just situational-specific.

The organisational challenge is to recognise that viewing settled units as functional, and units with a degree of chaos as dysfunctional, is not always appropriate without an understanding of the treatment being implemented.

The service should be well suited to those who use it and non-discriminatory

For many years, people with personality disorder have been discriminated against by being placed in inappropriate services and then deemed 'untreatable'. These experiences, and the media repeatedly referring to people with personality disorder as 'evil', 'monsters' or 'perverts', have led those with this diagnosis to experience stigmatisation and discrimination. The organisational challenge is to develop treatment services that are effective in reducing risk and bringing about changes in personality, thus reducing this prejudice and stigma.

Personality disorder is the consequence of psychological adaptations to life experience, the direction of which will be more or less determined by the person's genetic make-up. Thus, as the problem is primarily psychological, services best suited to the client group will be psychological and the clinical lead should be psychologically trained. In hospitals, units with non-psychiatric leadership have tended to be marginalised or belittled, or strategies have been implemented to 'bring them into line'. This means that those clients are discriminated against compared to clients within psychiatry-led services. This is ironic given psychiatry's problems with dealing with these clients (e.g. Fallon *et al.*, 1999). The organisational challenge is ensuring awareness of the potential for this and challenging inequity in the treatment of clients in these services.

Literature indicates that ethnic minority clients are less frequently given a diagnosis of personality disorder (Mikton and Grounds, 2007) and, thus, are discriminated against in terms of receiving appropriate treatment. Organisations need to actively raise awareness of the cross-cultural validity of this diagnosis and service managers should prioritise referrals of ethnic minority clients.

This then leads to the difficulty of treating people of ethnic minorities within a predominantly white client group. Unless carefully managed, this could lead to clients feeling isolated and experiencing further discrimination. We suggest that these issues are explicitly discussed on the unit with the client and with peers and that, where possible, more than one person from an ethnic minority is placed in the treatment group and that active recruitment of staff from ethnic minority groups is sought.

The service should be accessible so that help can be obtained when and where needed

Fazel and Danesh (2002) found that 65 per cent of male prisoners and 42 per cent of female prisoners suffered from personality disorder (not all antisocial). It is likely that many of these are disturbed enough to warrant intervention; thus, to provide accessible help when and where needed, prison units require the resources to deliver appropriate treatment. Carr-Walker and colleagues (2004) support developing services in prisons rather than hospitals, as their comparison of prison officers' and nurses' attitudes to working with people with personality disorder revealed more positive attitudes among prison officers.

Prison units should be multi-agency and include clinical staff working in partnership with prison officers. There is a precedent for this model (the Fens Unit, HMP Whitemoor). There are great opportunities for innovative work in such units; the organisational challenge is to set them up appropriately. In particular, senior managers of partner agencies need real ownership of the project. Formally establishing unit success as a performance goal contributes to managers taking ownership and provides genuine motivation for supporting the project.

Such a unit requires the collaboration of two institutions, the health and prison services, each of which has rigid systems for client care. Hybrid policies and procedures need developing and sanctioning by both prison and health trust to ensure that only one system of client care is followed.

Staff management is complex but, to minimise complexity, all clinical staff should be employed through one health provider and managed by the Clinical Director whilst all operational staff should be managed by the Operational Manager. Joint management of the unit requires these two managers to work co-operatively. This will be facilitated by the roles and responsibilities of each being explicitly defined in governance documentation. It is possible that within this relationship and in the unit, there will be a friction between the need for high levels of security and the fear that clinicians, unused to such environments, will not respect this. Thus, from the outset, and throughout service delivery, ongoing education of both groups, about security and treatment methods, is essential. Crucially, all decisions must be truly multidisciplinary, with prison staff being involved at every level in clinical and management meetings as well as the CPA process (Edgar and Rickford, 2009). Equally vital in relation to risk, confidentiality policies should incorporate the involvement of operational staff. Information sharing should take place at the beginning and end of each shift to ensure awareness of pertinent issues and for the containment of anxiety in staff and prisoners.

Given the hybrid nature of the unit, service commissioners should maintain financial control. Without ring-fencing, it is likely that resources will be plundered by either partner agency; however, magnanimity at times of real need will increase goodwill and prevent resentment.

There are advantages to implementing a model where experts in the dual needs of this group, security and therapy, are brought together. Difficult treatment can be delivered in an environment familiar to clients and progression through the system may be smoother. Despite appearing expensive, treatment provision is cheaper than keeping such prisoners on normal location as they often continue offending in prison (being assaultative, hostage taking, committing criminal damage, arson and 'dirty protest'), leading to segregation and numerous moves. Many also seriously self-harm, requiring extra staffing.

The service should promote safety of clients and their carers, staff and the wider public

Risk management

Due to the propensity of these clients to utilise highly dangerous behaviour towards themselves or others, risk management systems are crucial. Managers' responsibility has been highlighted with the advent of legislation holding them criminally responsible if activities are managed in a manner that results in death arising from a gross breach of duty of care to employees, the public or any other individual. Factors to be considered include: failing to ensure safe working practices; failure to comply with health and safety legislation; and the extent to which appropriate policies, systems and practices were in place to minimise risk. It is the responsibility of managers to ensure that there are systems and policies in place to continuously assess the risk of each client from referral through to discharge. The organisational challenge is to achieve risk management without being oppressive and inhibiting treatment opportunities.

Crisis management

An essential component of treatment for people with personality disorder is experiencing episodes of crisis (Livesley, 2003). Such crises occur when the client experiences significant distress and responds by resorting to dys-functional coping strategies including violence to self or others, substance abuse, prolific complaining, bullying, absconding, psychotic symptoms, pro-longed sleeping and promiscuous behaviour. When these clients present as most challenging, they are at their most distressed. Service response to crises varies from increased levels of observation to discharge of the client. The latter appears to be exclusive to people with personality disorder, who are often discharged for presenting with behaviours that are characteristic of their condition; this is equivalent to discharging a client with schizophrenia when floridly psychotic. Indeed, some services pre-empt this situation during admission of people with personality disorder by entering into a contract such that if the client presents with 'difficult behaviours', he will be dis-charged. As with people who are floridly psychotic, it is during crises that these clients are most in need of treatment.

Services may use crises to provide clients with healthy therapeutic oppor-tunities, or they may respond to crises in a fashion that colludes with psychopathology, thus perpetuating disorder. It is vital that service managers understand that effective treatment for people with personality disorder involves episodes of crisis that require sophisticated responses consistent with client formulations if therapeutic growth is to be promoted.

Robust risk management policies should: describe risk management within the context of the treatment model; convey understanding that management of short-term risks is detrimental to treatment and will be costly and ineffective; require staff to undergo specialist training to understand the complexities of risk management for personality disorder; necessitate the completion of individual risk assessments and crisis management plans contextualised within each client's clinical formulation; identify strategies to support staff in managing anxiety associated with such risk management approaches.

Healthy management of serious untoward incidents

Serious untoward incidents will undoubtedly occur with this client group, whether or not they are in treatment. Consequently, it is highly likely that serious incidents such as significant physical and/or sexual assaults, hostage taking and severe self-harm (including suicide) will occur. Organisations must accept that this client group pose risks, but the challenge is to learn what, if anything, could have been done to prevent the incident rather than finding someone to blame. Serious Untoward Incident Reviews should involve an independent chair and be inquisitorial rather than adversarial, resulting in a written outcome. It is the responsibility of the unit managers to ensure implementation of any action points that may arise from such reviews.

Monitoring services

Inspections by external authorities are essential in any service where there is one group of people (staff) who are in a position of power over another group of people (patients/prisoners). Zimbardo's seminal work across forty years shows that within situations of power imbalance, those carrying power, regardless of good character or intentions, can become hostile and punitive (Haney et al., 1973; Zimbardo, 2007). This is particularly important in environments where those without power are detained against their will, such as prisons and secure hospitals.

Inspecting services for people with personality disorder requires inspectors to have a thorough understanding of the requirements of effective services for this specific population. These services are, of necessity, different from standard mental health services and prison wings. Consequently, in-depth knowledge of the numerous presentations of people with personality disorder, their characteristic behaviours and the treatment model being implemented is required. Inspectorate bodies with more generic understanding of services and lacking full understanding of the complex dynamics involved in treating people with personality disorder often make ill-informed recommendations that, if implemented, would be antithetical to effective treatment. Clients also have access to these inspectors and if inspectors do not fully understand this client group, they can get drawn into colluding with their psychopathology.

Inspectorate bodies that interface with services for people with personality disorder include the Healthcare Commission, which inspects hospital services, and Her Majesty's Prison Inspectorate. Secure hospital services where people with personality disorder are detained under the Mental Health Act are also monitored by the Mental Health Act Commission and the validity of detention is subject to review by Hospital Managers and Mental Health Act Review Tribunals. Whilst members of these teams often have considerable expertise in specific aspects of standard service delivery, there is no requirement for team members to have specific expertise in the inspection of specialist services for people with personality disorder.

Mental Health Act Commission, Hospital Managers and Mental Health Act Tribunals

In relation to Commission visits, Managers Hearings and Tribunals, the challenge for managers is to ensure that the correct information is conveyed to the panels. The Mental Health Act 2007 changed the criteria for detention, which is particularly significant for people with personality disorder. Previously it was necessary to show that patients were treatable; now panels must be satisfied appropriate treatment is available. This means that service managers have increased responsibility to ensure that treatment offered is appropriate and, as both patients and their lawyers will become astute at challenging services, that treatment is evidence-based in relation to specific clients. If the panel are convinced that the treatment is inappropriate, patients may be discharged who pose a serious risk to themselves or others. In addition, successful judicial review, human rights and other legal challenges may follow in cases where people do not receive appropriate treatment.

Her Majesty's Prison Inspectorate

Inspection of services is vital due to the vulnerability of services to developing unhealthy dynamics. However, inspectors rarely have the specialist expertise to perform informed inspections. Although the inspectorate provide a level of monitoring that ensures some standards are maintained, without involving specialists their findings may be superficial and possibly unhelpful. Consequently, there is increased responsibility for managers to be proactive in auditing and regulating their own services. Managers should provide inspectors with documentation on the client group, their treatment needs and the treatment model in operation, and should be proactive in discussing issues with inspectors, without appearing patronising, over-defensive or dismissive.

The service should offer choices which promote independence

The issue of choice is complicated in relation to people with personality disorder. One of the defining characteristics of personality disorder is that the person has distorted cognition (perception and interpretation of self, others and events). Cognitive distortions develop through adverse life experiences and are maintained by choices made in adulthood. Many of these choices are self-defeating and damaging and reinforce their psychopathology. The organisational challenge is restricting the impact of self-defeating choices in order to facilitate treatment which will eventually enable clients to be capable of making healthy choices.

Contentious areas related to choice

Consent to assessment and treatment

Despite mental health services' ability to detain a patient against their will, psychological interventions require some degree of client participation. Consequently, managers need to ensure that clients are provided with adequate information, in oral and written form, concomitant with their intellectual ability, to enable them to give informed consent. Due to low self-worth, some clients will initially refuse treatment, believing they do not deserve it or will not cope. Despite wanting treatment, others rebuff it as they anticipate being rejected and manage their anxiety by pre-empting that rejection. Others reject it because they fear change. Lengthy assessment periods in inpatient settings provide a stronger basis for developing informed consent on the part of the client. They also enable staff to begin to build embryonic relationships through which they can motivate those reluctant to engage. Managers need to allow staff that time to emotionally engage clients so they can agree to treatment. Nevertheless, once they have agreed to treatment, clients' commitment will fluctuate and there will be times when they refuse treatment. At such times, it is essential that staff persist with engaging the client as it is often lack of worth or fear of rejection, change or emotional intimacy that motivates their refusal to engage. In addition to staff spending time with the client and explicitly discussing his or her fears, strategies should be employed such as the therapist sitting in the room for the whole of the therapy session even if the client does not attend. This sends a strong message about the therapist's belief in the client's worth and their commitment to the client. Staff should also persist in engaging the client when facing overt verbal hostility. Whilst those new to this client group may see these strategies as pressuring, if such measures are not employed, the client's dysfunctional schema will be reinforced; they will feel rejected, unworthy, unwanted.

Choice of therapist or therapy group

In some services, clients can choose or request a change of therapist. With this client group, such change is possible but usually only if the therapist has contravened a boundary. Most requests to change therapist are driven by the client's need to maintain control or fear of therapeutic progress. One of the aims of individual therapy is to develop an attachment relationship, an appropriate emotionally intimate relationship with the therapist, which is difficult for people with personality disorder since many are terrified of emotional closeness. This fear is managed in various ways including requesting a change of therapist, often in conjunction with formal complaints about the therapist. When struggling with interpersonal difficulties with facilitators or peers, clients often make well-constructed and coherent requests to change therapy groups. If managers allow these choices, the person's psychopathology may be reinforced and treatment impeded.

Leaving therapy

It is common for a client to volunteer for treatment, but when therapy begins to be challenging or effective due to raising the level of affect, the client may choose to disengage or withdraw. Another common motivation for this behaviour is testing the team to see if they really want to work with them. For example, one client disengaged from treatment for more than six months and repeatedly asked to leave the unit. After failed attempts at re-engagement, he was told he could go and he immediately took an overdose as he felt rejected and did not really want to leave. Another man regularly requested to leave but attended every therapy session, was emotionally engaged and made significant changes. Managers need to understand that the commitment of these clients does not remain consistent over time, that the choices they make are not straightforward, and often the choice they appear to be making is not what they actually want to happen. Consequently, at times, managers will be asked to support staff in decisions that initially appear contrary to client choice.

'Time-out'

It is regularly suggested that clients should be allowed the choice of 'time-out' of therapy. People with personality disorder ask for 'time-out' when 'stressed', but that episode of emotional arousal is necessary to bring about real change. Thus, clients are highly likely to ask for time-out at the stage when therapy can be most efficacious. Allowing these clients this choice undermines the therapeutic process.

The service should be well co-ordinated between all staff and agencies

Personality disorder services are always multidisciplinary and increasingly multi-agency. The organisational challenge is to develop a governance structure which facilitates effective communication, which is crucial for integration. Governance comprises the institutions and processes that determine how power is exercised, who is involved and how decisions are made. Therefore, governance effectively manages relationships of partner agencies at all levels to produce enhanced performance. That performance needs to be effectively assessed and monitored and those findings used to influence the strategy and direction of the unit. Effective governance requires an infrastructure that sustains co-operative and transparent decision making and planned change. This means that all professional groupings and partner agencies should be represented at meetings. All decisions impacting on any aspect of the functioning of the unit must be made within structured meetings. Decisions made outside of the meetings will result in managers being unaware that those decisions had been made and implemented. This results in poor leadership, negativity and a sense of disempowerment among staff.

The service should deliver continuity of care for as long as this is needed

People with personality disorder manage their distress in ways that are damaging to themselves or others. The fundamental change needed to remediate that damage cannot occur within brief interventions (see Chapter 4). The organisational challenge is to balance the pressure of continual referrals with the need of clients for long-term treatment. Consequently, it is important to ensure that those in treatment are able to use the place they are occupying. Whilst it is important to persist with those clients with shifting motivation, it is equally important to identify those clients who, after every effort has been made to engage them, are not currently emotionally able to use treatment. Systems need developing to ensure those clients can obtain supported appropriate transfers to free up places for new referrals.

Depending upon the extent of disturbance, some clients who have received institutional care will require ongoing treatment following discharge. Further services may need to be identified to provide ongoing support, and staff from the original service may be required to liaise with the new service until clients have formed supportive relationships.

Crucially, to ensure continuity of care, it is essential that there are systems developed for full information sharing. Most clients consent to disclosure. However, lack of consent should not prevent information sharing when clients have a history of destructive behaviour towards themselves or others and when sharing of information may prevent serious injury or damage to the health of a patient, a third party or public health. The client should be informed of this information sharing.

The service should empower and support staff

Personality disorder services are notorious for rapid turnover of staff and staff burnout. This is damaging for clients who need stability of relationships. The organisational challenge is to create a service within which staff feel safe, contained and valued. The leadership of such a unit is pivotal to achieving these aims.

Leadership in multi-agency/multidisciplinary services

The roles of leadership are to inspire and manage staff, to contain anxiety within the organisation whilst promoting change, to ensure effective structures and systems of communication, to provide vision and core values for the unit, and to influence those externally who are stakeholders and interested parties (e.g. Locke, 2003). As personality disorder services are multidisciplinary, and often multi-agency, the most likely model is distributed leadership. In distributed leadership, each manager negotiates the best interest for their organisation or section whilst having regard for the effective functioning of the service. However, distributed leadership can lead to 'uncertainties and ambiguities surrounding one's own role in relation to that of others, both vertical and lateral' (Huffington et al., 2004, p. 73). Whilst these uncertainties and ambiguities can be managed in some services, in services for people with personality disorder it is more likely to lead to damaging interpersonal dynamics which lead to feelings of personal vulnerability and conflict amongst the leadership team, or, alternatively, diffuse leadership with no one taking ultimate responsibility for decisions. Such dynamics can result in chaos, with senior management being vulnerable to splitting, thus mirroring dynamics within the client group. If this occurs, significant tension will be created within the service which will almost certainly be acted-out by the clients.

One person should carry leadership of the service. To earn the confidence of the staff team, this person must be a clinician with considerable knowledge and experience of working with these clients and who is able to demonstrate that in their work on the unit. The leader needs to be present on the unit and regularly engaged, but not over-involved, with staff and clients. Additionally, the leader should be able to contain, rather than react to, systemic anxiety ever-present on such units.

The leader should be confident enough in themselves and their senior staff team to mostly employ a democratic leadership style, encouraging their team to be part of decision making, informing them about everything that affects their work and sharing decision-making and problem-solving responsibilities.

This style requires the leader to take advice from staff, encouraging healthy debates among senior staff on all key issues, gathering information but holding the responsibility for the final decision. The leader needs to mentor senior staff into becoming highly skilled and experienced; it is when the senior team have such skill and experience that this form of leadership is most effective. Successful democratic leaders need to be able to thank staff for good work, challenge and manage those who are not being effective, and also be strong enough to apologise and admit when they are wrong. This form of leadership is most likely to ensure co-operation, team spirit, and high morale.

Even with strong leadership, there is potential for senior management teams to mirror client pathology and therefore it is essential that the team honestly engage in externally facilitated supervision. The unit leader needs to be part of that supervision and open to accepting both challenges and support equally alongside every other member of the group.

The challenge of supporting staff

'Leadership would be easy to achieve and manage if it weren't for the uncomfortable reality that without followership there could be no leadership' (Obholzer and Miller, 2004, p. 33). Developing the 'followership' in units for people with personality disorder is a definite organisational challenge. Whilst it is frequently articulated that some staff can be more difficult to manage than the clients, it is rarely formally addressed.

Collectively, the pattern of behaviours displayed by staff often mirror those of the client group. There is significant unconscious transference and countertransference whereby staff absorb the suffering and behaviour of the clients. When this goes unrecognised, staff may be drawn into damaging enactments, whilst awareness of these processes provides important insights into the clients. Emulated behaviour includes: complaining excessively about minor issues; jealousies between staff and/or staff groups; behaving in an entitled manner, for example expecting or demanding non-contributory training of their choice; acting in a grandiose manner, such as asserting competence beyond their level of training; or alternatively becoming incapacitated and unable to act up to their level of competence. Some staff become preoccupied thinking of their own stresses and distresses and become over-dependent on their supervisor or another colleague, whist others over-sexualise working relationships, and others become uncharacteristically passive aggressive or even overtly aggressive. Such behaviours need to be seen as a consequence of the environment and not a pathological behaviour located in the individuals. This brings considerable challenges for naïve managers who try to resolve the presenting problems individually, rather than considering them systemically. It is essential that this process is made explicit and that all staff have opportunities to engage in supervision to recognise the patterns and sources of their behaviours (see Chapter 13). When calculating staffing levels, consideration must be given to the extensive supervision required if staff are to be effectively supported in such environments. Whilst this may seem an expensive option, compared to the cost of long-term sickness, staff working below capacity due to burnout, and repeated recruitment drives due to staff resignations, it is cost-effective.

Sexual boundary violations

A significant organisational challenge involves creating environments which minimise the likelihood of sexual boundary violations. People with personality disorder are particularly vulnerable as many engage in flirtation as 'a type of faux-adult attempt to deny feelings of physical and psychological loneliness and to deal with the despair of perceiving themselves to be unwanted or not valued for themselves' (Sarkar, 2004, p. 317). They often have histories of repeated sexual abuse including abuse by professionals. Celenza (1998) identifies the staff most vulnerable to violating boundaries as narcissistically needy, requiring validation by others, finding negative transference such as hatred and anger unbearable, subjugating and 'lovesick', with histories of covert boundary breaches by parental figures. Staff have almost always experienced personal loss or crisis prior to the relationship. Research indicates that a minority are predatory offenders. More commonly, the motivation is unconscious and they describe themselves as 'in love' (Celenza and Gabbard, 2003).

To create safer environments, managers should ensure that there is a culture in which sex and love can be openly talked about rather than driven underground. There should be an open acknowledgement that sexual feelings towards patients and vice versa are commonplace within the therapeutic process and are a focus for supervision and treatment. Boundary violations must be included in training and regularly addressed in supervision (see Chapter 13). All staff need awareness that staff of any profession or position may breach boundaries. Recognising the ubiquitous risk, staff should regularly police each other's interactions with clients, recognising this as protective. Additionally, managers need to monitor the service culture, ensuring that sexuality is not being used as a coping strategy, between staff or between staff and clients. Flirtation can be used to distract from stress, form alliances, feel safe and manage fear of the clients. Such behaviour should be directly addressed and policies need to be rigidly adhered to, including a dress code to prohibit inappropriate clothing for men and women.

If a sexual boundary violation does occur, it is essential that the member of staff is suspended, investigated, reported to the professional body and, if possible, offered ongoing support from the unit. In many situations, the client is also removed from the service, but that can reinforce the damage as the client loses treatment at the time it is most needed. The client should be facilitated to work therapeutically on the abuse that they have experienced by the member of staff. Other clients on the unit need opportunities in therapeutic groups to talk about their feelings, which will be complex. Staff will also have complicated feelings which can be explored in group supervision. The detrimental impact on the trust of staff among clients as well as between different professional groups cannot be overestimated and will require managers to continually monitor the situation and offer time for further resolution as necessary.

The service should be properly accountable

Public accountability

There has been considerable government investment in personality disorder services and a commitment to ensure that the standard of care is of good quality and effective. The organisational challenge is to establish which specific performance indicators are appropriate, as the services have heterogeneous client groups and are diverse in their aims and objectives. Some services attend to management of symptoms and thus have short intervention periods; others address the disordered personality and have longer treatment programmes. Due to their different aims, they have different outcome targets. Consequently, each service needs to develop specific indicators and targets to measure performance against the established aims and objectives of the service.

Performance indicators need to focus on the following areas: clinical effectiveness and outcomes; efficiency; patient/carer experience; and capacity and capability. It is proposed that specific indicators can be determined by mapping them directly onto the operational model and business plan which reflect the priorities set by the treatment model. This structure enables every area of work in the service to be audited. For example, each component of treatment needs to be identified and methods instigated to collect data that indicate change. Data can be analysed annually, as can other data such as number, form and severity of incidents, providing an ongoing measure of clinical effectiveness and some indication of outcomes. Likewise other targets can be formed on the basis of the expectations of service delivery and regularly audited. Data should then be collated, analysed and included in the public annual report.

Importance of accountability for service commissioners

Despite commissioning services for people with severe personality disorder, commissioners are frequently anxious about such services and fluctuate in their support. The reaction of commissioners often follows a parallel process to that of the client group. Clients with severe personality disorder often initially fully commit to treatment but when experiencing any form of challenge want to take greater control or make attempts to devalue the experience, try to withdraw or even behave in ways that ensure removal from treatment, thus 'killing the service off'. When there are challenges of the kind that are inevitable in such services, commissioners tend to become more anxious and active than they do if similar situations arise in mental illness or learning disability services, by becoming more involved in the service, putting people they know into key posts or finding other ways to exert control. They may talk negatively about the service, with little if any evidence, and threaten the existence of the service by withdrawing resources or demanding more of the service than it can provide. In the most extreme cases, the destabilising pressure put on the service by the commissioners can result in service closure or reallocation to a different client group, thus 'killing the service off'.

All services for people with personality disorder inevitably experience situations that commissioners find challenging. As with clients (see Chapter 5), the most appropriate approach is to utilise explicit communication. When setting up the service, frank discussions should be had about the likelihood of this process occurring, but commissioners will also need reminding when this process occurs. The most important safeguard is the data that has been collected via the audit described above. No matter how 'successful' a unit is, if there are no data to support that contention then it is vulnerable.

Summary

By the very nature of their clients' symptoms, services for people with personality disorder will be faced with many challenges. The role of managers is to provide strong knowledgeable leadership whilst working to minimise inevitable tensions both within the service and with partner agencies. Knowledge of the dynamic that these clients generate will allow managers to contain their anxieties and make effective decisions. Managers need to ensure that systems are in place to facilitate strategic planning, governance arrangements, appropriate multidisciplinary decision-making processes, communication and cultural behaviour consistent with the objectives of the service, and to ensure that the environmental needs of staff and service users are met. In particular, they should ensure that the structural, relational and clinical risk management systems are working synergistically to ensure an optimally safe environment, both physically and emotionally.

References

Barlow, K.E., Miller, S. and Norton, K. (2007) Working with people with personality disorder; utilising service users' views. *Psychiatric Bulletin*, **31**, 85–88.

Carr-Walker, P., Bowers, L., Callaghan, P. *et al.* (2004) Attitudes towards personality disorders: comparison between prison officers and psychiatric nurses. *Legal and Criminological Psychology*, **9(2)**, 265–277.

Castillo, H. (2003) *Personality Disorder: Temperament or Trauma?* London: Jessica Kingsley.

Celenza, A. (1998) Precursors to sexual misconduct: preliminary findings. *Psychoanalytic Psychology*, **15**, 378–395.

Celenza, A. and Gabbard, G.O. (2003) Analysts who commit sexual boundary violations: a lost cause? *Journal of the American Psychoanalytic Association*, **51(2)**, 617–636.

Department of Health (1999) *National Service Framework for Mental Health: Modern Standards and Service Models for Mental Health*, HSC 1999/223. Crown Copyright. http://www.dh.gov.uk/en/Publicationsandstatistics/Publications/Publications PolicyAndGuidance/DH_4009598 (accessed October 2008).

Edgar, K. and Rickford, D. (2009) *Too Little, Too Late: An Independent Review of Unmet Mental Health Need in Prison*. London: Prison Reform Trust.

Fallon, P., Bluglass, R. and Edwards, B. (1999) *Report of the Committee of Inquiry into the Personality Disorder Unit, Ashworth Special Hospital*. London: HMSO.

Fazel, S. and Danesh, J. (2002) Serious mental disorder in 23,000 prisoners: a systematic review of 62 surveys. *Lancet*, **16: 359(9306)**, 545–550.

Haney, C., Banks, W.C. and Zimbardo, P.G. (1973) Interpersonal dynamics in a simulated prison. *International Journal of Criminology and Penology*, **1**, 69–97.

Huffington, C., James, K. and Armstrong, D. (2004) What is the emotional cost of distributed leadership? In C. Huffington, D. Armstrong, W. Halton, L. Doyle and J. Pooley (eds), *Working Below the Surface: The Emotional Life of Contemporary Organisations*. London: Karnac, ch. 4.

Livesley, J.W. (2003) *Practical Management of Personality Disorder*. New York: Guilford Press.

Locke, E. (2003) Leadership: starting at the top. In C. Pearce and J. Conger (eds), *Shared Leadership: Reframing the Hows and Whys of Leadership*. London: Sage, ch. 13.

Maltman, L., Stacey, J. and Hamilton, L. (2008) Peaks and troughs: an exploration of patient perspective of dangerous and severe personality disorder assessment. *Personality and Mental Health*, **2**, 7–16.

Mikton, C. and Grounds, A. (2007) Cross-cultural clinical judgment bias in personality disorder diagnosis by forensic psychiatrists in the UK. *Journal of Personality Disorder*, **21(4)**, 400–417.

National Institute for Mental Health in England (NIMHE) (2003) The personality disorder capabilities framework. http://www.spn.org.uk/fileadmin/SPN_uploads/ Documents/Papers/personalitydisorders.pdf (accessed October 2008).

Obholzer, A. and Miller, S. (2004) Leadership, followership and facilitating the creative workforce. In C. Huffington, D. Armstrong, W. Halton, L. Doyle and J. Pooley (eds), *Working Below the Surface: The Emotional Life of Contemporary Organisations*. London: Karnac, ch. 2.

Sarkar, S. (2004) Boundary violation and sexual exploitation in psychiatry and psychotherapy: a review. *Advances in Psychiatric Treatment*, **10**, 312–320.

Zimbardo, P. (2007) *The Lucifer Effect: Understanding How Good People Turn Evil*. New York: Random House.

Chapter 7

Effective transdisciplinary teamworking

Naomi Murphy

Introduction

The notion of working within multidisciplinary teams has become an intrinsic component of health and social care over the last thirty years. Recognition of the importance of co-ordinating services and policies stems back even further (Beveridge Report, 1942).

Within mental health services, the road towards robust multidisciplinary teamwork has proved challenging, and lack of shared understanding of what multidisciplinary teamwork is, as well as profession-specific anxieties about working collectively, has, at times, undermined the NHS drive towards improving co-ordination and delivery of integrated services. Consequently, NHS policy has become increasingly directive about the requirement for multidisciplinary teamwork (e.g. New Ways of Working, 2005) and has embedded the principles of multidisciplinary teamworking within papers designed to guide practice, particularly in relation to the care of people with personality disorder (e.g. *Personality Disorder: No Longer a Diagnosis of Exclusion* (NIMHE, 2003a); *Personality Disorder Capabilities Framework* (NIMHE, 2003b)); NICE guidelines for borderline and antisocial personality disorders (NICE, 2009a, 2009b).

No single definition of multidisciplinary team unites the literature on multidisciplinary teamworking. For some authors, multidisciplinary working is as simple a concept as 'fluid working arrangements . . . [that] consist of members from different professional groups . . . who are working towards a specific and sharply focused goal' (Biggs, 1997, p. 187). Others are more specific and emphasise the need for teams comprised of small numbers of individuals with regular contact between members sharing a collective identity (e.g. Øvretveit, 1985), or for members to have complementary skills and common aims and objectives (e.g. Katzenbach and Smith, 1993).

Since those responsible for developing and implementing services differ according to their understanding of multidisciplinary teamworking, confusion about what constitutes multidisciplinary teamwork is reflected within service provision and in the degree to which commitment to the principles of good multidisciplinary teamworking is demonstrated through preparation and implementation. Consequently, confusion about the roles of each professional group and the day-to-day operation and functioning of teams also persists. This can lead to teams that lack effectiveness and efficiency and can also contribute to the evolution and maintenance of teams that are dysfunctional services for staff to work within and for patients to receive care from. People with personality disorder often highlight existing flaws within mental health care services and exacerbate weaknesses in the operational policies and practices of services, due to a variety of reasons, including a willingness to articulate and pursue complaints (either with or without litigable consequences), and 'splitting' or polarised thinking about staff and their patterns of relating to staff. Therefore, inadequate attention to developing and maintaining strong multidisciplinary teams has the capacity to insidiously weaken the care and treatment that is made available to these patients. Hence, the attention to multidisciplinary teams within National Institute for Mental Health in England (NIMHE) guidance for those working with people with personality disorder.

Despite the focus upon teams within government documentation specific to personality disorder and also the frequent involvement with multiple care-providers which people with personality disorder often experience, there is scant attention to teamworking processes within the general literature base. One notable exception, edited by Sampson, McCubbin and Tyrer (*Personality Disorder and Community Mental Health Teams*, 2006), touches upon several issues that have been thus far neglected, yet only Sampson's excellent chapter specifically focuses upon the application of multidisciplinary teamwork to personality disorder, whilst the remainder of the text addresses more generic issues.

A multidisciplinary approach to personality disorder treatment is firmly endorsed by NHS guidance so this chapter will not be devoted to convincing readers of the legitimacy of multidisciplinary teamworking with these patients. Instead, there will be a brief discussion of the advantages of working within a multidisciplinary team followed by discussion of the challenges that arise in multidisciplinary teamwork across a range of settings highlighting how areas of vulnerability in generic teamworking can be exacerbated when applied to personality disordered individuals. Potential solutions are identified and this author will advocate for services specialising in the care and treatment of people with personality disorders to adopt higher level multidisciplinary teamworking processes to transform their multidisciplinary teams into high performing, transdisciplinary teams.

Why is multidisciplinary teamwork essential in working with people with personality disorder?

Teamwork has flourished within the business sphere due to associations with saving money and increased productivity. Whilst these factors may also be significant in setting up mental health teams, a further six strengths of team-work identified by Robbins and Finley (2000) indicate that teamwork could be even more of a necessity with patients who have more severe psychopathology.

1 Teams do work that one single individual can't

Most people with severe personality disorder have multiple needs requiring intervention. These needs are often interconnected. Multidisciplinary team-work offers a broader skill base to ensure that as many of the patient's needs as necessary can be addressed since no single discipline has the skills to address all of this client group's needs.

2 Teams enhance communication

Close teamwork enables staff to have the necessary communication they need to ensure that their interventions are co-ordinated and complementary rather than duplicated (Hallett and Birchall, 1992 as cited in Biggs, 1997) or undermining of the full treatment package (Moss, 1994).

All homicides by people who have had recent contact with mental health services have been subjected to thorough internal and external reviews since the Ritchie report (Ritchie *et al.*, 1994; Burns, 2006). The process of inquiry is stressful and impacts heavily upon individual caregivers in addition to the institution. Each inquiry has criticised the poor communication between agencies. Burns comments that due to the personality disordered patient's involvement with multiple agencies, there is endless scope for confusion and miscommunication that needs to be reduced.

3 Teams use resources more efficiently

The multiple professions that make up a multidisciplinary team create a wider social network that can be drawn upon for additional resources and knowledge.

4 Teams make higher quality decisions

West's (1994) study of decision making in groups found that although team decision making is inferior to that of the group's most competent member, decisions made by a group are superior to those made by the average group member.

5 Teams offer higher quality services

Opie (1997) highlights how the contribution of professionals offering differ-ent interventions and different knowledge of a client creates more holistic treatment and better informed care plans. Gaps in services are more likely to be identified by service providers and therefore addressed (Hallett and Birchall, 1992).

6 Teams mean improved processes

Good teamwork requires structured, clear processes thus leading to the evolution of more effective ways of working. Processes imported by one discipline may be enhanced when applied by disciplines with a different philosophical background which contribute a different analysis or skill set.

Further benefits

Teamwork is recommended in achieving tasks that require a high level of creativity (Moss, 1994; Fay *et al.*, 2006), and this is arguably the case when attempting to deliver treatment to a patient group who are notoriously difficult to engage and treat and for whom there is currently no single established treatment of choice. Teamwork promotes innovation through the cross-fertilisation of ideas which may raise the performance of some group members. Although West (1994) concluded that individuals working alone produced more ideas and better quality ideas when compared with those brainstorming in groups, Fay *et al.*'s (2006) review of team performance suggested that the impact of team members' diversity depended upon the task to be achieved, and found that when a high level of innovation was required, multidisciplinarity enhanced performance if teams had good team processes.

It has also been suggested that teamwork can be useful in alleviating the anxiety of individual staff members (e.g. Moss, 1994). Arguably, with a client group associated with raised levels of negative emotions in caregivers, teamwork plays an invaluable role in maintaining staff emotions within acceptable limits through opportunities to access emotional support and share responsibility for the well-being of patients who frequently pose a risk to themselves or others. Katzenbach and Smith (1993) highlight how teamwork also allows opportunities for more fun and enjoyment at work which can mitigate the effects of working with other difficult emotions.

People with personality disorder are not only notoriously litigious but many also engage in high risk behaviours (either to themselves or others) that if managed poorly can result in the death of the service user or a member of the public, thus leading to public inquiries into services or loss of professional registration for individual clinicians. Effective multidisciplinary working can offer some safety to service users and clinicians, as well as the larger organisation, by ensuring that the standards of care offered are as high as possible and that treatment decisions are subjected to screening for quality assurance.

The case for transdisciplinary teamworking

Multidisciplinary teamwork has come in for criticism and not solely from those suffering professional anxiety about the sustainability of their discipline. Teamwork has not been well researched for efficacy, which is perhaps unsurprising given the broad range of mental health teams in operation, but this lack of research can give a foothold to those reluctant to engage in teamworking. Analysis of literature on multidisciplinary teamworking exposes a number of vulnerabilities that may undermine the effectiveness of any team.

Lack of shared understanding of what a multidisciplinary team is has contributed to the perception at times that teams don't work. Katzenback and Smith (1993) observe that groups of individuals working together are too easily labelled a 'team', and describe a taxonomy of teams that has as its most efficient the 'high performing team' which entails not only the skills involved in a 'real team', i.e. 'a small number of people with complementary skills who are equally committed to a common purpose, goals and working approach for which they hold themselves mutually accountable', but also 'members who are also deeply committed to one another's personal growth and success' (p. 92).

Opie's (1997) literature review (drawing on Clark, 1994; Rosenfield, 1992; and Sands, 1993) differentiates between multidisciplinary teams, interdisciplinary teams and transdisciplinary teams by suggesting that transdisciplinary teams have a significantly higher level of integration than either multidisciplinary teams (primarily defined by task co-ordination) or interdisciplinary teams (retaining separate disciplinary orientation whilst engaging in joint collaborative work). There is no specific definition of transdisciplinary teamworking within the literature but, for the purpose of this chapter, transdisciplinary teamworking will be defined as a more complex approach to teamworking where team members perform unique roles and integrate their approaches to assessment, formulation and delivery of treatment in order to achieve mutually dependent goals. Transdisciplinary teamworking is characterised by clear channels of communication, robust decision making and good relations between team members and is underpinned by an integrated philosophy, shared values, and clear lines of accountability and responsibility outlined within an explicit operational policy. Opie notes that within transdisciplinary teams, the level of openness and subsequent 'scrutiny' of values and terminology enables the team 'to develop a common language' (1997, p. 263). Antoniadis and Videlock (1991, p. 162) suggest that effective transdisciplinary teamwork requires a strong theoretical base, clear intervention targets, appropriate tools, effective policies and procedures, opportunities for feedback, prescriptive supervision and training and validation of members, as well as a common knowledge base, presence of trust and respect, risk taking and clinical competence.

Teamworking as applied to services for people with personality disorder, or indeed any mental health service, meets the seven criteria that West *et al.* (1998) establish for a 'complex decision-making team' in that: (i) teams are operating in uncertain, unpredictable environments due to frequent changes in social and health care policy; (ii) teams work with uncertain, unpredictable technology due to frequently changing methods of clinical and risk assessment; (iii) teams are unclear how tasks should be performed on a daily basis due to conflict about the aetiology of mental health problems and the lack of a treatment of choice; (iv) teams exhibit a high level of interdependence among team members since no single discipline has the skills to meet all the patient's needs; (v) autonomy and control for teams are high despite policy-makers' attempts to standardise services; (vi) tasks are complex, requiring high levels of expertise and experience; and (vii) there are multiple components of effectiveness and the team is responsible to multiple stakeholders. One would anticipate that effective teamworking within a team forced to make complex decisions would require a higher level of practice than might be expected within services where tasks and decision making are more straightforward, and so one might advocate that high performing transdisciplinary teamworking is a more appropriate model for services catering for people with personality disorder than a simple, multidisciplinary team or inter-disciplinary team.

Creating and maintaining a high performing transdisciplinary team

Sampson (2006) has suggested that services often find it challenging to deal with people with personality disorder not because of the nature of their condition *per se* but rather because the services are not adequately set up to deal with their psychopathology. However, one could argue that such patients merely highlight and exacerbate vulnerabilities that already exist within teams. There are four categories of task involved in developing and maintaining a robust transdisciplinary team: preparing for a team, ensuring the team functions with clarity, reducing unhelpful differences between team members, and ensuring participatory safety. Clearly, the task of preparation needs to start before the other tasks, but all tasks are inter-related and dynamic and thus require continued attention and refinement via team-building and away-days in order that enhanced practices can evolve. Failure to attend to the tasks of transdisciplinary teamwork is likely to reduce any mental health team's effectiveness in meeting the needs of the patients, and this is likely to be more noticeable when the team caters for people with personality disorder.

Category 1: Preparing for a team

Plan team composition

Managers instigating new teams need to be clear about the necessary composition of the team, i.e. numbers of staff and disciplines to be represented in light of the needs of the client group. In many instances, new teams are created with generic posts that can theoretically be occupied by anyone from a core mental health profession. The idea of generic mental health workers is argued against under 'Roles' below. Although team members should have some freedom to establish how their roles will integrate, those instigating new teams should have some rationale for the team composition they have arrived at, rather than planning a team with generic posts.

Between five and eight members is identified as the optimum number of team members, as individuals feel less involved and committed in larger groups (Handy, 1993; Borrill *et al.*, 2000). Because the consequences of errors with this patient group can have disastrous effects, staff can attempt to avoid responsibility for decisions and try to hide within large groups, whilst staff new to this patient group, perhaps feeling deskilled, may find a large group too intimidating a forum within which to expose their lack of knowledge.

Staff selection

In Chapter 2, Murphy and McVey identify skills and qualities that are desirable in staff working with people with personality disorder (a desire to work with this client group, good emotional regulation skills, capacity for self-reflection including an ability to admit to errors, high self-esteem, a robust professional identity, possessing a psychological understanding of the patient, an ability to set limits empathically, a tendency to embrace therapeutic challenges, capacity to be emotionally honest, to see the vulnerability in the patient and to be able to identify true progress). When staff are required to work within teams, additional attributes are of benefit. Katzenbach and Smith (1993) highlight the need to ensure that teams are comprised of staff with a combination of strengths in the areas of technical expertise, problem-solving/decision-making skills and interpersonal skills (in order to ensure effective communication and constructive conflict). Having a robust but not rigid professional identity, being flexible, capacity to attach to a team, awareness that within a team the whole can be greater than the sum of its parts and that teamwork offers the potential for professional growth of the self and others, an ability to articulate professional knowledge in a way that is accessible to others, an ability to manage conflict in an open way and an ability to recognise when co-operation is in danger of becoming collusion might also be desirable attributes in transdisciplinary team members.

Katzenbach and Smith (1993) highlight types of staff who should not be selected for teams – those who lack conviction that teams work and those who are personally uncomfortable operating in groups. These characteristics are difficult to establish during interview as most clinicians are astute enough to recognise that the ability to 'teamwork' is valued and may not even recognise their own limitations in this area. However, an appreciation of the potential employee's capacity to function in groups can be gained by assigning an observable groupwork task to all applicants, thus providing richer information about each applicant's suitability for teamwork.

Staff training

Whilst it may be desirable to employ staff with experience of working within a specialist personality disorder team wherever possible, in reality, it is hard to attract enough experienced staff to fill an entire team. Murphy and McVey (Chapter 2) suggest that supporting staff in acquiring technical knowledge such as awareness of the aetiology, symptoms and treatment of personality disorder can be done in post if necessary and there are benefits in encouraging the team members to devise their own strategy for increasing their knowledge base (see 'Reducing unhelpful differences' below). More important, in the initial stage of establishing a new team, are opportunities for team members to participate in teamworking training.

It is often assumed that staff acquire the skills for teamworking when completing their core professional training. In practice, most disciplines do not receive team-specific training but are instead expected to learn the skills for effective teamworking by observing their supervisor. Until teamworking is routinely taught to all mental health professionals, preferably within a multidisciplinary environment as suggested in the *Personality Disorder Capabilities Framework*, it is likely that all professionals will have some outstanding teamwork training needs. Suggestions for training include team-building processes such as team dynamics, team goals, role expectations, problem-solving, decision making, communication skills, conflict management and interdependence (e.g. Abelson and Woodman, 1983; Alston, 1974; Anderlini, 1983; Butler and Maher, 1981). Whilst some of this training can be provided once the team is running, training in what a transdisciplinary team is, and how it functions, might be required to mould the expectations of new staff and enable them to participate in shaping up the team.

Orientation of new staff

Providing orientation for new team members in order for them to develop an understanding of the team's processes, philosophy and functioning is likely to improve the ability of new staff to be integrated within an existing team. However, the inclusion of new staff is also likely to require adjustments on the part of existing team members, as essentially a new group is formed with even one new staff member, and opportunities should be created that enable all to adjust by offering a period of reflection where members are encouraged to consider the impact the change will mean for them and their role.

Category 2: Establishing clarity

Membership

There need to be clearly identifiable members who commit to attending all core team activities if members are to establish trust amongst one another. Services operating with fluctuating members who 'bob in and out' are unlikely to get a commitment from these members and they are unlikely to be relied upon by core team members. Whilst part-time workers should not be excluded, Richards and Rees's (1998) study suggested that teams comprised mainly of part-time workers undermine team processes.

Accountability

Robust teams require clear lines of responsibility and accountability. Although intended as empowering, attempts to be non-hierarchical often lead to an absence of structure, and practices such as having a 'rolling chair' create operational difficulties and stress when staff are inadequately prepared for the task (Brown *et al.*, 2000). Lack of a clear leader is also associated with lack of clear objectives and team functioning (Richards and Rees, 1998). The absence of someone carrying additional authority within a team can mean that undesirable tasks are not fulfilled (Lang, 1982) and that incompetence is not addressed, as many profession managers pay less attention to staff assigned to teams than to staff whose day-to-day work they control directly. Therefore, lack of leadership within a team poses problems as management issues can go unnoticed outside the team and fail to be addressed (Øvretveit, 1997). Hierarchy is only problematic when associated with a rigid, top-down management style (Onyett, 2003).

Because work with people with personality disorder leaves little room for error, a team leader is required to ensure smooth functioning of the team. The leader's role is to optimise the performance of the team and its members by ensuring that, through liaison with profession managers when needed, the tasks for transdisciplinary teamworking are fulfilled and the requirements of the team, external managers and the broader service are met. The leader's role is not to manage team members but to ensure that all staff support the operational policy and contribute to its implementation as appropriate given their knowledge, skills and expertise. Leaders need to provide profession managers with adequate information for the member to be appropriately supported if necessary. Theoretically, leadership can be shared, but this will only be effective if each leader takes equal responsibility for performing the role.

In some teams it has been assumed, at least by medical members, that they will take the role of team leader (Reed *et al.*, 2000). This has caused friction with other team members as the burden of Responsible Medical Officer status and associated anxiety has led some psychiatrists to adopt behaviours that their colleagues find intolerably controlling. *New Ways of Working* (CSIP/NIMHE/CWP, 2005) clarifies what was previously established in the Nodder Report (DHSS, 1980), that doctors are 'not accountable for the actions of other clinicians in the team' (p. 17). Leaders should be selected for their personal qualities rather than perceived senior status, should be trusted by those above them and have authority from below (Onyett, 2003) as well as from within (Obholzer, 1994).

The skills of both transactional leadership (organising, planning and problem-solving) and transformational leadership (innovating, creating and challenging orthodoxy) are required in team leaders (Bass *et al.*, 1996; Alimo-Metcalfe, 1999). In addition, leaders require the ability to demonstrate effective involvement with patients, and should be able to communicate high expectations and confidence in staff and identify overall goals for the team (House, 1976 in Watts and Bennett, 1983). Katzenbach and Smith (1993) highlight the need for leaders to be industrious, to believe they cannot succeed without the combined contributions of the team members, and to be capable of striking the balance between guidance and relinquishing control. Leadership of the team also requires a calm enough temperament to be able to contain strong emotions that are evoked within a team (which is particularly pertinent in working with these patients) whilst absorbing pressure external to the team. Onyett (2003) draws attention to how difficult and lonely a position this is.

Other team members need to be clear about what their own responsibilities to the team are and these should be established within the operational policy (BPS, 2001), since explicitly stating who is responsible for each task makes accountability transparent (Watts and Bennett, 1983), thus enhancing performance and the likelihood of tasks being completed. Responsibility to the operational policy will need to be negotiated with the profession manager in order to enable the member to meet responsibilities outside the team.

Roles

A desire to ensure equal rights for all team members has often led to the assumption of (or aspiration towards) team members having equal skills, with some teams employing generic mental health workers in the main (Anciano and Kirkpatrick, 1990). Within such teams, referrals are primarily allocated according to team members' 'interest' or caseload rather than on the basis of expertise (Lang, 1982; Patmore and Weaver, 1991).

Some disciplines have been more attracted to the generic mental health role than others. Reports by the Department of Health (1994) and Sainsbury's

Centre (SCMH, 1997) found that occupational therapists, nurses and social workers were most prone to role blurring. There is little evidence to support the blurring of roles within teams. Indeed, role blurring is associated with role strain and confusion (Moller and Harber, 1996), poor relationships between team members (Brown and Wade, 1987) and lack of inter-professional collaboration (Norman and Peck, 1999). Typically, within role blurring, one discipline claims specialist skills that are traditionally part of another's core training. This raises anxiety among team members and leads to competitiveness or professional narcissism and may also result in some individuals offering work that is outside their sphere of competence. In addition, role blurring erodes professional identity, devalues those disciplines that opt for generic working and can lead to alienation from core professional groups. Within such teams, workers typically volunteer to take the patient and a worker's selection is rarely challenged.

Research by Deschamps and Brown (1983) found that groups are more successful when the social identities of their members are preserved, and the SCMH report concluded it was unhelpful to break down professional identities. It acknowledged that despite the need to address ideological differences, there was a need to celebrate differences and the varied contributions of each discipline. Whilst a significant proportion of skills are basic and belong to all, a healthy mix of specialist and generic skills must be maintained. Bowen et al. (1985) highlight the importance of every team member having a unique skill or knowledge base which is made explicit and respected within the team.

A team comprised of staff with diverse roles is essential when working with people with personality disorder. Because much of the treatment for this patient group is driven by psychological principles, there is a tendency for all staff to feel under pressure to offer psychological treatment. However, in the context of a disorder that can impair one's ability to form healthy, stable relationships, to accept adult responsibilities, to cope with emotions and to perform activities of daily living, it is undesirable that intervention consists entirely of medication and formal psychological therapy. There are appropriate roles for other disciplines in treating people with personality disorder. Arguably part of the role of the psychologist is to share their skills in order to enable other disciplines to use psychological principles to shape their own role (see Chapter 12) and for other disciplines to be creative about the form their role should take (guidance on the roles of key disciplines is included elsewhere within this book).

Confusion and misunderstanding of roles by all disciplines is rife, so explicit discussion of roles is important in the evolution of the team and should be a dynamic process to help inexperienced or singleton-post staff clarify their role with support from their own professional group.

Within forensic services, teams have the additional difficulty of finding ways for staff to resolve the role conflict that arises due to the competing requirements of caregiving and security. Regular discussions about these themes can assist inexperienced staff in finding a way to resolve this dilemma and ensure that, when applicable, the team are able to think about the patient as both a victim and an offender.

Operational policy and procedures

A clear operational policy which is regularly reviewed and updated is essential if a robust team is to be established and evolve. Lack of clear operational policies is linked to role strain due to ambiguity and causes reliance upon operational policies and procedures utilised in other areas of the service that may not account for the psychopathology of people with personality disorder.

An operational policy requires a clear definition of the team, the aims of the team and the core values on which those aims are based. The aims need to be translated into achievable and measurable objectives. Referral and discharge pathways need to be clearly identified as well as acceptance and exclusion criteria. The operational policy should include explicit statements about the core roles, responsibilities and accountability relationships of each discipline within the team as well as the team leader. The relationship between the team, the host institution and other service providers should also be clearly specified.

In providing a service to people who struggle with self-hatred, there are advantages to having clearly identified procedures for managing any routine tasks where discrepancies may indicate a patient falling back into the cycle of rejection. For instance, this author works in a service where all individual therapy sessions last exactly fifty minutes. Strict policing of this policy highlights cases where staff are frightened of patients (short-changing the patients) or struggling to manage their demands (providing extra time). The policy ensures that all patients are offered an equitable treatment package (all are offered weekly individual therapy and it is not acceptable to cancel a day's appointments – these must be re-arranged; therapists remain in the session even if the patient does not, thus ensuring patients do not feel discriminated against or prioritised). The focus of policies and procedures will vary from service to service depending upon the function and setting of the team but, at a minimum, we would argue for clearly written policies addressing each of the interventions on offer, formal complaints of patients, confidentiality and communication and decision-making pathways in support of the operational policy.

Communication and decision making

Teams require regular meetings with clear structure and format. Aids such as written agendas with some standard agenda items reflecting the context can help establish norms for effective and efficient participation. Staff whose experience of teams is restricted to participation in ward rounds may feel under pressure to discuss each patient each week. Since personality disordered patients are unlikely to show a rapid improvement, weekly discussion is not necessary unless the person is experiencing an episode of crisis. Instead, within an inpatient setting, it may be more practical to establish a rota to ensure each service user is discussed at regular intervals, and have standard agenda items such as applications for ground leave, bedroom access or visits, review of increased observations, forthcoming Mental Health Review Tribunals, and patients presenting as if in crisis. Appropriate documentation should be developed to ensure accurate records of reviews and decisions (including the rationale) are kept and systems established for the collection of appropriate data.

Since meetings require regular and punctual attendance by members, annual and study leave require co-ordination and non-attendance requires addressing. Good meetings are well chaired, identify the key questions and encourage the participation of all members whilst remaining focused. Whilst chairing the meeting may naturally fall to the leader, others may take responsibility for tasks such as completing a particular type of documentation. Teams have been criticised for the consistency of decision making (Ysseldyke and Algozzine, 1979) and level of participation of some staff (Abelson and Woodman, 1983), but De Dreu (2002) observed that teams which reflected upon their communication processes and working methods were better able to use ideas voiced by minority members. Adair (1986) identified ten processes that occur in teams when decisions are required. These range from avoidance of decision making ('apathy') through 'self-authorised authority' (where one individual decides and the group goes along with this for an easy life), 'topic-jumping' (confusing the group about what decision is being made) and 'majority views' (the team vote although there may still be significant dissent), to 'true consensus'. Whilst true consensus is time-consuming and may not always be possible,

> it occurs when communication has been sufficiently open for all to feel they have had a fair chance to influence decision and the 'feeling of the meeting' emerges without voting ... the most important test is that everyone is prepared to *act* as though it was their preferred solution.
>
> (Adair, 1986, pp. 68–69)

Willingness to act on decisions is used by Adair to differentiate between true and false consensus. If the team engages in poor decision-making processes, this should be discussed at the meeting to ensure that the team's ability to make decisions is protected. Teams should also avoid making decisions about patients outside the regular meetings where all staff are present, unless necessary to avoid imminent crisis. Failure to protect the team meeting as the appropriate decision-making forum contributes to staff being groomed for *ad hoc* decisions in the absence of fuller information which may be provided by other team members. This increases the chance of poor decision making which they may later be accountable for and which may impact negatively upon the patient's care and well-being as well as relationships with team members who may feel excluded and undermined.

Good decision making requires good information and consideration should be given to how much sharing of information is necessary when working with people with personality disorder. The idea that information should only be shared if directly related to risk is often too narrowly interpreted to be protective. For example, an inexperienced therapist failed to disclose to the team that an inpatient had been sexually abused by his mother as a child. Whilst the therapist was on holiday, the patient's mother visited. When a nurse encouraged the patient to hug his mother, the patient seriously assaulted him. Within an inpatient service, where all multidisciplinary staff will have at least some informal contact with the patient and be involved in decisions about his or her care, information should be shared as needed. This should be reflected within the confidentiality policy and discussed openly. Patients with a history of sexual abuse often associate secrets with abuse and shame and so can find increased openness reassuring and protective. At times, patients will 'test' staff by saying they wish to confide information that cannot be disclosed elsewhere. The staff member who responds by saying 'I can't promise that I won't need to disclose whatever you want to tell me to other team members' rarely finds this information being withheld from them and is often able to utilise this situation therapeutically.

Teams must consider how decisions are communicated to patients. Inexperienced team members, drawn into sharing their own opinions and leaking information about the views of others, can undermine the decision-making process and the safety of another team member. Inexperienced staff may feel there is nothing wrong with sharing their initial opinion about a decision prior to the meeting. However, to do so may lead to patients interpreting that someone else has been more powerful in the meeting (if the opinion offered is not the end outcome) rather than that their opinion changed due to healthy debate and the team member's attention being drawn to related but previously unconsidered issues. Disclosing to the patient the contributions of other members to the decision-making process can create the impression that some staff are 'soft touches' or others are 'tough', and leaves these members unsafe; they may be pressurised prior to forthcoming meetings or conversely receive all a patient's wrath when a decision is not the patient's desired outcome. Generally, it is good practice for two members to represent the team when disclosing decisions as this prevents the patient associating the decision with the news-bearer. Within a prison-based service, it has been helpful to ensure one member is employed by the prison and one by the NHS, to ensure that splits are not created between staff working for different agencies.

Relations with host organisation

Although teams are more likely to flourish within a nurturing, organisational environment (Webb and Hobdell, 1980), teams often lack clear guidance and support from external managers and the broader organisation (Sampson, 2006). Teams need to clarify relations with the host institution and identify resources they can access when necessary. Operational policies throughout mental health services rarely account for the psychopathology of personality disordered people, and the importance of ensuring that the specialist team's policies dovetail with those of other services cannot be overestimated. Collaborative work should be undertaken with other service providers to ensure that general organisational policies (e.g. complaints procedure) meet the needs of patients with both mental illness and personality disorder wherever possible.

Category 3: Reducing unhelpful differences

Ensuring common catchment/client group

New teams often inherit several acceptance criteria and catchment areas which need to be redefined, streamlined and owned by the team to ensure consistency.

Shared goals

Without shared goals, individual clinicians may undermine the overall treatment package and are unlikely to feel connected to other members.

Shared philosophy

Teamwork with personality disordered service users often entails multiple agencies and systems as well as multiple disciplines, so NHS employees may find themselves working with social service or National Offender Management Service employees. Education about the philosophical background of all team members is necessary for the team to arrive at a philosophy and statement of values that integrates and respects each philosophical background and can be incorporated within the operational policy. The team need to reflect upon differences that are not easily accommodated, consider the impact these have upon the team and practice and, where possible, reflect these within the operational policy. For example, within a prison setting, it is not unusual for prison officers to refer to prisoners by their surname, a practice which is antithetical to clinical care. One service overtly challenged the practice of clinical staff referring to the service user in this manner but did not comment on the practice when utilised by officers. The rationale was that the clinicians were employed within the territory of the officers, which should be respected, and that clinicians should role-model respect of their patients rather than impose their own philosophy. Over time most operational staff routinely referred to prisoners by their forename.

The team philosophy needs to embrace diversity and be intolerant of hostility and prejudice. A culture of openness and curiosity should be encouraged through non-confrontational discourse and inquisitive questioning. Reflection upon difference can reveal underlying attitudes and assumptions that can actually be resolved, or at least tolerated. Within the above example, referring to prisoners by their forenames carried the risk of clinicians being perceived as 'soft' and vulnerable to being groomed. Explaining the rationale for this practice to officers meant that even those who were most resistant to using forenames themselves were able to tolerate this practice by others.

People with personality disorder often elicit rejection from service providers, hence the need for *Personality Disorder: No Longer a Diagnosis of Exclusion* (NIMHE, 2003a). Much of the hostility of clinicians towards people with personality disorder stems from lack of understanding of personality disorder and confusion about whether it is treatable or untreatable. There is little sense to a personality disorder service that is unable to identify the vulnerability and need in this patient group and unable to be optimistic that treatment has something to offer. This should be reflected within the operational policy and within the discourse of the team.

Some shared knowledge

Theoretically different approaches to assessment and treatment have the potential to split a team if unresolved since objectives and working methods are often derived from these models (Norman and Peck, 1999) and professional identities are bound up in theoretical approaches. For all members to have identical knowledge and skills would be undesirable and remove the need for a multidisciplinary team. However, if team members are working with radically different ideas about causation and treatment, it is inevitable that conflicting interventions will be offered.

Teamwork needs to be completed to establish an integrated theoretical framework that all staff can work within. That is not to suggest that staff need to lay aside their theoretical orientation; instead team members need to establish whether there is overlap and where there is knowledge they could benefit from elsewhere within the team. An integrated approach ought to be holistic with different disciplines offering expertise in different areas of treatment. Theoretically diverse understandings of causation and approaches to assessment and treatment can be integrated successfully when a biopsychosocial model is adopted (e.g. Chapter 4). Engaging in knowledge sharing and actively discussing theoretical differences enables staff who remain sceptical about other theoretical approaches to focus their treatment efforts within an area that is most suited to their expertise, and allows differences to remain open for discussion.

Adopting an integrated theoretical framework and establishing *some* common knowledge does not necessitate duplication of roles. All staff should have some understanding of personality disorder psychopathology, aetiology and assessment as well as interventions offered by other team members. New knowledge can also be used to enhance existing roles. For example, Murphy and McVey (2001) describe how the principles of Young's schema-focused therapy can be used to guide nursing interactions, and they have since used this approach within prisons to shape the interactions of officers.

In addition to enhancing team cohesion, establishing a common theoretical framework allows scope for sharing generic treatment principles, for example formulation and evaluation of interventions. Murphy and McVey identify other important principles to optimise treatment (see Chapter 5) that cut across theoretical orientation and types of intervention.

Category 4: Participatory safety

Establish high frequency interaction

The importance of frequent interaction between members cannot be over-estimated. High frequency interaction is associated with increased sharing of ideas, opinions and perspectives and therefore greater creativity (Drach-Zahavy and Somech, 2001). This may occur because members feel safe which increases the ability of all members to feel able to contribute especially if the ideas are uncommon or risk is unpopular (Edmondson *et al.*, 2001). Resistance to novel ideas is reduced when staff interaction is high (Wilkinson, 1973).

Spatial proximity to others increases opportunities for interaction, suggesting that a shared base is advantageous. However, some effort is necessary to ensure that this assumption is actualised. Ensuring that all staff attend briefings/de-briefings allows staff to deepen their working relationships as well as enabling good channels of communication. Peer supervision, journal clubs and shared teaching all afford higher frequency interactions. Opportunities for informal contact are also necessary; when contact is limited to technical discussions, burnout is higher then when contact is of a more informal nature (Pines *et al.*, 1981).

Borrill *et al.*'s (2000) team research found that membership was associated with improved mental health particularly when there was clarity about team objectives and roles. Community staff rated teamwork among their strongest sources of reward (Carson *et al.*, 1995; Knapp *et al.*, 1992; Onyett *et al.*, 1995), and with patients who find it difficult to convey gratitude and make slow progress, peers may draw attention to small signs of progress that may be hard to recognise when one is immersed in treatment with the patient.

Teamwork has been highlighted as a way of coping (Jayaratine and Chess, 1984; Knapp *et al.*, 1992). Working with people with personality disorder elicits strong emotions in staff and having an identifiable peer group who relate to the issues that arise in relation to clinical practice can be invaluable and assist individual practitioners in managing their emotions honestly (by tolerating feelings of vulnerability) rather than diverting them into anger towards the patient.

Ensure adaptive conflict resolution

Some conflict is essential to ensure effective transdisciplinary teamworking, and there are problems associated with teams that lack conflict as well as those with excessive conflict (Onyett, 2003; Watts and Bennett, 1983). Lack of conflict is associated with poor decision making arising from collusion and may prevent rigorous debate, thus impacting upon creativity, sound decision making, team morale and productivity (Runde and Flanagan, 2008). Fay *et al.*'s (2006) analysis of theories on social identity suggests that team members may undermine the potential benefits of their multidisciplinarity by trying to simplify the world and establish sameness, thus losing the innovation that can be a feature of a robust team.

Strong team identification can lead to team boundaries being too sharply defined; team members are understood and shown respect, but outsiders may be misunderstood and denigrated. With a patient group characterised by hostility, there is the risk that the patient group become identified as the enemy, and this can be seen in the pejorative language (e.g. 'evil' and 'manipulative') adopted by some staff when discussing them.

Teams lacking conflict may be avoiding addressing power imbalances that exist within the group (Lang, 1982). Failure to address conflicts of power or competitive interests openly may cause tension and acting out within the team and reduces the opportunity for addressing underlying issues such as lack of trust. If conflict cannot be tolerated openly, there may be an accumulation of hostile and ambivalent feelings and this could lead to destructive processes such as scapegoating and the development of an in-group and an out-group. Conflict and competitiveness are likely to be significant features of teams working with people with personality disorder, as such patients often present as intensely angry and competitive and this can be experienced within the staff team (Thorndycroft and McCabe, 2008).

Healthy teams address conflict adaptively through management rather than suppression or avoidance (West and Farr, 1989; Runde and Flanagan, 2008). The whole team must take responsibility for addressing conflict. Much of the tension within teams arises from conflict about roles and responsibilities (Braga, 1972). Having these clarified explicitly within the operational policy allows potential sources of conflict to be discussed openly. Few professionals are taught skills for healthy conflict resolution (Runde and

Flanagan, 2008). By addressing conflict resolution within the operational policy and ensuring there is adequate space for open discussion of differences in opinion, attitudes and values, an environment is created that is better equipped to protect the team's capacity to make innovative, robust decisions whilst protecting the mental health of its members. Open discussion about the best way to resolve conflict also allows participants to acquire conflict resolution skills for future settings.

Protect integrity of team

People with personality disorder are prone to misinterpreting information or quoting information out of context in order to protect their dysfunctional beliefs (e.g. 'No one will ever care for me') and keep their world predictable and manageable. Teams with strong relationships between team members can generally tell when their colleagues may have been misquoted or misunderstood, which prevents staff inadvertently colluding with patients against their colleagues. Transference reactions may cause people with personality disorder to assume staff ineptitude in the absence of evidence. It is important that staff do not collude with the 'running down' of colleagues. If the patient has a genuine complaint they should be supported in making a formal complaint against the staff member, but unsubstantiated complaints should not be colluded with and should be discussed openly within the team in an attempt to understand the negative discourse. If staff perceive the patient's grumblings as reflecting reality this needs to be voiced.

Teamwork creates opportunities to maintain the physical safety of members as operational policies can be devised for home visiting that are relatively easy and practical to implement. Co-working is also a useful option with patients who routinely present as frightening, and decision making by a team (if processes are adhered to and decisions upheld) can protect staff from the risk to their professional integrity of litigation.

Summary

Transdisciplinary teams are an essential component of treatment of people with personality disorder with multiple treatment needs. Failure to attend to the tasks involved in transdisciplinary teamwork is likely to lead to a poorly functioning team and impact negatively upon the mental health of both service users and team members. In order to ensure the team functions effectively, work must be completed to ensure the team is adequately prepared for, has clarity of membership, accountability, roles, operational policies/procedures, communication and decision-making pathways, and clear relations with other services. Team members need a common catchment area/client group, common goals and philosophy, shared knowledge and participatory safety.

References

Abelson, M.A. and Woodman, R.W. (1983) Review of research on team effectiveness: implications for teams in schools. *School Psychology Review*, **12**, 123–136.

Adair, J. (1986) *Effective Teambuilding*. London: Pan Books.

Alimo-Metcalfe, B. (1999) Leadership in the NHS: what are the competencies and qualities needed and how can they be developed? In L.M. Annabelle and S. Dopson (eds), *Organisational Behaviour in Health Care*. Basingstoke: Macmillan Business, pp. 135–151.

Alston, P.P. (1974) Multidiscipline group facilitation training: an aid to the team approach. *Rehabilitation Counselling Bulletin*, **18**, 21–25.

Anciano, D. and Kirkpatrick, A. (1990) CMHTs and clinical psychology: the death of a profession. *Clinical Psychology Forum*, **26**, 9–12.

Anderlini, L.S. (1983) An inservice program for improving team participation in educational decision-making. *School Psychology Review*, **12**, 160–167.

Antoniadis, A. and Videlock, J. (1991) In search of teamwork: a transactional approach to team functioning. *The Transdisciplinary Journal*, **1(2)** 157–167.

Bass, B.M., Avolio, B.J. and Atwater, L. (1996) The transformational and transactional leadership of men and women. *Applied Psychology: An International Review*, **45(1)**, 5–34.

Beveridge, W. (1942) *Social Insurance and Allied Services*, Cm. 6404. London: HMSO.

Biggs, S. (1997) Interprofessional collaboration: problems and prospects. In J. Øvretveit, P. Mathias and T. Thompson (eds), *Interprofessional Working for Health and Social Care*. Basingstoke: Macmillan, ch. 9.

Borrill, C.S., Carletta, J., Carter, A.J. *et al.* (2000) *The Effectiveness of Health Care Teams in the National Health Service*. Birmingham: Aston University.

Bowen, W.T., Marler, D.C. and Androes, C. (1985) The psychiatric team: myth and mystique. *American Journal of Psychiatry*, **122**, 687–690.

Braga, J.L. (1972) Role theory, cognitive dissonance theory and the inter-disciplinary team. *Interchange*, **3**, 69–78.

British Psychological Society (BPS) (2001) *Working in Teams*. Leicester: BPS.

Brown, R. and Wade, G. (1987) Superordinate goals and intergroup behaviour: the effect of role ambiguity and status on intergroup attitudes and task performance. *European Journal of Social Psychology*, **17**, 131–142.

Brown, B., Crawford, P. and Darongkamas, J. (2000) Blurred roles and permeable boundaries: the experience of multidisciplinary working in community mental health. *Health and Social Care in the Community*, **8(6)**, 425–435.

Burns, T. (2006) An introduction to Community Mental Health Teams (CMHT): how do they relate to people with personality disorders? In M.J. Sampson, R.A. McCubbin and P. Tyrer (eds), *Personality Disorder and Community Mental Health Teams*. London: Wiley, ch. 9.

Butler, A.S. and Maher, C.A. (1981) Conflict and special service teams: perspectives and suggestions for school psychologists. *Journal of School Psychology*, **19(1)**, 62–70.

Care Services Improvement Partnership (CSIP)/National Institute for Mental Health in England (NIMHE), Changing Workforce Programme (CWP) and Royal College of Psychiatrists (2005) *New Ways of Working for Psychiatrists*. London: CSIP/NIMHE/CWP/RCP.

Carson, J., Fagin, L. and Ritter, S. (eds) (1995) *Stress and Coping in Mental Health Nursing*. London: Chapman and Hall.

Clark, P. (1994) Social, professional and educational values on the interdisciplinary team: implications for gerontological and geriatric education. *Educational Gerontology*, **20**, 53–61.

De Dreu, C.W.K. (2002) Team innovation and team effectiveness: the importance of minority dissent and reflexivity. *European Journal of Work and Organizational Psychology*, **11**, 285–298.

Department of Health (1994) *Working in Partnership: A Collaborative Approach to Care*. London: HMSO.

Department of Health and Social Security (DHSS) (1980) *Organisational and Management Problems of Psychiatric Hospitals*. London: HMSO.

Deschamps, J.C. and Brown, R. (1983) Superordinate goals and intergroup conflict. *British Journal of Social Psychology*, **22**, 189–195.

Drach-Zahavy, A. and Somech, A. (2001) Understanding team innovation: the role of team processes and structures. *Group Dynamics: Theory, Research and Practice*, **5**, 111–123.

Edmondson, A.C., Bohmer, R.M. and Pisano, G.P. (2001) Disrupted routines: team learning and new technology implementation in hospitals. *Administrative Science Quarterly*, **46**, 685–716.

Fay, D., Borrill, C., Amir, Z., Haward, R. and West, M. (2006) Getting the most out of multidisciplinary teams: a multi-sample study of team innovation in health care. *Journal of Occupational and Organizational Psychology*, **79**, 553–567.

Hallett, C. and Birchall, E. (1992) *Co-ordination and Child Protection: A Review of the Literature*. Edinburgh: HMSO.

Handy, C. (1993) *Understanding Organisations*. Harmondsworth: Penguin Books.

Jayaratne, S. and Chess, W.A. (1984) The effects of emotional support on perceived job stress and strain. *Journal of Applied Behavioral Science*, **20**, 141–153.

Katzenbach, J.R. and Smith, D.K. (1993) *The Wisdom of Teams*. London: McGraw-Hill.

Knapp, M., Cambridge, P., Thomason, C., Allen, C., Beecham, J. and Darton, R. (1992) *Care in the Community: Challenge and Demonstration*. Aldershot: Gower.

Lang, C.L. (1982) The resolution of status and ideological conflicts in a community mental health setting. *Psychiatry*, **45**, 159–171.

Moller, M.D. and Harber, J. (1996) Advanced practice in psychiatric nursing: the need for a blended role. *Online Journal of Issues in Nursing*. http://www.nursingworld.org/MainMenuCategories/ANAMarketplace/ANA Periodicals/OJIN/TableofContents/Vol21997/No1Jan97/ArticlePreviousTopic/AdvancedPracticePsychiatricNursing.aspx

Moss, R. (1994) Community mental health teams: a developing culture. *Journal of Mental Health*, **3**, 167–174.

Murphy, N. and McVey, D. (2001) Nursing personality disordered inpatients: a schema-focused approach. *British Journal of Forensic Practice*, **13(4)**, 8–15.

National Institute for Health and Clinical Excellence (2009a) *Antisocial Personality Disorder: NICE Clinical Guideline 77*. London: NICE.

National Institute for Health and Clinical Excellence (2009b) *Borderline Personality Disorder: NICE Clinical Guideline 78*. London: NICE.

National Institute for Mental Health in England (NIMHE) (2003a) *Personality Disorder: No Longer a Diagnosis of Exclusion*. London: NIMHE.

National Institute for Mental Health in England (NIMHE) (2003b) *Personality Disorder Capabilities Framework*. London: NIMHE.

Norman, I.J. and Peck, E. (1999) Working together in adult community mental health services: an inter-professional dialogue. *Journal of Mental Health*, **8(3)**, 217–230.

Obholzer, A. (1994) Authority, power and leadership. In A. Obholzer and V.Z. Roberts (eds), *The Unconscious at Work*. London: Routledge, p. 39–47.

Onyett, S.R. (2003) *Teamworking in Mental Health*. Basingstoke: Palgrave Macmillan.

Onyett, S.R., Heppleston, T. and Muijen, M. (1995) *Making Community Mental Health Teams Work*. London: SCMH.

Opie, A. (1997) Thinking teams thinking clients: issues of discourse and representation in the work of healthcare teams. *Sociology of Health and Illness*, **19(3)**, 259–280.

Øvretveit, J. (1985) *Organizational Issues in Multi-disciplinary Team Working*. Uxbridge: Brunel Institute of Organisation and Social Studies.

Øvretveit, J. (1997) How to describe interprofessional working. In J. Øvretveit, P. Mathias and T. Thompson (eds), *Interprofessional Working for Health and Social Care*. Basingstoke: Macmillan, ch. 1.

Patmore, C. and Weaver, T. (1991) Unnatural selection. *Health Services Journal*, **101(5273)**, 20–22.

Pines, A.M., Aronson, E. and Kafry, D. (1981) *Burnout*. New York: Free Press.

Reed, J., Conneely, J., Ranger, S. and Knibbs, J. (2000) A methodology to explore the functioning of multidisciplinary teams. *Clinical Psychology Forum*, **146**, 21–25.

Richards, A. and Rees, A. (1998) Developing criteria to measure the effectiveness of community mental health teams. *Mental Health Care*, **21(1)**, 14–17.

Ritchie, J., Dick, D. and Lingham, R. (1994) *Report of the Inquiry into the Care and Treatment of Christopher Clunis*. London: HMSO.

Robbins, H. and Finley, M. (2000) *Why Teams Don't Work*. London: Texere.

Roberts, V.Z. (1998) Is authority a dirty word? In A. Foster and V.Z. Roberts (eds), *Managing Mental Health in the Community: Chaos and Containment*. London: Routledge, ch. 4.

Rosenfield, P. (1992) The potential of transdisciplinary research for sustaining linkages between the health and social sciences. *Social Science and Medicine*, **35(11)**, 1343–1357.

Runde, C.E. and Flanagan, T.A. (2008) *Building Conflict Competent Teams*. San Francisco: Jossey Bass.

Sainsbury's Centre for Mental Health (1997) *Pulling Together: The Future Roles and Training of Mental Health Staff*. London: SCMH.

Sampson, M. (2006) The challenge community mental health teams face in their work with patients with personality disorders. In M.J. Sampson, R.A. McCubbin and P. Tyrer (eds), *Personality Disorder and Community Mental Health Teams*. London: Wiley, ch. 11.

Sands, R. (1993) 'Can you overlap here?' a question for an interdisciplinary team. *Discourse Processes*, **16(4)**, 545–564.

Thorndycroft, B. and McCabe, J. (2008) The challenge of working with staff groups in the caring professions: the importance of the 'team development and reflective practice group'. *British Journal of Psychotherapy*, **24(2)**, 167–183.

Thornicroft, G., Becker, T., Holloway, F. *et al.* (1999) Community mental health teams: evidence or belief? *British Journal of Psychiatry*, **175**, 508–513.

Watts, F. and Bennett, D. (1983) Management of the staff team. In F.N. Watts and D.H. Bennett (eds), *Theory and Practice of Psychiatric Rehabilitation*. London: Wiley, ch. 15.

Webb, A. and Hobdell, M. (1980) Co-ordination and teamwork in the health and personal social services. In S. Longsdale, A. Webb and T. Briggs (eds), *Teamwork in the Personal and Social Services and Health Care*. London: Croom Helm, ch. 6.

West, M. (1994) *Effective Teamwork*. Leicester: BPS Blackwell.

West, M.A. and Farr, J.L. (1989) Innovation at work: psychological perspectives. *Social Behaviour*, **4**, 15–30.

West, M.A., Borrill, C.S. and Unsworth, K.L. (1998) Team effectiveness in organisations. In C.L. Cooper and I.T. Robertson (eds), *International Review of Industrial and Organisational Psychology*, Vol. 13. Chichester: Wiley, pp. 1–48.

Wilkinson, G.S. (1973) Interaction patterns and staff response to psychiatric innovations. *Journal of Health and Social Behaviour*, **14**, 323–329.

Young, J.E. (1994) *Cognitive Therapy for Personality Disorders: A Schema-focused Approach*. Sarasota, FL: Professional Resource Press.

Ysseldyke, J.E. and Algozzine, B. (1979) Perspectives on assessment of learning disabled students. *Learning Disabilities Quarterly*, **2**, 3–13.

Chapter 8

The role of the nurse in treating people with personality disorder

Des McVey

Introduction

One of the greatest challenges for mental health nurses is that of providing effective nursing interventions to people with personality disorder (Bland and Rossen, 2005; Cleary *et al.*, 2002; James and Cowman, 2007; Moran and Mason, 1996), due to the complexity of this disorder and its manifestation via challenging behaviours that appear to defy rationality. The impact of the patients' behavioural and emotional difficulties and distorted cognitions upon their interactions with others leaves staff charged with their care experiencing intense emotions. These contribute to counter-therapeutic interactions that at worst are punitive and, at best, provide short-term symptom management. People with personality disorder are considered to be 'dislikeable' clients (Bowers, 2002; Brody and Farber, 1996; Lewis and Appleby, 1988; Nehls, 1999) and this has contributed to them being shunted from service to service often oscillating between community, prison and inpatient settings.

Prisons struggle to manage these clients due to their chaotic behaviour and apparent imperviousness to the rigid rules and disciplinary procedures that assist in the smooth running of prisons. The prison service fails to recognise that for some personality disordered individuals, behaviour is designed to orchestrate a move to extreme confinement. Whilst prison is intended as a place of punishment, for such prisoners it actually represents a place of safety or affirmation of their poor self-concept. Thus, detention within conditions of segregation can be the ultimate way for personality disordered prisoners to maintain their distorted cognitions. Attempts to return these prisoners to normal location are often met with escalating disturbance and eventually the prison may seek a hospital transfer (Edgar and Rickford, 2009).

Psychiatric hospitals admit these patients for treatment of their disorder. Yet, when patients present with symptoms of their disorder that staff experience as challenging, they have historically been discharged as 'untreatable'. The behaviour of people with personality disorder often generates high levels of anxiety among other patients and staff. Their behaviour is frequently subjected to moral scrutiny, resulting in the patient being labelled 'bad', rather than being considered within the context of a clinical formulation whereby the function may be understood (Gallop *et al.*, 1989; Nehls, 1999). Such patients become isolated, and their behaviour may be used to preclude them from accessing psychological or occupational therapy. However, all inpatients are subject to nursing care and require a named nurse who will be charged with providing a care plan to address their needs. The model for this plan is likely to be behavioural, as nurses tend to focus on this aspect when treating personality disorder (Woods, 2006). Unfortunately, since behaviour has an important survival function, a behaviourally targeted care plan will not impact effectively upon behaviour unless interventions simultaneously target the underlying motivations; indeed, the behavioural symptoms may be exacerbated. Typically, the patient modifies their behaviour in accordance with expectations within the environment (and is thus 'managed' rather than 'treated'), or appears unresponsive to the behavioural care plan and is deemed 'untreatable'. In both circumstances, the patient is discharged into the community without having received effective treatment. Within the community, such patients are frequently shuffled between services, often ending up in the more broadly accommodating voluntary sector.

Current literature pertaining to nursing interventions for people with personality disorder is focused upon providing management (e.g. Melia *et al.*, 1999; Moran and Mason, 1996) or psychological therapy (e.g. Byrt, 2006; Tennant and Hughes, 1997). Thus, the role of the nurse has become enmeshed with the roles of other professions and is undefined in relation to nursing's specific role in the treatment of personality disorder (Barker, 1999). This chapter makes a unique contribution to nursing literature by defining the distinct roles of nursing staff and outlining their contribution to the effective treatment of personality disordered patients.

Why current approaches often fail

The perception that nursing people with personality disorder is more difficult than conventional psychiatric nursing is well documented (Alhadeff, 1994; Bowers, 2002; Kaplan, 1986; Moran and Mason, 1996; Murphy and McVey, 2001; O'Brien and Flöte, 1997). The specific difficulties encountered by professionals involved in caring for this client group are explored in Chapter 2. It is acknowledged that interventions established as effective for other mental health problems will require adaptation if they are to be effective with people with personality disorder (Bateman, 2000). New initiatives for nursing care can be divided into those attempting to treat (Byrt, 2006; Noak, 1995; Tennant *et al.*, 2000) and those that manage (Melia *et al.*, 1999; Moran and Mason, 1996; Nielson, 1991). The two approaches are not mutually exclusive. However, many of these attempts to adapt nursing strategies may have unwittingly colluded with, rather than counteracted, the individual's psychopathology. This section will consider some of the most influential strategies that have been proposed and discuss why a new approach is needed.

Revisiting the nursing management of the psychopath

Moran and Mason (1996) offer some practical management techniques to use when inter-relating with patients with personality disorder. Whilst these strategies (outlined below) may at times contribute to more effective management, they are often iatrogenic.

Use of humour

Use of humour with a population prone to cognitive distortions and often holding a radically different perspective on the world compared to that held by staff can be dangerous. Humour is complex. It reflects personal taste and often requires specific 'understanding'; as such, not everyone 'gets it' or will find it funny. Humour also requires specific timing and relies on staff capacity to be humorous. Therefore, attempting to use humour can be risky, especially when the 'audience' is susceptible to misinterpretation and suspicion. Moran and Mason recommend using humour to prevent confrontation when telling uncomfortable truths, to diffuse tense situations and to avoid experiences of ridicule. Rather than helping the patient, employing this strategy keeps the member of staff safe whilst avoiding dealing with the real issue. Taken 'wrongly', humour can be perceived as belittling, devaluing, making light of something the patient perceives as serious, an attempt to ridicule the individual, collusive or grooming. Such perceptions can lead to significant interpersonal ruptures and even aggression. Many personality disordered patients will laugh at a comment a member of staff makes, only to make a formal complaint about the same statement when experiencing anger at a later date. Too much humour can also contribute to an erosion of boundaries between staff and patients as humorous interactions are vulnerable to over-familiarity, inappropriateness and flirtatiousness.

Ninety-nine per cent honesty

Moran and Mason provide little detail about what nurses should be honest about, and, more importantly, what issues would constitute the '1 per cent dishonesty'. Due to life experiences, people with personality disorder tend to be acutely sensitive to deception within relationships and thus this strategy is likely to lead to a pervasive lack of trust detrimental to both management and treatment of the patient.

Destabilising the static

It is recommended that nurses move up and down the hierarchical infra-structure of the patient group in an attempt to reduce the dominance of some patients. This appears more like 'game playing' and is a risky strategy with minimal chance of success. Many patients have developed expertise in such strategies to ensure personal survival. Thus, they are more proficient in such strategies than most nurses. It is difficult to see the value of this 'game' for either management or treatment. As a strategy, it is a poor substitute for the use of explicit communication to expose the hierarchy in order that it can be directly addressed.

Rule flexibility

The authors endorse rule-bending to create dysfunction within the patient hierarchy. However, utilising 'rule-bending' with a group of people who often create chaos will generate increased anxiety and further chaos. These patients have spent their lives bending, and of course breaking, rules to meet their own needs; using this as a management strategy is clearly counter-therapeutic. There is also the unanswered question of who decides when to bend the rules and which rules are flexible.

Vulnerability

Nurses are advised not to intervene spontaneously but to foster request mak-ing within the patient before responding to the patient's needs. In fulfilling this task, the nurse can then elicit gratitude and indebtedness from the patient. Again, this is a game-playing strategy that lacks authenticity. The authors mistakenly assume that all patients have the capacity to be grateful.

Usufruct – enjoy the dynamic

The authors suggest that staff should relish the therapeutic challenge and become explicit in communicating when they perceive the patient is being 'manipulative', thus allowing a constructive nurse–patient relationship to develop. This is indeed a healthy approach to take in addressing manipulation without resorting to blaming.

There is a particular irony in suggesting strategies to manage the behaviour of these patients that mirror the strategies commonly employed by these patients and result in them being criticised, i.e. the very strategies that we are attempt-ing to change. Use of humour in difficult emotional situations is an example of 'glib and superficial charm'; 99 per cent honesty smacks of 'conning' and 'lying'; destabilising the static is akin to being 'cunning and manipulative';

rule flexibility would encourage 'impulsive' decision making; and using times when the patient is vulnerable is blatant 'exploitation of a relationship'. The only healthy strategy described is usufruct, but used alongside the others this would be ineffective, as it would be received within a context of mistrust. Application of any of these strategies in an unstructured manner risks replicating insincere relationships the patients have experienced in the past and prevents the patients having authentic, healthy interpersonal experiences. Thus, it is likely their use will *increase* rather than *decrease* the patient's underlying distress. Although some of these strategies may at times have a role in managing patients, they would have to be applied with great skill and a thorough understanding of each patient's formulation. To list them as a set of strategies that can be drawn upon by all nurses could prove to be dangerous and counterproductive as, with the absence of sincerity and an honest therapeutic relationship, one could ask the question, 'Who is manipulating who?'

Triumvirate nursing

Melia *et al.* (1999) suggest using 'triumvirate nursing' to manage the patient. This involves each patient being allocated three nurses who only see the patient in pairs, after which they supervise each other. Although this triumvirate approach may be an ideal solution for protecting the nurses, it is difficult to identify what lasting benefit is offered to patients. One of the fundamental problems for personality disordered people is their fear of, and inability to develop, meaningful intimate relationships, due to the absence of these within their earlier lives. The triumvirate model precludes the patient experiencing opportunities for developing a healthy emotionally intimate relationship that may support them through the painful experiences of therapy. Many people with a diagnosis of personality disorder are understandably suspicious of others and lack a sense of self-worth. Such patients find it hard enough to trust one named nurse. To trust three working simultaneously would be exceptionally difficult for most people with this diagnosis. Even people without personality disorder might feel a little paranoid if they felt that every interaction they had with another was being subjected to intense scrutiny.

Many patients would feel vulnerable at being outnumbered in all interactions and might cope by attempting to split the nursing group. Two-to-one contact reduces the emotional intimacy associated with one-to-one nursing, therefore impacting upon the interpersonal projections that the nurses experience and diminishing the possibility of staff perceiving the interpersonal risk the person poses and the triggers that generated the risk behaviour. Triumvirate nursing may manage patients whilst they are detained but any behavioural modifications will be situationally specific. It is unlikely that factors underlying the disorder will be addressed. Like many strategies employed to manage those with personality disorder, the focus is upon keeping the staff group safe whilst the patient is incarcerated. This intervention restricts opportunities to address difficulties that underpin destructive behaviour and so fails to contribute to long-term improvements for the patient or for public safety.

Other influential literature

Woods *et al.* (2006) emphatically establish their intention to describe 'nursing interventions for people with personality disorder' (p. 1) within their book devoted to nursing people with this diagnosis. However, whilst they describe many salient contextual factors relating to personality disorder (aetiology, diagnosis and current psychological treatment approaches), they pay scant attention to the role of the nurse and then only within the context of a therapeutic community (Woods *et al.*, 2006, ch. 14). This is a useful guide to understanding the complexities of this disorder but unfortunately it does not offer new initiatives regarding the role of the nurse.

Noak (1995) describes the difficulties of nursing this client group and the importance of a good interpersonal relationship. He alludes to the role of the nurse being akin to that of a healthy parent but fails to detail how this can be achieved effectively.

Other literature pertaining to nursing these clients positions the nurse as either group or individual therapist and, as such, merely describes the strategies and processes associated with providing psychological therapy to these clients. Thus, there is only a tenuous link with the role of the nurse in the daily care and treatment of these patients (Doyle *et al.*, 2006; Tennant *et al.*, 2000).

The literature discussed suggests different strategies for managing two of the tasks required in caring for these patients, i.e. managing the patient and providing psychological therapy. Whilst both tasks are essential to the care of people with personality disorder, neither is unique to nursing and the full range of roles and responsibilities that are embodied within a well-functioning, modern nursing team is not captured. The roles represented within nursing include untrained support, therapist, primary nurse, associate nurse, charge nurse, ward manager, modern matron and nurse consultant. Each may have an important part to play in the management and treatment of patients with severe personality disorder but a single chapter is insufficient to fully describe each of these roles. Instead, this chapter will introduce an approach which aims to enable nurses to make a unique nursing contribution to both the management and treatment of these patients, by detailing the three most common roles of named nurse, nursing assistant and ward manager.

The need for a model of nursing for patients with personality disorder

In order to describe the practice of nursing people with personality disorder, it is essential to define the contribution offered by nursing that is distinct from that of other professions (e.g. psychologist, prison officer, occupational therapist). This feature was a clear omission from the reviewed texts where authors offered practical management strategies in the absence of a philosophy of care and failed to inform readers how these strategies could influence treatment outcomes.

It is through understanding their specific role that nurses can begin to develop a coherent philosophy and effective interventions to improve their practice and define their position within the clinical team. In addition to defining the role of the nurse, a coherent model of nursing care should also identify distinct tasks of nursing. This particular dynamic is not solely applicable to nursing care of people with personality disorder. Psychiatric nursing in general may be suffering from an identity crisis (Barker, 1999). Thus, this approach to nursing care may have applicability to all people whose mental health requires nursing care.

The tendency of these clients to highlight team fractures and ruptures is one of the most significant factors undermining treatment of people with personality disorder (Schafer, 2002; UKCC 1999). This process of 'splitting' exacerbates conflict within both the multidisciplinary team and the nursing team as the clients represent their needs differently depending upon the nature of contact with each staff member. In order to contain the impact of this phenomenon, it is essential that all professions involved in treatment not only have clearly identified roles but also have distinct tasks which complement one another and fulfil the needs of the overarching treatment model. The remainder of this chapter will define a coherent model of nursing for those working with personality disorder with the role and tasks clearly delineated.

The role of the nurse

Within the treatment of personality disorder, the psychiatric nurse's role can be clearly defined via the achievement of three inter-related goals.

I Enabling clients and staff to feel physically and emotional safe

It is the responsibility of the nursing department to provide an inpatient service that allows the client to feel both physically safe and emotionally contained. Providing such an environment reduces the likelihood of clients employing dysfunctional coping strategies to manage their anxiety. This is a sophisticated role and is guided by the treatment principles described in Chapter 5. To ensure the environment provides physical and emotional safety, the unit must operate within the context of a treatment model and all policies, practices and interactions must have a link to the theoretical principles of the treatment approach *in situ* (UKCC, 1999). Standard reactive approaches would not be considered in the absence of understanding both the formulation of the client and the unit dynamics. For example, placing a client on close observations after an act of self-injury may appear logical but may fuel anger and jealousy from other clients whose access to staff time or activities may become restricted. The client may then be scapegoated which could increase acting-out behaviour. Another factor for consideration is the use of bank nurses and agency staff and their potential as unfamiliar staff for exacerbating fear in patients who are chronically mistrustful. The importance of this component cannot be overestimated since the provision of safety facilitates all other interventions. Nurses at all levels should acknowledge this role and in particular their specific tasks that contribute to its maintenance.

The need for physical and emotional safety applies not only to clients but to all members of the unit's community and, as such, the more senior nurses have a responsibility for ensuring that this is extended to all members of the multidisciplinary team and the junior nurses.

2 Enabling clients to experience nurturance via a significant attachment figure

Poor early childhood attachments are considered significant in the development of personality disorder at both a neurobiological (e.g. Siegel, 2001) and psychological level (e.g. Page, 2001). Attachment relationships are vital in learning how to manage affect (Sarkar and Adshead, 2006) and provide the framework by which a person comes to know the self and predict the behaviour of others (Bowlby, 1969, 1973, 1980; Bretherton and Munholland, 1999). The difficult relationships that people with personality disorder have typically experienced during childhood lead to them developing distorted views of themselves and their relationships with others. These beliefs impact heavily upon their interactions (Young, 1994). Thus, it is asserted (Bateman and Tyrer, 2004; Hinshelwood, 2002) that the vehicle for effective treatment of personality disorder is the interpersonal relationship.

Richman (1998) noted that nurses spend the most time with patients and thus develop strong relationships. Therefore, a significant role for the nurse (particularly the primary nurse) is to provide the client with a healthy attachment figure. This allows for a healthy, intimate, interpersonal experience that challenges the negative core beliefs held. This is a demanding role and requires the use of sophisticated skills and qualities.

The intensity of emotions generated when working with these clients and the continual transference dynamics experienced by nurses (Doyle et al., 2006) make it essential that nurses have a framework in which to understand this process in order that responses remain appropriate and therapeutic. If these relationships have no therapeutic framework in which to develop, there is a significant risk that they become iatrogenic (e.g. as unearthed in the Fallon inquiry; Fallon et al., 1999) and result in dysfunctional relationships that may be characterised by sex, coercion or romance (Doyle et al., 2006) or that are angry and aggressive, thus confirming rather than disconfirming the beliefs of the patient about interpersonal relationships.

To provide a safe framework, nursing needs to adopt a more psychological approach to understanding the interpersonal relationship between nurse and patient since all interventions with successful outcomes for the treatment of personality disorder have been based within psychological models (Bateman, 2000; Linehan, 1993; Roth et al., 2005; Young, 1994) and there is an increasing trend for nurses to adopt more psychological principles to guide their delivery of care (Doyle et al., 2006; Hopkins and Ousley, 1999; Murphy and McVey 2003; Valinejad, 2001). This is not a new idea as the bedrock of Peplau's (1952) framework for nursing was an emphasis upon developing therapeutic skills that assist patients in understanding and recognising their situation.

Adapting psychological principles to meet nursing's aims requires a degree of sophistication if therapeutic opportunities are to be optimised. Careful deliberation is required in allocating named nurses to provide adequately therapeutic relationships. Particular consideration should be given to the gender of the named nurse. Not uncommonly in nursing practice, the gender of the named nurse is decided upon in relation to the patient's trauma or offending; for example, female patients who have been sexually abused may be primary-nursed by a female nurse. Although this may allow the patient to feel safe, it will do little to address her fear of men as the patient requires the experience of a healthy interpersonal relationship with a male in which she can access her fear, resolve it, and have an experience of intimacy with a male that is not abusive. Indeed, providing a female nurse could be viewed as collusive, as it implicitly communicates that men are not safe. Despite the female nurse providing immediate safety for the patient, she will not be able to provide a therapeutic experience that disconfirms the patient's fear of all men. Conversely, a patient who has committed a rape of a woman will often be provided with a male nurse. This may manage risk but will reduce the capacity of the team to address the patient's offending behaviour. It is unlikely that the male nurse will generate the underlying anger that may characterise the patient's interpersonal relationships with women. Providing the patient with a female nurse is likely to generate different affective states and thus be more therapeutically beneficial in reducing risk. This highlights a significant dilemma for nursing personality disordered patients: treatment is significantly more challenging than management for both staff and patients. Institutions caring for these people often rely more heavily upon managing the patient as opposed to treating him or her. Managing tends to be focused upon protecting the staff charged with caring for these patients, thus protecting the public, and indeed the patients themselves, only whilst the individual is detained. Treatment may be a more risky strategy for staff but offers greater potential for long-term protection of the public and the patients following release into the community.

3 Enabling therapeutic management of crisis

Mental health nurses so often remark, 'Psychologists open a can of worms that we have to manage', that it has become a cliché. This remark is most often made when a patient is experiencing an episode of crisis, manifested through disruptive or dangerous behaviours. Mental health services struggle to understand the concept of crisis with personality disorder and, as such, often resort to negativity and judgementalism to cope (Lewis and Appleby, 1988). Frequently, it is whilst experiencing crisis that patients are discharged from services and considered untreatable, attention seeking, unable to engage, or unworthy of treatment (Gallop *et al.*, 1989). As such, it appears that the whole concept of treatability is based upon the ability or inability of services to manage patients during episodes of crisis.

Effective treatment of patients with personality disorder involves them experiencing many episodes of crisis. Livesley (2003) considers crisis management as a vital aspect of treatment. Linehan (1993) refers to crises as maladaptive problem-solving. These maladaptive problem-solving behaviours for people with personality disorder include violence, bullying, drug and alcohol misuse, self-injury, psychotic episodes, sexual activity, flashback episodes, persistent complaining, disengaging from therapy and aggression. Many of these behaviours can make it difficult to view the patient as someone in need of care and support; however, it is essential for effective treatment that services understand crisis as a necessary stage in the therapeutic process rather than as the patient being 'difficult'. Interventions during crisis episodes should be based upon the assumption that the patient is attempting to get respite from emotional pain and should offer validation and understanding.

As people with personality disorder have almost always experienced extensive childhood abuse (Johnson *et al.*, 1999; Lee, 2006; Paris, 1998), it is important that these traumatic experiences are attended to in therapy. The maladaptive behaviours that constitute the crisis are often attempts to manage emotional pain associated with unresolved trauma. Attending to this trauma in session is likely to trigger crisis episodes and can leave the therapist feeling guilty and isolated when the nursing team hold them responsible for 'opening a can of worms'. Nurses should embrace this role in a positive light as opposed to viewing it as a negative by-product of working alongside psychologists. The nurse is in the pivotal position to take the lead role in managing the crisis in a clinically sophisticated manner, ensuring that the crisis episode is managed in a fashion that complements treatment and thus fosters growth through allowing the opportunity for a new experience and encouraging a healthy resolution to the crisis.

The tasks of the nursing team

The tasks of the named nurse

The named nurse is the pivotal role through which all treatment can be effective (Noak, 1995). The tasks associated with achieving each of the nursing goals are identified below.

Goal 1: Task 1 – Synthesise nursing approach with treatment model

Becoming familiar with psychological treatment models used within the transdisciplinary team enables a nurse to broaden their understanding of their patients and therefore select interventions that strengthen the therapeutic endeavours that the patient is engaged in via individual and group therapies. Chapter 7 discusses the importance of teams adopting a consistent theoretical model and, where one is *in situ*, the role of qualified nurses is to adapt nursing practices to ensure consistency with the treatment model utilised by the team, drawing upon the support of other team members to achieve this where necessary.

Goal 1: Task 2 – Provide training and support to junior nurses

The training of nursing assistants is mostly the responsibility of qualified nurses. Care needs to be taken in developing an on-the-job training schedule and ensuring that the nursing assistant has opportunities to develop an understanding of the clinical processes involved in treating these patients. Without this, apparently innocuous acts may generate unexpected critical events due to the sensitivity of this client group – for example, laughter as a group of staff share a joke in the office soon after a client has disclosed episodes of her abuse in a session may lead to misinterpretation of the laughter and possible acting out.

Goal 1: Task 3 – Develop a treatment plan

Within mental health nursing, much emphasis is placed upon the named nurse creating a care plan for their client. Care plans provide a structure within which all interventions can be steered (Rix, 1988). When these are synchronised with a theoretical treatment model, all interactions can be therapeutic and thus play a significant role in treatment. As such, developing a treatment plan that complements the overall treatment approach and team formulation is an essential task for the named nurse.

In the absence of a pre-existing, clear theoretical model to draw upon, Young's (1994) schema therapy is an integrated approach that has been demonstrated to have effective outcomes in the treatment of personality disorder

(Giesen-Bloo *et al.*, 2006), and is particularly useful for nurses as it is access-ible to those without professional psychological training and has previously been utilised to guide the interventions of nursing staff (McVey and Murphy, 2001; Murphy and McVey, 2003). It is easily utilised alongside most psycho-logical treatments since it bridges the gap between psychodynamic and cogni-tive behavioural models through the integration of principles from both schools of therapy and complements the fundamental principles underlying Peplau's (1952) model of nursing care.

Many clients with personality disorder have been raised in environments where adults were unreliable, dangerous and rejecting (Byrt and Woods, 2006), and thus they have developed strategies (such as being unhygienic, violent and disruptive) to prevent people from getting close to them in order to avoid emotional pain. A nursing treatment plan should emphasise the need for the behaviour's function to be understood from the client's perspective rather than from the logical world the team inhabit (Peplau, 1952). As such, the client will get a consistent response from their environment that dis-confirms their expectations of others as unreliable, dangerous and rejecting. For instance, rather than advising a client of the importance of personal hygiene to encourage cleanliness, nurses could acknowledge that in the client's world being unclean keeps people away from them and allows them to feel safe, but suggest that they may be protected enough by the staff to enjoy the benefits of feeling fresh and clean. This new experience would thus encourage the client to begin to recognise that their cognitions are distorted and enable them to see and experience the world from an alternative perspective.

The named nurse should not only devise the treatment plan (with colleagues where appropriate) but also take responsibility for ensuring her colleagues are aware of its existence and operationalise it appropriately. Maintaining a treatment plan thus ensures patients are provided with a predictable response that has therapeutic value and ensures all staff are working within the same formulation, thus providing safety for all involved.

Goal 2: Task 1 – Offer a new interpersonal experience

The relationship created between the client and the nurse is an essential dynamic relating to effective care (Simpson, 1991). Therefore, it is important that the named nurse has an understanding of the aetiology and function of each patient's interpersonal style. Many clients' early attachments will have left them with the belief that they are worthless and vulnerable and that adults are dangerous. This is the template through which these clients inter-pret all social interactions as they will have had little experience of healthy attachment and, as such, have no reason to reconsider this perspective or 'schema' (Young, 1994). Schemata are amenable to change but only within a significant attachment relationship where one is provided with an alternative experience. Thus, the only way in which clients can begin to challenge their negative beliefs is by experiencing interpersonal relationships that allow healthy attachments to develop and which present them with evidence that their beliefs may be distorted. For example, after receiving first aid for inserting a pen into his penis, a client with borderline personality disorder met with his named nurse. He joked with the nurse that he used his penis as a 'pencil case' (a joke he had shared with other staff). The named nurse responded in a manner that allowed for a new experience: 'I am aware that you use humour when you are feeling ashamed and it is important that you know that I am not disgusted with you but feel sad that you can be so punitive towards yourself. I am also aware that you self-injure when you are experiencing flashbacks. It is important that you discuss these with me so that I can help you.'

Goal 2: Task 2 – Provide 'limited re-parenting'

Peplau (1988) discusses the concept of the nurse as a surrogate figure and believes this concept offers an important infrastructure in which the client can grow. This approach is also encouraged by Young (2003) who refers to this as 'limited re-parenting'. A significant task for the named nurse is to provide the patient with the security of a parental figure who is able to resist the aspects of the patient's behaviour that could elicit rejection and understand this behaviour within the context of a damaged child. The nurse must also provide a healthy 'parental' response, thus encouraging the patient to develop a more positive view of him or herself. It is vital that the interpersonal style of the nurse provides the patient with such a healthy adult experience.

The emotional development of people with personality disorder has often been arrested due to early childhood trauma. It can be useful to ask the client to identify what age they 'feel' they are and for the nurse to adapt their own interpersonal approach accordingly. In some cases, the gender of the therapist may also be significant. For example, many female patients with personality disorder hold painful emotions towards men because they were physically, emotionally and sexually abused by men. These clients may believe that men are dangerous and unable to provide them with nurturance and healthy intimacy. Therefore, to experience effective nursing treatment, these clients require a healthy interpersonal experience with a male named nurse.

Goal 3: Task 1 – Expect and plan for crisis episodes

Crisis is an important process in the treatment of people with personality disorder and as such should be expected during the course of treatment. The named nurse should review any information from previous treatment periods to identify what behaviours represent crisis for the patient early in his admission, and collaboratively develop a management plan that can be implemented at times when the patient experiences crisis. It is likely that this management plan will require altering as the team develop a stronger formulation and it should therefore be evaluated after each crisis episode.

Goal 3: Task 2 – Act as therapeutic mediator between the therapist and the nursing team

The named nurse needs to liaise with the patient's individual therapist and have a full understanding of the patient's clinical formulation. It is his or her responsibility to communicate this to the nursing team together with the treatment approach, which will enable the patient to be supported through crises in a non-collusive manner. The named nurse should also encourage the staff team to understand the crisis episode as a progressive stage and offer support to the patient's therapist who may be experiencing isolation and scapegoating by poorly informed staff. The named nurse plays an instrumental role in supporting the patient as he or she may be experiencing symptoms associated with post-traumatic stress disorder.

Clients with extensive histories of trauma and reliance upon self-harm, sex and aggression to manage are likely to present with such behaviours during episodes of crisis. The named nurse should liaise with these clients' therapists to understand the function of each behaviour and should then ensure that this information is communicated to all those who directly care for the client to prevent a punitive response. Enabling colleagues to identify these clients' vulnerability through discussions of their experiences of trauma and flashbacks will enable understanding of, rather than punishment and revulsion for, their acts of self-harm. By explaining the clients' fear of intimacy and rejection, and their propensity to act in ways that push staff away in order to maintain control, the nurse will enable staff to maintain contact with these clients rather than collude with their dysfunctional strategies by avoiding and rejecting them.

Goal 3: Task 3 – Develop a management plan that supports the clinical formulation

When a patient is in crisis, it is essential that the crisis is managed in a manner consistent with the patient's case formulation. If crisis behaviours are managed inappropriately, maladaptive beliefs and behaviours will be perpetuated. Experiencing nurturance, validation and understanding rather than a punitive response at times of crisis will enable the patient to begin to feel safe enough to engage in a more meaningful change-orientated endeavour. The management plan should be designed so as to minimise risk but remain true to the patient's clinical formulation.

Goal 3: Task 4 – Support the development of new coping skills

The named nurse should also be involved in encouraging the patient to adopt healthier, effective management skills to get him through his crisis by suggesting and role-modelling more adaptive ways to manage.

As opposed to bemoaning the event of a crisis, it is important that named nurses learn to anticipate crisis as a stage of treatment, plan for it and applaud the fact that they can manage it in a therapeutic manner that is progressive for the patient. Nurses should view crisis support and management as a core responsibility in the effective treatment of personality disorder and work to develop sophisticated strategies to ensure that crisis episodes do not result in the ending of treatment. The named nurse will thus ensure that the nursing team are adequately prepared to understand and manage the crisis within the context of the treatment philosophy.

The role/tasks of the nursing assistant

Goal 1

Untrained nurses have a significant responsibility for the provision of safety due to their close proximity to the client. Ensuring the completion of a number of tasks can fulfil this.

Task 1 – Participate in in-house training

Whilst it is regularly stated that people with personality disorder are among the most difficult and least understood patients to manage and treat, it is the least trained staff with whom they spend the majority of time (Bowers, 2002). When hospitalised, they spend much of their time in the company of nursing assistants who carry out close observations, escort patients on walks, and engage in other recreational activities. In the absence of a coherent framework in which to understand psychopathology, this leaves nursing assistants in a precarious position where they may be vulnerable to being drawn into unhealthy relationships that can have long-term distressing outcomes as a consequence of their lack of formal training. They need to participate in sufficient training to understand the aetiology of the disorder, the coping strategies utilised and how the clients may impact on them and they in turn may impact upon the clients, in order to ensure that they and the clients are afforded a degree of security.

Goal 1: Task 2 – Ensure interactions reinforce rather than undermine treatment

Interactions with clients should be driven by clinical formulations and associated treatment plans. These staff should ensure activities are designed to meet therapeutic objectives. For instance, it may be counter-therapeutic to support a client in body-building if their core formulation indicates a fear of men and thus they should be encouraged to explore and resolve their fear *with* men, possibly by taking up running where they will be exposed to males in a sport that does not require an aggressive attitude.

Goal 1: Task 3 – Uphold service rules and policies

One of the aspects of caring for people with personality disorder that can be most challenging is when staff acts of kindness and generosity appear to be ungratefully received. Typically, this is because the well-motivated act was incongruent with the patient's clinical formulation. For example, a nursing assistant took a client (who had experienced sexual abuse in a care home) for an escorted trip into town and upon realising the client had insufficient funds to buy himself a burger the nursing assistant decided benevolently to purchase him a burger, despite this being against ward rules. Whilst many would view this as an act of care, the client's psychopathology and entrenched mistrust/ abuse schema caused him to perceive it as dangerous. The thought process developed as follows: (i) 'The assistant is eroding a boundary'; (ii) 'The assistant is creating a secret between me and him'; (iii) 'If the assistant breaks one rule, the assistant will break other rules'; (iv) 'The assistant is checking whether I can keep secrets and this is what happened in the care home'; (v) 'The assistant is planning to sexually abuse me'.

These are all logical conclusions for many clients, based on their experience of interpersonal relationships. Fear resulting from this apparent act of kindness could lead to the client managing that emotion by assaulting the nursing assistant and/or absconding. In this example, the client's anxiety was raised by an act of kindness, but rule breaking under any circumstances can exacerbate cognitive distortions in a similar fashion – for example, having a fly smoke, sleeping on nightshift, etc.

Goal 1: Task 4 – Be mindful of other interpretations of behaviour

In the above example of a client being bought a burger, we saw how apparent acts of kindness can be construed as malevolent and result in maladaptive responses when rules are broken. However, hyper-vigilance to abuse is so pronounced in people with personality disorder that even apparently innocuous events can trigger panic. For example, a nurse completed a difficult session with her client during which he managed to discuss his sexual abuse. She walked into the nursing office where two other nurses were sharing a joke. The client heard laughter from the office and looked round to see his nurse smiling. The client experienced overwhelming humiliation as he believed he was the subject of the laughter.

Goal 2: Task 1 – Familiarise self with formulation/care plan

It is essential that all staff have an understanding of their contribution as an attachment figure in order to provide the client with a healthy interpersonal experience. The nursing assistant therefore requires a detailed understanding of the clinical formulation and treatment plan of each client they are required to care for. In particular, they require knowledge of the kinds of relationships each client may find most difficult and the strategies the client uses to manage their interpersonal anxiety.

Goal 2: Task 2 – Participate in supervision

It is important that nursing assistants are aware of the impact their gender, age and interpersonal style may have upon their clients, and supervision is the most appropriate forum for staff to reflect upon this. Supervision also offers space for staff to access support to enable them to cope with the difficult emotions they experience in relation to the patients and recognise when they may be drawn into interactions with the patient that may be experienced by the patient as punitive.

Goal 3: Task 1 – Provide dignity in immediate crisis management

The untrained nurse can often be left for prolonged periods with clients who are experiencing crisis, particularly when clients are subject to close observations where the member of staff shadows the client. How this process is managed can determine whether it is a healthy therapeutic experience or an experience that evokes emotions such as shame and humiliation. It is essential at this time that the client experiences the close observations as a meaningful intervention. As such, the staff member should carry out their responsibilities within the context of the formulation and management plan. They must be aware of how their behaviours will be interpreted by the client by reflecting upon the formulation. For instance, reading a book whilst carrying out close observations can leave the patient feeling worthless and boring. Alternatively, in some instances, having a chat may be perceived as grooming. Using the principles outlined in Chapter 5 to guide their practice will also enhance their role within the crisis. The untrained nurse is often in a pivotal role where they can ensure that crisis management reinforces rather than negates treatment.

Whilst suggesting the need for caution when exposing untrained staff for long periods of time to men and women with extreme psychopathology, the author supports Bowers (2002) in acknowledging that there are many nursing assistants who despite lacking formal training possess the inherent skills, qualities and knowledge to offer meaningful interventions to such patients. However, it is essential that they have a clear understanding of the philosophical approach and their specific behavioural and interpersonal role within such a model.

Role of the ward manager/senior nurse

Within an inpatient service, the ward manager or senior nurse is the figure that motivates the nursing team. They are the pivotal link between the nurses and the rest of the multidisciplinary team and therefore hold a strong influence over the success or failure of treatment approaches. Patients on the unit will perceive the senior nurse as the 'head of the family' and, as such, they can often be subject to transference dynamics relating to parental figures from the past. With this weight of responsibility, it is important that the senior nurse adapts the philosophical approach underpinning treatment and ensures the nursing team are capable of meeting their three defining goals.

Goal 1: Task 1 – Ensure effective policies and practices

Clear policies and procedures are essential to ensure physical and emotional safety and it is important that these policies can be effectively operationalised within the context of the treatment model being used. The senior nurse should thus ensure that any policies introduced to the ward can operate effectively within the context. For example, a hospital risk management policy instructed that clients must have bedroom parole prior to being suitable for town parole. Although this policy may have some logic within the disease model of care where the patient gets progressively independent as they recover, it may not be applicable to a model that operates within the context of a formulation. A patient who always self-injures in her bedroom and has no history of self-harming in public may be safe to utilise town parole before she is safe in her bedroom. Therefore, the senior nurse must ensure that the principles of the hospital policies are adapted to accommodate the client group and their specific risks.

Goal 1: Task 2 – Maintain integrity of treatment approach

A significant hurdle in the treatment of personality disorder is the team's ability to maintain treatment integrity. Treatment integrity is challenged when staff alter their approach of care or when new procedures are introduced on a departmental-specific basis. In essence, treatment integrity is most at risk when any change is introduced without it going through a systematic change process. The senior nurse should therefore ensure that treatment integrity is maintained by sustaining an overview of the practices on the ward and ensuring there is a system for effective introduction of change.

Goal 1: Task 3 – Maintain effective teamwork

The complex psychopathology and associated maladaptive behaviours presented by this client group indicate that it is essential to maintain a high degree of teamwork and consistency (UKCC, 1999). In the absence of effective teamwork, it is likely to be the nurses who experience the brunt of the difficulties as the client group act out the chaos of the service. The senior nurse occupies a co-ordinating role in which he or she can ensure that all members of the transdisciplinary team are acknowledged and supported as they carry out their duties. Chapter 6 discusses the importance of effective teamwork in greater detail.

Goal 1: Task 4 – Reduce use and management of agency or bank staff

The use of agency and bank nurses has limitations in all fields of psychiatric nursing as most tasks should be carried out within the context of a trusting and developing relationship (Peplau, 1988). It is therefore important that the senior nurse limits the use of this resource. Introducing bank or agency nurses into a service where clients are anxious and suspicious can often increase risk rather than provide a meaningful contribution. On occasions when it is inevitable, the senior nurse should ensure that these nurses follow specific operational policies that allow the service to acknowledge the fear they may represent, for example ensuring that the nurses inter-relate with the clients within the context of the treatment approach.

Goal 2: Task 1 – Attend a weekly business meeting

The senior nurse of the unit often adopts the role of parental figure to the service and is the focal point for all members of the community. It is important that the senior nurse acknowledges this responsibility by delivering their practice in a manner that allows for the community to access a healthy experience of a 'good parent'. Organising and attending a weekly business meeting for the unit with an open invitation to both clients and staff will provide a forum where the senior nurse can listen to anxieties and offer support and solutions. This forum also protects less experienced nurses who are often met with difficult requests which they can refer to this meeting.

Goal 2: Task 2 – Have a brief understanding of each client

The senior nurse will be subject to transference dynamics among the client group who are likely to place them in a parental or previous carer's role. Consequently, it is essential that the senior nurse has a brief understanding of each client's clinical formulation in order to support treatment processes and also to prevent them colluding with client psychopathology.

Goal 2: Task 3 – Have a presence on the unit

This is an essential task for the senior nurse as it represents their willingness to invest in all the people under their charge. Spending time with both staff and clients on the unit allows for the development of healthy attachments and provides a state of security for the community. This is a very powerful dynamic as the senior nurse represents the head parent. The senior nurse should also make time for all members of the disciplinary team and acknowledge that some members can feel isolated, particularly lone practitioners.

Goal 3: Task 1 – Ensure efficient supervision and support structures

The senior nurse has a responsibility to ensure that all staff working on their unit have access to and attend clinical and managerial supervision. This supervision should be consistent with the treatment approach and it is essential that the experience of supervision is positive – for example, it would not be prudent to organise the nurse's supervision structure solely around a hierarchical model, since expecting a newly qualified staff nurse to provide supervision to an untrained nurse who has been working with clients for several years may generate difficulties.

Goal 3: Task 2 – Ensure training is provided regarding crisis

Continual training and education is an essential component of any health service and it is well documented that training opportunities for staff working with personality disordered clients are inadequate. It is essential that all staff working with clients who experience crisis episodes have access to effective training that allows them to manage and understand this process effectively.

Goal 3: Task 3 – Liaise with other managers

At times when there are crisis episodes on the unit, it is the senior nurse's task to ensure that any external managers who may have some on-call responsibility within the service are fully briefed and made aware of the management plans. This prevents these managers from making decisions that appear to be logical solutions but are antithetical to the treatment approach.

The role and tasks required of a senior nurse on a unit for people with personality disorder are complex and require a level of sophistication. It is a position with capacity to influence practice and policy and to facilitate an environment characterised by calmness and safety in which effective multi-disciplinary treatment can be delivered.

Summary

Providing effective nursing care to people with personality disorder is one of the greatest challenges for today's mental health nurses. The challenge is such that many nurses choose to avoid working with this client group and defend against their extreme psychopathology through a blaming and judgemental attitude (Tredget, 2001). There is an extreme paucity of education for nurses choosing to work with this disorder and many current practices are designed solely to protect the nurses who choose to engage in this particular field. Such strategies at best allow for these clients to be managed whilst detained, and at worst can be iatrogenic. Other developing approaches are often enmeshed with the role of other professions and therefore blur the identity of the nurse.

Mental health nurses have a significant role to play in the treatment of personality disorder and this chapter has briefly outlined and described the role of the nursing team, identifying specific goals and tasks. It is essential that practice is further developed within this field of nursing to ensure that personality disordered patients are exposed to sophisticated nursing care that allows them to feel contained enough to work through the difficult dynamics associated with their distress and maladaptive behaviours.

References

Alhadeff, L. (1994) Managing difficult populations. *New Directions for Mental Health Services*, **63**, 71–79.

Barker, P. (1999) *The Philosophy and Practice of Psychiatric Nursing*. London: Churchill Livingstone.

Bateman, A. (2000) Integration psychotherapy: an evolving reality in personality disorder. *British Journal of Psychotherapy*, **17(2)**, 147–156.

Bateman, A. and Fonagy, P. (2006) *Mentalisation-based Treatment for Borderline Personality Disorder: A Practical Guide*. Oxford: Open University Press.

Bateman, A.W. and Tyrer, P. (2004) Services for personality disorder: organisation for inclusion. *Advances in Psychiatric Treatment*, **10**, 425–433.

Bland, A.R. and Rossen, E.K. (2005) Clinical supervision of nurses working with patients with borderline personality disorder. *Issues in Mental Health Nursing*, **26**, 507–517.

Bowers, L. (2002) *Dangerous and Severe Personality Disorder: Response and Role of the Psychiatric Team*. London: Routledge.

Bowlby, J. (1969) *Attachment and Loss. Vol. 1*. New York: Basic Books.

Bowlby, J. (1973) *Attachment and Loss. Vol. 2*. New York: Basic Books.

Bowlby, J. (1980) *Attachment and Loss. Vol. 3*. New York: Basic Books.

Bretherton, I. and Munholland, K. (1999) Internal working models in attachment relationships. In J. Cassidy and P.R. Shaver (eds), *Handbook of Attachment*. New York: Guilford Press, ch. 5.

Brody, E.M. and Faber, B.A. (1996) The effects of therapist experience and patient diagnosis on counter-transference. *Psychotherapy*, **33**, 372–380.

Byrt, R. (2006) Nursing interventions in therapeutic communities. In P. Woods, A. Kettles and R. Byrt (eds), *Forensic Mental Health Nursing: Interventions with People with Personality Disorder*. London: Quay Books, ch. 14.

Byrt, R. and Woods, P. (2006) Introduction. In P. Woods, A. Kettles and R. Byrt (eds), *Forensic Mental Health Nursing: Interventions with People with Personality Disorder*. London: Quay Books.

Cleary, M., Seigfried, N. and Walter, G. (2002) Experience, knowledge and attitudes of mental health staff regarding clients with a borderline personality disorder. *International Journal of Mental Health Nursing*, **11**, 186–191.

De Zueleta, F. (2006) *From Pain to Violence: The Traumatic Roots of Destructiveness*. Chichester: Wiley Blackwell.

Doyle, M., Aiyegbusi, A. and Burbery, P. (2006) Personality disorder: specialist psychological approaches. In P. Woods, A. Kettles and R. Byrt (eds), *Forensic Mental Health Nursing: Interventions with People with Personality Disorder*. London: Quay Books, ch. 15.

Edgar, K. and Rickford, D. (2009) *Too Little, Too Late*. London: Prison Reform Trust.

Fallon, P., Bluglass, B., Edwards, B. and Daniels, G. (1999) *Report of the Committee of Inquiry into the Personality Disorder Unit, Ashworth Special Hospital*. London: Stationery Office.

Gallop, R. (1999) Personality disorder: finding a way in. In M. Clinton and S. Nelson (eds), *Advanced Practice in Mental Health Nursing*. Oxford: Blackwell Science, ch. 10.

Gallop, R., Lancee, W.J. and Garfinkel, P. (1989) How nursing staff respond to the label borderline personality disorder. *Hospital and Community Psychiatry*, **40**, 815–819.

Giesen-Bloo, J. and Van Dyckr Spinhoven, P. (2006) Outpatient psychotherapy for borderline personality disorder: randomised trial of schema focused therapy vs transference focused therapy. *Archives of General Psychiatry*, **63**, 649–658.

Hinshelwood, R.D. (2002) Abusive help – helping abuse: the psychodynamic impact of severe personality disorder on caring institutions. *Criminal Behaviour and Mental Health*, **12**, 20–30.

Hopkins, N. and Ousley, L. (1999) Clinical psychology and the forensic nursing role. In D. Robinson and A. Kettles (eds), *Forensic Nursing of the Mentally Disordered Offender*. London: Jessica Kingsley, ch. 7.

James, P.D. and Cowman, S. (2007) Psychiatric nurses' knowledge experience and attitudes towards clients with borderline personality disorder. *Journal of Psychiatric and Mental Health Nursing*, **14**, 670–678.

Johnson, J., Cohen, P., Brown, J. *et al.* (1999) Childhood maltreatment increases risk for personality disorders during early adulthood. *Archives of General Psychiatry*, **56**, 600–606.

Kaplan, C.A. (1986) The challenge of working with patients diagnosed as having a personality disorder. *Nursing Clinics of North America*, **21**, 429–438.

Lee, R. (2006) Childhood trauma and personality disorder: toward a biological model. *Current Psychiatry Reports*, **8**, 143–152.

Lewis, G. and Appleby, L. (1988) Personality disorder: the patients psychiatrists dislike. *British Journal of Psychiatry*, **153**, 44–49.

Linehan, M. (1993) *Cognitive Behavioural Treatment for Borderline Personality Disorder*. New York: Guilford Press.

Livesley, W.J. (2003) *Practical Management of Personality Disorder*. New York: Guilford Press.

McVey, D. and Murphy, N. (2001) Young's therapy for clients with personality disorders. *Nursing Times*, **97(16)**, 34–35.

Melia, P., Moran, T. and Mason, T. (1999) Psychiatric nursing for PD patients: crossing the boundaries safely. *Journal of Psychiatric and Mental Health Nursing*, **6**, 15–20.

Moran, T. and Mason, T. (1996) Revisiting the nursing management of the psychopath. *Journal of Psychiatric and Mental Health Nursing*, **3(3)**, 189–194.

Murphy, N. and McVey, D. (2001) Nursing personality disordered inpatients: a schema-focused approach. *British Journal of Forensic Practice*, **13(4)**, 8–15.

Murphy, N. and McVey, D. (2003) The challenge of nursing personality disordered patients. *British Journal of Forensic Practice*, **5(1)**, 3–19.

Nehls, N. (1999) Borderline personality disorder: the voice of patients. *Research in Nursing and Health*, **22**, 285–293.

Neilson, P. (1991) Manipulative and splitting behaviours. *Nursing Standard*, **6(8)**, 32–35.

Noak, J. (1995) Care of people with psychopathic disorder. *Nursing Standard*, **9(34)**, 30–32.

O'Brien, L. and Flöte, J. (1997) Providing nursing care for a patient with borderline personality disorder on an acute inpatient unit: a phenomenological study. *Australian and New Zealand Journal of Mental Health Nursing*, **6**, 137–147.

Page, T.F. (2001) Attachment and personality disorders: exploring maladaptive developmental pathways. *Child and Adolescent Social Work Journal*, **18(5)**, 313–334.

Paris, J. (1998) Does childhood trauma cause personality disorders in adults? *Canadian Journal of Psychiatry*, **43(2)**, 148–153.

Peplau, H.E. (1952) *Interpersonal Relations in Nursing*. New York: G.P. Putnam.

Peplau, H.E. (1988) *Interpersonal Relations in Nursing*, 2nd edn. Basingstoke: Macmillan.

Pietromonaco, P.R. and Feldman Barrett, L. (2000) The internal working models concept: what do we really know about the self in relation to others? *Review of General Psychology*, **4(2)**, 155–175.

Pretzer, J. (1994) Cognitive therapy for personality disorder: the state of art. *Clinical Psychology and Psychotherapy*, **1(5)**, 237–266.

Richman, J. (1998) The ceremonial and moral order of a ward for psychopaths. In T. Mason and D. Mercer (eds), *Critical Perspectives in Forensic Care: Inside Out*. London: Macmillan, ch. 9.

Rix, G. (1988) Care plan for an aggressive person based on Peplau's model of nursing. In B. Collister (ed.), *Psychiatric Nursing: Person to Person*. London: Arnold, ch. 10.

Roth, A., Fonagy, P. and Parry, G. (2005) *What Works for Whom? A Critical Review of Psychotherapy Research*. New York: Guilford Press.

Royce, L. (2006) Childhood trauma and personality disorder: towards a biological model. *Current Psychiatry Reports*, **8**, 43–52.

Sarkar, J. and Adshead, G. (2006) Personality disorders as disorganisation of attachment and affect regulation. *Advances in Psychiatric Treatment*, **12**, 297–305.

Schafer, P. (2002) Nursing interventions and future directions with patients who constantly break rules and test boundaries. In A. Kettles, P. Woods and M. Collins (eds), *Therapeutic Interventions for Forensic Mental Health Nurses*. London: Jessica Kingsley, ch. 4.

Siegel, D.J. (2001) Toward an interpersonal neurobiology of the developing mind: attachment relationships, 'mindsight' and neural integration. *Infant Mental Health Journal*, **22(1–2)**, 67–94.

Simpson, H. (1991) *Peplau's Model in Action*. London: Macmillan.

Tennant, A. and Hughes, G. (1997) Issues in nursing care for patients with severe personality disorders. *Mental Health Practice*, **1**, 10–16.

Tennant, A., Davies, C. and Tennant, I. (2000) Working with the personality disordered offender. In C. Chaloner and M. Coffey (eds), *Forensic Mental Health: Current Approaches*. Oxford: Blackwell, ch. 6.

Tredget, J.E. (2001) The aetiology, presentation and treatment of personality disorders. *Journal of Psychiatric and Mental Health Nursing*, **8**, 347–356.

UKCC (1999) *Nursing in Secure Environments*. London: United Kingdom Central Council.

Valinejac, C. (2001) A model for in-house psychological training. *Mental Health Nursing*, **21(6)**, 18–21.

Woods, P. (2006) Types of personality disorder. In P. Woods, A. Kettles and R. Byrt (eds), *Forensic Mental Health Nursing: Interventions with People with Personality Disorder*. London: Quay Books, ch. 2.

Woods, P., Kettles, A. and Byrt, R. (eds) (2006) *Forensic Mental Health Nursing: Interventions with People with Personality Disorder*. London: Quay Books.

Young, J.E. (1994) *Cognitive Therapy for Personality Disorders: A Schema Focused Approach (Revised)*. Sarasota, FL: Professional Resources Exchange.

Young, J. (2003) *Schema Therapy: A Practitioner's Guide*. New York: Guilford Press.

Chapter 9

The role of the occupational therapist in treating people with personality disorder

Leanne Jones

Introduction

As its name suggests, occupational therapy is concerned with 'occupation', that is, activities of daily life that have value and meaning to individuals and their cultures. Occupation encompasses caring for oneself, enjoying life and contributing socially and financially to one's community (Law *et al.*, 1998). People have an innate need to be active and express their occupational nature through engagement in a range of activities that are uniquely human in their diversity and complexity (Wilcock, 1993). Being unable to fulfil this intense drive to act is detrimental to individuals' physical and mental health and is associated with an increased risk of mortality (Glass *et al.*, 1999).

Occupational therapy enables people to overcome difficulties with day-to-day functioning in order to enable them to participate in activities that enhance their health and well-being (World Federation of Occupational Therapists, 2004). Occupation is used as the therapeutic medium and therefore forms both the means and the end of therapy (Trombly, 1995). Occupation is employed therapeutically to enable clients to address problems with skills, capacities, habits and beliefs, and to support them in overcoming the environmental barriers that restrict them.

Occupational therapy is a relatively young profession. It was established early in the twentieth century in response to emerging health needs within a period of rapid industrialisation and population growth in American society following World War I. The American Society for the Promotion of Occupational Therapy was founded in 1917 by individuals from a range of backgrounds including nursing, social work, teaching and medicine. Their work was informed by centuries of the therapeutic use of activity; as early as AD 172 the Greek physician Galen pronounced that 'employment is nature's physician and essential to human happiness' (Kloss, 2005).

In today's society, the significance of occupation for health remains widely underestimated. Some commentators have suggested that this may be because occupation is perceived to be rather unremarkable and mundane as it forms the fabric of daily life (Wilcock, 2003). There is also widespread misunderstanding of the occupational therapy role. This may be particularly prevalent within personality disorder settings, where historically occupational therapy has been under-represented. Common misconceptions are that occupational therapists merely organise activities to occupy clients, provide psychological skill-based interventions (such as anxiety management) or teach activities such as art or cooking. Such perceptions fail to recognise that occupational therapy is a complex therapeutic intervention (Creek, 2003) with its own specialised focus, thus contributing to other disciplines expecting occupational therapists to work outside their role.

This chapter outlines the unique role of the occupational therapist in the transdisciplinary treatment of people with personality disorder, and specifically focuses on issues relating to occupational therapy practice. Readers are encouraged to consult other chapters of this book for discussions of generic issues pertinent to occupational therapy treatment.

The need for occupational therapy within personality disorder services

The occupational needs of people with personality disorder are frequently overlooked. For instance, the recent guidelines for treating antisocial and borderline personality disorders fail to discuss the role of occupational therapy (NICE, 2009a, 2009b). As trauma is central to personality disorder (Soloff *et al.*, 2002; Zlotnick *et al.*, 2003), services tend to focus upon working with client' traumatic experiences and their impact upon psychopathology. However, experiences of trauma have significant consequences for individuals' occupational functioning and these difficulties need effective treatment if the individual is to reach a state of health and well-being.

'Impairment in social, occupational or other important areas of functioning' is an integral feature of personality disorder (DSM-IV; APA, 1994). Personality disorder is associated with significant functional impairment across a range of performance areas including work, leisure and social relations (Skodol *et al.*, 2002, 2005; Calabretta-Caprini, 1989). There is no evidence to suggest that personality disordered clients are any less occupationally impaired than people with mental illness; indeed, Zanarini *et al.* (2005) suggest the presence of greater functional impairment in borderline clients.

Salz's (1983) study of vocational histories of individuals with borderline personality disorder provides a useful illustration of the difficulties they experience. She identified inconsistency as the most significant feature, with 'a work-school pattern characterised by intense involvement followed by abrupt termination, often at the brink of success' (1983, p. 34). Other issues included dysfunctional interpersonal relationships, perfectionistic standards, lack of recognition of high level of ability, lack of enjoyment and satisfaction, reliance on grandiose fantasies, and habitual avoidance and procrastination.

People with personality disorder lack a clear, stable and realistic occupational identity or 'composite sense of who one is and wishes to become as an occupational being generated from one's history of occupational participation' (Kielhofner, 2008, p. 106). Construction of a positive occupational identity is essential to adaptive 'doing' as it acts as both a means of self-definition and a determinant of future action. People with personality disorder have an impaired sense of identity, including extensive maladaptive ideas about self, poor interpersonal boundaries, difficulty differentiating self from others, an impoverished self-concept, uncertainty about personal qualities, an unstable sense of self and a sense of inner emptiness (Livesley, 2003). Consequently, individuals have difficulty forming an adaptive future image of how they want their life to be. This results in a struggle to establish and work towards life goals and difficulty identifying meaning, purpose and order in their lives.

Occupational therapists' specialist training enables them to address these difficulties by providing therapeutic interventions that enable the client to become 'competent', 'a social being' and 'I' (Fidler and Fidler, 1983).

Challenges involved in working with clients with personality disorder

Whilst working with the client group is undoubtedly rewarding, it is also testing for occupational therapists. Personality disordered clients are hard to treat and personality disorder services can be difficult to work in. Having an understanding of what issues are likely to arise enables therapists to recognise tricky situations as they develop and deal with them before they become overwhelming. In this spirit, this section will explore some of the key challenges involved.

An illusion of competence

Identifying the nature and extent of the occupational needs of people with personality disorder presents a challenge for therapists, in that they may fail to recognise when occupational therapy is required. Occupational functioning in personality disordered clients is frequently characterised by an illusion of competence, whereby individuals can appear to achieve a higher level of occupational adaptation than actually exists. People with personality disorder are often able to achieve competence in specific life roles, for example within a leisure or work role. As people tend to choose to engage in activities they are likely to succeed at (Christiansen et al., 2004), this can give the impression of overall competence. Further investigation, however, can reveal deficits in other areas that result in the individual struggling to maintain a balanced routine of work, leisure, self-care and social occupations, indicating that occupational therapy intervention is required.

In addition, the occupational functioning of people with personality disorder can vary significantly according to the social or physical environment. Assessing individuals in a limited range of settings may mislead therapists into concluding that occupational therapy is not required. This issue is illustrated by a male client in a prison setting, who successfully performed a work role as shower-room cleaner but experienced significant difficulties when he switched to kitchen cleaner. Being in this environment triggered childhood memories of his parents neglecting to feed him and he resumed childhood behaviours such as stealing and hoarding food.

Individuals' functioning may also fluctuate greatly over time. Consequently, initial assessments of competence may require revisiting. During times of crisis, personality disordered individuals' participation in occupation can become grossly disrupted and routines may disintegrate or an obsessive focus upon valued occupations may develop. For instance, during a period of crisis a female client attempted to paint twenty-four hours a day in order to distract herself from overwhelming thoughts and feelings. The ensuing lack of sleep impacted on her ability to maintain her habitual routine.

Occupational needs may not always be immediately apparent. Superficial analysis may indicate that a client's engagement in occupation is adaptive when it is actually pathologically driven. For example, a female borderline patient seemingly participated in a structured routine of healthy activities. Violin playing, which she described as her most significant interest, was revealed on further exploration to be solely motivated by her desire to please her abusive mother. This warranted occupational therapy intervention as the activity served to maintain the unhealthy dynamic in her relationship with her mother and undermined the development of her own interests and preferences.

An issue that further serves to obscure individuals' difficulties is the fact that people with personality disorder can possess a chronic mistrust of others that can lead them to attempt to conceal their areas of vulnerability from their therapists. Shame is also a powerful dynamic contributing to individuals hiding their difficulties. Clients with narcissistic personality disorder are reliant on their positive self-image to defend against shame so are likely to be resistant to engaging in a process which exposes their weaknesses. Clients can also lack insight into their own difficulties, making it difficult for them to provide an accurate self-report.

These factors contribute to an illusion of competence that masks individuals' occupational needs. Limited occupational participation may be perceived as a deliberate and wilful refusal to engage in activity. Occupational therapists may fail to recognise that occupational therapy intervention is required and clients experiencing pathologically-driven occupational difficulties may be thought lazy or awkward. Where an occupational therapist has developed an accurate formulation, other team members may find it difficult to see the occupational deficits of the client due to their own negative feelings towards the individual, and become resentful towards the occupational therapist.

Difficulties forming therapeutic relationships

A further challenge for the therapist is establishing a therapeutic alliance that will enable occupational therapy to take place. People with personality disorder frequently find it difficult to trust others, experience significant interpersonal difficulties and struggle to tolerate close relationships. Whilst this section focuses on issues pertinent to occupational therapists, Chapter 5 offers more extensive guidance on how to address issues impacting on the therapeutic alliance.

Occupational therapists tend to be a minority group within personality disorder services, and individual therapists are often professionally isolated. This can negatively impact on individuals' self-esteem, leaving them vulnerable to forming 'special relationships' with clients, whereby the client idealises the therapist and both parties believe only the therapist truly understands the client. In this scenario, therapists can over-identify with the client, reject views of other multidisciplinary team members and become split from the rest of the team. Here, the therapist risks developing an unhealthy relationship with the client and becoming unable to assess his or her occupational needs objectively.

Occupational therapists new to the field of personality disorder may be ill-equipped to manage the sexual dynamics often present in relationships with people who have experienced childhood sexual abuse (as is the case with many people with a diagnosis of personality disorder). People with a history of sexual trauma may inject sexuality into therapeutic relationships, for example by behaving in a flirtatious manner in order to prevent the therapist being displeased with them. In their anxiety to maintain professional boundaries within the relationship, therapists may respond in a critical manner, leaving the client feeling humiliated. Alternatively the therapist may unconsciously reciprocate the client's flirtatiousness, therefore failing to help the individual feel safe within the relationship. In both situations, valuable opportunities to help the client recognise and address the issue are lost.

A further challenge is that aspects of the occupational therapy role may mirror grooming behaviours used by childhood abusers. Providing equipment and materials for sessions, accompanying clients to community resources and displaying unconditional positive regard for clients are all legitimate occupational therapy interventions. However, inexperienced therapists may not consider that buying things for individuals, taking them to nice places, being pleasant and attentive are all strategies abusers use to prepare children for sexual abuse. Therapists may be unaware that clients are anticipating that the relationship will become sexual and therefore neglect to provide the reassurance to help them feel safe.

Therapists may wrongly assume they understand what the client is thinking or intending to communicate. The disparity between therapists' life experiences and those of people with personality disorder means therapists cannot take this for granted. For instance, a client described his parents as people who did leisure activities with him when he was a boy. When questioned further, he stated he used to watch television with his drunken mother who was liable to beat him if he drew her attention to him.

People with personality disorder have different logics compared to other people as a result of their extreme formative experiences. An example is individuals who have been sexually abused in childhood neglecting their self-care. Whilst most people would have difficulty seeing the benefits of being dirty and smelly, for some clients, making themselves repellant to potential abusers to defend against future abuse is a logical strategy.

Inadequacy of simple formulations

Therapists need to be mindful of the fact that conducting a simple formulation of clients' problems is insufficient when working with people with personality disorder. Without thorough consideration of how issues develop and persist, treatment is unlikely to be successful. An example is a therapist's attempt to challenge a borderline individual's low self-efficacy through facilitating successful experiences. As Neville-Jan *et al.* (1991) observed, such individuals' negative perceptions of their own capacity are often so firmly entrenched that they remain fixed, even after repeated successes. A more effective formulation allows a client to recognise the disparity between her view of herself and her actual performance on a rational level, addresses deep-seated beliefs and considers the client's emotional experience (that is, supports her to allow herself to experience pride).

Clients' lack of motivation

People with personality disorder are frequently uninterested in developing their occupational functioning and can be actively opposed to engaging in occupational therapy. Individuals often view life as a day-by-day battle to maintain their own safety and survival in a hostile and frightening world. Developing healthy engagement in occupation is likely to be viewed as insignificant in comparison to the perceived magnitude of this struggle to avoid harm and individuals may dismiss occupational therapy as a result.

This problem can be exacerbated by confusion regarding the occupational therapy role and the lack of credibility sadly attached to the profession in some settings. Clients can share the commonly-held misconception that occupational therapy merely involves arts and crafts activities to occupy one's time and thus perceive it to be unappealing or irrelevant to their needs. A further issue is that occupational therapy may be wrongly perceived to be an intervention for clients who have significant and obvious difficulties performing activities across the areas of work, leisure and self-care. Personality disordered clients, who frequently function well in some areas, can be hurt and offended when referred for a treatment which they perceive has these connotations.

Clients' reluctance to engage can be compounded by a tendency for individuals to view themselves as unworthy of positive attention and experiences. For some individuals, developing their occupational functioning directly conflicts with their own agendas. For example, the dependent client who desperately seeks to avoid abandonment is likely to resist developing her ability to live independently, being fearful it will result in her receiving less support. Negotiating with the client to develop shared treatment aims that focus on occupational needs can prove challenging, as addressing occupational deficits can involve asking the client to relinquish long-held coping strategies.

For people with narcissistic personality disorder, occupational therapy may threaten their perception of themselves as highly competent. Such individuals frequently work hard to impress others with how capable they are and may attempt to subtly steer the therapist away from activities that reveal them to be otherwise. They often struggle to receive feedback that challenges their maladaptive positive self-concept and may vociferously oppose the therapist or disengage from therapy.

Being pulled away from an occupational focus

Therapists working with personality disordered clients may find maintaining an occupational focus challenging. Clients may seek to ventilate thoughts and feelings and obtain emotional support, particularly when they have difficulty recognising how occupational therapy could benefit them. Employing the therapeutic use of an activity that is valued by the client – a core skill of occupational therapy – is frequently problematic as personality disordered individuals often lack clarity as to what their interests are (Livesley, 2003) or have antisocial interests that are not appropriate for use within therapy.

Working within services where occupational therapy is misunderstood and undervalued can lead therapists to experience role confusion, self-doubt and professional defensiveness (Wright and Rowe, 2005). A consequence can be that therapists abandon their professional focus and provide interventions in which they are not trained, whilst neglecting the occupational needs of their clients. Many occupational therapists function as 'gap fillers' and 'fragment towards specialisations in other professions with a growing incoherence between practice and philosophy' (Fortune, 2000, p. 226).

Lack of credibility of the profession

Research has shown that mental health workers use black humour as a means of coping with the emotional demands of their work. This may be amplified in personality disorder services, given the high level of expressed emotion present. This, combined with occupational therapy's traditional role as butt of others' denigrating jokes (about 'basket weaving' and the like), can pose a threat to the credibility of the occupational therapist, particularly when voiced in front of the client. Unassertive characters may struggle to communicate the value of their work within such a climate and may collude with their detractors to fit in.

Providing occupationally focused interventions can create resentment and hostility in other professionals. Without a clear understanding of occupational therapy's role, staff members may perceive offering activity (particularly leisure) as over-indulgent. This is particularly likely to be an issue within forensic settings where some staff members hold punitive attitudes towards clients. For other staff, there may be issues around jealousy as resources available to occupational therapists are not accessible for other professions.

Lack of training to work with trauma

Unlike clinicians from other disciplines, most occupational therapists will not be required to work with trauma and consequently the topic is generally excluded from occupational therapy curricula. However, most personality disordered clients have experienced significant trauma including sexual, physical and emotional abuse. Traumatic experiences significantly impact upon clients' identities and their current occupational functioning. Abrahamson (1998) argues that, for occupational therapy to be relevant, therapists must consider how experiences of trauma continue to impact on clients' day-to-day realities. This presents a challenge for therapists who have received inadequate training on trauma and how to work with it from an occupational therapy perspective.

Occupational therapists working with trauma may cause anxiety within the multidisciplinary team. To be effective, occupational therapists need to explore the impact of traumatic experiences on clients' occupational functioning (Zemke and Clark, 1996), but others may assume they are trying to treat the trauma itself and are working outside their sphere of competence.

Working with dangerous people

Effective occupational therapy with violent offenders involves examination of their offending histories. This process is potentially traumatising as it involves reading and listening to descriptions of horrific crimes including rape, murder and sexual offences against children. Therapists often struggle to reconcile that clients are simultaneously victims of abuse and perpetrators of violent crimes. Where this is the case, therapists may selectively relate to one side of a person, thus failing to work effectively with the other. Retaining a view of the client as perpetrator may be a particular challenge for occupational therapists, whose philosophy emphasises maintaining a positive view of the client.

Occupational therapy involves the therapeutic use of everyday activities to bring about positive change in individuals' occupational functioning. Therapists select activities on the basis of their therapeutic potential to address the needs of the client. Therapists working with people with personality disorder must additionally consider whether using an activity would pose a risk to the individual or to others. Personality disordered individuals have a higher than average risk of engaging in acts of self-harm, suicide and violence towards other people. Therapists need to accurately risk assess any activity they plan to use with an individual and determine whether any risks can be safely managed. Failure to effectively do so has the potential to result in serious harm to the client or another and litigation or de-registration of the therapist.

Personality disorder services operate strict risk management strategies to reduce the potential for harm to their clients and other people, including control of environments, equipment and materials available for use by clients. This presents a significant challenge for occupational therapists, who require the use of such resources to conduct their interventions. Whilst the use of occupation with clients can provide clinical teams with a means of assessing risk in a controlled setting, litigation-conscious managers may be reluctant to embrace this, restricting the range of activities available to use with clients.

The occupational therapy role involves being exposed to a higher level of risk than other team members. Within forensic settings, it is not unusual for occupational therapists to use sharp equipment with individuals who have been convicted of serious acts of violence using weapons. Therapists need to manage their own fear without resorting to macho denial, which is likely to leave risk issues unacknowledged and unaddressed. Therapists can find the prospect of talking openly to clients about the risk they present awkward or frightening and can avoid or rush through such discussions. They may believe that they need to maintain a 'cosy' relationship to keep themselves safe and may fear that discussing risk will anger or offend the client and increase the risk of being harmed. In reality, failing to engage clients in open discussion increases risk as issues are left unaddressed.

When discussing risk with clients, therapists need to be prepared for the deception that individuals can display. Clients may attempt to be misleading regarding their level of risk and view occupational therapy sessions as an opportunity to secrete tools.

Working effectively with people with personality disorder

Having explored the challenges faced when working in the field, it could be reasonably concluded that working with very demanding clients, in unaccommodating and sometimes overtly hostile environments, presents an insurmountable task for occupational therapists.

The purpose of this section is to equip the reader with strategies to ensure safe and effective practice, to deliver a varied occupational therapy programme within restricted environments and to develop positive working relationships within which occupational therapy is understood and valued.

When working with people with personality disorder it is vital therapists stringently follow the principles of good practice outlined within the documents *Professional Standards for Occupational Therapy Practice* (2007) and *Code of Ethics and Professional Conduct* (2005). Due to the litigious nature of the client group, failure to do so will inevitably be exposed. Further to this, strategies for effective working are outlined below.

Maintaining credibility

Developing others' understanding of occupational therapy is arguably the responsibility of every practitioner. Therapists need to be prepared to clearly explain the occupational therapy role; brief reference to research evidence can help give credence to such descriptions. It is particularly helpful to highlight the outcomes most likely to be valued by the listener – for example, by telling clients how they personally can benefit, by highlighting how interventions reduce risk within a forensic setting and by informing service providers about how occupational therapy can increase the throughput of clients.

Therapists need to capitalise on opportunities to educate others about the profession. A bare minimum is unfailing representation at multidisciplinary team and Care Programme Approach meetings, which afford opportunities for promotion of the role during the handover of client-related information. Attending senior management meetings enables occupational therapy services to ensure their agenda is heard and to reinforce the need for resource investment. Services currently excluded at strategic level may have to lobby for their inclusion. Unit-wide training programmes, journal clubs and away-days provide obvious forums for education delivery whose usefulness should not be underestimated. Where such arrangements are not already in place, organising department open days and training sessions should be considered.

A further public relations opportunity is the circulation of occupational therapy client reports. These should include clear explanations of the impact that untreated occupational needs have on health, well-being and (often most influentially) risk and why occupational therapy is required to address these areas.

Therapists need to pre-empt misunderstanding of the role. When introducing new clinical initiatives such as a new therapy group, it is helpful to prepare by educating staff from other disciplines about the aims and rationale of the group in the weeks prior to it starting in order that colleagues don't focus exclusively on the activity at the expense of therapeutic content. Providing non-therapeutic activity needs to be approached with caution. Offering diversional activity can give the impression that this is all occupational therapy has to offer and, once this idea has taken hold within a service, it can be difficult to counteract.

Derogatory remarks about occupational therapy, made in jest or otherwise, should be directly addressed by the therapist (Melton and Creek, 2006). Ignoring or laughing along with such comments can appear to condone this behaviour which demeans the profession. Statements that reflect a lack of understanding of the occupational therapy role (for example, when others casually refer to their own activity-based sessions as 'OT') should be corrected.

By maintaining an awareness of the occupational therapist stereotype of 'basket weaver', therapists can ensure that they behave in a professional manner that lends no credence to such perceptions. Using occupational therapy terminology is a simple means of conveying that occupational therapy is a profession with its own technical knowledge. Occupational therapists at consultant level need to be seen to be taking responsibility for the development of the service as a whole and shouldn't be afraid to offer direction to other practitioners, whatever their discipline.

Identifying clients in need of occupational therapy

Services need to have clearly defined referral criteria based around the tenet that clients need occupational therapy when they have occupational needs that impact upon their health, well-being, personal development, life satisfaction and/or risk of harm to self and others.

Screening assessments provide a useful aid to assessing clients' appropriateness for therapy as they collect a broad range of information and ensure the assessment remains occupationally focused. *The Model of Human Occupation Screening Tool* (Parkinson *et al.*, 2006) is recommended as it allows for information to be gathered from a range of sources. Relying on clients' self-report alone is insufficient because of their lack of insight and reluctance to expose their vulnerabilities (Lima, 2008). Interviewing other staff and, with the client's permission, family and friends enables the therapist to gain insight into the client's functioning in a range of physical and social environments. Therapists should supplement screening tool findings with reference to clients' risk assessments and/or risk histories in order to gain some understanding of the relationship between clients' occupational adaptation and risk.

Maintaining an occupational focus

The aim of occupational therapy is to enable the client to construct a positive occupational identity and enact it in day-to-day life by sustaining a congruent pattern of occupational participation. Therapists need to help their clients to overcome the legacies of their childhoods and re-craft their daily lives so that they contain meaning, worth and fulfilment. Offering interventions outside the occupational therapy role, be it via anger management groups, counselling sessions or diversional activities, deprives clients of the occupationally focused interventions they require and therapists risk attempting to provide interventions they are not trained to deliver.

Using an occupational therapy conceptual practice model is helpful in maintaining an occupational focus. Clearly explaining the role of occupational therapy assists clients to develop accurate expectations about the focus of sessions, which increases the probability of staying on task. Structured assessments are also useful to ensure occupation remains the focal point of discussion and prevent the therapist being taken off on irrelevant tangents.

Developing motivation

In order to be motivated for change, clients require an awareness of their occupational difficulties and the ways in which they impact upon their health, well-being, survival and/or risk. Therapists need to be open and honest with clients regarding the range and severity of their occupational needs. Discussing findings of standardised assessments is a useful means of facilitating this. Inexperienced therapists may worry that this will hurt or offend the client and elicit a hostile response or damage an already fragile therapeutic relationship. In practice, clients frequently respond well to explicit yet non-judgemental observations about their needs. The process can actually strengthen the therapeutic alliance as it can enable clients to experience being understood and validated and develops the credibility of the therapist.

Therapists need to communicate confidence in the efficacy of occupational therapy. Psycho-education regarding the benefits of engagement in a balanced routine of healthy occupations is also likely to be needed.

Where clients seek to avoid facing their own deficits by disregarding feedback, therapists need to persist with raising the issue, using examples to evidence their views. Neglecting to do so would mean colluding with clients' avoidance and would negatively affect treatment outcomes as key issues would be left untreated. The therapist needs to judge how much feedback a client can manage (which is often in direct proportion to the strength of the therapeutic alliance). This principle should be applied with all clients including those with narcissistic personality disorder, regardless of any outrage they may display. Providing more positive feedback than negative helps the client to 'save face' and enabling clients to participate in occupations they value is helpful in maintaining their motivation.

Dependent clients should be reassured that developing their functioning won't result in them receiving less support until they are ready to relinquish it and although therapy will enable them to develop greater independence, they will increase their social networks and opportunities to develop supportive relationships.

Building effective therapeutic relationships

Initially, building a therapeutic alliance forms the primary focus of occupational therapy because of the extent of clients' difficulties with forming trusting relationships. Even when formal assessment and treatment have commenced, therapists must be prepared to postpone this work in order to address relationship difficulties as they arise (Livesley, 2003).

When building relationships with clients, it is important not to interpret resistance as a sign that they are not ready for therapy. Many have a fear of rejection and will try to avert abandonment by pushing their therapist away. Persistence is not only crucial to relationship development but is also therapeutic in that it challenges individuals' beliefs about themselves and others. Where clients avoid contact, informing them that the therapist will wait in the location where the session is due to take place for its duration is a helpful strategy (see Chapter 5 for further discussion).

Establishing boundaries with regard to the frequency and duration of sessions helps manage clients' expectations and is particularly useful to pre-empt dependent clients' attempts to engineer more time with their therapists. Where resources are stretched, therapists need to be open about the fact that intervention will be time-limited, to reduce clients' disappointment and feelings of abandonment when sessions end.

Holding sessions in environments where individuals feel as safe as possible will aid the development of the therapeutic alliance. This may involve adapting the treatment setting to suit the individual's needs, for example by initially having a person the client trusts in or outside the room.

During early sessions, it is important to identify clients' fears around therapy and provide appropriate reassurance. Therapists should always reassure clients who have been victims of systematic sexual abuse that they will not have sex with them or otherwise harm them, as these are very real fears and expectations for these people (see Chapter 5). Whilst some therapists may balk at engaging in such frank discussion, it is important to be explicit because clients may not share the same logic as their therapist. Personality disordered individuals lack experience of feeling safe with others and thus erroneously predict abuse.

Using activities valued by clients can help them tolerate time with their therapists when they are feeling unsafe. Care needs to be taken when choosing activities, however; introducing an activity that an individual dislikes or struggles to perform could potentially damage the relationship if the person is left feeling coerced, exposed or humiliated.

Consistency in maintaining boundaries is essential in order to challenge clients' negative expectations and build trust. Being seconds late is significant due to many personality disordered individuals' over-sensitivity to rejection. Clients are likely to struggle to rationalise tardiness or tolerate the emotional consequences of their therapist being late.

Clients' attempts to inject sexuality into the relationship need to be addressed promptly and directly. Formulating the behaviour as an effort to connect with others provides an opportunity to reassure clients that this is a common consequence of childhood sexual abuse and enables exploration of more functional ways of bonding with others. Being aware of one's own discomfort helps the therapist to avoid responding in an unintentionally punitive manner or behaving in a way that could be interpreted as reciprocating the client's flirtatiousness.

Clearly linking activities used in therapy to clients' occupational needs and treatment goals enables them to understand the therapeutic value of what they are doing and reduces the likelihood of them dismissing occupational therapy as pointless or irrelevant. This approach also helps reassure clients that they are not being groomed; explicit discussion around this is likely to be of benefit. Therapists need to avoid trying to foster closeness by creating a sense of being 'in cahoots together', for example by implying that they are offering clients special treats which must be kept a secret. A more likely outcome here would be the client fearing abuse or spotting an opportunity to split the therapist from the rest of the team.

Clients' level of engagement within the therapeutic relationship needs to be considered when deciding what assessment methods to use. In the absence of a trusting and collaborative relationship, people with personality disorder are likely to present inaccurate information about themselves to either please or mislead the therapist (Barris, 1985). In-depth explorations of clients' difficulties are best saved until there is sufficient trust within the relationship.

Conceptualising issues and guiding treatment

An occupational therapy model of practice is an invaluable resource when formulating clients' functioning as it helps identify salient issues amongst what can be a mass of information. The *Model of Human Occupation* (Kielhofner, 2008) is recommended as it considers intra-personal factors such as self-efficacy, values and interests, all of which are significant issues for the client group. The model's relevance for this population is well documented (Cara, 1992; Froehlich, 1992; Neville-Jan *et al.*, 1991; Salz, 1983).

Understanding the client's perspective

Asking clarifying questions – such as 'You describe your father as doing things with you when you were young. Can you give me an example of a time you did something together?' – is recommended to ensure that the therapist and client are utilising concepts such as 'strict' and 'loving' in a similar manner.

Working with trauma

Traumatic experiences are prevalent within the histories of people with personality disorder. Occupational therapists working in the field need to develop an awareness of issues such as childhood sexual abuse in order to be able to respond appropriately (Foulder-Hughes, 1998). Understanding the impact trauma has upon a person's identity enables the therapist to treat problems with present-day occupational functioning.

When responding to disclosures relating to trauma, therapists must be mindful of the nature of their training and experience, to ensure they remain within their sphere of competence. Whilst it is important to enable clients to share their experiences, it is equally vital to avoid encouraging further disclosure or to attempt to offer psychological analysis. Therapists should limit their interventions to providing validation, supporting clients to establish a connection with their emotional experience and exploring the impact of trauma upon current occupational functioning. Lentin (2002, p. 145) advocates 'talking with a focus on the things one does, has done, wants to do and could do', to facilitate 'the construction of a self who is an agentic and masterful occupational being who tackles the challenges of ongoing life'.

Clear and regular feedback to the team regarding such interventions should alleviate others' anxieties about occupational therapists remaining within their professional role.

Working with risk

Addressing issues head on is the key to effective risk management. Where clients have histories of harming themselves or others, comprehensive risk assessments need to be carried out and multidisciplinary team agreement obtained prior to embarking on any intervention. Where risk is present – for example when conducting cooking sessions in a forensic environment – clear risk management strategies should be identified and followed stringently. Therapists should set and enforce boundaries around when it is not safe enough to proceed.

Therapists need to be open with clients about the risks involved in a session. Being explicit about risk management strategies can help them feel contained (thus further reducing risk). Therapists also need to be emotionally honest, for example by telling clients when they feel frightened of them, as this aids individuals to develop their understanding of their own dangerousness and the impact it has on others. This also reduces the likelihood of therapists acting out, for example by resorting to macho or ingratiating behaviour.

Occupational therapy facilitates opportunities for positive risk taking whereby clients' risk can be tested and reduced within a controlled environment. Occupational therapists must present multidisciplinary teams with robust protocols around the use of 'controversial' interventions that include strong rationales and comprehensive risk management strategies.

Clinical supervision

The challenges inherent in personality disorder working create a requirement for quality supervision (Couldrick, 2003) within which both parties openly and frankly discuss the supervisee's performance. Supervisors need to offer direct feedback and challenge, whilst maintaining a non-judgemental stance which enables the supervisee to be reflective and honest.

Secondary traumatisation caused by listening to distressing accounts of abuse or offending behaviour can be addressed through working through the therapist's emotional response within supervision. Supervisors need to oversee supervisees' formulations of clients and to intervene where necessary, particularly in forensic services where therapists may struggle to hold both the victim and perpetrator parts of the client in mind.

Participation in multidisciplinary group supervision provides an opportunity for therapists to develop shared understanding with other team members and can reduce feelings of professional isolation, particularly where individuals can be open about their experience of working within the team.

Occupational balance

Occupational therapists are encouraged to use their knowledge around the health benefits of occupation in order to manage their own work-induced stress. Winwood *et al.* (2007, p. 862) found that 'active and fulfilling non-work-time behaviours are more significant in maximising recovery from work strain than is commonly recognised'; engagement in exercise, creative and social occupations is particularly beneficial.

Conclusion

Occupational therapy is an important component of the transdisciplinary treatment of clients with personality disorder due to the prevalence of occupational dysfunction within the population. The need for occupational therapy however is yet to be widely recognised across personality disorder services. This is likely to be detrimental to overall treatment outcomes due to the negative consequences functional deficits have for health. It is argued that the occupational therapy profession needs to develop a distinct identity and role and the ability to clearly articulate its contribution to the treatment of people with personality disorder.

Working with clients with personality disorder is a challenging undertaking for occupational therapists, both in terms of providing effective clinical interventions and managing the difficult dynamics that exist within personality disorder services. Having an awareness of issues that are likely to arise enables occupational therapists to pre-empt potential problems and/or address them promptly in order to minimise their impact.

References

Abrahamson, V. (1998) Do occupational therapists feel equipped to deal with the adult legacy of childhood sexual abuse? *British Journal of Occupational Therapy*, **61(2)**, 63–67.

American Psychiatric Association (1994) *Diagnostic and Statistical Manual of Mental Disorders – 4th edn.* Washington, DC: APA.

Barris, R. (1985) Psychosocial dysfunction. In G. Kielhofner (1985), *A Model of Human Occupation: Theory and Application.* Baltimore: Williams & Wilkins.

Calabretta-Caprini, T. (1989) Contracting with patients diagnosed with borderline personality disorder. *Canadian Journal of Occupational Therapy*, **56(4)**, 179–184.

Cara, E. (1992) Neutralizing the narcissistic style: narcissistic personality disorder, self-psychology and occupational therapy. *Occupational Therapy in Health Care*, **8(2/3)**, 135–156.

Christiansen, C., Townsend, E. and Bing, R.K. (2004) Occupation and well-being. In C. Christiansen and E. Townsend (eds), *Introduction to Occupation: The Art of Science and Living.* Upper Saddle River, NJ: Prentice Hall, ch. 1.

College of Occupational Therapists (2005) *Code of Ethics and Professional Conduct.* London: COT.

College of Occupational Therapists (2007) *Professional Standards for Occupational Therapy Practice.* London: COT.

Couldrick, L. (2003) Personality disorder – a role for occupational therapy. In L. Couldrick and D. Aldred (eds), *Forensic Occupational Therapy.* London: Whurr Publishers, ch. 20.

Creek, J. (2003) *Occupational Therapy Defined as a Complex Intervention.* London: College of Occupational Therapists.

Fidler, G.S. and Fidler, J.W. (1983) Doing and becoming; the occupational therapy experience. In G. Kielhofner (ed.), *Health Through Occupation: Theory and Practice in Occupational Therapy.* Philadelphia: F.A. Davis. ch. 13.

Fortune, T. (2000) Occupational therapists: is our therapy truly occupational or are we merely filling gaps? *British Journal of Occupational Therapy*, **63(5)**, 225–230.

Foulder-Hughes, L. (1998) The educational needs of occupational therapists who work with adult survivors of childhood sexual abuse. *British Journal of Occupational Therapy*, **61(2)**, 68–74.

Froehlich, J. (1992) Occupational therapy interventions with survivors of sexual abuse. *Occupational Therapy in Health Care*, **8(2/3)**, 1–25.

Glass, T.A., Mendes de Leon, C., Marrotoli, R.A. and Berkman, L.F. (1999) Population based study of social and productive activities as predictors of survival amongst elderly Americans. *British Medical Journal*, **319**, 478–483.

Kielhofner, G. (2008) *Model of Human Occupation: Theory and Application*, 4th edn. Baltimore: Lippincott, Williams & Wilkins.

Kloss, D.M. (2005) *Occupational Health Law.* Malden, MA: Blackwell Publishing.

Law, M., Steinwender, S. and Leclair, L. (1998) Occupation, health and well-being. *Canadian Journal of Occupational Therapy*, **65(2)**, 81–91.

Lentin, P. (2002) The human spirit and occupation: surviving and creating a life. *Journal of Occupational Science*, **9(3)**, 143–152.

Lima, A. (2008) 'The colours of my being' – a community intervention for a person with borderline personality disorder and co-morbid minor depression. *Mental Health Occupational Therapy*, **13(3)**, 109–112.

Livesley, W.J. (2003) *Practical Management of Personality Disorder*. London: Guilford Press.

Melton, J. and Creek, J. (2006) Occupational therapists and power. *British Journal of Occupational Therapy*, **69(10)**, 441.

National Institute for Health and Clinical Excellence (2009a) *Antisocial Personality Disorder: NICE Clinical Guideline 77*. London: NICE.

National Institute for Health and Clinical Excellence (2009b) *Borderline Personality Disorder: NICE Clinical Guideline 78*. London: NICE.

Neville-Jan, A., Bradley, M., Bunn, C. and Gehri, B. (1991) The model of human occupation and individuals with co-dependency problems. *Occupational Therapy in Mental Health*, **11(2/3)**, 73–97.

Parkinson, S., Forsyth, K. and Kielhofner, G. (2006) *The Model of Human Occupation Screening Tool (MOHOST) (Version 2.0)*. Authors.

Salz, C. (1983) A theoretical approach to the treatment of work difficulties in borderline personalities. In D. Gibson (ed.), *Occupational Therapy with Borderline Patients*. New York: Haworth Press, Inc, ch. 3.

Skodol, A.E., Gunderson, J.G., McGlashan, T.H. *et al.* (2002) Functional impairment in patients with schizotypal, borderline, avoidant or obsessive-compulsive personality disorder. *American Journal of Psychiatry*, **159(2)**, 276–283.

Skodol, A.E., Oldham, J.M., Bender, D.S. *et al.* (2005) Dimensional representations of DSM-IV personality disorders: relationships to functional impairment. *American Journal of Psychiatry*, **162(10)**, 1919–1925.

Soloff, P.H., Lynch, K.G. and Kelly, T.M. (2002) Childhood abuse as a risk factor for suicidal behaviour in borderline personality disorder. *Journal of Personality Disorder*, **16**, 201–214.

Trombly, C.A. (1995) Occupation: purposefulness and meaningfulness as therapeutic mechanisms. The 1995 Eleanor Clarke Slagle lecture. *American Journal of Occupational Therapy*, **49**, 960–972.

Wilcock, A. (1993) A theory of the human need for occupation. *Occupational Science: Australia*, **1(1)**, 17–24.

Wilcock, A. (2003) Occupational science: the study of humans as occupational beings. In P. Kramer, J. Hinojosa and C.B. Royeen (eds), *Perspectives in Human Occupation: Participation in Life*. Baltimore: Lippincott, Williams & Wilkins, ch. 6.

Winwood, C.P., Bakker, A.B. and Winefield, A.H. (2007) An investigation of the role of non-work-time behavior in buffering the effects of work strain. *Journal of Occupational and Environmental Medicine*, **49(8)**, 862–871.

World Federation of Occupational Therapists (2004) *Definition of Occupational Therapy*. Forrestfield, Australia: World Federation of Occupational Therapists.

Wright, C. and Rowe, N. (2005) Protecting professional identities: service user involvement and occupational therapy. *British Journal of Occupational Therapy*, **68(1)**, 45–47.

Zanarini, M.C., Frankenburg, F.R., Hennen, J., Reich, B. and Silk, K.R. (2005) Psychosocial functioning of borderline patients and Axis II comparison subjects followed prospectively for six years. *Journal of Personality Disorders*, **19(1)**, 19–29.

Zemke, R. and Clark, F. (1996) *Occupational Science: The Evolving Discipline.* Philadelphia: F.A. Davis.

Zlotnick, C., Johnson, D.M., Yen, S. *et al.* (2003) Clinical features and impairment in women with borderline personality disorder (BPD) and post-traumatic stress disorder (PTSD), BPD without PTSD and other personality disorders with PTSD. *Journal of Nervous and Mental Disease*, **191**, 706–713.

Chapter 10

The role of the prison officer (dangerous and severe personality disorder in the prison system)

Stephen Fox

Introduction

Historically, responsibility for protecting the public from the dangerous mentally ill has been placed upon the shoulders of psychiatry. The burden of public protection was relieved with Fallon's recommendation for abolition of hospital orders in favour of penal sentencing (Fallon *et al.*, 1999) and the introduction (Criminal Justice Act 2003) of 'renewable' indeterminate sentences for dangerous offenders whose release is dependent on the level of risk of sexual and/or violent re-offending posed (Eastman, 1999). Whilst the future for the psychiatrist had become uncertain, the prison officer was becoming increasingly responsible for dealing with those classified as *dangerous and severely personality disordered* (a non-diagnostic label for those contained within specialist services), with the implementation of Dangerous and Severe Personality Disorder Units at HMP Whitemoor and HMP Frankland.

The 'dangerous' and 'disruptive' prisoner is no stranger to the prison officer. At any one time, between 0.2 per cent and 5 per cent of prisoners fit this classification (Coyle in Coid, 1998). The Joint Home Office/Department of Health Working Group's estimation is that there are approximately 2,000 people, mainly men, in prisons and secure hospitals who would meet the criteria for Dangerous and Severe Personality Disorder (DSPD) (DoH, 1999). Coyle, the Home Office and the Department of Health are tentative about the accuracy of these estimates. However, since more people labelled DSPD will be accommodated in prisons, there will be an increasing expectation that officers will be involved in the process of treating DSPD prisoners in addition to being responsible for their safe custody. It is suggested that the future for working with this difficult client group now centres on a 'situational approach' to 'problem behaviour' where operational staff collaborate with mental health care professionals to establish new therapeutic regimes (Coid, 1998). The notion of 'treating' rather than 'managing' this population became a reality for prison officers in 2002 with the creation of a treatment-orientated unit for DSPD prisoners at HMP Whitemoor.

The primary tasks of security and control

Thomas asserts in his dated, yet authoritative and cyclically prophetic, analysis of the conflict inherent in the role of the English prison officer that 'the uniformed officer *is* the English prison service' and that, without the support of officers, reform is 'doomed to certain failure' (Thomas, 1972). Prison officers are acutely aware of the significance of their compliance for prospective reforms. However, this axiom of prison life may be overlooked, discounted or underestimated by the uninformed or uninitiated reformer.

The current authoritative, overtly appreciative, standard text about the role of the modern prisoner officer introduces us to a benign, 'close knit' workforce of typically middle-aged men from military backgrounds, only comparatively recently diluted by a slow but significant intake of women, younger, unmarried staff and those with no military background, whose concept of job satisfaction is essentially a 'good day', either free of crisis, or a 'good day' where a crisis has been successfully resolved. For these staff, conflict between care and control is not quite as profound as for their more militaristic forebears (Liebling and Price, 2001). However, the creation of a prison-hosted DSPD Unit (one of four units: two hospital sites and two prison sites established under the auspices of the Health Partnership Directorship), with its highly specialised multidisciplinary clinical team, aggressively promoting a treatment model, explicitly challenged the traditional officer role and thus posed perhaps as great a perceived threat to the control of prisoners as some of the ambitious reforms in the late nineteenth century.

HMP Whitemoor is a high security prison shadowed by the escape of six prisoners from its Special Secure Unit in 1994 during which one of the officers from this 'close knit group' was shot and wounded. In the aftermath, HMP Whitemoor 'amended' for its failure to provide secure containment by embracing 'very properly a reliance on strict adherence to written security procedures and regulations' (Excerpt ES3, HMCIP, 2000). HMP Whitemoor became an exemplary high security prison with a clear understanding of its primary task. To compound this, officers at HMP Whitemoor were aware of the ability of offenders with dangerous and severe personality disorder to compromise the security and control of a secure institution because of the high profile failures at Ashworth high secure hospital (see Fallon *et al.*, 1999).

On the other hand, the iconoclastic clinical team who were to bring their reforms to HMP Whitemoor very properly relied upon strict adherence to a coherent treatment model and possessed an equally clear understanding of *their* primary tasks. Inevitably, there was potential for inter-professional conflict.

The alienation of the prison officer and 'the basics'

Reconciling the often contradictory tasks of control and treatment is, perhaps, the greatest stumbling block to introducing treatment-orientated reforms into a prison. However, there is a more insidious pair of hazards which threaten the maintenance, if not the introduction, of a treatment model: the de-skilling of officers (due to specialists taking over officer-led rehabilitative functions) and the perception that specialists treat prisoners more favourably than prison officers. Thomas observes that the prison officer has largely been excluded from the implementation of successive reforms. Since the late nineteenth century, prison staff have been viewed as the agents of punishment who are impediments to reform. Prison officers have tended to be reduced to 'mere fetchers and carriers of men for people who come inside from the various bodies which interest themselves in prison work' (Thomas, 1972).

The officers' historically *normative* primary task of control has been repeatedly undermined by successive reforms, with the task of control surviving in the form of an *existential* and *phenomenal* primary task (see Roberts, 1994). In 1966, the Mountbatten Report unequivocally reasserted control as the Prison Service's normative primary task, where it has firmly remained (despite the Prison Service briefly entertaining Woolf's (1991) ill-implemented and ill-fated liberal, optimistic reformism) until this present day. The escape from Whitemoor (and escapes from Parkhurst in 1995) instigated the robustly implemented Learmont Report (Home Office, 1995), thus shifting the Prison Service's focus away from Woolf's reforms and back upon secure control. However, Woolf did pave the way for the 2002 launch of the Prison Service's Decency Agenda. At the beginning of the new millennium, the primary task of control was, at least, to be tempered with decency.

Exercising control over the prisoner population has been the enduring primary role for the prisoner officer. In 1963, the Prison Officers' Association published a document, 'The role of the modern officer', which depicted a typical day's duty as comprising of 'nothing more or less than unlocking the men and locking them up again; escorting them to exercise, to the workshops and back again inside the prison; feeding them and, at the end of the day, finally locking them up and checking them for the night' (Prison Officers' Association, 1963, pp. 330–332).

The 'typical day' is as familiar to today's English prison officer as it would have been to the prison subordinate in 1875. There are prison officers throughout the prison system who are to some extent involved in a wide range of reforms, but the description above encapsulates what the modern officer still recognises as 'the basics' – those non-discretionary tasks, the delivery of the 'core day', that all officers are expected to perform, without question, when required to do so.

Assessment and observation – role model officers and the management model

What was the profile of officers who volunteered to work in the newly formed DSPD Unit? Liebling and Price (2001) observed that prison officers often gravitate to a particular wing or section of a prison which is compatible with their working style and their own personality. Prior to the creation of the DSPD Unit, their study of staff–prisoner relationships at Whitemoor identified a range of working styles throughout the prison. They found common factors shared by a group they identified as 'role model officers': known and consistent boundaries; moral fibre; awareness of the effects of their own power; an understanding of the painfulness of prison; a professional orientation; and an optimistic, but realistic outlook.

These role model characteristics were evident in a significant proportion of the staff who commenced work on the DSPD Unit. They had been drawn from diverse prison environments ranging from the highly boundaried, security-focused environment of the Special Secure Unit, to those who had worked closely and flexibly with prisoners in the Sexual Offenders Treatment Programme (Fox *et al.*, 2006). Despite their contrasting professional histories, these staff 'enjoyed' working with DSPD prisoners and rated themselves as truthful, industrious and open thinking. They were secure and enthusiastic about working with DSPD prisoners and took the opportunity to engage in high frequency officer–prisoner interactions. Bowers (2002) found that these officers spent 42 per cent of their time talking to prisoners, whereas other research has indicated that psychiatric nurses spend just 18 per cent of their time with patients. Importantly, these staff did not fit the profile of Gilbert's (1997) 'reciprocators' who are inclined to work in clinical settings but tend to 'go along to get along', may be inconsistent and may be reluctant to use coercive authority or physical interventions even when it is fully legitimate. The role model officers who gravitated to the DSPD Unit were especially conscious of their primary tasks of security and control.

The officers' initial enthusiasm was rewarded with the DSPD Unit enjoying a remarkable degree of secure order considering the profile of the prisoner population. In the early formative period, a group of fifty-five prisoners were responsible for just ten violent incidents whereas thirty-seven were anticipated (Taylor, 2003). Studies that rely on recording prison adjudications need to be analysed critically as there are other factors, other than successful 'management', which may account for a decrease in recorded violent incidents. However, officers charged with observing and supporting the prisoners (some of whom had personal experience of particular prisoners' dangerousness and disruptiveness from their former posts in Segregation Units and Closed Supervision Centres) were confident that it was *their* contribution on the unit that was responsible for the secure controlled environment. According to the assessment officers, these gains may have been correlated to successful prisoner management and interventions that were focused through utilisation of the Daily Behaviour Rating Scale (DBRS; Hogue *et al.*, 1998). The DBRS was argued to be the 'glue' that bonded the assessment programme together. The provision of a coherent assessment tool enabled staff to appreciate the functions of prisoners' behaviour rather than merely reacting to it (Fox *et al.*, 2006).

At this point, the DSPD Unit had not formulated and articulated its treatment model. Indeed, the Assessment and Observation Unit officers were keenly focused on *not* clinically treating prisoners. Despite this, officers were observing significant behavioural improvements in the prisoners and understood these gains as arising from an awareness of the function of prisoners' behaviour. Officers, despite self-consciously *managing* the prisoners, were already beginning to integrate treatment principles within their professional practice.

Reflecting upon Thomas's (1972) caveats about tension between prison officers and any influx of specialists, it seems appropriate to consider the relative absence of conflict between officers, specialists and their conflicting primary tasks of control and treatment during the early development of the unit.

Essentially, there was no 'influx' of specialists to overwhelm the officers' roles. It amounted, rather, to a steady 'trickle'. Furthermore, the officers were not, consciously, doing anything especially novel. Officers were running the Assessment and Observation Spur as a sophisticated Close Supervision Centre or Special Unit. Unlike some of their forebears in Special Units who felt at times they 'were not doing anything' but 'getting through the day' quietly (Walmsley *et al.*, 1991), DSPD Unit officers had the luxury of perceiving they were 'in [such] an appropriately resourced environment [they] could make unprecedented progress with this profoundly challenging prisoner group' (Fox *et al.*, 2006).

However, this phase of development in the unit proved to be the calm before the storm. The steady trickle of clinicians increased until it became an influx of Thomasonian scale. Moreover, the influx were intent on commencing therapeutic intervention with a treatment model that was profoundly 'cognitive-interpersonal' and appeared, to some officers, to threaten the hard-won continuity of secure order on the unit.

Intervention–role model officers and the treatment model (relinquishing control to gain control)

The work on the Intervention Spur rapidly became more clinically therapeutic than the work on the Assessment and Observation Spur. In a study of the social climate of the unit, the officers on the Assessment Spur were found to rate their environment as having higher levels of order and organisation and clearer rules than staff working on the Intervention Spur rated their environment (Cooper, 2005). Predictably, within the officer group, concerns were being expressed that by making too great a departure from the traditional officer role, the good order and discipline of the unit might be compromised. Enthusiasm to 'make a difference' through therapy continued but the officers cautiously utilised a 'mediating function where [they] endeavoured to support the treatment of prisoners', provided that 'explicitly and unequivocally it did not pose a threat to security or good order' (Fox *et al.*, 2006).

It appeared that the 'adaptations made by the prison officers [on the Intervention Spur were] not so much an intellectual response to a more appropriate model, but rather . . . an adaptive strategy to cope with inter-professional tensions related with relinquishing some elements of the role that had, previously, proven to manage prisoners effectively' (Fox *et al.*, 2006). In the initial stage of development, the Intervention Officers tended to vacillate uneasily between the role of quasi-therapist and gaoler, depending upon how each therapeutic measure impacted on their perception of the secure order of the unit. It was not until the introduction of the formal treatment model in 2004 that a core group of Intervention Officers was able to reconstruct a role which authentically supported treatment for its stated aims.

As therapeutic intervention progressed under the formal treatment model, officers observed significant behavioural improvements above and beyond that which had been achieved on the Assessment Spur. Whereas those staff involved in assessment were proudly confident that the behavioural improvements observed on their spur were related to their high quality prisoner management, officers involved in intervention discovered that within their more overtly therapeutic milieu, the application of the prisoner management model could be problematic. There were even occasions where it 'appeared to collude with the prisoner's personality disorder, undermining his treatment and, moreover, tending to compromise good order rather than facilitate it' (Fox *et al.*, 2006). It became clear that the rigid application of the management model functioned potently to encourage the prisoners to see themselves primarily as victims and lose sight of their own offending behaviours, past and present.

This was a period of 'growing pains' for the identity of the officers. The logic of working with dangerous and severe personality disorder was perverse. For example, whilst many prisons are now successfully challenging aggressive behaviours in mainstream locations, it is a given that when these behaviours reach a certain magnitude, especially when the prisoner actively pursues segregation, they virtually guarantee that the prisoner is 'segged-off' (relocated in the Segregation Unit). In the 'upside down world' of the DSPD Unit, the extremely threatening, dangerously violent prisoner is, counter-intuitively, included on the unit even when he aggressively requests to be segregated. On the DSPD Unit, 'segging-off', in all but the most extreme cases, is considered anti-therapeutic and offending-collusive (see Box 10.1).

Box 10.1

Richard had spent the larger part of his life sentence in Segregation Units and was well known in the system as a 'hard man'. Richard made repeated concerted aggressive efforts on the DSPD Unit to be 'segged-off'. However, rather than colluding with him, officers, directed by his formulation, expressed to Richard that they felt that rather than being 'hard', he was treating the Segregation Unit like the sanctuary his bedroom had been in his childhood. He was told he was behaving like a 'frightened little boy'. Richard was terrified of therapy and 'remembering the past'. Officers told him they cared for him and appreciated how frightening therapy can be. It was made clear to Richard that, despite him using overt aggression that victimised staff, staff would strive to keep him included on the unit and he would not be rejected. He was also told that if he wanted to be 'tough', the best way to prove this would be to engage in therapy.

Eventually Richard communicated to officers that he was frightened and stated that the Segregation Unit was somewhere safe to 'hide'. He began to appreciate that although he had felt like the victim and saw the officers as abusers, his actions to get relocated to the Segregation Unit actually served to victimise the officers. Richard wanted to be the victim in this process, but the officers' formulation-driven language and actions challenged the maintenance of this role and encouraged him to reflect upon his dangerousness. Richard has not 'hidden' in the Segregation Unit in the four years he has spent on the DSPD Unit and his acts of aggression have significantly reduced.

Some officers adapted quickly to the paradoxes of working with DSPD prisoners. However, for those officers whose professional practices were heavily orientated around the traditional prisoner management model, the counter-intuitive way of working with this client group was not only perverse, but frightening and, at times, repugnant.

Until this point, officers achieved their professional objectives with some success by using their traditional role (albeit in 'Role Officer' form). There was a process of some adaptation whereby the officers mediated between the management and treatment models, but ultimately, when there was a significant perceived threat to the good order and safety of the unit, the management model prevailed. On these occasions, officers would step robustly back into their roles as gaolers, the therapeutic bubble burst and the unit resurrected itself unambiguously as a prison wing. Liebling and Price (2001) compare this process to a 'cinema projector breaking down in the middle of a film . . . you can be immersed . . . but when the picture breaks and the lights come on, you remember that the screen was showing only a superficial fiction, and you were brought back to reality'.

On the DSPD Unit it had become increasingly unclear which model was the 'reality' and which was the 'superficial fiction'. Some officers expressed ambivalence towards *both* models as neither model offered a panacea for dealing with prisoners who have dangerous and severe personality disorder. The role of the officers, on the Intervention Spur, if not on the Assessment Spur, was becoming increasingly confused. Hay and Sparks asked in 1991 whether 'the role of the [typical] prison officer . . . [is] so contradictory, as to make it unusually hard for anyone to occupy it satisfactorily'. Indeed, on the DSPD Unit in 2004, it appeared to be extraordinarily problematic for a DSPD Unit prison officer to occupy a role that satisfied the polarised objectives of an 'exemplary' high security prison *and* an authentic therapeutic unit.

The deepening role crisis fortunately abated. The multi-factorial causation for this requires further analysis but an increased understanding about personality disorder and the introduction of schema-focused therapy (Young *et al.*, 2003) provided officers with insight into the counter-intuitive nature of managing and treating this prisoner group and lessened the dilemma experienced by operational staff. As officers became increasingly competent at making sense of prisoners' behaviour in the context of personality disorder and schemata, they began to find that the 'perverse logic' of the treatment model empowered them to manage prisoners *through* treatment, rather than *in spite of* it. A paradigm was in ferment that recognised that by working towards the treatment model's objectives of '*emotional* safety and containment' the officers could realise the prison's requirement for '*physical* safety and containment'. Astutely, the officer group heuristically discovered that the treatment model, when used knowledgeably and confidently, could provide a tool that facilitated, rather than compromised, secure order. This may have been the watershed for the officer group to authentically support the treatment model. Like the observation of Sykes (1958), the officers discovered they might have to lose one form of control to gain another form of control.

Balancing short-term risk and long-term risk: staff protection versus public protection

> The fact that [the prisoner] was highly dangerous and could attack us at any time didn't seem to matter so much as the fact that there were signs of him improving [in the longer term]. We could see the effect that we're having on this person and wanted to keep him [despite the fact he was frightening us].
>
> (Officer, DSPD Unit, HMP Whitemoor, cited in Savage, 2003)

Officers who work with DSPD prisoners place themselves at real risk of psychological and physical harm. Managing risk according to clinical formulations, in this milieu, is orientated to achieving sustainable long-term risk reduction to protect the public. Whilst the DSPD Unit has witnessed a remarkable reduction in violent incidents among its prisoner group, there have been individual incidents where using formulation-driven risk management strategies has increased short-term risk (see Box 10.2).

Box 10.2

David regularly touched male and female staff on the arm, shoulder or leg. Sometimes these actions were accompanied by flirtatious comments ranging from the subtle to the salacious. Generally, officers hesitated to challenge him explicitly for fear of his explosive temper. However, many officers used banter to remind him to respect other people's personal space and that his behaviour was 'against the rules'. This approach occasionally worked for short periods.

David's formulation prescribed that these behaviours needed challenging more explicitly in order to address long-term risk and public protection. David needed to know how his 'grooming' was experienced by others. Officers who experienced his touch as distressing were directed to explicitly express to him how they felt. This direction frightened officers as they were reluctant to expose their vulnerability to him.

Some officers followed this direction. Rather than just telling him that he should not inappropriately touch others because it is 'against the rules', they expressed how they felt, using terms such as 'frightened' and 'invaded'. However, the officers still felt unable to go as far as to express to him that they felt as if they were being groomed for a sexual relationship.

As predicted and feared, David's response to being challenged more (if not absolutely) explicitly was initially extremely aggressive. However, over time, David became more aware of the impact that he had on others and reduced his use of physical touch.

Officers who work with this prisoner group are required to appreciate that while physical safety on the unit may be significantly improved overall, there will be occasions when the protection of the staff will be consciously sacrificed for the protection of the public through the use of interventions guided by clinical formulations.

'Jail craft'

'Jail craft' is a term used by prison officers to encapsulate a range of interpersonal skills that empower individual officers to 'craft' their working environment and those within it. Thomas (1972) cites a *Times* article (8 May 1950) which concisely captured the spirit of jail craft as 'being clever'. 'Being clever' in the prison context means managing prisoners by being 'resource-ful', 'persuasive' and, at times, 'crafty'. It is an art, for example, that assists two officers to lock away 100 reluctant prisoners on a landing in a large local prison three times a day, 364 days a year, in just a few minutes.

In dealing with prisoners on the DSPD Unit, strictly adhering to the pris-oner management model gave way to *being clever*. In this context, being clever meant learning about each individual prisoner and understanding *why* he behaved in such a way; being clever meant not colluding with prisoners' unhelpful schemata; being clever meant using the perverse logic of working with DSPD prisoners to achieve secure order as well as public protection. The great irony became that being clever meant managing prisoners by treat-ing them. While Caplan (1993) believes that role conflict can result in an emphasis on orderliness and clarity, Cooper's (2005) study indicates that on the DSPD Unit the officers can, and do, flexibly 'utilise relationship factors to aid maintenance of both security and therapeutic roles within their work', despite the potential for role conflict.

Crucially, officers are more likely to adapt to a reform when it clearly offers some benefits in terms of secure control. Historically, in terms of large-scale reforms such as the DSPD programme, this has been rare. Implementing the treatment model on the DSPD Unit, like the separation system (see Forsythe, 1987, pp. 24–29), was an uncommon reform that far from being perceived as a threat to secure order, was discovered to have the potential to be a powerful tool to achieve it. It is not suggested that this specific treatment model is unique in its efficacy to achieve secure control. However, it is transparent and prescriptive enough to make the perverse logic of working with DSPD prisoners accessible to the pragmatic prison officer who is new to the clinical milieu. Moreover, it does not incorporate the sentimental optimistic liberal-ism that, with good reason, evokes caution in prison officers.

A licence to care

Prisoner officers are not permitted to be 'friends' with prisoners. In training, prison officers are informally encouraged to 'develop a suspicious "mindset"' and 'not to trust the bastards' (Crawley, 2004). This restriction extends beyond the prison's walls (Home Office Staff Handbook, 2005) and staff are directed not to be friends, customers, clients or affiliates even to former prisoners. To be observed to care for a 'con' (or even 'ex-con'), no matter how appropriate the intentions are, makes the officer profoundly vulnerable to censure from his peers, managers, security department and the public. In practice, this means the 'caring' officer might be derided as a 'care bear', or 'tree hugger' by fellow officers and even prisoners. In some locations, the officer may be deemed a threat to secure order as his ability to maintain 'appropriate' boundaries is questioned, and he may ultimately be shamed out of his role, if not his employment. This places even the most professional and appropriate treatment-orientated officer in security-orientated prisons (especially in the high security estate) in a dilemma. Treatment requiring the officer to 'emotionally engage' with prisoners may serve to alienate him not only from his peers, but from his friends, family and society. Therefore, it is crucial that officers who treat DSPD prisoners are *visibly* granted *formal* permission to emotionally engage with prisoners: '[We were] given the licence [by the treatment model] to act as you feel as opposed to being suppressed on other wings . . . more of a family than a team. The interaction we now have with prisoners is unique [in this prison] . . . we are breaking down barriers' (Officer, DSPD Unit, HMP Whitemoor, cited in Savage, 2003).

To 'act as you feel', however, was not seen as a licence to 'act out' or be 'mates' with prisoners. Officers remained conscious of the dangerousness of their prisoner group:

> On other wings you can switch off . . . [but on the DSPD Unit] sometimes it is difficult to step back [into being a prison officer] when talking to them [at an emotionally engaged level] . . . you have to try and tell yourself you are also a discipline officer. You are more focused on here. You can read situations more. You watch out for your colleagues more.
> (Officer, DSPD Unit, HMP Whitemoor, cited in Savage, 2003)

The formalised, published treatment model not only provided a guide to appropriate and effective relating with DSPD prisoners but provided officers with a legitimate and tangible 'licence to care'. While the officer could still expect to be treated with suspicion by his peers outside the therapeutic milieu, and sometimes within, he could at least be confident that he was relating in a way that was officially sanctioned by his employers and the state.

The price of caring: role conflict and burnout

The 'licence to care' comes at a price. A consequence of greater emotional engagement with this prisoner group is 'burnout', 'a syndrome of emotional exhaustion, depersonalisation, and reduced personal accomplishment that can occur among individuals who "do people work of some kind"' (Maslach and Jackson, 1986). Those who work in emotionally demanding roles, in terms of frequency and intensity of interpersonal interactions, have been suggested to be more vulnerable to higher levels of burnout than those who work in less emotionally demanding roles (Cordes and Dougherty, 1993). Prison personnel are considered to be a group susceptible to burnout (Pines and Maslach, 1978). Moreover, DSPD Unit officers are expected to be much more 'emotionally engaged' than typical staff, with 'the role of the prison officer working within . . . the Dangerous and Severe Personality Disorder

Unit . . . [being] considered as that of a quasi treatment specialist' (Sands, 2005), which might place them at elevated risk.

Sands (2005) found higher levels of burnout among DSPD Unit officers than among their clinical co-workers. Officers reported higher rates of emotional exhaustion and depersonalisation and lower rates of personal accomplishment (Sands, 2005). The disparity between officers' and clinicians' levels of burnout may be correlated to a higher degree of role conflict for officers. Sands suggests there is 'something about the external experiences of the prison officer . . . that might impact on the incidence of burnout' (2005). Another consideration may be Morgan's (2006) observation that officers have more in common with the prisoners than specialists have. Furthermore, officers spend significantly more time interacting informally with the prisoners and these interactions may be in larger groups of competitive and demanding prisoners (rather than in 'contained' individual sessions (Ackerley *et al.*, 1988)), and they may work a large number of 'contracted hours' (overtime) incorporated into shift patterns that are antisocial. In short, officers have been more likely to experience burnout than clinicians, and this may arise from role conflict, 'external experiences' and longer periods of contact with prisoners.

The unit offers a number of interventions to address burnout. Some interventions might be familiar to officers in other prisons – for example, regular and *ad hoc* debriefings or 'care team' support. Other interventions such as compulsory 'counselling' sessions and 'supervision sessions' may be less familiar. Supervision is promoted within any mental health service as the main defence against burnout (see Chapter 13).

Sarason *et al.* (1977) suggested that professional support groups may prevent or reduce burnout. On the DSPD Unit, every group session is followed by peer supervision for the facilitators; facilitators receive supplementary monthly supervision sessions for each group they work with; and all officers are expected to attend tri-weekly supervision sessions. The group-work-orientated supervision is tightly focused on the dynamics in that particular group. However, the tri-weekly large group sessions are more 'open' and are 'considered to be helpful in discussing and exploring difficulties within therapeutic work and developing recognition that others share one's experiences' (Sands, 2005). Individual supervision sessions support the officer to 'explore, reflect and receive feedback on work related issues . . . [and the] impact of prisoners' behaviour and stressors' (Sneath, 2006).

Banter and explicit communication

Crawley observes that, 'in the lives of prison officers, humour is as important as it is ubiquitous'. She adds that the practice of banter, the ritualised exchange of insults, 'generally lightens the atmosphere of a wing', 'functions as a defence mechanism', 'sharpens the wits' and importantly establishes status in the hierarchy of a group (Crawley, 2004). However, banter can also serve to exclude or oppress others and within the context of DSPD prisoners can be profoundly anti-therapeutic (see Box 10.3).

Box 10.3

Charlie would invariably greet officers with banter. His way of saying 'Hello' was to shout abusive phrases, often juxtaposed with a beaming childlike smile. Some officers who liked Charlie would reciprocate by shouting back an equally abusive greeting. Superficially, the exchanges seemed to lighten the relationships between Charlie and the officers. However, Charlie discreetly communicated to some staff that their responses hurt his feelings and made him feel rejected (Charlie has a primary diagnosis of borderline personality disorder). These feelings of rejection would build up and he would eventually 'explode' aggressively on the unit.

Through his formulation, it was communicated to officers that reciprocating banter with him colluded with his personality disorder, compounding his sense of rejection and fuelling his aggressive out-bursts. Officers began to refrain from meeting Charlie's banter with banter and highlighted how his use of banter set him up to be rejected. He was encouraged to initiate conversations without recourse to banter and to express clearly to others how he felt. Charlie was also encour-aged to tell those staff who used banter with him that he felt hurt and rejected by their comments.

While Charlie finds it difficult to challenge those who use abusive banter to him, he does use significantly less banter now and is more likely to express his feelings to staff and prisoners explicitly. His explosive episodes have dramatically reduced.

In the context of DSPD, both in its treatment and management, our experi-ence of banter has been that it is largely, if not exclusively, negative in its impact on this prisoner group. A strategy that has been found to be more effective has been the adoption of 'explicit communication' (see Chapter 5). Box 10.4 illustrates the potential effectiveness of explicit communication.

Box 10.4

Henry was sexually abused by his foster carers as a child. When officers attempted to perform a 'strip search' during routine cell searches, he would become extremely distressed, passive-aggressive and uncooperative. Officers attempted to make light of the process by using humour, but this aggravated the situation. Some officers experimented with communicating to him explicitly by stating they had not come to sexually abuse him before commencing search procedures. He appeared suspicious about the explicit reassurance, but seemed less distressed and co-operated with the search. On subsequent searches, staff explicitly stated that they had not come to sexually assault him and observed less distress and greater co-operation.

Whilst this case study illustrates a successful example of using a therapeutic initiative that complemented the management of a prisoner, the reader is again reminded that being directed by such clinical formulations may, on occasion, increase short-term risk.

Prison officers as treatment facilitators

Although conflict between control and treatment may be the greatest stumbling block to treatment programmes in the prison context, the de-skilling of prison officers also poses a significant threat to maintenance of a therapeutic milieu. When officers are directed to actively support treatment, whilst being excluded from being part of its delivery, there is the risk that officers will come to resent and mistrust the professionals they work *under* and the treatment programme they champion. Officers may respond in a variety of ways that are harmful to the effective maintenance of a treatment programme. At best they will try to accommodate therapists, therapy and the 'patient' by exploiting their 'jail craft' to have what Liebling and Price (2001) identify as a 'good day'. However, more problematic responses include attempting to survive the conflict and alienation by contracting out of the 'culture conflict' and refusing to participate in the development of a treatment culture or by resorting to the 'last defence of diminishing status' (Thomas, 1972), which is a focus on the dangerousness of their work, and taking refuge in the rigid application of the 'management model' at the expense of the treatment programme. The more officers see their role as maintaining order and security, the greater their tendency towards disciplinary authority, negative beliefs about prisoners and antagonism towards non-custodial staff (Fenwick, 2005). Furthermore, such officers are more likely to define themselves as being in conflict with prisoners and, ultimately, may find themselves sharing a 'collective hatred' with those prisoners (Fenwick, 2005).

It is thus paramount that within any prison-based treatment programme, especially where the primary task is secure order (e.g. High Security Estate and Close Supervision Centres), prison officers are not used merely as 'fetchers and carriers' but are authentically incorporated into the treatment programme. Therapists must willingly share their skills and knowledge with the officer group and ensure that there is a nexus between the treatment model and the officer's role as both an officer and (quasi-) therapist. Gilbert (1997) states that 'the 24-hours-a-day treatment provided by . . . line officers [is] the primary and most influential treatment program offered by any prison'. In practice, this means officers need to be appropriately trained and *fully* involved in the treatment programme, from being part of multidisciplinary team meetings through to being therapeutic co-facilitators (rather than essentially being 'security guards') in group therapies.

Transition from inter-professional tension to intra-professional tension

Validating and developing the skills of those officers with 'the right experience and abilities' served to relieve some tensions between this sub-group of officers and the clinical team. However, it appeared that the 'specialism' of those officers who developed programmes, policies and training and those who co-facilitated groups served to increase intra-professional tensions between 'specialist' officers and 'operational' officers. For some, 'specialist' officers were seen not only as an impediment to having a 'good day', but as advocates of unwelcome reforms that could compromise good order and discipline on the wing: '[Group work officers] screw up the prisoners' heads and we are the ones who have to put the pieces back together on the spurs . . . so that this place doesn't fall apart' (Officer, DSPD Unit, 2005).

Moreover, for some officers, the 'specialist' officers were viewed as being 'precious', 'the prisoners' friends' and the clinicians' 'favourites'. The language used to deride the DSPD officer 'care bears' resonates with the sense of disaffection that was expressed by officers when the Gladstone Committee remodelled Governors as reformative agents. Governors, formerly the allies of officers, joined the reformers' and prisoners' partisanship, compounding the officers' sense of being less important than prisoners. Governors' partisanship with prisoners has ceded to new managerialism. However, the creation of the 'specialist' treatment officer inflamed the longstanding professional hurt of being less cared for than prisoners. More painfully still, it was not the remote figure of the Governor who was prioritising prisoners over officers, but rather his 'close knit' group of friends and colleagues who were 'betraying' him.

The struggle for professional recognition and the tension between the *real* therapists and *quasi*-therapists

Generally, prison officers consider themselves professionals. However, they have not enjoyed the status and rewards typically associated with belonging to a professional group. Salary is perhaps the most popular rating used to compare conditions of employment. In 1999, prisoner officers were paid marginally less than the average of all occupations and significantly below the non-manual average (Liebling and Price, 2001). There has been a trend for officers' salaries to decline relative to other occupations. Recent trends have hit long-serving officers the hardest. Although prison officers consider themselves to be professionals, they do not receive a professional's salary (Liebling and Price, 2001).

Professional groups also expect to enjoy a certain amount of social prestige. However, the public image of prison officers 'is hardly [a] fertile ground for the construction of a stable and favourable conception of self' (Colvin, cited in Liebling and Price, 2001). DSPD Unit officers suffer the double jeopardy of being labelled, in their traditional role, as 'bullies' and 'thugs' and being derided, in their quasi-therapeutic role, for 'pandering to prisoners'.

Academic training and eligibility to join professional bodies is yet another benefit of being a professional. A small number of prison officers are individually supported to pursue training at graduate and postgraduate level but generally this tends to be in the fields of criminology, security studies or management studies. There is no undergraduate or postgraduate course that is specific to working as a prison officer. The officer's aspirations to custodial professional academic recognition are limited to the attainment of National Vocational Qualifications which, although accredited, are seen by some as tokenistic or another unwelcome hurdle to jump over to gain promotion.

On the DSPD Unit, officers have a strong sense of professionalism and have grown acutely aware that the service they deliver is significantly 'above and beyond' their former generic professional role. For some staff, this has heightened awareness that despite the professional service they deliver, they do not enjoy the equivalent status, qualification and remuneration that are associated with some of the other professional groups with whom they co-facilitate therapy.

Conclusion: meeting the challenge of working with personality disordered prisoners

While this chapter has focused on the work of the DSPD Unit at HMP Whitemoor, many of the learning experiences may be transferable to other prison contexts. Arguably, a more psychologically insightful prisoner officer role would be useful in all prisons. Segregation Units, Special Units and Close Supervision Centres appear to be particularly suitable for developing the officer roles described in this chapter.

A number of themes have been identified which appear to be positively related to the operational staff group's ability to effectively manage and treat personality disordered individuals. A sufficient number of role model officers should already be in post in the prison and the host prison should be able to tolerate the migration of a significant number of these officers to the DSPD Unit or other therapeutic initiative. The staff-to-prisoner ratio needs to be high and the development of a multidisciplinary ethos within such a service is essential. Staff require high quality training in the subject area of 'personality disorder', and opportunities for career development within the programme are necessary to develop and retain skills within the staff group. The provision of quality supervision is essential to reduce levels of 'burnout' and to support further staff development. Crucially, a treatment model is required which is accessible, transparent and prescriptive. This treatment model must offer the flexibility to accommodate the multiple needs of a diverse group of prisoners and the multifarious contributions of a broad range of professionals whilst being understood and accepted as conducive to achieving control.

Furthermore, the possibility of successfully managing and treating this challenging prisoner group is greatly enhanced when the operational staff group is comprised of individuals with specific personal characteristics. These characteristics include a personal commitment to transdisciplinary working and the courage to support interventions that, in the short term, appear risky; the ability to adopt a psychological understanding of risk and firmly embed psychological thinking within everyday 'jail craft'; and the inclination to co-treat prisoners, in conjunction with a range of clinicians, with a focus on public protection rather than maintenance of a quiet prison. Staff must also possess a willingness to undertake effective supervision since an officer who is not willing to be supervised places himself and those around him at significant risk of harm and, just as the psychologist must model therapeutically appropriate behaviour to the officer, the officer must model this appropriate behaviour to the prisoner. The officer will be required to develop his communication skills further since the use of explicit communication will often have to displace the traditional reliance upon banter. The officer must also be willing to form relationships and attachments with prisoners to a level he may be unaccustomed to, and must be capable of appreciating that one of his roles is to represent the prisoners' victims – past, present and prospective. The 'vulnerability' this implies may be in conflict with his traditional role, but it is a role that is essential if the protection of the public is genuinely our aim.

In short, when treating prisoners with personality disorder, we make demands in requiring them to courageously tackle their familiar but dangerous ways of coping and invest energy in exploring new ways to address the challenges of life. The demands of creating a service that is fit for supporting this growth also require that both the host organisation and the staff working within such a service are brave enough to take calculated risks and are open to exploring new strategies to successfully rehabilitate people who have posed a serious threat to the safety of society.

References

Ackerley, G.D., Burnell, J., Holder, D.C. and Kurdek, L.A. (1988) Burnout among licensed psychologists. *Professional Psychology: Research and Practice*, **19(6)**, 624–631.

Bowers, L. (2002) The right people for the job: choosing staff that will adjust positively and productively to working in the new personality disorder services. *Feedback Report*, November. London: City University (St Bartholomew School of Nursing and Midwifery).

Caplan, C.A. (1993) Nursing staff and patients' perceptions of the ward atmosphere in a maximum security forensic hospital. *Archives of Psychiatric Nursing*, **7(1)**, 23–29.

Coid, J. (1998) The management of dangerous psychopaths in prison. In T. Millon, E. Simonsen, M. Birket Smith and R. Davis (eds), *Psychopathy: Anti-social, Criminal and Violent Behaviour*. New York: Guilford Press.

Colvin, E. (1977) Prison officers: a sociological portrait of the uniformed staff of an English prison. PhD thesis, University of Cambridge.

Cooper, J. (2005) The social climate of the Dangerous and Severe Personality Disorder unit at HMP Whitemoor: staff and prisoner perceptions. HMP Whitemoor, unpublished.

Cordes, C.L. and Dougherty, T.W. (1993) A review and an integration of research on job burnout. *Academy of Management Review*, **18**, 621–656.

Crawley, E. (2004) *Doing Prison Work: The Public and Private Lives of Prison Officers*. Cullompton, Devon: Willan Publishing.

Department of Health (1999) *Managing People with Severe Personality Disorder: Proposals for Policy Development*. http://www.dspdprogramme.gov.uk/media/pdfs/Proposals_for_Policy_Development.pdf (accessed 21 April 2008).

Eastman, N. (1999) Who should take responsibility for antisocial personality disorder? *British Medical Journal*, **318**, 206–207.

Fallon, P., Bluglass, R., Edwards, B. and Daniels, G. (1999) *Report of the Committee of Inquiry into the Personality Disorder Unit, Ashworth Special Hospital*. London: HMSO.

Fenwick, S. (2005) The impact of working in segregation. *Prison Service Journal*, **158**, 3–8.

Forsythe, W.J. (1987) *The Reform of Prisoners: 1830–1900*. London: Croom Helm.

Fox, S., Jones, A., Meadows, L. and Savage, R. (2006) Prison officers in a multi-disciplinary team: the role of operational staff in the DSPD Unit at HMP Whitemoor. *Prison Service Journal*, **168**, 27–32.

Gilbert, M.J. (1997) The illusion of structure: a critique of the classical model of organisation and the discretionary power of correctional officers. *Criminal Justice Review*, **22(1)**, 49–64.

Hay, W. and Sparks, R. (1991) What is a prison officer? *Prison Service Journal*, **83**, 2–7.

Her Majesty's Chief Inspectorates of Prisons (HMCIP) (2000) Report on a full announced inspection of HMP Whitemoor, November, HM Chief Inspector of Prisons. http://www.justice.gov.uk/inspectorates/hmi-prisons/docs/whitemoor001-rps.pdf (accessed 1 February 2010).

Hogue, A., Liddle, H.A., Turner, R.M., Dakof, G.A. and Lapann, K. (1998)

Treatment adherence and differentiation in individual versus family therapy for adolescent drug abuse. *Journal of Counselling Psychology*, **45**, 104–114.

Home Office (1966) *Report of the Inquiry into Prison Escapes and Security – The Mountbatten Report (Cmnd 3175)*. London: HMSO.

Home Office (1995) *Review of Prison Service Security in England and Wales – The Learmont Report*. London: HMSO.

Home Office Staff Handbook (2005) Issued by the Directorate of Personnel, HM Prison Service, Cleland House, Page Street, London.

Liebling, A. and Price, D. (2001) *The Prison Officer*. Leyhill, HM Prison Service: Waterside Press.

Maslach, C. and Jackson, S.E. (1986) *MBI: The Maslach Burnout Inventory Manual (Research Edition)*. Palo Alto, CA: Consulting Psychologists Press.

Morgan, R. (2006) Turnkey or role model. *Prison Service Journal*, **168**, 11–13.

Pines, A. and Maslach, C. (1978) Characteristics of staff burnout in mental health settings. *Hospital and Community Psychiatry*, **29**, 233–237.

Prison Officers' Association (1963) The role of the modern officer. *Prison Officers' Magazine*, November, 330–333.

Report of the Departmental Committee on Prisons (1895) The Gladstone Committee C.7702. London: HMSO.

Roberts, V.Z. (1994) The organisation of work: contributions from open systems theory. In A. Obholzer and V.Z. Roberts (eds), *The Unconscious at Work*. London: Routledge.

Sands, J. (2005) Burnout and coping styles on a Dangerous and Severe Personality Disorder unit: prison officers' and clinicians' experiences. HM Prison Whitemoor, unpublished.

Sarason, S.B., Carroll, C.F., Maton, K., Cohen, S. and Lorentz, F. (1977) *Human Services and Resource Networks*. San Francisco: Jossey-Bass.

Savage, R. (2003) The role of prison officers on the DSPD unit at HMP Whitemoor. HM Prison Whitemoor, unpublished.

Sneath, E.L. (2006) Strategy for building a positive supervision culture – the Fens unit. HM Prison Whitemoor, unpublished.

Sykes, G. (1958) *The Society of Captives*. Princeton, NJ: Princeton University Press.

Taylor, R. (2003) An assessment of violent incident rates in the Dangerous and Severe Personality Disorder Unit at HMP Whitemoor. Findings 210, Research, Development and Statistics Directorate, Communications Development Unit, Room 264, Home Office, 50 Queen Anne's Gate, SW1H 9AT.

Thomas, J.E. (1972) *The English Prison Officer since 1850: A Study in Conflict*. London: Routledge & Kegan Paul.

Walmsley, R., Evershed, S., Fry, C., Coid, J., Roberston, G. and Gunn, J. (eds) (1991) *Managing Difficult Prisoners: The Parkhurst Special Unit*. London: HMSO.

Woolf, H. (1991) *Prison Disturbances April 1990: Report of an Enquiry by Rt. Hon. Lord Justice Woolf (Parts I and II) and His Honour Judge Steven Tumin (Part II) Cm 1456*. London: HMSO.

Young, J.E., Klosko, J.S. and Weishaar, M.E. (2003) *Schema Therapy: A Practitioner's Guide*. New York: Guilford Press.

Chapter 11

The role of the psychiatrist in treating personality disorder

Val Hawes

Introduction

This chapter will consider theoretical and practical aspects of the role of psychiatrist in an inpatient service providing lengthy psychological treatment for individuals with severe personality disorder. Theoretical aspects will include consideration of general changes to the role of psychiatrists, psychiatrists' attitudes to personality disorder and a summary of models and theories of personality disorder. Practical aspects include the psychiatric contribution to formulations of individuals with complex psychopathology, the role of medication in facilitating psychological treatment, the contribution of the psychiatrist to risk assessment and the psychiatrist as member of the multidisciplinary team.

Theoretical aspects

The changing role of psychiatrists

Traditionally, the psychiatrist was a hospital consultant who, like consultants in other specialities, had responsibility for a number of inpatients/beds and for the assessment and treatment of outpatients referred by general practitioners. Such consultants formed the upper layer of the hospital hierarchy and, in asylums, the most senior doctor was the medical superintendent. The Mental Health Acts (1959, 1983) added the legal responsibilities of the 'responsible medical officer' (RMO) to the role of the consultant.

Under these arrangements, all patients were under the care of a named consultant and all other professionals working in mental health settings were considered to be members of the consultant psychiatrist's team. The tendency for senior members of most professions to move away from direct clinical care into management contributed to the continuation of medical leadership.

With the closure of inpatient beds and the development of community mental health teams (CMHTs), non-medical professionals had the opportunity to escape from the hierarchy of the hospital and to develop alternative service models without overtly challenging the role of psychiatrists. However, the NHS reforms of the early 1990s (with changes in funding arrangements) led to CMHTs becoming the main route of access to mental health services (Onyett, 2003), with psychiatrists acting as gate-keepers as they usually brought with their contribution the understanding that they retained clinical and legal responsibility for all the patients under the care of the team.

The involvement of psychiatrists in CMHTs in this way led to high patient caseloads for consultants with increasing risk of 'burnout' and increasing difficulties in recruiting and retaining psychiatrists. Some of these difficulties were pinpointed by Kennedy and Griffiths (2001) who carried out in-depth interviews with consultant colleagues in northeast England. Some worked in traditional ways but others were moving towards new roles with a clearer separation of emergency work and fixed sessions. These new roles were well supported by the chief executives of the Trusts involved.

This small piece of qualitative research was one stimulus to two conferences of consultant psychiatrists held during 2003, the results of which were published as *New Roles for Psychiatrists* (National Working Group, 2004). This led to further work and to a final report in 2005 entitled *New Ways of Working* (NWW). This described the essence of NWW as being about using the skills, knowledge and experience of consultant psychiatrists to best effect; about promoting distributed responsibility and leadership across teams to achieve a cultural shift in services; and also about willingness to embrace change and to work flexibly with all stakeholders. More pragmatically, NWW was considered to provide a solution to recruitment and retention difficulties that were increasingly evident in psychiatry, and an opportunity to streamline budgets by reducing the number of consultant posts.

The theoretical and pragmatic aspects of NWW were consolidated with the extension of the concept to all mental health professionals in *New Ways of Working for Everyone* (2007) and included an emphasis on the benefits to users and carers. This document emphasises the aim to work with the current workforce but with a strong emphasis on competence, dispersed leadership and shared skills within a team approach. It also refers to extending the roles and scope of existing professions, for example non-medical independent and supplementary prescribing and the development of new assistant and practitioner roles.

These developments, alongside the changes in medical training (Modernising Medical Careers and the Postgraduate Medical Education and Training Board (PMETB)) and further changes in service structures (the development of foundation trusts), have led to expressions of concern that these changes represent a threat to psychiatry as a profession (Gee, 2007) or to the professionalism of psychiatrists (Brown and Bhugra, 2007).

The NWW approach has been developed mainly in the context of mental health services for adults of working age. However, the 2007 report includes chapters relating the developments to mental health services for children and adolescents and also for older people. Thus far there has been no specific reference to forensic services but it is likely that these will see relatively slower change in professional roles, particularly in those services with wholly or mainly inpatient emphasis. There has likewise been no specific reference to services for people with personality disorder. An increased emphasis on teamworking is likely to benefit users who are already linked with a team but the still limited confidence of many mental health professionals in dealing with these individuals may contribute to continued effective exclusion.

Attitudes to personality disorder

Although DSM-III (1980) incorporated a separate axis (Axis II) for personality and specific developmental disorders and diagnostic criteria for several personality disorders including borderline personality disorder, it was not until the late 1980s and early 1990s that the latter diagnosis began to be used more widely in the UK. By then, psychiatrists had become familiar with frequently presenting patients who had harmed themselves (by overdose or cutting) and who showed marked affective instability and impulsivity. These features became the main evidence of personality disorder for many psychiatrists and other mental health professionals. Once a diagnosis of borderline personality disorder had been made, such individuals were often excluded from services on the basis that they did not have a mental illness, and some of those who were offered follow-up often effectively excluded themselves by failing to keep appointments. Individuals whose personality disturbance was mainly or partly evident through criminal activity and other antisocial behaviour were labelled as having antisocial personality disorder and considered to be the responsibility of the criminal justice system. Individuals who with detailed assessment would clearly meet criteria for one of the other personality disorders were usually only offered treatment for co-morbid mental illness, for example anxiety or depression. In many services, both general adult and forensic, little specific attention was given to personality disorder issues that not infrequently complicated the treatment of that co-morbid illness.

Within the older model of service provision, consultant psychiatrists were often key to the decision as to whether or not a service continued to be offered to any individual with clear personality disorder. Whilst this led to many exclusions, there were individual psychiatrists who developed and maintained a specific interest in personality disorder, often pursuing research interests alongside clinical work – for example, Peter Tyrer's development of the Personality Assessment Schedule. Psychiatrists and medical psychotherapists have played a major role in the development and maintenance of therapeutic communities at the Henderson and Cassel Hospitals, and in the development of newer psychotherapeutically oriented outpatient services, for example the Complex Cases Service in Cambridge. In forensic personality disorder services, consultant psychiatrists have varied in the extent to which they have been involved in psychological treatment but they have nearly always had the final say in decisions about admissions and discharges from such services. In this regard, like many other consultant forensic psychiatrists, they have tended to perpetuate the traditional role of the psychiatrist. An alternative model in which the psychiatrist functions as a member of a team in such a setting is described in the last section of this chapter.

The exclusion from mainstream services described above was only officially acknowledged with the publication of *Personality Disorder: No Longer a Diagnosis of Exclusion* (NIMHE, 2003). Using this as a springboard, the National Institute of Mental Health in England, succeeded by the Care Services Improvement Partnership, commissioned and funded a number of pilot projects covering various aspects of services for people with personality disorder and training for professionals in agencies working with such individuals. It is unclear to what extent these initiatives have led to a change of attitude towards personality disorder in those with previously negative attitudes. It seems more likely that they have been most effective in providing development opportunities for services and professionals who had an existing interest in these disorders whilst mainstream services and mental health professionals are relatively unchanged.

Despite most psychiatrists, and other mental health professionals, acknowledging that they do find some service users 'difficult', relatively little has been written about how to understand and then work with such individuals. Hinshelwood (1999) specifically includes those with severe personality disorder as 'difficult patients'. Although it seems that many are reluctant to look beyond the 'difficult' presentation, it is clear to professionals who choose to work with personality disordered individuals that there are understandable reasons for the 'difficult' side and that there is virtually always some aspect of the individual's personality that is available for engagement.

Models and theories of mental disorder and personality disorder

Most psychiatrists appear to remain very conscious of their original training as doctors and rarely question the applicability of the medical model to an understanding of mental disorder. These assumptions have contributed to the dominance of the major mental illnesses (schizophrenia and major affective illness) in psychiatric thinking and to the role of the psychiatrist in administering mental illness as a social institution. Questioning these mainstream views has usually been left to psychiatrists who have held radically different perspectives. These include the anti-psychiatrists such as Thomas Szasz and R.D. Laing, post-psychiatrists like Bracken and Thomas (2001), and those who have considered other models from the perspective of non-Western cultures. Psychodynamic models have had very limited influence in British psychiatry, with some specific exceptions – for example, some acceptance of Freudian understanding of melancholia and hysteria, and Bowlby's work on attachment.

Personality disorders inevitably cause difficulties for any approach based on the medical model as they are not clearly developmental disorders in the sense of having a clear genetic or neuropsychiatric cause. By definition, they are assumed to be continuous from adolescence onwards rather than episodic like mental illnesses (although mental illness runs a chronic course in many individuals and more recent longitudinal studies show discontinuity of personality disorder diagnoses over time).

Instead, there is a multitude of models and theories providing approaches to understanding of personality disorder. In terms of models, both main classification systems (DSM and ICD) have used a categorical approach although increasingly there is recognition of the flaws in this approach, including a lack of theoretical underpinning and inadequate psychometric properties (Livesley, 2001). Despite these drawbacks, psychiatrists perhaps feel comfortable with the categorical model as it sits close to the medical model and is congruent with the overall categorical approach of both classification systems (although DSM-IV includes dimensional aspects for some disorders, for example bipolar disorder).

The main alternative to categories is the dimensional model, of which there are two main types – those based on normal personality traits, for example the five factor model, and those based on studies of personality disorder. Although many researchers in the field agree that trait models potentially provide a more coherent representation of the individual differences in personality disorder, Livesley (2001) notes that personality disorder involves more than maladaptive traits and is wary of creating a concept that applies to a sizeable proportion of the population.

There are many theories of personality disorder. Each seeks to explain the aetiology and typical adaptive/maladaptive functioning of personality disorder. Within their (1996) book on major theories of personality disorder, Clarkin and Lenzenweger include cognitive, psychoanalytic, interpersonal, evolutionary and neurobiological theories. Whilst individual clinicians will tend to favour theory that most closely reflects their own theoretical perspective, many of the theories are most applicable to those individuals in whom one (or at most two) personality disorders are present. Among an inpatient/residential group of individuals with personality disorder, there will be many with multiple personality traits (meeting criteria for several personality disorders) and clear evidence of other co-morbid mental disorders. Some of these individuals (particularly those who have offended) may also meet criteria for a diagnosis of psychopathy in terms of Hare's Psychopathy Checklist-Revised (PCL-R; Hare, 1991). For such individuals, an understanding based on a neurobiological framework (Depue and Lenzenweger, 2001; Blair *et al.*,

2005) can help to shed light on complex psychopathology. Such an approach is likely to appeal to psychiatrists (particularly those with an interest in developmental and neuropsychiatric disorders), with the expectation that this understanding will complement psychological approaches to current dysfunction.

Practical aspects

Psychiatric contribution to psychological formulation

Introduction

For the psychiatrist working in a personality disorder service, the main contribution to formulation will be the exercise of traditional psychiatric skills in carrying out detailed assessment based on past history, including past records and informant account (if available), and current presentation (ideally observed over a period of time and in more than one setting rather than a single interview). In many cases, this assessment will suggest at least one area of co-morbidity with developmental and/or Axis I disorders. In those cases where the psychopathology is restricted to aspects of personality disorder/ psychopathy, the psychiatrist's clinical findings will provide evidence that is complementary to the findings from psychometric assessments.

Awareness of self and context

During the stage of initial assessment, the psychiatrist should be aware of how his role, personal characteristics and demeanour may impact upon the individual being assessed and the outcome of assessment. In terms of the psychiatrist's role, many individuals may be anxious about the purpose of assessment – for example, that the aim is to find evidence of mental illness that will lead to being detained in hospital under the Mental Health Act. Individuals who have not previously had any contact with mental health services may repeatedly deny symptoms and/or refuse to engage with the interview for fear that the psychiatrist may detect symptoms. Alternatively, the individual may see the assessment interview as an opportunity to stress the severity of symptoms in the belief that the psychiatrist will then arrange the hospital admission sought. For an individual who has had previous contact with mental health services, there may be fears of either another rejection or a repeat of a traumatic admission.

The personal characteristics in terms of gender, age and ethnicity of both the psychiatrist and the individual being assessed will also affect the conduct and outcome of the interview. As an older White woman I know that I will be regarded differently than would be the case if I were a middle-aged Asian man. I also know that I may experience quite a hostile response from a young woman in the community but that my presence may be reassuring to a young man in custody.

Flexibility of interview style

For many individuals with complex personality pathology, the emphasis in their previous contacts with professionals is likely to have been on one or more aspects of their outwardly maladaptive behaviour such as self-harm, drug abuse or offending. Many will have had little or no opportunity to describe in any detail either their early lives or their complex internal experiences. In assessing these individuals, the psychiatrist will need to draw on all his past experience and interpersonal skills, adapting these to complex and variable clinical presentations. Some practical examples are as follows:

- For individuals who are very ready to disclose past victimisation, it will be necessary to strike a balance between providing reassurance that the account is heard and setting a limit on the extent of disclosure until ongoing therapy is in place, ensuring support in the interim.
- For individuals who are dismissive of their past trauma and/or clearly distrustful of others (including professionals), it will be important to note but respect their wariness and to begin to establish trust through concentration on 'safe' topics. Attention to any relevant physical health issues can provide a safe area for discussion, with referral for appropriate investigation or treatment.
- With some individuals, there will be clear evidence of affective dysregulation, for example marked anxiety or easily-triggered anger. In such situations, it may be important to arrange short interviews or to allow the individual to leave an interview in order to manage his affect. It will then be helpful for the psychiatrist to find an opportunity to chat informally with the individual to reassure him that his abrupt departure is not viewed negatively and to re-establish an interpersonal foundation for ongoing assessment.
- Some individuals may describe violent and/or sadistic fantasies and the psychiatrist will need to be sensitive to the manner in which these are disclosed – whether with an intense awareness of the interviewer's reactions (with intent to frighten, seduce or repel) or whether with shame and/or anxiety about both the content and the risk of acting out.
- Other individuals may describe strange mental experiences and again the psychiatrist should pay attention to the manner of disclosure as well as to the content – the individual may be puzzled and interested in her own experience, or fearful that these experiences are evidence that she is 'going mad'. In these situations, it will be important to take plenty of time to listen to the individual (several interviews and making verbatim notes if possible) and to reserve judgement about diagnosis. With time,

reflection back and further exploration with the individual, experiences that initially sounded like psychotic symptoms may be more appropriately 'labelled' as schizotypal perceptions or dissociative states.

Box 11.1

Colin was referred by his probation officer after he reported hearing voices urging violence and violent dreams. At the first appointment he talked fast and readily about many topics but kept coming back to his preoccupation with violence including daydreams and fantasies of himself as both victim and perpetrator of serious violence. He also talked readily of having been drunk and/or stoned for much of the time. He was tall but of very slim build and it was not surprising that, as a child, he had been skinny and frequently bullied until an uncle taught him how to fight back. From then on he was apparently fearless and frequently tackled stronger boys. He was proud of his reputation for continuing to fight after being injured. It seemed clear that he had overcompensated for physical disadvantage by learning to anticipate threat and to be always ready to respond with violence, and also that his daydreams and fantasies functioned to maintain vigilance.

Margaret was referred by a social worker who was trying to sort out her benefits after she had spent a short period in custody. The first appointment was arranged at a city centre office that involved a long bus journey for Margaret. At that appointment, she sat on the far side of the room and gave monosyllabic responses at first. She spoke of having been alcoholic for several years and was guarded about her life before that, referring explicitly to her distrust of professionals. She was then asked about her current practical difficulties including loss of benefits and she began to talk more freely. The psychiatrist offered to write a letter to the benefits agency to back up the one sent by the social worker and suggested that the next appointment could be arranged at her GP surgery, a few minutes' walk from where she lived. She responded positively to this suggestion and attended two more appointments but then stopped attending after the psychiatrist arrived late for the next one.

Jack was seen in a secure setting and from the start was both mentally and physically active. On direct questioning, he reported regular amphetamine use in the community but with a paradoxical response – when he took it with friends, they 'speeded' off within minutes while he was able to relax and watch TV. Subsequent specialist assessment confirmed the diagnosis of adult attention-deficit hyperactivity disorder (ADHD). He described past psychotic symptoms including delusional beliefs of having Jesus-like power to affect the lives of passers-by. It was unclear whether these symptoms were feigned (he readily acknowledged a past admission to a psychiatric hospital with feigned psychosis) or whether they had been induced by heavy use of amphetamines. There were several other aspects of his complex psychopathology, one of the more unusual being his description of physical sensations – for example, he spoke of being aware of his blood circulating round his body and described his intense mental activity as being like 'thousands of worm holes'. Despite Jack's undoubted capacity for deception, it seemed to the psychiatrist that such descriptions were a genuine and spontaneous expression of unusual perceptions associated with schizotypal personality disorder.

Identification of co-morbid psychiatric disorders

In addition to complex personality pathology, a significant proportion of individuals will have co-morbid disorders. These may include developmental and neuropsychiatric disorders including learning disabilities, autistic spectrum disorders, the sequelae of head injuries, ADHD and Tourette syndrome. This author has also found a higher than expected number of sex chromosome abnormalities and an individual with primary hypogonadism among a cohort of offenders undergoing personality disorder assessment.

The other large group of co-morbid disorders will be Axis I disorders. A significant proportion of individuals with a diagnosis of borderline personality disorder will have a history and/or ongoing symptoms of affective disorder – either depression or lengthy mood swings – in addition to the typical affective instability of the borderline personality. Many individuals with borderline personality disorder also describe hearing voices, but more detailed description and/or observation of the individual reveals these experiences to be dissociative and based in early traumatic experience rather than psychotic.

Completing the formulation

Following assessment, the psychiatrist should be in a good position to either confirm personality pathology as the main factor requiring treatment or indicate the degree of co-morbidity and complexity of overall psychopathology. For individuals with the most complex psychopathology (i.e. diagnostic criteria for many disorders being fulfilled), the task of clarifying how the different elements of pathology contribute to the formulation can seem overwhelming. In such cases, it can be tempting to simply list the various diagnoses rather than attempting to identify the most important aspects in terms of past (e.g. linked to past offences) and current functioning. However, both the psychiatrist and therapist involved with the individual will need to remember that the formulation is dynamic rather than fixed. As the individual begins to progress in treatment, aspects of his psychopathology that have been quiescent may become active, usually in an attempt to maintain psychological defences and avoid vulnerability. In some cases, these changes will indicate reactivation of a previous pattern but sometimes behavioural change may indicate the presence of new or previously unrecognised difficulties – for example, frank obsessive-compulsive cleaning in someone who has previously been only tidy.

An important contribution of the psychiatrist at the stage of completing assessment and formulating treatment needs will be to give advice about the individual's suitability for lengthy psychological treatment. Even in a service with capacity to adapt the treatment model to the diverse needs of a very heterogeneous population, there may be individuals who, due to issues related to co-morbidity, are not suitable to start treatment or who may become destabilised during treatment. This issue may be particularly relevant for individuals with a clear history of episodes of mental illness, for example episodes of paranoid psychosis or of psychotic symptoms in the context of affective disorder. In some services (particularly those where there is reluctance to use medication), individuals with such a history may routinely be excluded. However, given the lack of access to psychological treatment for individuals with a primary diagnosis of personality disorder but co-morbid episodic mental illness, it is this author's view that such individuals should have an opportunity to engage in treatment, with recognition that it may be necessary at times to provide additional support and/or to arrange a 'treatment break' during an episode of illness. Crises of various types are inevitable in a lengthy treatment programme and episodes of mental illness can usually be accommodated as one type of crisis. With this approach, there may also be occasions when the process of psychological treatment triggers a prolonged destabilisation of mental state and, in such cases, it may be necessary to arrange transfer to a mental illness service.

Other situations where the psychiatrist is likely to be involved in decisions about suitability for treatment are those relating to active substance abuse and significant learning disability. While many individuals accepted into a personality disorder service have a significant history of substance abuse, the majority will have had an opportunity for detoxification and achievement of a period of abstinence before admission to the service. However, some individuals, even in the most secure conditions, have not yet made any commitment to abstinence and will use every opportunity to subvert security measures and to continue substance use. In such circumstances, it may be necessary to exclude such an individual as not ready for treatment and for the sake of other service users.

The situation for individuals with significant learning disabilities will depend considerably on the individual concerned and on the treatment approach. Clearly a treatment programme requiring frequent use of written materials, including homework assignments, will not be suitable for an individual with limited literacy. However, a below-average measured IQ does not necessarily imply an inability to benefit from an adaptable treatment approach and such individuals may be as able to grasp applied psychological concepts as a bright but emotionally stunted peer.

In addition to specifically psychiatric/psychological issues affecting suitability for treatment, it will sometimes be important to consider other individual and situational issues. These might include the timing of treatment in relation to serious physical health issues. For example, it would be unwise to start lengthy psychological treatment while an individual is receiving anti-viral treatment for hepatitis C, whereas with an individual already engaged in treatment who has a physical health crisis, it may be more appropriate to arrange a break from treatment rather than discharge from the treatment programme. In an inpatient setting, situational crises such as the terminal illness of an attachment figure or legal proceedings over access to children may be double-edged in relation to ongoing psychological treatment. The crisis may so preoccupy the individual that in effect only supportive work is possible for a time. On the other hand, such a crisis can have an energising effect through disruption of previously fixed thoughts and feelings.

Situational issues are particularly important for individuals with personality disorder who are living in the community. Such individuals, particularly those with a borderline component to their disorder, are likely to be sensitive to situational stress and to frequently experience crises of various sorts. For these individuals, supportive management may be the most realistic option unless there is an experienced team involved who can provide consistent treatment beyond support.

Box 11.2

George had a history of substance abuse and psychotic episodes in addition to a diagnosis of personality disorder. He had been on long-term antipsychotic medication but consistently complained of side effects. After admission to the personality disorder service, he began to engage well with his therapist and continued through a negotiated reduction in medication. He stopped the remaining medication but soon afterwards, following news of his mother's serious illness, he developed acute psychotic symptoms (actively conversing with unseen people and believing that pigeons were bringing threatening messages). After a short period of increased observation and support, he agreed to restart low-dose medication and continued therapy.

Sam was seen at the request of hostel staff after his release from a custodial sentence. Whilst in prison, he had been able to abstain from heroin after ten years' dependency and he wanted to understand himself better. The psychiatrist referred him to an experienced mental health nurse who was looking for a patient for psychodynamic therapy. Sam was enthusiastic and engaged well with therapy assessment but soon defaulted from both therapy and psychiatric follow-up. A few months later, he contacted the psychiatrist again. At this stage he was clear that he knew there were many aspects of his early life that had been problematic but that he must concentrate on coping with present difficulties. He requested monthly appointments and used these well for support.

The contribution of the psychiatrist to risk assessment and management

In this section, no attempt will be made to address the important and sometimes contentious issue of the link between the risk of violence and mental disorder. Actuarial risk assessment, clinical risk assessment and the value of a combined approach based on structured clinical judgement have been repeatedly debated and written about by researchers and clinicians over recent years (e.g. Maden, 2003; Hart *et al.*, 2007).

The focus here will instead be on issues of dynamic risk assessment and management as they arise in settings in which individuals with personality disorder are in treatment or at least in contact with mental health services. In order to respond appropriately to varying dynamic risks in inpatient settings, it is important that members of the team have a clear understanding of the formulation of the individual concerned. While this will particularly involve those therapists working directly with that individual, a psychiatrist who was involved in initial assessment and has some ongoing contact with the individual may usefully contribute to multidisciplinary discussions and care planning.

A variety of situations might necessitate a review of dynamic risk – for example, a significant incident affecting a close associate of the individual under discussion; intelligence that the individual may have used illicit drugs; awareness that an individual has received a letter ending a relationship. The manifestation of increased risk may be anticipated or become evident in various ways – for example, decreased participation in therapy, clearly dysfunctional behaviour such as damaging property or interpersonal aggression, or increased risk of self-harm or suicide. In these situations, the psychiatrist's knowledge of the individual, combined with careful listening to both the individual and colleagues, may enable the psychiatrist to help the team in the exacting task of assessing and managing risk for that individual for that day – for example, discerning whether an individual is threatening self-harm because of anger at staff, as distraction from flashbacks or whether he is truly despairing.

Box 11.3

Tony was referred by his supervising probation officer following his release from prison on licence (sentenced for an impulsive violent offence) and it was agreed that the psychiatrist would see him for follow-up. He often spoke quite dramatically about his current circumstances, including thoughts of suicide, but stated that he could not act on these due to concern for his parents (one of his brothers had committed suicide) and his son. At one appointment he was more agitated than usual. That day he had visited his ex-partner and discovered she had a new partner and wanted to change arrangements for contact with his son. He talked at length, making threats towards his ex-partner and expressing that he did not care about the consequences of his actions for his parents and son. Following the appointment, the psychiatrist discussed the situation with a senior probation officer and the decision was made to recommend recall to prison. Tony was arrested the next day. When the psychiatrist saw him in prison, he expressed considerable anger but then moved on to a more considered discussion with evidence of an ongoing therapeutic alliance. Tony's capacity to maintain the alliance was considered a major protective factor in the psychiatrist's updated risk assessment.

The role of medication in facilitating psychological treatment

Previously, many psychiatrists were doubtful that medication had any significant role in the treatment of those with personality disorder, other than in situations where it was used to manage seriously disruptive and aggressive behaviour. Whilst NICE guidelines (2009a, 2009b) for antisocial and borderline personality disorder do not recommend the use of medication with these diagnoses, the benefits of medication have been acknowledged in people with more complex personality pathology (Tyrer and Bateman, 2004). In a service including users with complex psychopathology, there are two main roles for medication: the treatment of co-morbid disorders, and the management of symptoms directly related to personality disorder that tend to interfere with therapy. It is also vitally important that service users have adequate access to a primary care service for physical health issues as these can be a significant concern with some personality disordered individuals – for example, diabetics whose self-harm repertoire may include compulsive overeating and deliberate mismanagement of blood sugar levels.

Treatment of co-morbid disorders

Where a co-morbid disorder requiring medication is already established before the individual arrives in the personality disorder service or where such a diagnosis is made after arrival in the service, it is important to achieve optimum control of symptoms related to that disorder. This might include continuation of anticonvulsant medication for epilepsy and ongoing or intermittent treatment of episodes of mental illness. For individuals with residual symptoms of ADHD, a trial of stimulant medication may contribute to the individual's stability and engagement in treatment.

Management of therapy-interfering symptoms

There are two main groups of symptoms directly related to personality disorder that may significantly interfere with aspects of treatment. These are high arousal (including hyper-vigilance with ideas of reference) often associated with paranoid personality disorder and the affective dysregulation associated with borderline personality disorder. Those who have lived in a state of heightened arousal for some time may complain of difficulty in sleeping which is not helped by short-term use of hypnotics. They may well benefit from low-dose antipsychotic medication, carefully titrated to avoid over-sedation which might decrease the individual's awareness of threat before he is ready for this. Unfortunately some of those who might well benefit from such medication may be the most resistant to this suggestion due to both anxiety about any loss of vigilance and their fundamental mistrust of professionals. Individuals with significant borderline personality difficulties are usually more amenable to pharmacological treatment, and mood stabilisers, antidepressants and low-dose antipsychotics may all be useful, alone or in combination, in achieving improved self-management and stability. One further type of therapy-interfering symptom that may be relevant in some offenders with personality disorder is that related to sexualised coping, influencing both cognitions and affect. This type of maladaptive coping may respond well to a selective serotonin reuptake inhibitor (SSRI) antidepressant or to medication with direct antilibidinal effect.

Abuse of medication

Professionals working in personality disorder services quickly become aware that there is always potential for misuse of whatever substances or systems are in place, and prescribed medication is a very obvious target for abuse. From experience of working in a service with relatively high usage of medication, it usually becomes clear that only relatively few individuals are regularly engaged in misuse of their own medication or trading medication with others. If trading with associated intimidation/bribery becomes very marked, it may be necessary to exclude the main culprit from treatment for the protection of others. However, more usually it will be sufficient to make clear to the individual that this is a problematic behaviour to be targeted as part of her treatment.

Negotiation and duration of pharmacological treatment

Probably the most vital aspect of the use of medication with personality disordered individuals is discussion and negotiation around the likely benefits and side effects of any proposed medication. Occasionally, in a crisis situation when the safety of the individual or of others is in jeopardy, the psychiatrist may need to be very directive about the use of medication, but the more usual situation would be open discussion of the issue, initiated by the individual or by the psychiatrist. Sometimes the suggestion of medication may be readily taken up, but at other times it will be more appropriate to approach the issue slowly, often on more than one occasion. The psychiatrist will usually be aware of those individuals who definitely do not wish to consider this option and he will usually wish to respect that decision – on the whole these will be individuals who experience relatively little subjective distress.

For individuals on medication for co-morbid conditions and those who need a combination of medications to achieve optimum stability, it is likely that at least some medication may need to be continued long term. For others, a time will probably come in the course of treatment for the individual to request a reduction of medication. The optimum time for such a reduction is when the individual has already made considerable progress and wants to experience and manage a greater range of affect than his medication may have enabled him to access. Such reductions or withdrawal of medication should, whenever possible, be completed in a managed way to avoid withdrawal effects.

Box 11.4

Clive had a history of serious violent offending and his personality disorder diagnosis had components from all three clusters. In the treatment setting, his attitude towards peers and staff appeared quite arrogant, for example he complained that no one wanted to have serious conversations. He was very sensitive to slights, would ruminate on these and, when discussing such an incident, would become intensely angry, then isolate himself. Between such episodes, he showed commitment to therapy with evidence of slow but definite progress and a clear recognition of the benefits of being in a containing environment. It was he who suggested to the psychiatrist that medication might be helpful. He was started on a very low dose of atypical antipsychotic medication and there was definite improvement in his level of engagement with others. However, angry episodes continued and he then spoke of feeling anxious and depressed. An SSRI antidepressant was added to his prescription and over the next months there was a marked change in his interpersonal behaviour – any anger was brief and he socialised with peers, becoming regularly involved in card games etc.

The psychiatrist as member of the multidisciplinary team

The preceding practical sections of this chapter are written with the assumption that the psychiatrist working in a personality disorder service will be functioning as a member of a multidisciplinary team. In this final section some practical outworkings of that assumption will be described.

In an inpatient service providing intensive treatment for personality disorder based on a psychological treatment model, it is this author's view that clinical leadership should be with those who are best equipped to mould the service and team to the evolving needs of both patients and staff in ways that are consistent with the psychological model. It is thus most likely that one or more psychologists will take that clinical leadership role(s). With this in mind, it will be very important in the early stages of development of the service and/ or when a psychiatrist joins such a service, that the psychiatrist should be clear in his own mind that his role does not include clinical leadership of the service. Instead, the role of the psychiatrist will be as one of the senior clinicians, i.e. one of those with other professionals of consultant grade who form the core leadership team in a large service (or the whole team in a smaller service). Both within the team and the service as a whole, the psychiatrist should understand that his authority stems from his experience and the exercise of his particular skills (as above) rather than from his profession or title. Alongside his specifically psychiatric contributions to the team and service, it will be important that he shows a consistent commitment to teamworking and group decisions – and in this respect he will not be so very different from other psychiatrists working in very different mental health settings.

The extent of specifically psychiatric work as described in previous sections is likely to vary depending on the size and type of service – for example, frequency of new admissions and the extent of any exclusion criteria. In an inpatient service with a lengthy treatment programme, the demands of such work are likely to allow for the psychiatrist to also become directly involved in psychological therapy. Such involvement increases the breadth of professional interest and experience and can greatly strengthen links with the team.

Although the psychiatrist himself may be very clear that his role is that of a member of a team, he will need to be aware that for at least some of the patients and staff with whom he is in daily contact, there may be some expectations of a medical doctor based on past experiences. These may include too ready acceptance or rejection of the views of the psychiatrist, past experience of a doctor/psychiatrist who behaved in a hierarchical manner, or too readily discussed medical symptoms. The psychiatrist will hope to negotiate each of these expectations in a sensitive way, establishing his own boundaries concerning informal consultation together with the level of accessibility and informality with patients and staff that is comfortable for the psychiatrist and consistent with overall team practice. In most settings nowadays, this will include the use of first names in all informal conversations, with use of surnames and titles reserved for more formal settings and reports.

Two specific aspects of the psychiatrist's interpersonal function are listening and apologies. Careful listening to the emotional and psychological experiences of patients has been mentioned in the sections above on assessment and risk. All clinicians working with individuals with severe personality disorder will hear disturbing accounts and will necessarily develop their own ways of guarding against being personally overwhelmed. There is a risk of becoming hardened and the psychiatrist may be wise to monitor his responses – an indication of healthy responses may be that there are still some interviews that leave the clinician feeling emotionally drained or feeling sad, angry or frightened by what he has heard. As well as listening to patients, it will be important for the psychiatrist to listen to colleagues of all ranks and disciplines and for the listening to include listening/participation in light-hearted conversations as well as serious discussions.

Doctors have sometimes been thought of as incapable of apologising (Sellar, 2007) but apologies can play an important part in building and maintaining trust with both service users and colleagues. Many individuals with personality disorder have grown up with harsh carers who were always 'right'. A simple apology – for example, for a factual mistake in a report or for a too-complicated explanation – may make a small contribution to increased trust in staff. At the other end of the scale, the psychiatrist, either alone or with some other colleagues, may reach a decision about an individual patient without considering all relevant factors. If there is reason to re-examine the decision-making process, it may be appropriate for the psychiatrist to apologise to other team members and to the individual concerned.

Conclusion

The role of the psychiatrist in a personality disorder service as described may be rather different from both traditional and more usual current job descriptions for psychiatrists. To occupy this role may lead to a sense of isolation in several ways – it may be difficult/impossible to fully explain to colleagues either the satisfactions or difficulties of the job, and where the job is truly stretching, it may be difficult to fully empathise with colleagues in more mainstream services. Nevertheless, it will be important for the psychiatrist to maintain at least some links with a peer group and with professional developments. Any such sense of isolation will be offset by the support and stimulus of the multidisciplinary team and by the ongoing opportunities to exercise and develop the wide range of skills and interests involved in working with individuals with personality disorder.

References

Blair, J., Mitchell, D. and Blair, K. (2005) *The Psychopath: Emotion and the Brain.* Oxford: Blackwell.

Bracken, P. and Thomas, P. (2001) Postpsychiatry: a new direction in mental health. *British Medical Journal*, **322**, 724–727.

Brown, N. and Bhugra, D. (2007) 'New' professionalism or professionalism derailed? *Psychiatric Bulletin*, **31**, 281–283.

Care Services Improvement Partnership/National Institute for Mental Health in England, Changing Workforce Programme and Royal College of Psychiatrists (2005) *New Ways of Working for Psychiatrists: Enhancing Effective, Person-Centred Services through New Ways of Working in Multidisciplinary and Multi-Agency Contexts. Final Report 'But Not the End of the Story'.* London: Department of Health.

Clarkin, J.F. and Lenzenweger, M.F. (1996) *Major Theories of Personality Disorder.* New York: Guilford Press.

Depue, R.A. and Lenzenweger, M.F. (2001) A neurobehavioural model of personality disturbance. In W.J. Livesley (ed.), *The Handbook of Personality Disorder.* New York: Guilford Press.

Gee, M. (2007) New Ways of Working threatens the future of the psychiatric profession. Letter in *Psychiatric Bulletin*, **31**, 315.

Hare, R.D. (1991) *The Hare Psychopathy Checklist – Revised.* Toronto: Multi-Health Systems.

Hart, S.D., Michie, C. and Cooke, D.J. (2007) Precision of actuarial risk assessment instruments: evaluating the 'margins of error' of group v. individual predictions of violence. *British Journal of Psychiatry*, **190**, Suppl. 49, s60–65.

Hinshelwood, R.D. (1999) *Thinking about Institutions.* London: Jessica Kingsley.

Kennedy, P. and Griffiths, H. (2001) General psychiatrists discovering new roles for a new era . . . and removing work stress. *British Journal of Psychiatry*, **179**, 283–285.

Livesley, W.J. (2001) Conceptual and taxonomic issues. In W. John Livesley (ed.), *Handbook of Personality Disorders.* New York: Guilford Press.

Maden, A. (2003) Standardised risk assessment: why all the fuss? *Psychiatric Bulletin*, **27**, 201–204.

National Institute for Health and Clinical Excellence (2009a) *Antisocial Personality Disorder: NICE Clinical Guideline 77.* London: NICE.

National Institute for Health and Clinical Excellence (2009b) *Borderline Personality Disorder: NICE Clinical Guideline 78.* London: NICE.

National Institute for Mental Health in England (NIMHE) (2003) *Personality Disorder: No Longer a Diagnosis of Exclusion*. London: NIMHE.

National Working Group on New Roles for Psychiatrists (2004) *New Roles for Psychiatrists*. London: British Medical Association.

New Ways of Working (2007) *Mental Health: New Ways of Working for Everyone*. London: Department of Health.

Onyett, S. (2003) *Teamworking in Mental Health*. Basingstoke: Palgrave Macmillan.

Sellar, W. (2007) When sorry seems to be the hardest word. *BMJ Careers*, 15 Sept.

Tyrer, P. and Bateman, A.W. (2004) Drug treatment for personality disorder. *Advances in Psychiatric Treatment*, **10**, 389–398.

Chapter 12

Beyond therapy – the wider role of the psychologist in treating personality disorder

Jo Ramsden

Introduction

The role of the psychologist within any service is to provide psychological therapies and, traditionally, the emphasis in clinical psychology literature has been on how best to deliver these in the context of work with individuals. In this chapter, the focus is removed from the psychologist-as-therapist. Instead, the chapter is concerned with the role of the psychologist as someone who has the necessary skills to maximise the therapeutic potential of the multidisciplinary team. Knowledge of psychological theory and practice enables the psychologist to harmonise care by embedding psychological thinking into the everyday work of the team in an effort to ensure consistency and, ultimately, optimal conditions for growth and change as recommended by NICE (2009).

Although the importance of service development is acknowledged in clinical psychology training, these skills tend not to be fostered until post-qualification and then, usually, not until a psychologist's career is well established. During placements, psychologists in clinical training are usually exposed to their supervisor's well-defined role and service development issues may not be prioritised given the transient nature of placements. Once qualified, service development skills are not typically considered to be within the remit of junior posts. However, it is argued here that for work with individuals with 'personality disorders', service development is a key role and that psychologists at every level within these services need to consider their role as extending beyond the therapy room.

The use of psychological theory and therapy and the importance of team coherence are understood within many specialist teams catering for people with 'personality disorders' (e.g. Bateman and Fonagy, 1999, 2001). However, individuals who fulfil the necessary DSM-IV criteria for 'personality disorder' do not always fall within the remit of specialist services. For example, government guidance on best practice indicates that all substance misuse and eating disorder services are catering for significant numbers of people with 'personality disorder' (NIMHE, 2003), as are inpatient psychiatric services (e.g. Zimmerman *et al.*, 2005) and forensic services (e.g. Brinded *et al.*, 1999).

Despite the diversity of these services, it is vital that all teams work in an integrated and coherent fashion (Bateman and Fonagy, 2000) and traditional multidisciplinary working with multiple perspectives has the potential to obstruct this type of approach. Disagreement and conflict are more likely within teams working with service users with personality disorder as this client group tend to elicit polarised responses from the variety of professionals they come into contact with. Diverse views and conflicting ideas about service users are, therefore, understandable but this typically leads to confused or erratic treatment or stagnation. Little is achieved in terms of helping the service user to find emotional stability, and consistent ways of coping are likely to elude him or her given that these have not been modelled by the team.

As service developers (or systemic practitioners), clinical psychologists have the capacity to fulfil a unique role and consolidate thinking across disciplines by providing a framework (or formulation). Psychological formulations reconcile what may seem inconsistent about the individual by illuminating the *function* of behaviour. However, it should be acknowledged that the implications of working within a psychological framework are not always readily understood and welcomed. Teams comprised of individuals from diverse disciplines may resist integration, perhaps fearing the blurring of professional boundaries or loss of power. For example, in some services the dominance of psychiatry has led to non-medical professionals feeling subordinate and struggling to exert their 'expert' status. In such a climate, transdisciplinary working (where teams comprising individuals from different disciplines have integrated aims, objectives and philosophy) may be perceived as particularly threatening to professional distinctiveness and resisted.

It is important to stress that the unique role that the psychologist fulfils within these teams is one which, whilst working towards consensus, agreement and integration, also has the capacity to augment, rather than dilute, diverse disciplinary roles. Generally speaking, the psychologist's role is one which defines the problem (not 'what?' as a diagnosis does, but 'why?') and also, therefore, the goal. Using unique disciplinary skills, each professional within the team is then working towards the achievement of that goal.

Transdisciplinary teamworking is addressed more rigorously in Chapter 7 but in this chapter the unique role of the psychologist is considered. The analogy of the psychologist as a parental figure is employed and some of the processes implicit to that role are identified, as are some of the likely challenges. The aim is also to outline practical steps which may be used as a guide to service development, to aid the communication and support which are necessary when embedding psychological principles into everyday care.

The psychologist as parental figure

Treatment for personality disorder is primarily psychological and effective dissemination of psychological knowledge is crucial for all disciplines to be able to work in a theoretically coherent manner (NICE, 2009). Inevitably, the psychologist is placed in a parental role in that it is *their* knowledge that allows the concepts to be applied, *their* assessment and formulation (albeit drawing on the experiences and conclusions of those from other disciplines) that guide and direct the work. Additionally, the operationalisation of psychological principles will for many disciplines be new territory and there is an onus of responsibility on the psychologist to model and 'teach' how to interact and work with core problems (rather than, for example, reacting intuitively to how someone is presenting).

The model of the psychologist as a parental figure defines the position within the team in terms of alliances and boundaries. By expecting other disciplines to operationalise psychological principles there is a need for the psychologist to be available, supportive, validating, respectful of and knowledgeable about diverse practitioner roles. There is a need for the psychologist to model reflective practice, to voice their own struggles, to be open to learning and developing, to be fallible and non-oppressive (i.e. to allow the 'space' for others to take what they need from psychology and to apply it to their own discipline).

The other task of the parental figure role, however, is that of someone who guides and teaches. Implicit within this, then, is the need for the psychologist to be distant and distinct from other disciplines; to be outside the interpersonal politics which inevitably exist amongst ward-based staff. Objectivity and neutrality allow the psychologist to be a safe person and this emotional safety (so essential for work with service users) is modelled through professional boundaries.

Establishing coherence within the team

The coherent working of a team comprised of individuals from diverse disciplines is most likely to come from a rigorous understanding of *why* a service user presents in the way they do. Medical discourses which prevail in many services would suggest that simply knowing *what* (i.e. having a diagnosis) is enough to indicate treatment (as it is for many physical ailments), and for some teams this tradition will present a significant obstacle.

In the majority of cases, there is some recognition that service users are more complex than their diagnosis would suggest or that there are misunderstood motivations for an individual's challenging interpersonal behaviour, and the task for the psychologist is to provide a framework for simplifying what may feel like overwhelming complexity. This task of providing a framework will frequently be a case of validating the intuitive perspectives of various team members. Indeed, when it comes to drawing up individual formulations, the psychologist needs to be acutely aware of the validity of differing opinions and views. In other words, the formulation (whilst utilising core psychological skills) needs to be owned by the team and individual perspectives need to be integrated within it.

Given the client group in question, it is likely that diverse perspectives will need to be reconciled. Considering this as a dialectical challenge, where the 'truth' of each opinion needs to be drawn out, is another indication of the unique role held by the psychologist and so there needs to be a distance from the team that facilitates an overview of the processes being exhibited. An example might be where a team is split over their assessment of risk, with some team members assessing an individual as safe and manageable while others express fear and concern over the same individual. In this example, the 'truth' in both perspectives may be identified by the psychologist as relating to the positions held by the disparate team members. Those with less contact with the service user, and who are perceived by that individual to be holding more power (and, therefore, more responsibility for decisions regarding their treatment or detention), may see an angrier, volatile side of the service user. Others who spend more time with the same person, who maybe have the freedom to be more nurturing and responsive, may well find that individual calmer and more reasonable.

In this way, the instinctive, but often discordant, perspectives of the team are validated and reconciled into a coherent picture of the service user that is more likely to facilitate a consistent and therapeutic approach. Acknowledging how an individual's behaviour tends to instinctively impact upon how other people feel and react (for example, acknowledging that a service user's behaviour is likely to elicit natural responses of anger, fear or disgust) is implicitly non-judgemental about what may be perceived as 'unprofessional' reactions. It may also help the team to identify maladaptive coping. For example, the team may come to recognise that when they feel scared or angry with a particular person it is likely to be indicative of that service user's own fear (Murphy and McVey, 2001).

Establishing formulations that are as inclusive as possible when it comes to team perspectives is more likely to render the formulation holistic and, therefore, more useful and applicable. As importantly, it is likely to increase the engagement of the team through a sense of shared ownership and facilitate effective implementation. Not only are team members more likely to feel validated but challenges that are presented, perhaps uniquely, to someone from a particular discipline can be addressed (see, for example, Box 12.1). Consequently, the formulation is perceived not just as a framework for psychologists but as a tool for the whole team.

Box 12.1

Medical and nursing staff were continually approached by Grace with various physical ailments. Few of these had any basis in reality. Grace was taking up a lot of time and resources and staff were becoming resentful. It was hypothesised that this was the only 'safe' way for Grace to access nurturance as she was frightened of having her emotional needs dismissed. To avoid reinforcing this behaviour, regular time for Grace was planned for every shift, thereby providing her with some appropriate nurturance. When approached for unfounded health problems, medical staff took time to suggest gently to Grace that this might be her safe way of accessing support.

The process of developing formulations will be unfamiliar to many non-psychologists and it is therefore necessary for the psychologist to remember key aspects that may need to be made explicit to avoid confusion and/or may need to be addressed obliquely through modelling. For example, team members may assume that, like a diagnosis, a formulation is rigid and unchanging (or that changing it threatens the expertise of the professionals involved). Stressing that the dynamism of a formulation is part of its strength is, therefore, important. Perhaps more powerfully, psychologists need to convey the message implicitly through remaining open to change, to admitting to being wrong, confused or unknowing. Similarly, the process of drawing up a formulation transparently and, wherever possible, with the expertise of the service user, is a core skill for psychologists but may be less common for other professionals and may not fit easily into some cultures (e.g. forensic and inpatient settings). The process of doing this challenges the traditional notion of expertise and its implicit oppressiveness.

Practically speaking, to enable team members to work within their own discipline, in a way that is integrated with the rest of the team, driven by the formulation and consistent with the treatment model, there needs to be a degree of planning. It is implicit within the model that instinctive interpersonal responses tend to ultimately confirm maladaptive core beliefs and that disconfirming, explicit communication comes less naturally given the presentation of the service user. As a consequence, challenges need to be anticipated by the team and responses considered and prepared. Care plans are more helpful when they are explicit about how practitioners should respond and under what circumstances, preferably linking an 'ideal' response to observable behaviour. Below (Box 12.2) is one such specific example which was drawn up with the full involvement of the service user's primary nurse.

Box 12.2

Sally is spending a lot of time on her own and blocking any interaction, e.g. isolating herself, covering her face, eating her meals alone, etc.

- Sally has many strategies that allow her to avoid relationships within which she fears that she will be abused. Staff need to remember that these are designed to keep her safe because she feels so scared. Sally, therefore, needs to be regularly approached. There should be no pressure for Sally to interact but staff should remind Sally that they are there for her to talk to if she needs it. Staff should stress that they very much want to listen and understand how she is feeling.
- When approaching Sally, staff could comment on the fact that she is alone and that this makes them worried that she is feeling unhappy, frightened or vulnerable. Sally should be reminded that she is safe and that staff are there to protect her and they want to listen etc.
- Sally should never be ignored and, although she may be unlikely to respond, staff should always say 'Hello' or acknowledge her in some way when they see her.

Providing emotional containment

As a parental figure, the psychologist is a team member whose role may well provide a degree of emotional containment and the need for this is likely to be significant given that many services cope in maladaptive ways with the significant emotional demands of the work (thereby mimicking the behaviour of the service users). Most notably, services tend to be concerned primarily with risk assessment and management. This priority is strengthened given the current climate and the concept of 'personality disorder' which is often employed to support a government agenda concerned with controlling 'dangerousness' and prioritising public safety (Pilgrim, 2001). Behaviourally, risk management (which is often reactive) inadvertently leads to the reinforcement of maladaptive behaviours and chaotic ways of coping, as seen in Box 12.3.

Box 12.3

Sue's parents were inattentive and often unavailable for emotional support. As a child, Sue received attention only after she had become aggressive, loud and hostile. For Sue, this was the only time she felt important and powerful. As an adult, Sue found it hard to get attention and the time she needed from others in functional ways. Angry, demanding behaviour was rigidly controlled and immediately attended to on the ward and Sue's tried and tested methods of getting attention always resulted in her having plenty of staff time. As a consequence, Sue never had the opportunity or the need to learn alternative ways of feeling special and valued within relationships.

Within many services, empathic, emotionally congruent interactions are often considered problematic as it means engaging with a service user's overt distress which is viewed as uncontrollable, impulsive, irrational and, therefore, 'risky'. Other, non-psychology practitioners may not naturally consider themselves equipped to deal with these types of 'dangerous' interactions (maybe fearing that they may 'stir things up' or 'open a can of worms'). Similarly, Bell and Evershed (2004) discuss subcultures, such as prison environments, where a 'tough containment' approach is favoured and where the expression of emotion is inhibited due to fears that staff may appear emotionally vulnerable.

Kurtz (2005) refers to social defences and the ways in which organisations may structure themselves so that group members may avoid or minimise emotional pain. She outlines how these defences ultimately undermine the organisational task. For example, Kurtz (2005) suggests that staff may adopt a moralistic stance towards individuals with a 'personality disorder' label, thereby creating distance. Goodwin and Gore (2000) examined the social defences at work in a long-stay psychiatric ward and found 'social distancing' to be one of the 'anti-tasks' which were undertaken and which appeared to have a social defence function in undermining emotional engagement with patients. Social distancing was achieved through the minimisation of intimacy and reduced contact time with residents (through administrative tasks and engagement with other staff). Other examples might include staff who are sometimes required to work across services or wards or have regular changes in keyworking responsibilities, thereby minimising the opportunities for, and undermining the importance of, attachments.

The trauma that has been experienced by many service users who attract a 'personality disorder' label is often so extreme and pervasive that it is intolerable not just for the service user but for staff also. The prioritisation of risk management could be thought of as a social defence mechanism in that systems are created which ultimately work to silence the expression of unbearable emotion. The physical management of volatile, emotive or hostile situations and the 'machismo' often inherent within cultures that seek to address interpersonal violence prevent reflection and shift the emphasis away from an individual's inner world, their vulnerabilities, victimisation and fear. The psychological framework works to contain some of these emotions and facilitate more therapeutic ways of working. Risk assessment is directly addressed through formulation, meaning that hostility, for example, can be re-defined so that staff can interpret it as protective for the service user (rather than directed at them personally), enabling a less reactive or defensive stance.

In addition, risk assessment can, through a psychological formulation, become more finely tuned, appropriate and useful and replace knee-jerk responses (for example, that mental illness is directly associated with dangerousness (Pilgrim and Rogers, 2003)). In this way, service users are experienced as less erratic and unpredictable. Risk management strategies can be more accurately applied to genuinely dangerous situations and staff may have the freedom to experiment with other ways of containing volatile emotions (see Box 12.4 for example).

Box 12.4

It felt very dangerous to talk to Karen – who alleged sexual abuse within the family from an early age – about her sexual feelings given that she often assaulted staff in a sexual manner. Staff preferred to manage these assaults with physical restraint and discussing in any detail why an assault of this nature had happened was viewed as having the potential to 'stir things up'. Staff would simply remind Karen that they had a 'professional relationship' with her. However, the psychological formulation suggested that her sexual assaults were her way of pre-empting the abusive situation she feared. Non-sexual relationships were terrifying for Karen because she expected sexual abuse at all times. It was also suggested that talking about 'professionalism' may have no meaning for someone whose relationships in the past have not conformed to the boundaries that might be expected of a 'professional'. Given this formulation, staff found that explicitly reassuring Karen that they were not going to have sex with her actually reduced her anxiety and her risk of committing sexual assaults.

In practice, the disconfirming effect of psychologically based interventions means that risk may be increased in the short term but, again, a psychological understanding will allow this to be predicted. Services (which generally have short-term risk management as a priority) can be reassured that the work has longer-term risk management implications, that any dangerous behaviour can be anticipated and that there is a measure of certainty and control. In this way, the risk assessment is containing and the psychologist is able to demonstrate a knowledge and understanding of the situation that might be considered protective. To put this another way, the psychological understanding of risk might be viewed as positively working to help staff stay safe and reduce risk over time rather than expecting them to intuitively manage situations as they occur.

The risk assessment aspect of the formulation simplifies what may initially have appeared complex and may help to address some of the conflict staff sometimes experience given that traditional risk management strategies can seem to be counter-productive and undermining of more therapeutic interventions. Nursing staff, for example, often express concern over the contradictions of trying to convey to a frightened patient that they can be trusted, only then to be required to restrain that patient should they become violent, or to forcibly medicate should they become non-compliant. Kurtz (2005) refers to ambivalence on the part of government and society about what is required from services that cater for those with a diagnosis of 'personality disorder' (i.e. do they want to treat, punish or contain?) and suggests that this intensifies conflict and confusion for staff working within these services. She highlights the responsibility that service managers have in communicating a coherent sense of purpose for their staff in order to immunise them against diverse external demands and facilitate stability. In the absence of coherence of this sort, the psychologist trying to effect these types of changes at a service delivery level may feel themselves to be in a vulnerable position. It can feel hazardous and exposing to advocate therapeutic approaches which sit awkwardly alongside rigidly held, traditional risk management strategies.

To conclude this section, it needs to be acknowledged that risk may also be tied to issues around structure and organisation which can present significant challenges to service development. Clearly, there are numerous permutations but, as an example, communal areas such as smoking areas may be out of immediate staff sight making it difficult for staff to monitor the hostile, bullying or exploitative encounters which inevitably take place between traumatised people. Even where efforts are made to establish interventions that enable therapeutic discussion about the interpersonal dynamics between those involved in a service, the physical layout of the building may therefore allow for re-traumatising encounters.

In addition, there may be sudden and unforeseen changes that can frustrate service delivery – abrupt prison transfers, for example, or emergency ward admissions that may not only have the effect of disturbing the stability of the ward but may also necessitate inappropriate moves to free up bed space. There is also the issue of staffing. Where staffing levels are low and resources stretched, risk management is likely to be prioritised and distance created between overburdened team members and service users. Again, this can feel insurmountable and frustrating to the psychologist trying to effect change at a service level, but it indicates, again, the importance for the psychologist to have an appreciation of the demands placed on other disciplines by the organisation, to be supportive and emotionally containing.

Modelling

Part of being sensitive to distinct professional roles is maintaining respect for social defences, appreciating the protective purpose that they serve and the difficulties other professionals may have with operationalising psychological concepts. Often, in asking non-psychologists to engage in explicit communication, there is a requirement that these other professionals engage in therapeutic interactions which may feel bizarre, incongruous, and hazardous to their relationship with the service user, to their status or to their emotional invulnerability. Some of the examples that have been used to illustrate this chapter are typical, and include asking a team to reassure a hostile service user that they are safe, and talking about fears of emotional deprivation with someone who has a somatic complaint. In one example, team members were required to be explicit about the fact that they were not going to have sex with the service user. This required that team to voice the individual's fears and to acknowledge within themselves her perception of them as potential abusers. For many people this may be deeply threatening and it is maybe not surprising that, although the formulation allows the team to feel knowledgeable about the purpose of an individual's behaviour, there may be resistance to explicit communication.

Obviously there are training implications as staff need to be familiar with the theory underpinning the work. A theoretical understanding is likely to increase confidence and facilitate creativity in its application. However, the parental role is one of modelling appropriate behaviour and it is likely that this modelling may have a more powerful impact in terms of helping staff operationalise the theoretical principles. It is, therefore, necessary for the psychologist to be available. This means being on the end of the phone, being physically present on wards, regular attendance at meetings and handovers and scheduling time for support/advice or *ad hoc* supervision. Essentially, the psychologist, who is likely to be considered a senior member of the team no matter how newly qualified they are, needs, nevertheless, to be fully integrated, approachable and accessible. Opportunities are then likely to be created for influencing a culture and demonstrating how psychological principles can best be applied. There is also likely to be an element of containment if explicit communication (which might be distrusted and/or feared by non-psychologists) is witnessed as having been tried and tested (see for example Box 12.5).

Box 12.5

Martin was a difficult person to have on the ward. He refused to attend to his personal hygiene; he was rude and blatantly flouted ward rules. He was not well liked by the staff who found him repugnant. As a consequence, there were few attempts to engage him or to spend time with him. With the psychologist, Martin would request sessions only to be unavailable at the agreed time, and staff would consider this 'typically disrespectful'. The formulation suggested that a profound sense of defectiveness and social isolation lay at the heart of Martin's presentation, but a lack of warmth within the staff team towards Martin made addressing this impossible and tended only to confirm his expectations. Having a presence on the ward meant that the psychologist had informal opportunities (often in front of staff) to comment on the fact that Martin had, once again, missed his psychology session. The psychologist was able to gently wonder with Martin if he wanted the session but didn't feel as if he deserved the time and attention. The appropriateness of Martin's response and his gradual engagement with psychology were noted by the staff who then felt more able to talk with him in this way.

It may be useful for psychologists to consider the impact of an absent parent or how uninterested parenting is communicated. Examples may include not attending meetings (maybe because particular patients are not under review), arriving late or, for some services, having to take on other commitments or work across wards. All of these things impact on the presence of the psychologist and, therefore, on their perceived commitment and interest. Under these circumstances, it is likely that non-psychologists will feel that they don't have the necessary support, the work will seem less vital and the psychologist's influence will be undermined.

Conversely, it needs to be acknowledged that many psychologists (probably because of their own interpersonal anxieties) will strive to be well liked within the team, meaning that some professional boundaries are transgressed. Again the parental analogy may be useful in helping to clarify what would be inappropriate and undermining of the emotional safety that needs to be upheld as part of the role. A parental figure should not, for example, become involved in gossip or conspicuously favour one individual above another. Maintaining professional boundaries permits the modelling of safe, clear relationships that facilitate personal and professional growth. In other words, a boundaried professional relationship models that of a therapeutic one in that it maintains the core conditions (Rogers, 1961) allowing for safe feedback.

It has been acknowledged that some of the concepts and the expectation of explicit communication may leave teams feeling vulnerable, uncertain and lacking in skills. Under these circumstances, social defences are likely to be strong and the psychologist may feel themselves to be isolated, mistrusted, marginalised, etc. Again, this might be helpfully resolved through modelling and psychologists will need to be aware of their own discomfort and employ strategies to assist in overcoming this (see Box 12.6). Handovers, peer supervision and other meetings provide plentiful opportunities for psychologists or other team members who are 'on board' to voice their acceptance (albeit reluctant at times), their uncertainties, misgivings and fears. This also gives an opportunity to the psychologist to provide explicit reassurance and validation as well as guidance.

Box 12.6

When reinforcing the psychological model and offering support for nursing staff during handovers, the psychologist in the team often felt foolish. The nursing team subtly communicated their disdain for her ideas and would, for example, giggle if sexual matters were ever discussed or be dismissive if she talked empathically about a violent service user. Eventually, the psychologist and a senior member of the nursing team arranged to always attend handovers together. The nurse was then able to sit opposite the psychologist and model appropriate consideration of the psychological concepts as well as voice the unspoken fears of the nursing team.

There is an implicit requirement when working within a psychological framework that team members acknowledge their intuitive reactions to service users to inform their understanding of that individual's presentation, and reflective practice is intrinsically supportive. For example, junior staff often report relief and a sense of validation when senior staff reflect on what are often very similar difficulties to those they experience. Equally, staff report relief at being able to talk about what is inevitably a stressful job (Bowers, 2002) and particularly about their fears around overtly hostile or aggressive patients. Often this is something they have previously had to manage in isolation for fear of de-motivating or creating anxiety amongst the rest of the team.

Reflective practice may not always come naturally, especially to teams with rigid social defences, and, again, this is an area where modelling may be useful. A general sense of non-defensiveness and fallibility is likely to be extremely powerful, especially where teams are used to a psychiatric parental role and its inherent 'expertise'.

Supervision

Peer group supervision (preferably facilitated by someone outside of the team) is one useful arena for this type of modelling. Within supervision, the psychologist can be explicit about their uncertainties. Through being candid about what might be perceived as 'unprofessional' thoughts and feelings (e.g. dislike, anger), the psychologist facilitates safety in allowing others to explore their own biases, reactions and misconceptions.

Bell and Evershed (2004) refer to the importance of supervision as a forum for checking just such personal reactions to a client and, once recognised, preventing those feelings from interfering with the therapeutic process. This would seem to be particularly important when working with a group of individuals who have the capacity to be extremely needy, vulnerable, distressed and hostile, where there may be traumatic histories not only of abuse but also of offending (Bowers, 2002) and where there is increased potential for the environment to be oppressive and punitive (Kurtz, 2005). Bell and Evershed (2004) also indicate that supervision can be viewed as having various purposes by different professionals and by diverse settings. They give the example of forensic settings where supervision is viewed less as a forum for the development of the practitioner and more as an appraisal process through which standardised practices can be maintained. Working to introduce reflective supervision that encompasses support, professional growth and personal development can potentially be challenging and, therefore, creating opportunities to model the use of supervision in this way can be invaluable.

The benefits of group reflection and support are probably most eloquently defined by Main (1968, p. 27) who argues that

> The patient's distress can be dramatically resolved if the disagreeing staff can meet, disclose and discuss their hidden disagreements, and reach genuine consensus about how the patient could be handled in any particular manner.

Group supervision is often more effective than individual supervision at facilitating the openness needed for achieving consensus. Group supervision allows for peer support which can often feel safer if individuals within teams fear being judged or 'psychoanalysed'. The support of peers who work alongside each other experiencing the same day-to-day difficulties often has more intrinsic value and is more validating than support offered from an 'outsider'. In addition, group supervision allows for the sharing of multiple perspectives which Kurtz (2005) argues is useful not only for facilitating a co-ordinated approach (as described by Main, 1968, above) but also for understanding complicated relationships amongst the patient group on the ward. Similarly, the patient group in question, in attempting to manage their interpersonal anxiety, may present differently given changes in context and company, and multiple perspectives can facilitate a more holistic view of the individual, as described in Box 12.7.

Box 12.7

Regular supervision group members discussed a patient they were struggling with only to find that two students (on time-limited placements) in the group had a very different experience. The students felt empathic and warm towards the female patient while the permanent staff members felt irritated with and frustrated by her alternating superficiality and hostility. It was concluded by the group that, where a relationship was certain not to progress, the patient felt safer and more able to sustain a genuine connection, whereas her fears of rejection meant that potential long-term relationships with permanent staff were too threatening.

For a supervision group to facilitate the disclosure of emotions which may seem 'unprofessional' such as those above, it needs to be as safe and non-judgemental as possible, and good group practice, such as the establishment of group rules and agreed boundaries, is necessary. Again, sharing the ownership of the group as much as possible also helps for it to be seen as safe. Group rules, for example, may need to be constantly reviewed and explicitly re-negotiated. Frequent evaluation of the group, and acknowledgement of the feedback, is another way in which it can be indicated to the group that members have an unambiguous role in terms of ownership.

Individual supervision, especially with key members of staff who have influence and can disseminate knowledge and model effective practice, may also be useful to establish. Again, there is the need for the psychologist to be wary of professional dominance (Cheshire and Pilgrim, 2004) and the different demands placed on those from diverse disciplines. It may be useful to draw up contracts which acknowledge this and make explicit that discussion about the diversity of roles is welcomed where necessary.

Individual supervision is often a more appropriate place for the giving of direct feedback, although it highlights and is suggestive of a power differential, which needs to be carefully negotiated as this is not an evaluative role. Maintaining openness to receiving feedback can be helpful not only for personal growth but also to minimise real or perceived power differences and maintain successful working alliances. Additionally, opportunities are afforded to ensure that psychological plans and ideas are appropriate and workable in real life.

Training

It has been acknowledged that being available and modelling practice might be more powerful for influencing service delivery than training. Nevertheless, for the effective operationalisation of psychological concepts there are, clearly, training implications. Training is needed to increase knowledge and understanding of psychological concepts and theory and, given high staff turnover, this can be a resource-intensive undertaking requiring the psychologist to provide frequent updates and repeated workshops. Ideally, the training component would become procedural (e.g. a regular part of inductions, away-days or other training events), so that existing knowledge can be built upon and refreshed and new staff given the necessary learning opportunities. However, it is not essential that this remains a purely psychological role and input from other disciplines often means that the theories and concepts being disseminated can be taught in a more applied fashion. Training may become co-delivered, for example, by the psychologist and a member of the nursing team who is able to usefully apply the concepts to the unique challenges presented to this discipline.

Training in psychological concepts may not be the only place where the psychologist is implicated as having a role in terms of disseminating knowledge or facilitating discussion. Kurtz (2005) argues that the difficulties with the concept of personality disorder highlight an additional training need. She suggests that critical discussion around the concept as well as the impact of psychiatric classification is needed to facilitate an awareness of how power is negotiated through discursive practices and to minimise the use of oppressive language. For Pilgrim (2001), critical discussion which highlights the uncertainty that the academic community has about 'personality disorder' has the potential to reassure practitioners whose confusion and conflict are evident through the often contradictory views they hold about their service users (Parker *et al.*, 1995; Webb, 2005).

Implicit within this is the importance of language and how the psychologist may be able to raise awareness within the team of the role that language plays. Specifically, awareness may need to be heightened about the 'personality disorder' label and how it works to distance the team from service users as well as obstruct creative therapeutic working. For example, the 'personality disorder' label implies (as do psychiatric classifications) that the disorder in question is a discrete, 'non-normal' category, and has the tendency to lead a team away from a formulation-based approach. Kurtz (2005) suggests that the pathology inherent in the labelling of 'personality disorder' creates distance between staff and service users and increases the likelihood that staff will have pessimistic expectations about the possibility of change. Pilgrim (2001) argues that inherent within the concept are moral judgements about behaviour which effectively render the 'personality disordered' individual marginalised, mistrusted and disliked. He cites an argument put forward by Mann and Lewis (1989) that those unlucky enough to attract the diagnosis have neither the respect for being 'normal' nor the care and empathy that comes from being viewed as sick. Webb (2005) found that amongst various attitudes held towards those with a 'personality disorder' by a community mental health team was the sense that 'personality disorder' differed from mental illness through the implication that the individual was culpable and could be held accountable for their actions. Those with a diagnosis of schizophrenia, by contrast, were perceived as 'unfortunate' and 'blameless'.

Equally, many services that cater for individuals with 'personality disorders' will accommodate individuals with co-morbid mental health problems and those who present with psychotic symptoms tend to attract straightforward 'illness' labels that can make it hard for staff to appreciate the psychological components of that presentation. The wellness/illness discourse locates the 'problem' within the individual, their organic structure and brain chemistry. The solution is, therefore, medical and the impact of the environment is implicitly undermined, as is the importance of interpersonal interactions and psychological approaches in general. This can be problematic for those trying to influence service delivery in a more psychological direction. In some instances, asking teams to consider talking to a distressed, psychotic service user as a first choice of intervention when medication has been prescribed as required when needed is often felt to be, at best, an optimistic ideal. Where the service user has a history of violence or hostility this type of intervention may be disregarded as foolhardy or even dangerous.

There is, then, an onus on the psychologist to raise awareness amongst team members about language so that the team begin to naturally consider the impact of their speech. The issue that language is powerful and potentially oppressive needs to be grounded in mundane, everyday conversation as well as in the use of discourses that may pervade throughout the institution. For example, the team may need to think about commonly used terms which are unthinkingly based on their response to the patient and which might be anti-therapeutic. Referring to a service user as 'manipulative' or 'attention-seeking' for example may well simply reinforce beliefs that others will respond in an emotionally depriving manner. The impact on a service user of hearing about a staff member's own history of abuse and self-harm, their troubled sex life or even their enjoyable overseas holiday may also need to be brought into the team's awareness. Implicit within this is an appreciation for the impact that everyday interactions are likely to have and, therefore, their potential therapeutic value and importance.

Evaluation

Clearly, there is a need for feedback and systems for evaluating progress. Supervision, attendance at ward handovers and various other clinical team meetings are all opportunities for informal feedback from team members. There is evidently also a need for more formal evaluation. However, qualitative indicators including references within reports, incident reports, clinical discussions in team meetings, etc. are all extremely useful and may be more available and insightful than data gathered more formally. Monitoring progress in terms of interpersonal functioning of individual service users is also important, as are evaluations of staff morale and/or ward atmosphere.

It is important that the psychologist, as well as the whole team, is mindful of and attentive to small indicators of change. An example might be a team gradually talking more about an individual in terms of their experience of safety (rather than their overt hostility). Service development may be frustratingly slow and with both the psychologist's and the team's motivation in mind it is important, therefore, to remain alert to what might be dismissed as insignificant indicators of change.

Conclusion

The essential psychological work required for service users who have attracted a 'personality disorder' label cannot be effectively conducted within individual sessions with a psychologist. The work needs to be considered a task for the multidisciplinary team. It has been argued that the psychologist within the team is able to facilitate the coherent working of a group of disparate professionals as a transdisciplinary team by illuminating the function of maladaptive behaviour thereby clarifying the logic behind a service user's often complex and bewildering communication and defining the goals of the team. In addition, the psychologist is able to embed psychological work into everyday interactions by providing a degree of emotional containment and modelling explicit communication.

The psychologist in a team working with individuals with 'personality disorder' is in a privileged and unique position. Fundamentally, the psychologist has the luxury of working to understand the service user's worldview unburdened by the need to engage them in activity, enforce medication or enforce various rules other than those necessitated by professional boundaries. It is this position that affords the psychologist the ability to contribute a new and useful perspective. In this chapter, the psychological role has been compared to that of a parent and it may be that this unfettered perspective permits the adoption of such a position. The psychologist's role is one of giving permission: to say and engage with what may feel dangerous; to use relationships that may previously have been purely functional to be therapeutic; indeed, to have relationships and attachments at all.

It has been acknowledged that many services are likely to have rigid social defences which can be extremely powerful and have the capacity to fundamentally undermine the task. Regular support and supervision for the psychologist should, therefore, be highlighted and, given the importance placed on integrated teamworking, it would seem incumbent on clinical psychology training programmes to ensure that this type of service development is something that psychologists feel comfortable with and fully equipped for.

References

Bateman, A.W. and Fonagy, P. (1999) The effectiveness of partial hospitalisation in the treatment of borderline personality disorder: a randomised control trial. *American Journal of Psychiatry*, **156**, 1563–1569.

Bateman, A.W. and Fonagy, P. (2000) Effectiveness of psychotherapeutic treatment for personality disorder. *British Journal of Psychiatry*, **177**, 138–143.

Bateman, A.W. and Fonagy, P. (2001) Treatment of borderline personality disorder with psychoanalytically oriented partial hospitalisation: an 18 month follow up. *American Journal of Psychiatry*, **158**, 36–42.

Bell, R. and Evershed, S. (2004) The management of difficult clients. In A. Needs and G. Towl (eds), *Applying Psychology to Forensic Practice*. Oxford: BPS Blackwell.

Bowers, L. (2002) *Dangerous and Severe Personality Disorder: Response and Role of the Psychiatric Team*. London and New York: Routledge.

Brinded, P.M.J., Mulder, R.T., Stevens, I., Fairley, N. and Malcolm, F. (1999) The Christchurch prisons epidemiology study: personality disorder assessment in a prison population. *Criminal Behaviour and Mental Health*, **9(2)**, 144–155.

Cheshire, K. and Pilgrim, D. (2004) *A Short Introduction to Clinical Psychology*. London: Sage.

Goodwin, A.M. and Gore, V. (2000) Managing the stress of nursing people with severe and enduring mental illness: a psychodynamic observation study of a long stay psychiatric ward. *British Journal of Medical Psychology*, **73(3)**, 311–325.

Kurtz, A. (2005) The needs of staff who care for people with a diagnosis of personality disorder who are considered a risk to others. *Journal of Forensic Psychiatry and Psychology*, **16(2)**, 399–422.

Main, T. (1968) The ailment. In E. Barnes (ed), *Psychosocial Nursing: Studies from the Cassel Hospital*. Oxford: Tavistock Publications.

Mann, A. and Lewis, G. (1989) Personality disorder. In P. Williams, G. Wilkinson and K. Rawnsley (eds), *The Scope of Epidemiological Psychiatry*. London: Routledge, ch. 14.

Murphy, N. and McVey, D. (2001) Nursing in-patients with personality disorder: a schema focused approach. *British Journal of Forensic Practice*, **3(4)**, 8–15.

National Institute for Health and Clinical Excellence (2009) *Borderline Personality Disorder: NICE Clinical Guideline 78*. London: NICE.

National Institute for Mental Health in England (NIMHE) (2003) *Personality Disorder: No Longer a Diagnosis of Exclusion*. London: NIMHE.

Parker, I., Georgaca, E., Harper, D., McLaughlin, T. and Stowell Smith, M. (1995) *Deconstructing Psychopathology*. London: Sage.

Pilgrim, D. (2001) Disordered personalities and disordered concepts. *Journal of Mental Health*, **10(3)**, 253–265.

Pilgrim, D. and Rogers, A. (2003) Mental disorder and violence: an empirical picture in context. *Journal of Mental Health*, **12(1)**, 7–18.

Rogers, C. (1961) *On Becoming a Person: A Therapist's View of Psychotherapy*. London: Constable.

Webb, E.C. (2005) A focus group survey of CMHT staff views on the meaning of personality disorder. *Clinical Psychology*, **48**, 3–7.

Zimmerman, M., Rothschild, L. and Chelminski, I. (2005) The prevalence of DSM-IV personality disorders in psychiatric outpatients. *American Journal of Psychiatry*, **162(10)**, 1911–1918.

Issues and challenges for the clinical professional

Elizabeth Sneath

Introduction

Ensuring sustainable effective treatment programmes requires a workforce with a thorough understanding of people with personality disorder and the responses that they experience in relation to them. Providing robust treatment for people with personality disorder requires clinicians not only to develop particular skills and draw on specific personal qualities (see Chapter 2) but also to have access to good systems for support and supervision (NICE, 2009a). Without this, staff may experience burnout and exhaustion (NIHME, 2003b, p. 43). This is reflected in the difficulties experienced by many personality disorder services in recruiting and retaining staff. To work effectively, staff must feel safe and purposefully occupied. Workforce development needs to move beyond selection and training and include provision for support and well-being if those working with these patients are to avoid being subjected to chronic exposure to potential risks. A healthy workforce is characterised by staff who are competent, autonomous, understand the difference they can make to their workplace, have personal values and beliefs that are congruent with the roles they undertake and have increased resilience to risk.

Staff selection

Employers repeatedly experience difficulties in 'screening out' and 'selecting in' staff who are resilient and competent with patients with personality disorder. Clinical experience suggests a high degree of personal resilience is needed and that some staff are more suited to this work than others. Either current selection processes are inadequate or other post-recruitment factors are influential in whether staff members remain resilient and effective in their work. Key qualities and skills that maintain competence and resilience in working with personality disordered patients can be derived from the literature. The ideal person needs to possess: a desire to work with this client group, good emotional regulation skills, a capacity for self-reflection, robust self-esteem, a robust professional identity, a psychological understanding of the disorder, an ability to identify both the vulnerability of the client and true progress, a capacity to present as 'healthy parent', an ability to set limits, and a capacity to be open to new experiences (see Chapter 2). Because of the potential for 'splitting' and being drawn into unhealthy interpersonal dynamics when treatment is delivered via a team, clinical professionals also need to be comfortable with multidisciplinary teamworking.

For clinicians treating personality disordered patients, warm interpersonal skills are essential. It is vital that staff undertaking this work have an ability to bear hostility without being drawn into retaliating. Equally, it is essential for staff to be able to manage internal and external conflicts without becoming over-involved. Some of these characteristics are intrinsically related to the personality of staff (e.g. openness to new experience) whereas others can be developed, such as knowledge and experience.

Essential personal characteristics are not the domain of one profession and neither are they easily developed. They clearly relate to an individual's own personal history, security of attachment pattern and personality. For example, Dozier et al. (1994) found that case managers with secure attachment styles were able to respond appropriately to patients' underlying needs and to resist patients' pull to behave in a manner that confirmed their schematic expectations. Whilst all of these personal characteristics are clearly involved, they form only part of the whole picture. At times, even the most experienced or personally suited clinicians become vulnerable to the interpersonal dynamics and pull of the personality disordered patient. Staff behave uncharacteristically or develop burnout, which can manifest as apathy, negativity and over-reliance on set patterns of relating to patients. Thus, staff who appear inherently resilient can still be affected by the nature of the work and the wider environment and, over time, become less resilient.

Current selection practices have room for improvement. Interviews are routinely used despite their poor ability to predict job performance. Staff selection could involve a variety of other methods including interviewing by service users, job simulation exercises, psychometric tests, assessment centres, biodata and guided references, but there is a reluctance to use these more complex methods. These might allow better assessment of attitudes towards patients, resilience under interpersonal pressure, or response to hostile and aggressive situations. These could add value to the selection process but such methods can be expensive and time-consuming and are not validated as a good indicator of future performance with these clients. It may be beneficial for efforts to be devoted to improving recruitment procedures and perhaps developing new approaches which might screen staff for individual difference in susceptibility and reactivity to risk or pre-existing psychopathology.

Given the obstacles to successful staff selection, the greater challenge for clinical professionals is to look at other processes such as induction and orientation, preventative training, robust supervision, coaching, mentoring, counselling, debriefing, and behavioural protocols, which can be put in place to maintain staff's resilience, ameliorate the influence of personality disordered patients' interpersonal dynamics and prevent difficulties from arising.

Preparing and developing staff

Identifying training needs

The Personality Disorder Capabilities Framework (NIHME, 2003b) offers a framework of specific capabilities required for working with personality disorder in a range of settings and at different stages of a career. Four capability domains are outlined: *promoting social functioning and obtaining social support*; *improving psychological well-being*; *assessing and managing risk to self and others*; *management and leadership*. NICE (2009a) emphasises the need for all staff to be familiar with these capabilities. However, efforts to educate and develop staff also need to reflect the individual needs of both organisations and staff, which can vary considerably depending on discipline and experience. Training needs to be regularly available, accessible, core competency-driven and sensitive to the needs of different professional groups. The specific roles of different disciplines have been discussed earlier in the book and competencies and training needs can be inferred from these (Chapters 8–12). Unidisciplinary training still plays an important role in staff development but there is also a need to build a culture of shared values and understanding between different staff groups (DoH, 1999). Training must also address the needs of both inexperienced and experienced staff, which can be a challenge in providing generic or core training. Conducting a training needs analysis and the use of structured competency-based appraisals such as the Knowledge and Skills Framework alongside reflection upon the Personality Disorder Capabilities Framework enables training programmes to be focused upon the unique needs of each individual within each distinct service.

Knowledge required across staff group

Any training programme for staff working with these clients must meet four key knowledge-based aims: ensure all staff have an understanding of the disorder; change any negative attitudes; ensure interventions are integrated (at least within specialist services); and improve understanding of team processes in team-based services. Managers of such services require additional training. Whilst a number of skills may be influenced by raising the knowledge base of the staff, skills may be more readily enhanced via other strategies such as supervision, mentoring and support.

As a priority, staff need to have an understanding of the aetiology and manifestation of personality disorder and an awareness of the impact of poor emotional regulation skills and cognitive distortions on relationships with others, thus ensuring all staff understand the behaviours, attitudes and emotions presented and are able to respond effectively. Training can indirectly reduce negativity towards people with personality disorder (Bowers, 2002; Krawitz, 2004). In particular, attention has increasingly focused on the value of providing staff with a psychological understanding of the personality disordered patient's challenging behaviour, to achieve more effective management (e.g. Murphy and McVey, 2003; Bowers, 2002). Thus, assisting staff in understanding that self-harm, complaining behaviour, aggression, isolative or sexualised behaviour may represent the client's best efforts to get his or her needs met (no matter how dysfunctional a strategy this appears) should form an important focus for training programmes (see Chapter 4 for greater discussion).

Additionally, training should *directly* address attitudes towards the patient (NICE, 2009a), including beliefs about 'treatability' and willingness to work with the client group, and ensure staff are aware of how their own attitudes and belief systems contribute to interpersonal transactions with patients (see Chapter 5 for greater discussion). It is important to consider attitudes on a regular basis as these vary in accordance with both patient dynamics and also the organisational and political climates. Thus even staff who are positively inclined may become resentful of patients when feeling neglected by managers.

Within specialist services, it is important that there is a coherent treatment model that all staff have understanding of and are confident to use to guide their own interventions and ensure consistency across the team (see Chapter 6 for greater discussion; NICE, 2009a). Attention must be given to ensuring that this model is accessible to staff of different disciplines and levels of experience. Core information needs to be delivered in such a way that other disciplines can access and use it to enhance their own role. For example, schema therapy may be predominantly utilised by psychological therapists but concepts can be taught to non-therapists (e.g. prison officers and nurses) to facilitate their understanding of the patient and guide their own interactions via schema-focused treatment plans (Murphy and McVey, 2003).

Ensuring interventions are integrated also requires that staff in specialist services have an understanding of team processes, goals, role expectations, and team problem-solving and decision-making strategies, and have their communication and conflict management skills strengthened (see Chapter 7).

Training for managers is also important as, in the absence of leadership capabilities, there is likely to be a high level of burnout, absenteeism, sickness and disillusionment in teams working with personality disordered patients. There is a generic need for preventative training in handling difficult situations, and managing staff emotions. A new initiative could introduce training in psychological self-maintenance. There is also the challenge of staff adopting the characteristics of their clients and acting out issues within management supervision (e.g. persistent complaining), which managers would benefit from being able to predict and manage effectively.

Overcoming practical difficulties in training delivery

There are several difficulties to overcome in delivering staff training within a personality disorder service. This has contributed to an inadequate supply of in-post training to support effective practice and is exacerbated by staff being poorly prepared by professional training and limited availability of high quality post-qualification training (Duggan, 2002). There is also an ongoing resource dilemma to navigate – providing care and treatment to patients whilst staff are being taught or are delivering training to other staff. Attitudinal difficulties can prevent staff from discussing subjects that they find difficult – for example, talking about relationship/boundary violations, burnout, sexualised dynamics, the functioning of multidisciplinary teams, or their own emotional responses to the patient. Training focused on attitude change can encounter resistance. Strategies need to be employed to desensitise staff or decrease resistance, such as tailoring training to the audience, or finding ways to gradually desensitise staff – for example, by experienced staff drip-feeding information into conversations and briefings.

The experience of service providers often points to the lack of success of formal training programmes and a greater reliance on mentoring or other aspects of on-the-job training to develop staff. Those responsible for the delivery of formal training need to ensure that there is a clear relationship between knowledge and skills. Training providers should be encouraged to make clear and practical links so that participants are able to identify ways to improve their skill base.

Organisations are very important in determining how learning is implemented and can foster or inhibit the process. There are clearly challenges in embedding skills, attitudes and knowledge within the prevailing culture, which need to be considered when setting up services for personality disordered patients. For example, in the Fens Unit at HMP Whitemoor, a key aim was to develop a large multidisciplinary team of 150 staff (including prison officers, nurses, occupational therapists and psychologists) to use a greater amount of explicit communication – a technique where staff put into words their personal responses to a patient or the perceived unspoken words of the patient or staff group (for example, 'I feel frightened of you', 'I am not going to hurt or abuse you'). This goes against the prevailing secretive ex-military culture of 'loose lips sink ships' in a maximum security prison. Staff were initially given formal training on why explicit communication is important to personality disordered prisoners, and practical guidance. This was followed up with role-modelling of explicit communication by senior clinical staff within therapeutic interventions, which was then discussed explicitly at group debriefings/team briefings. Staff were encouraged to try out explicit communication techniques in their interactions with prisoners and report back at briefings. Selected staff were offered mentoring and coaching on using explicit communication techniques and putting them into practice. Over the course of two years, a large number of staff have adopted this practice and it is now routinely used as part of interpersonal interactions on the prison landings.

The need for teamwork training to meet the increasingly complex needs of service users is well recognised and has highlighted the need to change the way in which health care professionals are educated. As professionals team up, rivalries and misconceptions about respective roles and responsibilities become evident. There is also a danger that inter-professional learning may erode professional values or entrench negative stereotypes that professionals hold about one another. Personality disordered patients (and sometimes their families) can exploit all of these conflicts. However, the advantages of multi-disciplinary training outweigh the disadvantages, particularly when supported with protocol-guided practice. What is clear from the literature on education in this area is that there is currently a lack of robust data on the effectiveness of inter-professional education (Golding and Gray, 2006) and that the most beneficial team learning seems to be in the workplace, based around common service-related needs.

In preparing staff for integration into established teams, teamwork is regularly cited as being central to well-being. In situations where cohesive, well-functioning teams can make the difference between safe practice and serious injustice, staff rely heavily on working with effective like-minded colleagues. Anecdotal evidence suggests that new staff on units take time to become integrated into their teams and for the new individual this has important and potentially challenging psychological consequences. Without the almost unconditional protection afforded to established team members, the individual is likely to experience a heightened sense of vulnerability. Issues around personal acceptance and integration may be provoked, leaving the individual questioning their personal worth and contribution, which may create a vulnerability to being singled out for a 'special relationship' by the patients. Realistic preparation of staff for assimilation into their new teams may negate or reduce these effects – for example, orientation visits, establishing a buddy system, attendance at team training prior to joining. Further research is needed to identify which strategies are effective in facilitating the integration of new team members.

Addressing treatment-interfering behaviours

There are many challenges in the interface between clinician and patient. Treatment-interfering behaviours, i.e. behaviours that impede treatment, come from a broad range of sources including patient, therapist, other staff, and the environment (family, culture organisations and institutions). Patient-generated treatment-interfering behaviours compromise the effectiveness of treatment, restrict the patient's ability to access therapy or decrease the clinician's motivation to treat the patient, and increase the clinician's risk of burnout. However, it is arguably even more important to treatment success with personality disordered patients to consider the clinician-generated interfering behaviours.

Most staff do their best in their job and have not set out to become therapists, nurses, social workers or prison officers in order to spend their days being punitive, aggressive or over-involved. However, staff can get drawn into interpersonal cycles which lead them to behave negatively or with hostility. Kiesler (1996) suggests that analysing therapist–patient transactions and supervisor–therapist transactions in structured ways in clinical supervision can help identify what causes the staff member to behave punitively. For example, a patient repeatedly requesting help may be experienced as insulting, aggressive, undermining of our efforts and belittling, therefore testing the patience and tolerance of most staff, who may respond to the strong emotion they are experiencing rather than overt signs that the patient wants help.

Cognitive behavioural therapists (e.g. Linehan, 1993; Leahy, 2006) have helped to progress focused exploration of therapist-interfering behaviours and their potential impact on the practitioner–patient interface. A clinician's treatment-interfering behaviours might take the form of disrespectful behaviour, a lack of consideration or contempt for the patient – for example, being late, becoming judgemental or forgetting important material. Alternatively, they may be driven by the therapist's own schema or difficulties in regulating affect. Leahy explores how a therapist's personal schemas of unrelenting standards, autonomy/control or abandonment/rejection may interfere with emotional expression and processing or the ability to safeguard one's own personal limits. For example, a hurtful hostile attack from the patient may be experienced as overwhelming and lead to a lapse in emotional regulation in the therapist. The therapist's vulnerability to lapses can, and does, lead to therapeutic stalls and impasses, which can be frequent with personality disordered patients and are anxiety-provoking as they challenge a therapist's sense of competence and efficacy. The challenge for clinicians is to remain willing and able to consider one's own contributions to ruptures so that an alternative response to the patient's behaviour can be provided and thus avoid the treatment being impeded. The therapist's own maladaptive interpersonal cycles can be interrupted or avoided by the use of targeted explicit communication, such as proactively informing the patient early in a transaction when feeling frightened, rather than reacting at a later point when emotions may have become overwhelming. The importance of taking into consideration the idiographic logic of a personality disordered patient has been argued elsewhere in this book. The challenge for practitioners is to keep this idea foremost in their minds. It is the meaning of behaviour to the patient and not the intentions of the clinician that can determine the reactions or harm and upset to the patient.

Sometimes ruptures are caused by the therapist's failure to synthesise the extremes of treatment, for example becoming too rigid, too flexible, too change-oriented or too accepting, which might trigger hopelessness and/or behavioural passivity within the patient (Leahy, 2006). This can lead the therapist to respond with attempts to control other caregivers or the environment in order to protect the patient from stress, which in turn reinforces the patient's helpless behaviour, leading to increased passivity, rejection of help and unrealistic expectations of others. For clinicians working with personality disordered patients, it could be useful to incorporate an analysis of both the patient's and the clinician's treatment-interfering behaviours (within the context of interpersonal cycles) into the supervision process. For example, a therapist may be fearful of the patient self-harming when he is emotional or that if the patient becomes too distressed she will not attend subsequent sessions or may attack the therapist with hostility. In these circumstances, therapists may avoid subject matter for fear of upsetting the patient, which could be perceived by the patient as lack of interest/rejection and create further distress. A more effective intervention would be to discuss the therapist's fear that upsetting the patient may lead to non-attendance.

Another area of psychological research and theory that may be relevant to how clinicians manage their responses to the practitioner–patient interface with personality disorder is attribution theory, whereby people search for causal attributions concerning events that provoke emotion along the dimensions of locus of control and stability. The attributions that clinicians use to explain serious incidents involving themselves or others (and the consequences) influence how well the individual adjusts. A key contributor to adjustment is whether responsibility for the incident is located within the patient or external to the patient. Weigel *et al.* (2006) found that when staff working with learning disabled patients with challenging behaviour focused upon their own contribution to a situation they had a tendency to engage in damaging self-blame. However, when they located responsibility solely within the client, staff experienced increased anxiety as they viewed the behaviour to be in control of the client and out of their own control. Using a psychological framework in supervision enables staff to understand how the environment and interpersonal interactions work together with the patient's internal world to drive the patient's response, and can thus assist the clinician to feel in greater control and that similar incidents can be avoided.

Work or organisational environments can also give rise to therapy-interfering behaviours. For example, if a client is aware that their therapist has seen all her other patients that week, but hasn't seen them because their session was on a public holiday or the therapist was away on a single training day, what seems fair and reasonable on the surface can have an implicit message to the patient – i.e. that they are neglected and uncared for. A competent clinician will adjust their schedule accordingly and also point out the implications to inexperienced or less mindful colleagues.

Another key challenge is the 'reluctant' patient. Within community, inpatient and prison settings, reluctance may be demonstrated by behaviours including failure to attend, failure to complete homework tasks, double-scheduling appointments or turning up in an intoxicated or aggressive state. Such behaviours may lead to the therapist withdrawing their offer of therapy or the prisoner being ejected from a treatment programme. In hospital settings where patients are detained against their will, such a situation has in the past led to discharge from section of many personality disordered patients due to the treatability clause of the 1983 Mental Health Act. Engagement is a complex process, involving motivation, resistance, and responsivity to treatment. According to Howells *et al.* (2007, p. 330),

> clinical observation suggests that offenders with personality disorders are very often 'unready' for treatment in part because of their internal characteristics (beliefs, emotional reactions, identities and behavioural deficits that undermine engagement and the forming of a therapeutic alliance) and in part because of external, situational influences such as perceived coercion into treatment.

The challenge for clinicians is to accurately assess treatment readiness on an ongoing basis and to revisit individual formulations in order to ensure that treatment not only reflects readiness to change but is aimed at understanding, predicting, monitoring and overcoming reluctance where this is appropriate. Supervision has an important role in highlighting treatment-interfering behaviours and identifying strategies to minimise their impact.

Issues for supervision

Supervision is integral to safe and effective clinical practice. It improves self-efficacy and job satisfaction, enhances the learning of complex skills, improves communication between staff, and supports the maintenance of high quality practices. For clinicians working with personality disordered patients, an additional benefit is enabling practitioners to stay sane in the face of ongoing emotional onslaught that can challenge even the most robust of staff. There are emotional consequences of hearing and seeing a patient's distress or seriously harmful behaviour (offending, self-harming, suicide, aggression, subjecting themselves to sexual exploitation) that can elicit feelings of disgust, abhorrence and hostility from staff. There are several challenges to be avoided: inappropriate relationships, boundary blurring, becoming exhausted and burntout, under-performing, behaving in ways that are harmful to the patient, and engaging in rivalry with patients for special care or attention (e.g. Bowers *et al.*, 2005).

Supervision offers a reflective space to contain emotions, explore and address therapist-interfering behaviours, learn complex skills and gain support. In the therapeutic milieu of treating patients with personality disorder, supervision has a vital role as a containing relationship to counteract the effects of working with challenging clients (NICE, 2009b). Supervision therefore needs to be robust but flexible enough to be able to focus and explore multiple areas. Supervision discussions should include:

- client-based formulations;
- application of therapeutic strategies and therapy processes;
- the clinician's own emotional reactions to the patient;
- the clinician's own development and attachment experiences;
- the clinician's own interpersonal style;
- review of relationship boundaries.

Supervision of teams is also necessary when multiple practitioners from one team are involved with a personality disordered patient. Regular formal and informal discussions with colleagues are invaluable for overcoming the difficulties associated with multiple practitioners being involved with the same patient and can draw attention to splitting processes or manipulation. Regular supervision helps a team develop a shared framework for understanding personality disorder and highlights the presence of a variety of attitudes towards the patient.

A climate of openness and transparency needs to be created within the supervision and management processes. This is taken for granted in some professions but needs fostering in staff who are unused to the idea of supervision in order to overcome resistance. It is preferable to slowly create a learning culture in which people want and value supervision and understand its role in facilitating practice and protecting clinicians from boundary transgressions or dysfunctional responses to personality disordered patients, rather than attempt to coerce reluctant staff to engage. One approach to building a culture of supervision with professionals unused to supervision (e.g. prison officers, health workers, social care teams) is to develop key staff as 'supervision champions' to be involved in implementing and supporting the development of a supervision culture. Experience in the Fens Unit highlighted the importance of a long lead-in time for implementation and the value of providing supervisee training to prepare staff for supervision and enable them to be open to the experience. Supervision practices have to be accessible and embedded in regular structures to allow a culture to develop in which staff can feel supported, receive emotional validation, grow in patient awareness, and self-awareness, and develop their expertise.

Careful consideration needs to be given to who is the most appropriate individual to conduct supervision. Services often opt for the expert model where clinicians more experienced in the treatment of personality disorder, or the prevailing treatment model, supervise less experienced staff. However, in larger services, particularly those in secure settings, there are often insufficient senior clinicians to deliver supervision at the front line. Supervision needs to be planned strategically to enable each profession within a service to develop sufficient expertise to deliver their own supervision rather than relying on psychologists due to the psychological nature of treatment. A process-orientated or consultative type supervision may be more suitable for staff not used to supervision and a mentoring scheme might also be necessary, until supervision practices are well established.

The key difficulties likely to be experienced in supervision of clinicians working with personality disordered patients are: inability to adapt practices within a formulation, harm of patients, reluctance to disclose emotions, defensiveness, personalisation of attacks, unwillingness to work on own schemas or resistance to reflection, competing with clients for special care, working outside of relationship boundaries and other boundary violations. A limitation of conventional supervision based on psychotherapeutic models is that the focus of supervision can be restricted – only focusing on the things we are conscious of or bring to supervision. Given the strong emotional reactions to working with personality disorder this might create a distorted self-focus. This highlights the importance of knowing the supervisee beyond the supervising relationship, despite NICE's (2009a) recommendation that an external supervisor is acceptable. A cognitive interpersonal model of supervision offers an opportunity to reflect the fact that clinicians bring their own schemas and interpersonal styles into all aspects of their work. Cognitive interpersonal supervision utilises therapeutic techniques of the therapy model, i.e. empathic confrontation, explicit communication, and exploration and reflection to explore the clinician's own interpersonal dynamics and attachment styles and how these impact on their interactions with their patients. This allows the effectiveness of the clinician to be tailored and monitored for adherence to the service's treatment programme, the emotional and interpersonal responses of the clinician to the patient to be explored, and awareness of how the clinician is feeling towards the personality disordered patient to be enhanced.

Another challenge is attaining quality assurance within the supervision process so that difficult or taboo subjects such as sex, violence, and feelings towards the personality disordered patients are discussed and explored. Recording sessions (as endorsed by NICE (2009a)) can allow closer scrutiny of clinician behaviour and allow unnoticed reactions to be focused on. This needs to be applied to all staff, including experienced staff, as even the most senior and experienced clinicians have blind spots or areas of vulnerability and prejudice. Supervisors will need to raise clinicians' awareness of their own treatment-interfering behaviours and impact on the personality disordered patient. Having a structure within the supervision process could assist with this. The expectation and experience of many staff is that supervision will consist of positive validation endorsing their therapeutic endeavours with the patient and only offering constructive criticism when the staff member ventures wildly off course. To focus on the therapist's treatment-interfering behaviours can be a difficult experience for some staff and preparation is needed to ensure that supervisees have an understanding of the supportive value of this focus and that supervisors are capable of creating adequate trust for this task to be possible.

Employers and colleagues are repeatedly surprised when members of staff (even experienced members) succumb to relationship boundary violations with personality disordered clients. NICE (2009a) recommend that all staff are taught about the potential for boundary violations when working with antisocial clients. Vamos (2001) demonstrated that awareness could be greatly increased with very little intervention and could contribute greatly to protecting against future violations. Learning about relationship boundaries is often not enough to protect staff as most staff are aware that their professional bodies disapprove of boundary violations and understand why. Active review of boundaries is required to spot the smaller boundary crossings or boundary pushes before they develop into full-blown boundary violations. This requires open and honest discussion of feelings and thoughts towards patients, including sexual attraction, liking, hostility and the behaviours that these feelings may be driving in professionals, such as favouritism, comforting, flirtation or seduction, pacifying, or acting punitively. Making boundary management an open process and exposing key issues 'on the table' enables a culture of honesty and responsibility to be created, as recommended within NICE (2009a), rather than a culture of blame. This requires giving people permission to acknowledge that boundary crossings and pushes occur as a normal process in working with personality disordered patients so that they can disclose instances of boundary crossing for discussion and learning. Other preventative strategies are to use checklists within supervision to normalise boundary checking and review. Sneath (2008) adapted Hamilton and Spruill's (1999) risk management checklist (which identifies risk behaviours associated with sexual misconduct) for use in clinical supervision. The checklist aims to support boundary policing or monitoring by being explicit and ensuring defined risk behaviours are more routinely checked out with the supervisee. The regular use of a checklist enables supervisors to feel more confident in raising this theme and allows the supervisee to feel less personally threatened.

Optimising support opportunities

Given the highly emotional nature of the work, its impact on staff and the high likelihood of serious untoward incidents such as self-harm or aggression, supervision alone may be insufficient to meet staff support needs, particularly in working with psychopathic clients (NICE, 2009a). Frequent and flexibly delivered support needs to be available and accessible to staff within the organisation. A holistic staff well-being strategy optimises organisational support practices by integrating them with the prevailing models of treatment, supervision, management and training to provide the maximum benefit and support to staff, but needs monitoring to ensure effectiveness. Key organisational interventions that should be included in a staff well-being strategy are outlined below.

Maximising informal support opportunities

A variety of formal and informal support opportunities can be made available to staff (e.g. staff briefings, debriefings, multidisciplinary team meetings, and creating regular opportunities for teams to work, have breaks or engage in training together). To be effective, these aspects of work must be predictable and reliable so that they can provide a containing function for the organisation whether in a secure setting or the community. If staff do not regularly attend briefings or meetings, or are not familiar with the normal practices, outcomes and expectations, then this will not be a good source of support or containment. Senior staff or managers should ensure there is regular and reliable attendance at staff debriefings and consider making attendance at briefings mandatory to provide the necessary predictability for containment, or arrange meetings at a time when there is least opportunity for avoidance. Staff working with personality disordered populations learn to manage incidents as they occur, but rarely learn to reflect on the effectiveness of their strategies and the impact on their own emotional states. A frequent complaint from staff is that they are expected to just 'get on with it', moving from responding to one incident to another in quick succession, with a fear that at some point they will be blamed for making a mistake. This fear leads to staff wanting to avoid the workplace when they sense an impending crisis, or paralyses them during crisis periods. To prevent this, a system of debriefs post-incident and support mechanisms can enable staff to remove themselves from the environment even for a twenty-minute tea break, whilst knowing that they are not leaving their fellow team members in the lurch. A debrief for the team organised within a matter of hours or days rather than weeks or months can help with reflection, normalising and reducing feelings of guilt, anger or fear. This is not always easy but time invested early on can reduce sickness absence and staff resignations in order to avoid repeats of traumatic events.

Active management interest

Active interest of managers and colleagues is essential for staff morale, particularly when staff perceive they are not appreciated by the client group. Staff benefit from believing that what they are doing matters and that it is valued by the organisation. This can be enhanced by managers noticing what staff do and taking an active interest by commenting on what staff do, following up events and enquiring positively about outcomes. Regular, positive feedback is also important to validate staff and to counter the parallel processes that come from patient dynamics, such as negativity, mistrust, critical attack, self-focus and entitlement, which can frequently transfer from the patients and permeate staff interactions. Another strategy is to publicise and give staff recognition. If staff are thanked for their efforts and achievements and their commitment is appreciated, staff are more likely to want and seek responsibility.

Positive adaptive behaviours and pro-active coping can be role-modelled by senior clinical staff discussing their own emotional responses to the client, getting support from the team, expressing relief about sharing and discussing their reactions whilst acknowledging that their feelings were driven by the patient's maladaptive coping strategies. Therapists can also take a lead in briefings or intervene to ensure that difficult issues are not being avoided. By sensitively facilitating full discussions and the verbalisation of difficulties and emotional reactions, staff can be supported and allowed emotional relief.

Sensitive enquiry and awareness

Providing the right support at the right time requires an ongoing focus on what is going on and what to do to support staff. It is vital to be alert to signs that someone is not coping well and to explore unusual behaviours as early as possible. This requires an understanding of what is 'usual' and the ability to identify when additional support or action is needed – for example, when a member of staff's mood, response or behaviour is incongruent with what would normally be expected and especially if the person seems unaware that their response is unusual. Obvious clues include changes in work patterns, unexplained sickness absences, isolating or withdrawal from social contacts, unusual emotional displays and difficulties in relationships at work.

In a community setting this could manifest as staff being absent from team activities; being absent from the office because they are 'too busy'; focusing excessively on one particular client over and above the rest of their caseload; avoiding dealing with matters to do with a particular client; not sharing information regarding particular cases with the rest of the team; acting as an 'intermediary' between other team members or agencies and the client; or denying any emotional impact by the client on themselves but raising that they have noticed that another colleague appears to be struggling. Kinder *et al.* (2008) advocate a straightforward approach involving non-controlling or open questions such as 'I've noticed you've been quieter than usual' or 'I am wondering how you are doing at the moment', and allowing staff freedom to choose what to divulge.

Interventions to counter parallel processes

Personality disordered patient dynamics are often observed in the staff groups that work with them. For example, patients who struggle with feeling emotionally low and overwhelmed with hopelessness, or avoid affect by diverting it into anger, sometimes manifest this as complaining rather than overtly angry behaviour. This can appear to be replicated in the service as a parallel process – for example, complaining by staff, or specific individuals becoming a scapegoat for problems or difficulties. Similarly, groups of staff can adopt the egocentric, entitled and self-focused behaviour of the narcissistic personality disorder. Interventions to counter parallel processes can be at organisation, team or individual level and may include exposing staff responses and behaviours as parallel processes (using sensitive enquiry or facilitative questioning) and highlighting to staff or teams how they have adopted the behaviours of the personality disordered patients. This helps open up exploration within the team in the face of difficult situations and resistance. Interventions can also be targeted to elicit more adaptive responses – for example, directed perspective taking, team reflection exercises, staff sensitivity groups, team-building events focused on building trust, acceptance of imperfections and enjoyment at work. Multidisciplinary team ward rounds or case reviews can be structured in a way to allow expression and reflection on the impact of patient dynamics on team members.

Coaching and mentoring

Experienced staff can also provide coaching and mentoring as additional mechanisms of support to staff, either by facilitative enquiry to create awareness and self-directed learning or by using their own experiences and knowledge to empower and motivate staff.

Counselling

Specific support in the form of counselling or stress reduction schemes can be used to help people deal with emotional distress that is reducing their ability to function as well as they might. However, organisations must be careful to manage the potential difficulties in blurring the boundaries between supervision, personal support, and organisational or managerial support. In such instances, it can be helpful to have different individuals or organisations providing different aspects of support.

It is clear that a preventative approach to secondary stress and burnout needs to be included which highlights the importance of individual clinicians knowing their client, themselves, the likely dynamics to expect from personality disordered patients, the likely transferences and their own limits. Preventative education could utilise staff training and awareness initiatives to encourage staff to develop positive adaptive behaviours to cope with the stresses of working with personality disordered patients and strategies for noticing and counteracting the parallel processes.

Maintaining positive cultures

Positive attitudes towards personality disorder have systemic origins (Bowers, 2002). An individual's attitude is often unwittingly affected by the prevailing attitudes within the organisation. Many staff start with a positive attitude towards treating personality disorder but, as they experience the challenges of working with this client group and the interpersonal dynamics of the patient are projected into the treatment milieu, negativity and hopelessness can develop. It can be hard for staff to maintain a psychological understanding of why someone they are trying to help would want to insult, hit or reject them. Instead, the milieu can drift into one where making negative judgements about patients (such as references to attention-seeking, manipulative or childish behaviour) becomes permissible. Consequently, staff may feel powerless to effect positive changes, and can become disillusioned and depressed. Being in receipt of clinical supervision is strongly associated with a positive overall attitude to personality disordered patients (Bowers, 2002). Other practical strategies for achieving positive support might include role-modelling by senior staff (conveying hope but also being able to reveal their own frustrations and experiences of dealing with the client group). Encouraging staff to check and follow up colleagues who have had difficult or demanding interactions to see if they are 'ok' conveys care and shared responsibility and also counters negativity and another parallel process of 'nobody cares about me', or 'no one cares enough'.

Liaising with similar organisations

Making links with like-minded organisations can assist with maintaining a positive treatment ethos, validation, sharing good practice and normalisation of experiences.

Further developments

The therapeutic milieu and organisational context can have a huge impact on how treatment is delivered and maintained. The organisational culture can be supportive or counter-productive. Vicarious trauma, intimacy and the structure of the working day can all have an important influence. The level of exposure to the patient, differences between working on a closed unit versus in the community, job rotation, fear, sickness, role blurring versus team cohesion, dynamics such as scapegoating and complaints can all contribute to a toxic environment. A key preventative challenge is to identify how the organisational climate and culture can be used to protect staff from the toxicity of the client group. Organisational interventions need to be targeted at keeping toxicity to a minimum by challenging parallel processes such as scapegoating, blaming of staff for human error, boundary violations, and complaining, and ensuring that hope is kept to an optimum. Training programmes can create awareness but monitoring and regular challenge are required by clinicians to maintain positive treatment cultures in which personality disordered patients are treated in a manner that conveys acceptance and compassion for the patient with a minimum of emotionally laden terminology (e.g. manipulative, naïve, etc.). These key principles need to be embedded and reinforced in service policies and protocols.

Organisational climates need regular monitoring to assess for negative influences. With many influences and factors interacting with each other, it can be difficult to assess what the most significant factors are. Monitoring levels of positivity and hopelessness in the environment in conjunction with other staff well-being indicators would offer a starting point.

It would be useful to apply evidence about the characteristics of resilient people to clinicians working with personality disorder. Research could be targeted at factors underpinning resilience and factors that enable and maintain people working with this client group; for instance, an exploration of whether there are key attachment styles associated with clinicians who work successfully with this client group and whether these are related to the duration of service with any particular client group; or examination of how positive attitudes of staff are maintained and what the environmental influences on this are. Studies involving critical incident analysis might provide more understanding of this complex interaction.

The risk of boundary violations within therapeutic relationships is unlikely to disappear and more use could be made of risk management tools within clinical and managerial supervision to assess risk of boundary crossings. Investment in preventive education could also be useful.

In conclusion, the complexity of personality disorder psychopathology, staff and organisational culture interactions necessitates both an emphasis on the importance of services working together and an exploration of and focus on systemic influences. It is important that the strands of recruitment, induction, training, mentoring and supervision are brought together in a comprehensive, flexible workforce development strategy to enhance the contribution of all staff.

References

Bowers, L. (2002) *Dangerous and Severe Personality Disorder: Response and Role of the Psychiatric Team*. London: Routledge.

Bowers, L., Carr-Walker, P., Paton, J., Nijman, H. *et al.* (2005) Changes in attitudes to personality disorder on a DSPD unit. *Criminal Behaviour and Mental Health*, **15(3)**, 171–183.

Department of Health (1999) *Continuing Professional Development: Quality in the New NHS, HSC 199/54*. Department of Health, London.

Dozier, M., Cue, K. and Barnett, L. (1994) Clinicians as caregivers. Role of attachment organization in treatment. *Journal of Consulting and Clinical Psychology*, **62**, 793–800.

Duggan, M. (2002) *Developing Services for People with Personality Disorder: The Training Needs of Staff and Services. Report of a Scoping Project*. London: Author.

Golding, L. and Gray, I. (2006) *Continued Professional Development for Clinical Psychologists: A Practical Handbook*. Chichester: Wiley-Blackwell.

Hamilton, J.C. and Spruill, J. (1999) Identifying and reducing risk factors related to trainee-client sexual misconduct. *Professional Psychology: Research and Practice*, **30**, 318–327.

Howells, K., Krishnan, G. and Daffern, M. (2007) Challenges in the treatment of dangerous and severe personality disorder. *Advances in Psychiatric Treatment*, **13**, 325–332.

Kiesler, D.J. (1996) *Contemporary Interpersonal Theory and Research: Personality, Psychopathology and Psychotherapy*. Toronto: Wiley.

Kinder, A., Hughes, R. and Cooper, C.L. (2008) *Employee Well-being Support: A Workplace Resource*. Chichester: John Wiley and Sons Ltd.

Krawitz, R. (2004) Borderline personality disorder: attitudinal change following training. *Australian and New Zealand Journal of Psychiatry*, **38**, 554–559.

Leahy, T. (2006) *Roadblocks in Cognitive-behavioural Therapy: Transforming Challenges into Opportunities for Change*. New York: Guilford press.

Linehan, M. (1993) *Cognitive-behavioural Therapy of Borderline Personality Disorder*. New York: Guilford Press.

Murphy, N. and McVey, D. (2003) Nursing personality disordered patients: a schema-focused approach. *Journal of Forensic Practice*, **5(3)**, 21–27.

National Institute for Health and Clinical Excellence (2009a) *Antisocial Personality Disorder: NICE Clinical Guideline 77*. London: NICE.

National Institute for Health and Clinical Excellence (2009b) *Borderline Personality Disorder: NICE Clinical Guideline 78*. London: NICE.

National Institute for Mental Health in England (NIHME) (2003a) *Personality Disorder: No Longer a Diagnosis of Exclusion*. London: NIHME.

National Institute for Mental Health in England (NIHME) (2003b) *Breaking the Cycle of Rejection. The Personality Disorder Capabilities Framework*. London: NIHME.

Sneath, E.L. (2008) Management of therapeutic boundaries. Unpublished document.

Vamos, M. (2001) The concept of appropriate professional boundaries in psychiatric practice: a pilot training course. *Australian and New Zealand Journal of Psychiatry*, **35**, 613–618.

Weigel, L., Langdon, P., Collins, S. and O'Brien, Y. (2006) Challenging behaviour and learning disabilities: the relationship between expressed emotions and staff attributions. *British Journal of Clinical Psychology*, **45**, 205–216.

Index

MIX
Paper from
responsible sources
FSC
www.fsc.org   FSC® C013056

Printed and bound in Great Britain by
TJ International Ltd, Padstow, Cornwall